Social Work Practice with Refugee and Immigrant Youth in the United States

Melvin Delgado

Boston University

Kay Jones

Boston University

Mojdeh Rohani

International Institute of Boston

Boston • New York • San Francisco
Mexico City • Montreal • Toronto • London • Madrid • Munich • Paris
Hong Kong • Singapore • Tokyo • Cape Town • Sydney

Series Editor: *Patricia Quinlin*
Editorial Assistant: *Annemarie Kennedy*
Marketing Manager: *Kris Ellis-Levy*
Manufacturing Buyer: *JoAnne Sweeney*
Cover Designer: *Joel Gendron*
Production Coordinator: *Pat Torelli Publishing Services*
Editorial-Production Service: *Lynda Griffiths*
Electronic Composition: *TKM Productions*

For related titles and support materials, visit our online catalog at www.ablongman.com.

Between the time Website information is gathered and then published, it is not unusual for some sites to have closed. Also, the transcription of URLs can result in typographical errors. The publisher would appreciate notification where these occur so that they may be corrected in subsequent editions.

To obtain permission(s) to use material from this work, please submit a written request to Allyn and Bacon, Permissions Department, 75 Arlington Street, Boston, MA 02116 or fax your request to 617-848-7320.

Library of Congress Cataloging-in-Publication Data

Delgado, Melvin.
    Social work practice with refugee and immigrant youth in the United States / Melvin Delgado, Kay Jones, Mojdeh Rohani.
        p. cm.
    Includes bibliographical references and index.
    ISBN 0-205-39883-9
    1. Social work with immigrants--United States. 2. Social work with youth--United States. 3. Youth--Services for--United States. 4. Refugees--Services for--United States. 5. Immigrants--Services for--United States. I. Jones, Kay. II. Rohani, Mojdeh. III. Title.
    HV4010.D45 2005
    362.87'53'0973--dc22   2004048533

Printed in the United States of America

10 9 8 7 6 5 4 3 2 1   08 07 06 05 04

To Denise, Laura, and Barbara,
a continued source of inspiration and support.
M.D.

To my family.
And to all the refugees and immigrants
who demonstrate such courage and strength
as they rebuild their lives, and who
contribute so greatly to our country.
K.J.

To my loving and supporting family
and to immigrants whose courage
and determinism continue to inspire me.
M.R.

Contents

PART II • *Major Elements and Building Blocks of Youth Development*   **97**

5 *Best Practice Principles with Newcomer Youth*   **99**

PART III • *Youth Development Paradigm:
Elements and Practice*   **163**

Preface

Book Goals

Major structural changes occurred in the latter part of the twentieth century in the United States at a time when record numbers of newcomers sought refuge here. These demographic, economic, technological, and political changes have effectively changed the newcomer experience in such a way that it is impossible to compare newcomer adjustment to society with those newcomers who entered this country in the nineteenth and early part of the twentieth centuries, even when they shared the same country of origins. The United States is on the cusp of incredible changes in the next 50 years—changes that will alter the composition of the country as we now know it and bring with it numerous languages that will be an integral part of the nation's social fabric.

Social Work Practice with Refugee and Immigrant Youth in the United States contextualizes the newcomer experience and provides a guide for social workers developing interventions using a youth development paradigm. This book does so through four interrelated goals:

1. Provide the reader with a contextualization of the unique experience faced by refugee and immigrant youth when they resettle in this country.
2. Provide a definitional and conceptual grounding of a youth development paradigm with particular applicability for use with newcomer youth.
3. Identify the potential facilitating and hindering forces for utilizing a youth development paradigm with newcomer youth.
4. Illustrate through the use of case studies and examples how organizations and programs targeting newcomer youth can effectively use a youth development paradigm.

Outline of Book

This book consists of 5 parts and 10 chapters: Part I, Context Setting (4 chapters); Part II, Major Elements and Building Blocks of Youth Development (3 chapters); Part III, Youth Development Paradigm: Elements and Practice (1 chapter); Part IV, Reflections from the Field of Practice (1 chapter); and Part V, Themes for Future Directions (1 chapter). Each of these parts and the corresponding chapters systematically build on each other. However, each section addresses a particular aspect of practice with newcomer youth. We have endeavored to provide the reader with case illustrations in each of the chapters as a means of concretizing key theoretical points. These examples help to ensure that the book is grounded in the operative reality of life in the United States for newcomer youth, their families, and communities.

Special Conditions of Book

Books having a practice focus encounter a wide range of challenges and as a result generally have inherent limitations. For example, we struggled with the perennial issue of depth versus breath in addressing content. The subject is immense in scope and ever changing in character. This dynamic process highlights the importance of the topic and the need to stay abreast of new developments globally. Rarely will a day or two go by without some print or television news story on some aspect of immigration and refugee status. The newsworthiness of the subject matter has brought with it increased attention from policymakers, academics, and the general public.

We endeavored to update all chapters throughout the writing process. Unfortunately, however, some material becomes dated as soon as it gets published. Natural, political upheavals and wars, for example, create a state of crisis and uncertainty, resulting in displacement of large numbers of people across national boundaries. These events can result in large numbers of newcomer groups entering this country without the requisite infrastructure to assist them in their resettlement. Each of the wide range of refugee and immigrant groups that falls under the rubric of "newcomers" has unique histories and circumstances, making generalizations arduous or impossible to make: "Much in the immigrant experience is shared—from emigration to immigration, including reactions to and from the receiving country. However, many experiences are unique to a particular immigrant group and to a specific individual" (Segal, 2002, p. 37).

Constraints on manuscript length make the in-depth treatment of any one group impossible. We believe that providing a general perspective is far more important than providing in-depth specificity on any one group. Our hope is that readers will be able to bring a group-specific perspective into broader discussions concerning social work practice with newcomer youth. Assets, issues, and needs that are common and unique can then be sorted out, allowing each group to be a part of the entire picture of immigration and refugee status but still being able to maintain its uniqueness in the process.

Finally, our use of literature was not restricted to scholarly sources. We relied on newspaper articles, videos, Internet sources, and unpublished materials. Sole reliance on scholarly sources would be a dated and too narrow approach to writing this book. Use of more "user-friendly" sources of information increases the likelihood that we would be tapping into the latest facts, opinions, and perspectives on the subject of newcomer youth. It is also our hope in writing this book that readers will discover new sources of information, particularly easily available and free or inexpensive, that can assist them in their practice with newcomer youth.

Use of Terms

Readers will encounter numerous terms in the course of reading this book. Some of these terms will be quite familiar and well accepted in the field of practice; some terms will be new and, upon review, will become widely accepted. However, there may be terms that readers would prefer not to use or legitimize, and there will be cases where readers will totally object to the use of certain terms or the meaning we ascribe to them. We struggled in selecting and widely using some of the terminology.

There were instances when we attempted to create new terms because we believe that some of the conventional terms did not do justice to the conditions or points of view we tried to convey. At times we were successful in this quest; at other times we were not. The field of practice with newcomers is ever expanding and as a result is quite dynamic. New groups have started to emerge where the previous use of terms applied but do not in these new instances. In essence, we wish to convey to the readers our awareness of the viability and controversial nature of how terms can attract and repel practitioners. At no time did we take this duty lightly because it was expedient to do so.

The promise of a youth development paradigm for positive transformation with newcomer youth is predicated on these individuals receiving needed instrumental, expressive, and informational support from community-based organizations, education systems, and government. A youth development paradigm must be conceptualized as a stage after which basic human needs are met, not as a substitute for interventions stressing these needs. It is imperative to emphasize this point in an age of government retrenchment and redefinition of what constitutes a "safety net." Although this book will highlight the numerous assets newcomers bring to this country, by no means should these assets be viewed from the perspective that this society withdraws instrumental support from this population group.

The subject of newcomers—and more specifically newcomer youth—as an overlooked group is exciting and challenging for social work practitioners, policymakers, and scholars alike. It is not often that these three groups can both share and learn from each other. When we bring newcomer youth to the table to be a part of the decision-making process, the potential for youth and the field of social work to be transformed is immeasurable. Nothing short of this collaborative partnership can achieve meaningful and lasting change.

We sincerely hope that readers are able to capture the joy we experienced in researching and writing about this topic. We have spent many years practicing with newcomers and believe that the social work profession can make important and lasting contributions in assisting newcomers to make the United States their home.

Acknowledgments

We would like to thank the following people for their invaluable help in making this book a reality: Sara Bruno, Cristina Weeter, Wilma Peebles-Wilkins, and Susan Hogan at Boston University's School of Social Work; Molly Baldwin, Sayra Pinto, Omar Ortez, Susan Ulrich, Mehrnoush Bakhshandeh, and all the other staff and youth participants at ROCA; and Marcela Klicova at International Institute of Boston. Our appreciation also goes to the following reviewers for their helpful comments on the manuscript: Frederick L. Ahearn, Catholic University; Betty Garcia, California State University, Fresno; and Susan P. Robbins, University of Houston.

Context Setting

Give me your tired, your poor,
Your huddled masses yearning to breathe free,
The wretched refuse of your teeming shores.
Send these, the homeless, tempest-tossed to me,
I lift my lamp beside the golden door!

—Emma Lazarus, 1883, Engraved on Statue of Liberty

1

Overview

A receiving country's readiness to accept immigrants in general or a single immigrant group in particular is itself a complex matter. When immigration is viewed as inextricably bound to a nation's political, economic, and social well-being as well as to its future security interests, it is more likely to be welcomed than if it is not.

—Segal, 2002, p. 24

Introduction

The twenty-first century ushered in a series of challenges unlike any other epoch in this nation's history. Although the United States has developed an international reputation for receiving immigrants and refugees over the past 150 years, this current period of history is unprecedented (Oldfield, 2002; Sommer, 2002). Newcomers in the United States are increasingly becoming a group that is being feared and the subject of intense scrutiny by government and community alike (Audi, 2003; Jacoby, 2002; Jaret, 1999; Kuthiala, 2001; Lichtblau, 2003; Liptar, 2003; Mask, 2002; Sharry, 2002; Sullivan, 2002). The passage of the Illegal Immigration Reform and Immigrant Responsibility Act in 1997 reflected a heightened concern on the part of the federal government and caused widespread fear in newcomer communities (Dugger, 1997a).

After the events of September 11, 2001, concerns combined with a slowing economy raised serious questions about what immigrants and refugees mean for this country's social and economic future (Chen, 2002; Gori, 2002; Gutfeld, 2003; Marquis, 2002b; Sachs, 2000a, 2002b; Sadowski-Smith, 2002b; Sutner, 2002). The number of refugees admitted into the United States during fiscal year 2002 was supposed to be 70,000. However, due to increased stringent requirements after September 11th, the actual number admitted was only 27,000 (*Boston Globe*, 2002; *U.S. Newswire*, 2002).

Although addressing post–Communist Europe, Zolberg (2001) sums up this fear quite well: "The massive movement of human beings across international borders has come to be regarded as one of the most intractable problems the United States and the other affluent democracies face in the strange new post–Communist world. Long a marginal subject even for demographers and social scientists, international migration quickly ascended to the status of security issue, imperatively requiring attention in the highest places" (p. 1). Fear of newcomers translates into official and unofficial policies that effectively hamper their adjustment process in this country. Although newcomers arrive in the United States with numerous personal assets, successful adjustment requires a concerted and comprehensive approach involving formal and informal resources in the host country.

The demographic profile of the United States changed dramatically over the past five decades and is projected to continue to do so well into this century, and this will have tremendous implications for the social work profession. This country is not only getting older but also more ethnically and racially diverse—trends that have been referred to as "graying" and "browning." These two trends are projected to continue unabated unless major unanticipated changes occur to alter the composition of the United States (Camarillo & Bonilla, 2001; Murdock, 1995; Pear, 1992; Sandefur, Martin, Eggerling-Boeck, Mannon, & Meier, 2001). The social work profession will be thrust into providing services that take into account a continued shift in population profile, and one that will increasingly bring it into contact with newcomers.

Population growth in this nation is expected to increase by 129 million between 2000 and 2050. If immigration is halted, the growth increase would be reduced to only 54 million (Doyle, 2002). Immigration has played a significant role in making this country—especially some states and cities—much more ethnically and racially diverse. This increased diversity, as it will be noted in Chapter 2, has occurred very rapidly by historical standards, further making this country's immigration and refugee policies highly charged and controversial.

The challenge of social work practice with diverse populations has never been more apparent than it is today (Agbayani-Siewart, 1994; Amodeo & Jones, 1997; DeMonchy, 1991; Gopaul-McNicol, 1993; Greene & Watkins, 1998; Le-Doux & Stephens, 1992; Nanji, 1993; Stevens, 2002). Successful transition of newcomers to this society is considered a complex and multifaceted phenomenon that has consistently challenged policymakers, practitioners, and scholars (Sam, 2000; Shapiro, Douglas, Rocha, Radecki, Vu, & Dinh, 1999).

Sociocultural developments within the United States in the last decade have witnessed the emergence of two distinct and yet potential beneficial trends: the increased presence of immigrant and refugee youth and the popularity of youth development as a paradigm and field of practice. These developments have not crossed paths in the professional literature, although they have in the practice arena. This is one of the primary motivations for writing this book. The convergence of these two trends brings forth exciting new possibilities that will be beneficial to both newcomers and the field of youth development.

Types of Newcomers to the United States

Who are newcomers? Newcomer groups are not monolithic in composition. Immigrants come from many different parts of the world, including repressive situations, making them feel like refugees in the traditional sense of the word (Tambiah, 2000).

Refugees, in turn, are fleeing repression and dangerous circumstances. Although the term *newcomer* has served as a means of grouping together people from very disparate backgrounds and circumstances, it is still necessary to define the two major groupings within this umbrella concept.

Immigrants are defined as those individuals who depart their country of origin voluntarily in search of better economic and living arrangements. African slaves brought to the United States during this nation's slavery period can best be classified as "forced immigrants." Unfortunately, the forced immigration of slaves into this country has either been totally overlooked in the treatment of immigration or only touched on in passing (Indra, 1999; Ogbu, 1994; Patterson, 1982). This bias has effectively rendered the subject of forced immigration out of any discussion of how immigrants have shaped this nation, and has become the subject of a book specifically devoted to forced immigration and the social-economic-political factors that operate overtly and covertly to bring this about (Indra, 1999). This book, the reader is advised, will only touch on this topic. *Undocumented immigrants*, in turn, are those individuals who enter this country without proper (legal) documentation, and have done so for reasons similar to those who are in this country as immigrants.

Refugees are those individuals who are forced to leave their country because of human rights violations and threats to safety. Furthermore, this book will also address *asylum seekers* who are youth. The status of refugee is very much determined by political considerations of the U.S. government (Coutin, 2000; Levine, 2001; Padilla, 1997). Refugees and asylees seek protection in the United States from persecution in their homeland. The former applies for protection before entering this country and the latter does so after entering this country. The legal status of newcomers, as will be addressed in Chapters 3 and 4, plays a critical role in how they view themselves and the role government plays in helping them adjust to life in this country (Swarns, 2003b). In 2002, over 9,000 asylum seekers were detained in detention centers awaiting adjudication of their claims, which can take anywhere from months to years for a determination to be made (Swarns, 2003a).

Who Is a Youth and Who Is a Newcomer Youth?

Youth is defined as anyone under the age of 18 years old. However, there will be circumstances in this text when youth between the ages of 18 and 21 years will be addressed. The term *youth* will be used in the broadest sense for the purposes of this book. However, every effort will be made to define the age grouping when appropriate to contextualize the discussion. The term *newcomer* will be used interchangeably when referring to broad statements involving refugees and immigrants. When specific reference involves the unique circumstances of either of these groups, then the proper designation of *refugee* or *immigrant* or *undocumented immigrant* will be used.

The challenges that newcomer youth face are quite formidable and have long-range implications for their eventual success. Those challenges are also present for policymakers, practitioners, and scholars (Balgopal, 2000; Devore & Schlesinger, 1995; Drachman, 1995; Padilla, 1997; Potocky, 1996; Potocky-Tripodi, 2002; Zhou, 1997). The circumstances leading to displacement and resettlement are brought with these individuals to this country with immense implications for the adjustment process (Scheinfeld & Wallach, 1997). For example, there are over 400,000 victims of torture living in the United States, raising challenges for how best to identify them and meet their needs (Levine, 2001). Places such as Bellevue Hospital in New York City, for instance, can best be conceptualized as refugee camps with elevators rather than hospitals, for it is here that one can easily see the consequences of past torture (Hoffman, 2003).

Virtually all public and scholarly discussions of immigrants and refugees generally center on a very limited scope of topics (Board on Children and Families, 1995):

> Discussions about immigration, focused on such policy issues as labor force participation and use of welfare programs, frequently fail to include considerations of children's well-being. Even those debates which center on programs that benefit children—such as schools, public assistance, and social welfare programs—are often based on issues related to short-term costs and societal impacts, neglecting considerations of well-being and future contributions of immigrant children. Hence, immigrant children have been rendered largely invisible in policy spheres. Yet first- and second-generation immigrant children are the fastest-growing segment of the U.S. population under age 15. (p. 72)

The Board on Children and Families (1995) concluded, not surprisingly, that there is a glaring absence of research on newcomer youth and their families. This lack of research increases the real possibility that existing programs and policies might be dismissive rather than culturally appropriate, inclusive, and effective. This gap is particularly evident when addressing the needs of young newcomer children. The fate of newcomer youth cannot be artificially separated from that of family and community, since these two arenas greatly shape the destinies of youth (Grindle, 2002). The development of practice models that focus on newcomer youth within a community context is in tremendous need in the human service and education fields (Fabricant & Fisher, 2002; Gonzalez-Ramos & Sanchez-Nester, 2001; Johns, 2001; Lowry, 2002; Padilla, 1997; Specht & Courtney, 1994). These models must rest on the reality youth face in day-to-day living, however, with topics such as intergenerational conflict, identity formation, and post-traumatic stress, for example, very often being a part of their lives (Levine; 2001; Potocky, 1996).

Being new to this country substantially separates the issues and needs of immigrant and refugee youth from those of other youth. In the case of refugee youth, for example, the stresses associated with flight, refugee camp interment, and resettlement increase the likelihood that they can experience a multitude of post-migration stressors that can translate into problems (Casanova, 1996; Hyman, Vu, & Beiser, 2000).

Since a large proportion of immigrants and refugees are of color, this raises challenging and delicate issues for how these individuals relate to or are integrated into existing communities of color, since newcomers very often find themselves living in the same neighborhoods (Graham, 2002). The 1990s witnessed over 25 million immigrants whose national origins qualified them as official "minorities," thereby qualifying them for affirmative action programs (Graham, 2002). The development of separate services focused on the unique needs and backgrounds of newcomer youth, versus integration within existing services targeting youth of color who are native to this country, raises important questions about how services, be they youth development or otherwise, need to be planned. What set of values and goals need to be in place to direct the focus of interventions? To what extent are resources redirected from natives to newcomers and at what political costs?

At-Risk Youth and the Field of Youth Development

A number of scholarly books have been published in the last decade devoted to at-risk youth (Besharov, 1999; Burt, Resnick, & Novick, 1998; Collingwood, 1997; Furstenberg, Cook, Eccles, Elder, & Sameroff, 1999; National Academy Press, 1993, 1999; Schulenberg, Maggs, & Hurrelmann, 1997; Witt & Crompton, 1996). Newcomer youth, by virtually all definitions in the field, can well fall into a category of being at risk.

The attractiveness of viewing youth as potential problems competes with views of youth as assets (National Assembly and the National Collaboration for Youth, 2000):

> Today, proponents of youth development still see the reduction of existing problems through prevention as vitally important. But they also hold that while we develop strategies to prevent dangerous activities, we must be equally adamant about stating positive goals that we wish all young people to achieve and then begin helping them to reach those goals. They see youth development as an ongoing process that promotes positive outcomes for all youth. Youth development programs are important for youngsters who have taken their first drink and for teenagers already undergoing treatment for drug addiction. Kids from inner-city, lower-income families need to have the same needs met and acquire the same competencies as their peers from suburban and upper-income neighborhoods. When needs are not met and competencies are not acquired, any young person can be "at-risk." (p. 1)

Youth who are labeled as "at risk" have been the subject of numerous commission reports in an effort to minimize or eliminate problems when they achieve adulthood. However, scholarly publications and task force reports, with some notable exceptions, have largely ignored the plight of refugee and immigrant youth, yet these youth can also be categorized as being "at risk" for failure in this society (Hernandez, 1999; Hernandez & Charney, 1998). This oversight also applies to the field of child welfare (Potocky, 1996; Roberts, 2002). As a result, social workers must endeavor to embrace a paradigm that can effectively identify and mobilize the assets of youth while at the same time recognizing their struggles and needs.

The youth development field has enjoyed a tremendous amount of success in programming, in scholarship, and as a field of practice taught in this nation's schools of higher education. The paradigm systematically and strategically builds on youth and community assets and does so by encouraging their active participation in the development of program goals and activities (Hellison, Cutforth, Kallusky, Martinek, Parker, & Stiehl, 2000; Lakes, 1995; Lerner, 1995). However, although appealing for practice with this country's marginalized groups, particularly those of color who are living in this nation's cities, its applicability and potential for newcomer youth is still in its infancy and largely unexplored and untapped. Roffman, Suarez-Orozco, and Rhodes (2003), in a rare publication on youth development and immigrant youth, articulated a vision as to why youth development is so important for newcomer youth. The stresses associated with being uprooted and relocated to a foreign country, combined with a pervasive exclusionary climate, make newcomer youth an important population group for the field.

This book fills this important gap by addressing how a youth development paradigm can be used to meet the emerging needs of newcomer youth and their families. Barker, Knaul, Cassaniga, and Schrader (2000), in their book entitled *Urban Girls: Empowerment in Especially Difficult Circumstances*, for example, illustrate the varying ways of operationalizing the concept of empowerment throughout the world based on local conditions. A youth development paradigm, like empowerment, cannot be applied without considerable adjustments, taking into account a set of social-political-cultural factors inherent in the backgrounds of these youth. In addition, this book provides the reader with a number of examples of successful programs and identifies the rewards and challenges associated with youth development and newcomer youth.

The profession's work with newcomers started early in this country's history in the late nineteenth century and should continue well into this century. The following chapter will highlight key demographic trends that have all the elements of positioning the profession to continue its historical origins into yet another century. The magnitude of the demographic forces related to newcomers can best be appreciated through an in-depth understanding of the trends, profiles, and migration/dispersal patterns of newcomers to the United States.

It is appropriate to end this introductory chapter with a response to Emma Lazarus's poem at the foot of the Statue of Liberty (quoted on page 3). Kempler (2002), an immigrant to this country himself, captures the meaning of Lazarus's poem for newcomers in this country:

> Stop and think for a moment about these words. I believe you will see that they are somewhat "tongue-in cheek," even ironic. "Yes," the great lady seems to be saying, "I know very well that you are tired. I know very well that you come with little or no money or material wealth. I know that you have been treated like refuse, that you have been homeless, and have been tossed from place to place. But it is you, especially you, that I welcome. I know that here your energies, your spirit, your pent-up aspirations and resourcefulness will find a place to express itself and grow. And, so, I hold up my lamp of welcome to you." (p. 2)

2

Demographic Profile and Trends

Immigrants constantly infuse new life into our economy and culture. As any of the elected officials here today can attest, their cities and counties thrive precisely because of their vibrant immigrant communities.

—New York City Mayor Rudolph Giuliani, June 1997, Ellis Island Conference

Introduction

Population movements within and between countries are a phenomenon that has taken on great significance in the early part of the twenty-first century, drawing increased attention of scholars and politicians globally (Sadowski-Smith, 2002a; *The Economist*, 2002). To understand the complex challenges facing immigrant and refugee youth in the United States, it is necessary to have a solid grasp of demographic profiles as well as current and projected trends (Little & Triest, 2001). These statistics, however, need to be appreciated within global, national, local, and historical contexts. After all, we are truly living in a global age.

As noted earlier in Chapter 1, statistics on refugees and asylum seekers, for example, can vary widely depending on the goals of gathering the data. "Statistics on refugees and other uprooted people are often inexact and controversial. One country's refugee is another's illegal alien. As such, government tallies cannot always be trusted" (U.S. Committee for Refugees, 2002, p. 1). The same can be said for counting those who are undocumented within a country (Population Resource Center, 1997). Technical, methodological, and political factors all influence the outcome of any data gathering methods, and no more so than with these population groups (Bakewell, 2000). Statistics gathered on newcomer groups are generally done in a highly charged political context, and a failure to understand this reality is to do a serious disfavor to any meaningful dialogue on the subject of newcomers to this country.

The subject of refugees and immigrants (or "foreign-borns") has touched all sectors of this country and the world and has deep historical roots and significance. All regions of the United States have experienced the increased presence of newcomer groups, particularly in the latter part of the twentieth and early part of the twenty-first century (U.S. Census Bureau, 2002d). Historically, some sectors of the country, particularly cities, have had greater contact with immigrant and refugee groups, however (Phillips & Straussner, 2002). This chapter pays specific attention to one state (California) and three urban areas (Los Angeles, New York City, and Miami), since the vast majority of newcomers to the United States have settled in these areas.

The reader is warned that this chapter, unfortunately, commits the "sin" of providing statistics on newcomers in a manner that makes them lose their individuality and stories. Practitioners, probably better than any other group, are well aware of how newcomers' stories are all unique and that any effort to group them is bound to fail in conveying their journey and circumstances. Colson's (1999) comments on this very point are accurate, with some exceptions, anytime discussion of population movements are addressed in the literature: "The refugee literature is still biased toward undifferentiated 'people' without gender, age, or other defining characteristics except ethnicity" (p. 23). Demographic statistics can minimize differences at the expense of providing a broad conceptualization of a phenomenon, almost like seeing the forest but not the trees. Being able to see the trees is critical in the work done by social workers. The authors apologize for this perspective and hope that the following chapters redress this characterization.

Global Perspective

The average American believes that no country in this world except the United States faces the challenges presented by newly arrived immigrants and refugees. Nothing could be further from the truth (*The Economist*, 2002). European countries also face considerable challenges in addressing and, in some cases, actively stemming the flow of newcomers (Bloch, 2002; Bruni, 2002; Cross & Moore, 2002). However, this is not universally the case, as Americans are often led to believe by the popular media. Canada, for example, has instituted a new immigration policy with a goal of attracting young and preferably large foreign-born families to rural sections of the country (Krauss, 2002). An aging population, combined with a dramatic fall in birthrates have largely fueled this policy.

Global displacement of populations is probably as old as civilization itself. "Migration is as old as humans wandering in search of food, but international migration is a relatively recent phenomenon. It was only in the early 20th century that the system of nation-states, passports, and visas developed to regulate the flow of people across national borders" (Martin & Widgren, 2002, pp. 3–4). Population transfers between countries in the modern era have dimensions to them unlike those of previous historical periods. Nevertheless, most of the world's population will never cross a national border—its people spending their entire lives within their respective countries of birth. Migration is the exception rather than the rule.

The world's population has increased significantly over the past 50 years and is projected to continue to do so in the near future (U.S. Committee for Refugees, 2002).

In 1998, there were over 2 billion youth under the age of 20 years in developing countries of the world, 400 million being adolescents between the ages of 15 and 19 years old (*Market Europe*, 1998). In 1998, the world's population stood at 5.9 billion; it is projected to increase to between 8 and 9 billion by the year 2025 (Kritz, 2001), 11.2 billion by 2050, and 27 billion by 2150 (*Market Europe*, 1998).

Most of this population increase, it must be emphasized, is centered on African, Latino, and Asian countries. The latter two sets of countries are major sources of newcomers to the United States. The U.S. population increased at a more rapid rate during the 1990s than most demographers had predicted and may overtake Europe in population by 2040 (*The Economist*, 2002). It was estimated in 1990 that the U.S. population in 2000 would be 275 million; instead, it increased to 281 million.

The potential increase in the world's population, particularly within developing countries, combined with political conflict, will undoubtedly place immigration and refugee-related issues at or near the top of most country's social agendas (Schmeidl, 2001). Some of these movements are predictable, based on past historical events. Others are unpredictable, and few nations, if any, will be prepared for the chaos that follows natural events and conflicts (Frelick, 2002a; U.S. Committee for Refugees, 2002). In essence, no year will go by without some form of population upheavals somewhere in the world.

It is estimated that there are approximately 40 violent national conflicts at any one period of time (Summerfield, 2000). In 1999, there were an estimated 14 million refugees fleeing persecution in their homeland, and few, if any, industrialized countries are the destination of immigrants, refugees, asylum seekers, and asylees (Kerwin, 2001). Over 80 percent of all refugees remain in developing countries. However, over 4 million sought asylum in western European nations in the decade of the 1990s (Summerfield, 2000). In 2001, it is estimated that over 923,000 people applied for asylum worldwide. The United Nations High Commissioner for Refugees (2001) reports that the United States led all nations in the number of asylee applications with 68,400, followed by Canada (12,200), Australia (6,500), Norway (1,300), and Sweden (1,100) rounding out the five major destinations of asylum seekers.

Although worldwide statistics on immigration are arduous to find, it is estimated that in 2000, between 150 and 160 million people (or 2.5 percent of the world's population) lived outside the country of their birth, an increase from 120 million in 1990 (Doyle, 2002; Martin & Widgren, 2002). In 1965, it was estimated that 75 million people (or 3 percent of the world's population) lived outside their country of birth (Martin & Widgren, 2002) (see Figure 2.1). Annually, almost 3 million people cross national boundaries, of which 1.8 million do so without legal authority (Martin & Widgren, 2002). According to the United Nations High Commissioner for Refugees (2001), there were 6.1 million refugees in 115 countries in 2000.

The percentage of immigrants and refugees is relatively small when placed within a global scale, although it masks the disproportionate impact it has on some countries. Another perspective places all of these displaced persons within a distinct geographical boundary and calls it a nation, making it the world's sixth most populated nation, ranking behind China, India, United States, Indonesia, and Brazil (Martin & Widgren, 2002). Select nations account for a major share of immigrants, with China (14 percent) and Mexico (8 percent) being the two largest sources of immigrants in the world.

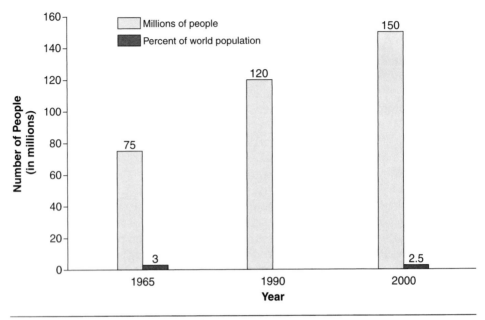

FIGURE 2.1   *People Worldwide Living Outside Their Country of Birth*

Historical Overview of Newcomers to the United States

It is tempting to draw profound comparisons between the influx of newcomers to the United States a century ago with the wave of newcomers in the late twentieth and early twenty-first centuries. However, similarities are few and far between when new technologies, transportation, employment patterns, and the characteristics of the newcomers are taken into account.

Historically, it was relatively easy to know the formal educational level a newcomer possessed based on his or her job in U.S. society. Lack of credentials, combined with limited or no English-language skills and familiarity with the culture, essentially tracked newcomers into factory and service jobs. However, the latest migration phase does not fit this pattern. The case of Luiz Velez Gutierrez, once a judge and law professor in Colombia, South America, illustrates this point:

> Five years ago, Luiz Velez Gutierrez had a driver. He had a secretary, too. His colleagues and staff referred to him in Spanish as "doctor," "judge," and "professor." These days, Velez wakes and puts his crimson shirt and pants on, walks from his rented room . . . and arrives at his job at Harvard Divinity School: cleaning bathrooms, swabbing railings, vacuuming rugs, wiping tables. (Jennings, 2002, p.1C)

Luiz Velez Gutierrez, who came to the United States to be reunited with his wife and child, is part of a growing population group of newcomers who cannot make a lateral position shift from the country of origin to this country. Newcomers with technical skills have an easier time of doing so when compared to those whose professions are "language intensive," as in the case of lawyers. Technically, these newcomers can be considered "working class" because of their occupations and income. However, in reality they are very different from natives who occupy similar strata.

The emergence of the concept of dual citizenship, particularly among Caribbean and Central and South American nations such as Mexico, is one effort at helping newcomers adjust to life in this country without giving up their concept of nationality (Larkin, 1999). Critics of dual nationality, however, are quick to raise concerns about this type of identity in a world that is so dominated by nation-states (Feldblum & Klusmayer, 1999). Further, previous waves of newcomers did not have this option, and that is why they became "Americanized."

Nativist concerns were present then and are present now, however (Little & Triest, 2001). If the circumstances and characteristics of these two immigration periods (100 years ago and today) are so different, then why are there still strong national sentiments against newcomers? The answer to this question is both simple and complex at the same time.

The phenomenon of newcomers to the United States is not new in this country's history (*Christian Science Monitor*, 2002; Flores, 2002; Suarez-Orozco & Paez, 2002a). It is virtually impossible to graduate from a U.S. school and not have been exposed to this country's history involving immigrants and refugees from all corners of the world. Unfortunately, the reality of what awaited this nation's newest residents was far from ideal (Bayor, 1978; Ehrlich, Biderback, & Ehrlich, 1981; Miller, 1969). The recent wave of immigrants and refugees must be cast into a historical context to better understand the similarities and significant differences between this modern period of newcomers (1980–present) and previous waves. The period 1900 through 1970 witnessed the continued decrease of the overall percentage of the U.S. population being foreign-born, from a high of 13.6 percent to a twentieth-century low of 4.7 percent (Immigration Policy Reports, 2001a).

Figures 2.2 and 2.3 provide a vivid graphic depiction of the waves of newcomers to the United States over a 150-year period. Scholars generally divide the nation's immigration and refugee history into four historically distinct periods: (1) First Wave (prior to 1820), primarily consisting of English-speaking immigrants from the British Isles; (2) Second Wave (1840s to 1850s), primarily consisting of Irish and Germans; (3) Third Wave (1880 to 1914), primarily consisting of southern and eastern European countries and averaging 650,000 per year for a total of 20 million; and (4) Fourth Wave (1965 to present), the most significant period of immigration from a numerical viewpoint and consisting primarily of Latinos, Asians, and Pacific Islanders.

These categories are rarely mutually exclusive or exact, but they do provide a perspective on understanding previous immigration waves and how the current wave compares historically (Steinberg, 1981). An understanding of common trends makes appreciating the differences that much more rewarding, particularly when examining the latest wave of newcomers. There are numerous reasons why this country has attracted newcomers over the course of its history. Employment, however, is universally accepted as a key factor influencing immigration waves, and common fear of new-

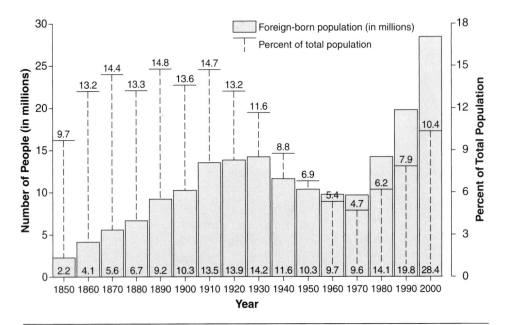

FIGURE 2.2   *Foreign-Born Population and Percent of Total Population for the United States: 1850 to 2000*

Note: (For 1850–1990, resident population. For 2000, civilian noninstitutional population plus Armed Forces living off post or with their families on post.

Source: U.S. Census Bureau (1999a, Table1; 2001, Table1–1).

comers becoming "public charges" is largely unmerited (Hondagneu-Sotelo, 2002; Immigration Policy Reports, 2001a).

Newcomers to the United States must be viewed from a long-term perspective to better understand their economic contributions to the country. Initially, they may not contribute economically to the extent natives would like. However, over an extended period of time they do become contributors to the economic base of the country (Andino, 2002). The age of newcomers upon entry to this country is a key factor in making them economic contributors because many are in their prime working years (more than 70 percent are 18 years of age and older). In 1997, for example, newcomer workers contributed an estimated $133 billion in direct taxes (National Immigration Forum, 2000).

A term such as *immigrant* is too broad and hides within-group differences (*Credit Union Journal*, 2003). Portes and Rumbaut (1997), for example, divide immigrants into three distinct categories depending on their primary motive for entering this country and their socioeconomic characteristics:

1. *Labor migrants:* This category usually symbolizes what the average person thinks about when the word *immigrant* is mentioned. These individuals can be in the United States without proper documentation or as contract laborers.

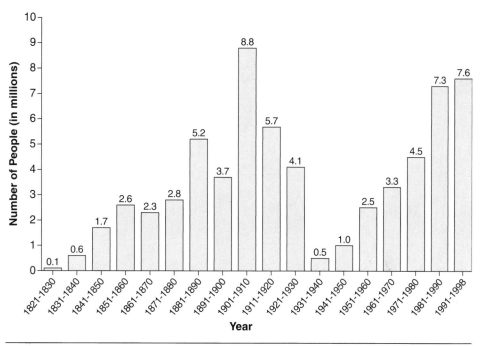

FIGURE 2.3 *Immigrants to the United States by Decade: Fiscal Years 1821 to 1998*

Source: U.S. Immigration and Naturalization Service (2000, Table 1).

2. *Professional immigrants:* These individuals have favored status in the United States because of their educational backgrounds and employment competencies.
3. *Entrepreneurial immigrants:* These immigrants entered the United States with proper documentation and have managed to develop businesses that very often serve their own communities.

Each of these categories of immigrants faces a different set of challenges, and to lump all under an umbrella of "immigrant" does a disservice to their unique circumstances. A similar argument can be made for refugees and asylum seekers.

Current anti-immigrant sentiments or nativism is not a new phenomenon in the United States (Aarim-Heriot, 2003; Roy, 2002). Anti-newcomer slogans, policies, and perceptions are an integral part of this nation's history and can be traced back to the origins of this country. However, the popularity of the term *nativism* can probably best be traced back to the nineteenth century, a period in U.S. history that witnessed tremendous upheavals and unprecedented immigration. Nativism represents a "fear and loathing of foreigners" and reaches heightened levels when a nation's social problems are considered intractable and there is widespread efforts to identify scapegoats (National Immigration Forum, 2001).

A number of outstanding publications exist that specifically highlight anti-immigrant sentiments in this country dating back to the colonial period to the present. Jaret

(1999), however, warns that any effort to focus on studying anti-immigrant sentiments without also studying pro-immigrant sentiments and actions provides a distorted perspective of history. In studying anti-immigrant sentiments and actions during the two eras of high immigration (1880 to 1924 and 1970 to 1998), Jaret concludes that nativism in the 1990s was particularly widespread and strong and that nativism was no longer restricted to the "traditional conservative" sector of the country. The "Red Scare" period, the "Palmer Raids" of the 1920s, and the internment of 120,000 Americans of Japanese ancestry were also periods of tremendous anxiety about foreigners living in this country.

The presence of undocumented immigrants has played a significant role in the "crisis of immigration" in present-day United States. Nativism is predicated on any one, combination, or all of the following perceived threats: (1) political order, (2) economic system and (3) social and cultural aspects of Americans.

The state of California, probably more than any other state in the 1990s, best epitomizes these sentiments (Hernandez, Siles, & Rochin, 2000). Three California voter propositions stand out as examples of "immigrant bashing" that have drawn national media attention: (1) Proposition 187 ("Save Our State"), an initiative restricting social, medical, and educational services to undocumented immigrants, received 59 percent of the vote; (2) Proposition 209 (California Civil Rights Initiative) dismantled affirmative action; and (3) Proposition 227 ("English for the Children") severely limited bilingual education programs.

Each of these propositions addresses common public perceptions of newcomers—they are a drain on state and national resources; they are unbalancing key social, economic, and political conditions; and they exhibit a total disregard for becoming assimilated like prior newcomer groups and this tendency severely undermines American values and identity. Failure to learn English is one example of this disregard.

However, a historical view will uncover anti-immigrant sentiments in California dating back to the nineteenth century, and show how this state wielded a prodigious amount of influence in the passing of national laws prohibiting immigration to this country and in targeting Chinese and Japanese immigrants. McClain (1998) uplifts the struggle of Chinese people in the United States and particularly in California. However, McClain presents a compelling picture of a community that was politically astute and committed to achieving social and economic justice by effectively using the judicial system.

Miller (1969) notes how stereotypes permeated much of what was known about this community: "Finally, the arrival of the Chinese in California provoked editorial fears across the nation, fears that can only be explained in terms of the unfavorable image of these people that preceded them to American shores. The presence of the Chinese on the West Coast reinforced many of the negative stereotypes of them, which in turn interacted with other anxieties affecting nineteenth century American society" (p. 15). Chavez (1998) goes so far as to warn us that the "state of emergency" in which we live is not the exception but the rule historically, particularly in California.

The U.S. Congress prohibited immigration from China for 10 years between 1892 and 1902, and in 1902 banned it permanently. The Chinese Exclusion Act of 1882 was this nation's first law restricting immigration to the United States. The law had strong backing of West Coast, particularly Californian, national elected officials in the Congress. Aarim-Heriot (2003), in turn, argues that the passage of the Chinese Exclusion Act of 1882 ("Chinese Question") cannot be effectively separated from the broader issues pertaining to the "Negro Problem" of the nineteenth century. In 1907, President Roosevelt, in an agreement with Japan, excluded Japanese from immigrating to this country. In 1924, Congress passed the National Origins Act, which discriminated against newcomers from southern and eastern Europe; Asian immigrants, in turn, were almost totally excluded from entering the United States.

National Perspectives, Profiles, Trends

The United States (1996–2001) with a net migration of 960,000, leads the world as a destination for immigrants, or 27 percent of the world's international immigrants (Doyle, 2002). An average of 600,000 newcomers entered the United States every year during the 1980s, not counting those who were undocumented. The 1990s will go down as the period in time when more immigrants entered this country than any other decade in the nation's history (Margolis, 1998; Szanisko, 2002).

A 1999 report by the U.S. Department of Justice Immigration and Naturalization Service (1999) notes that in fiscal year 1997 there were 85,866 cases filed or reported for naturalization, a decrease of 33 percent from the previous year's total of 128,190. Six groups accounted for almost two-thirds the amount (64 percent of all new asylum claims): Chinese (People's Republic of China), Haitians, Indians, Iraqis, Mexicans, and Salvadorans.

A 1998 *Wall Street Journal*/NBC national opinion poll found that 50 percent of the respondents believed that immigration served to undermine the American character, whereas 36 percent believed it strengthened it (Murdock, 1998). Unfortunately, newcomer contributions to this nation have taken a backseat to their costs, politically, economically, and socially (Endelman, 2000; Feder, 1995; Millman, 1997). For example, almost 27 percent of adult newcomers possess a bachelor's degree, which is similar to the U.S. national average, and 42 percent of all naturalized immigrants since 1988 have completed a four-year level of higher education, which is 15 percent higher than the U.S. national average (Immigration Policy Reports 2001b). It is estimated that newcomers add $10 billion to the national economy every year (Endelman, 2000). Newcomers in the United States are generally occupying jobs at the bottom of the labor market. Newcomers fueled half of the labor growth during the period from 1990 to 2000. More specifically, they made up 79 percent of the male civilian labor force, with newcomer women accounting for 30 percent (Armas, 2002). About 10 percent of immigrants identify themselves as self-employed or entrepreneurs, similar to the percentage among native-born Americans (*Credit Union Journal*, 2003).

Since 1975, almost 2 million refugees have been admitted to the United States, although the number per year has decreased since September 11, 2001 (Mayadas & Segal, 2000). In 1995, a total of 114,664 refugees were granted admission, with the largest number originating from Europe (46,998) and Asia (43,314). California, New York, and Florida were the most popular resettlement destinations (Mayadas & Segal, 2000).

In 2000, these states continued to be the most popular destination for immigrants, too (U.S. Immigration and Naturalization Service, 2002). Major cities within these states were the primary destination of the newcomers. However, many others states and regions experienced significant increases, such as Maryland, Colorado, and the Midwest (Aguilar, 2001; Roylance, 2001; Simon, 2002).

It is important to reemphasize that the difference between a *refugee* and an *immigrant* or a *undocumented person* may have more to do with political considerations of the United States than any other factor (Portes & Rumbaut, 1997):

> Being a refugee is therefore not a matter of personal choice, but of governmental decision based on a combination of legal guidelines and political expediency. Depending on the relationships between the United States and the country of origin and the internal context of the time, [there is] a particular flow of people of economically motivated immigrants. Given past policy, it is thus not surprising that there are few escapees from rightist regimes living legally in the country. (p. 23)

According to the U.S. Census Bureau (2002d) (see Figure 2.4), in the year 2000 there were 9.3 million legal permanent residents (LPRs) in the United States, representing 33 percent of all foreign-born (3.3 percent of the total U.S. population). Naturalized citizens accounted for almost 9.2 million, or 30 percent of all foreign-born. Finally, humanitarian immigrants (refugees, asylees, Amerasians, Cuban-Haitians, and certain parolees) accounted for 7 percent, or 2.3 million (Immigration Policy Reports, 2001b). In the past 30 years, immigrants to the United States have accounted for over one-third of the total population growth of the country (U.S. Census Bureau, 2002d;

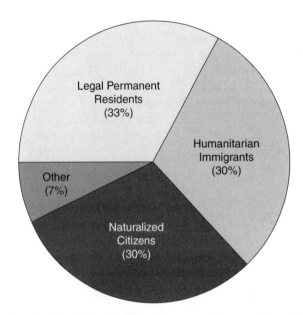

FIGURE 2.4   *Percent of All Foreign-Born U.S. Residents: 2000*

Zhou, 2001a). Some 27 states had a foreign-born population of at least 5 percent in 2000, almost doubling that of 1980 when 14 states had that percentage. New York, for example, would have lost population during this 10-year period if it were not for newcomers (Haughney, 2002; Szanisko, 2002).

In 1990, the foreign-born numbered 19.8 million, representing 7.9 percent of the total population. Historians and demographers could argue that this percentage is still considerably lower than the 17.4 percent in 1910 (Portes & Rumbaut, 1997). Between 1991 and 1998, a total of 7.6 million immigrants settled in this country, with 3.1 million (40 percent) originating from Latin America (Population Resource Center, 2002). Between 1990 and 2000, the number of foreign-born in the United States increased by 57 percent to 31.3 million, or three times the number in 1970, which was the lowest point in the past 100 years (Cheng, 2002a). Newcomers accounted for the largest proportion of the nation's population since 1930, constituting 42 percent of this nation's entire population growth during the 1990s, compared to 35 percent between 1900 and 1910 (Cheng, 2002b; Szanisklo, 2002). The percentage of the nation's total foreign-born population averaged 13 to 15 percent during the 1860 to 1920 period (Hendricks, 2002a).

According to the 2000 U.S. Census Bureau, an estimated 28.4 million foreign-born residents live in the United States, or 10.4 percent of all U.S. residents (Poe, 2002). When combined with their children, they number 56 million, or 20 percent of all U.S. residents. Eighty-five percent of immigrant families have at least one or both parents who are noncitizens and one or more children who are citizens (Immigration Policy Reports, 2001b). By contrast, 19.0 percent of Switzerland's population is foreign-born, followed by Austria (9.0 percent), Belgium (8.9 percent), and France with (6.3 percent) (Feldblum & Klusmeyer, 1999).

In 2000, Latinos officially became the largest group of color in the United States, numbering 35.3 million (13.2 percent), or 600,000 more than African Americans/Blacks, and were the fastest-growing demographic group in the country. In 2001, the Latino population increased to 37 million, up almost 5 percent from April 2000, with the African-American/Black population accounting for 36.1 million, or a 2 percent increase from April 2000 (Armas, 2002; Clemetson, 2002; Hendricks, 2003). In 2002, the number continued to increase, with Latinos numbering 38.8 million (Navarro, 2003c).

Latinos gained 13 million people in the United States between 1990 and 2000 (U.S. Census Bureau, 2001). They are expected to increase their representation to 18 percent of the U.S. population by 2025 and triple in size by the year 2050, accounting for 25 percent of the nation's population (Population Resource Center, 2002). By 2025, the Latino population of Arkansas, Delaware, Georgia, Kansas, Maryland, Nebraska, and North Carolina will increase by at least 70 percent (Yeoman, 2000). With the possible exception of parts of Maryland, these states historically have not been destination points for Latinos. Numerically, the Latino community in the United States would rank fifth among Spanish-speaking countries in the world (Scott, 2002). Their influence can be felt throughout the social fabric of the country (Navarro, 1999).

It is helpful to take two perspectives on the population increase of the Latino community within the United States—its impact on organized religion and its buying power. It is predicted that by 2050, for example, 86 percent of all U.S. Catholics will be Latino, up from 30 to 38 percent in 2000 (Levitt, 2002; U.S. Conference of Catholic Bishops, 2001). This increase is largely fueled by high birth and immigration rates. Approximately 47 million people spoke a language other than English in the home in 2000, an increase from 31.8 million in 1990 (Hendricks, 2002a). Over 100 languages are spoken in the school systems of Chicago, Los Angeles, New York, and Fairfax County, Virginia (McDonnell & Hill, 1993).

Nationwide, the Latino buying power has increased dramatically as this population group has increased numerically. The Latino purchasing power increased to $580.5 billion in 2000, up from $223 billion in 1990 (an increase of 160 percent); it is projected to increase an additional 60 percent by 2007 and account for $926.1 billion (almost *one trillion dollars*) (Schneider, 2002). Latino newcomers to the United States constitute a significant sector of this market purchasing power increase. This demographic shift has had a tremendous influence in academic circles, too (Lee, 2003).

Newcomer Youth in the United States

Almost 10 percent of all newcomers are under the age of 18 years, compared to the average age of 28.3 years for U.S. citizens (Dianne, 2001). Since 1990, the number of immigrant families in the United States has increased seven times faster than the corresponding number of native-born families. One of every five youth under the age of 15 had at least one foreign-born parent in 1995 (Huang, 2002). The implications of this trend will be far reaching in states such as California, Florida, New York, and Texas (Hernandez, Siles, & Rochin, 2000). In the early 1990s, 78 percent of all newcomer youth were concentrated in California, Florida, Illinois, New Jersey, New York, and Texas. California alone had 45 percent of all newcomer youth in the country (Board on Children and Families, 1995).

The youthfulness of foreign-born parents increases the likelihood of this group having more children. The 25 to 54 years age group, for example, accounted for 58.7 percent of the immigrant population, compared to 41.7 percent for the U.S. population. Youth who were either immigrants themselves or the children of immigrants grew to 13.7 million in 1997 from 8 million in 1990, making them the fastest-growing segment of the U.S. population under the age of 18 years old (Dugger, 1998). It is projected that by 2010, over 9 million newcomer children will reside in this country, or 22 percent of all school-age children (Fix & Passel, 1994). The vast majority (77.7 percent) of children living in foreign-born households were born in the United States (Cheng, 2002a).

In the case of newcomer youth who are being reunited with their parents in the United States, there are many emotions associated with this journey, as illustrated in the case of Grace Zeng:

> Coming to America was my parents' hope to seek a better life. I came to America when I was eight, so I didn't know where America was and how things were in America. All I knew was I'm going to move somewhere far away from my relatives and friends. Before I came to America, adults around me told me how good America was and how fortunate

our family was to go to America. So I got really excited about going to America, but also upset. I don't know how to describe that feeling of happiness that I finally would get to live with my mom. My mom immigrated to America when I was four, and for a long time I had a feeling of loneliness and of losing valuable people. So up until the day that I left China I was still wondering what America was really like. And if you want to know what happened to my family and me then you please wait until you can continue to read my next journal entry. (KQED, 2002)

Clearly, reunification with parents brings both joy and sorrow for newcomer youth. Any statistic on reunification will never capture the range of feelings and experiences of these youth and their parents.

Newcomers' Countries of Origin

Recent newcomers to the United States are overwhelmingly non-European in national origins, differing significantly from newcomers in the nineteenth and early twentieth centuries. Since 1960, the majority of all newcomers have come from Latin America and the Caribbean (52 percent), with Asian and Middle Eastern countries accounting for 28 percent, and the remaining percentage (20 percent) coming from Canada and European countries (Foner, Rumbaut, & Gold, 2000). In 2000, Latino, Asian, and Pacific-Islander countries accounted for 9 out of the 10 top countries of foreign-born residing in the United States (U.S. Census Bureau, 2002a). African refugees made up almost 3 percent of all refugees in the United States in fiscal year 1990 and this increased to 30 percent by 2001 (Swarns, 2003c). However, since September 11, 2001, thousands are still awaiting security clearance before being granted entrance into this country, primarily from Somalia and Sudan.

"New" immigrant groups, such as Arabs, Haitians, and Colombians, are increasingly entering the United States. In 2000, there were 1 million Arab Americans residing in this country. The states of California (169,000), New York (107,000), and Michigan (97,000) had the largest concentration of these groups (Population Reference Bureau, 2002). Haitians numbered 385,000, and increased by over 33 percent during the 1990s (Martin & Widgren, 2002). Since 1996, Colombia has sent 1.1 million to the United States (due to persistent civil violence), or almost 3 percent of its population. In 2001, Washington, DC, had 8 percent of its Black population being foreign-born, up from 1 percent in 1970 (Fears, 2002). Maryland (5 percent) and Virginia (2 percent), too, experienced an increase of Black foreign-born, from .50 percent and .50 percent, respectively, in 1970.

By 1997, Mexicans represented 35 percent of all immigrants, documented and undocumented, in this country. By the year 2000, they accounted for 33 percent of all immigrant children in the United States (Graham, 2002). The Mexican proportion of the U.S. population is the largest of any nationality in this country's history since the census of 1890, surpassing that of Germans with 30 percent (U.S. Census Bureau, 2002a). Some 39 percent (12.8 million) of Latinos in the United States are foreign-born, with 43.0 percent having entered in the 1990s and 29.7 entering in the 1980s—27.3 percent entered prior to 1980 (U.S. Census Bureau, 2001).

Undocumented Newcomers and the Consequences of Deportation

Probably very few topics can raise the ire of a nation's public more than discussion of its "undocumented" (more commonly referred to as "illegal aliens"). The term *illegal alien* is insidious and places the undocumented into a criminal category, and unjustifiably so. Their presence in the United States is overwhelmingly motivated by a desire to achieve a standard of living that meets their basic human needs as well as that of their families (Thompson, 2002). The payment of taxes raises a series of conflicts for those who are undocumented and working. On one level, they wish to pay taxes to demonstrate "good moral character" and to show that they are contributors (Hernandez, 2003a). However, payment of taxes opens them up for the possibility of being discovered by the government and deported. Although tax information is not routinely shared with the Homeland Security Department or the Department of Justice, this possibility does exist if there is cause to think that the taxpayer is a potential terrorist.

Those who actually engage in illicit activities or who are potentially terrorists are but a small percentage of this group. Although the United States Constitution does not grant the right to newcomers to enter the country, it does protect them from racial and national origin discrimination and from arbitrary treatment by the government once they have entered (ACLU, 2002). Several states, most notably New Mexico, North Carolina, Tennessee, and Utah, have passed laws allowing undocumented immigrants to obtain driver's licenses (Calvan, 2003). Several other states (California, Georgia, and Illinois) are debating similar legislation.

Another dimension that is often overlooked is organ donation by undocumented immigrants. According to the United Network of Organ Sharing based in Richmond, Virginia, 1 percent of all U.S. transplants in 2001 were performed on undocumented immigrants. However, during the same period, they represented 2 percent of organ donors (*Associated Press State & Local Wire*, 2003a).

The total number of undocumented newcomers in the United States at any one time varies, with the government generally being unsuccessful in stemming the tide of the unwelcome (Nevins, 2002). However, as noted in Figure 2.5, the undocumented immigrants in the United States numbered over 5 million in 1996, up from 3.9 million in late 1992, with estimates as high as 10 million in 2000 (Kuthiala, 2001; Martin & Widgren, 2002; Zhou, 2001a).

According to a 2003 U.S. Immigration and Naturalization report, undocumented immigrants increased by more than one million in less than four years. California, once again, led the nation in the number of undocumented residents (Malone, 2003). It is estimated that California has over 2.5 million undocumented immigrants as of 2003 (Calvan, 2003). Texas, ranked number two, broke the 1 million mark in 2000. Arizona's undocumented newcomers increased by over 300 percent to 283,000. Georgia witnessed a 600 percent increase to 228,000. North Carolina, in turn, increased fourfold to 206,000. Finally, Florida experienced a less dramatic but still sizable increase to 337,000 from 239,000 in 1990.

In 2000, there were 1,815,000 undocumented persons apprehended and 185,000 deportations (Martin & Widgren, 2002). Peter Schey, a nationally known immigration

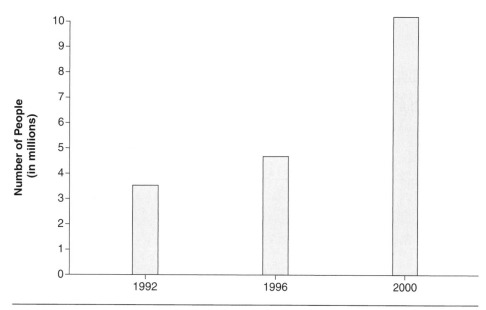

FIGURE 2.5   *Undocumented Immigrants in the United States: 1992–2000*

lawyer, argues that there are very good reasons why undocumented people continue to seek entry into this country: "Every 10 years the INS has a new set of reforms and every 10 years the INS says there are 5 [million] to 10 million undocumented people here. No matter what they do, the numbers stay the same.... The reasons people come to the United States are more powerful than the laws intended to stop them" (Goldsmith, 2002, p. 1).

Forty percent of all those who are undocumented entered this country "legally," meaning they overstayed the length of time authorized prior to admittance. They are students, tourists, business persons, or have some other temporary visa status and remained in the country after their visas expired (*Arizona Republic,* 2001). The public's image of the undocumented, however, is largely shaped by the deaths of those who were unsuccessful in crossing the Mexican border (Fountain & Yardley, 2002; Nieves, 2002; Zernike & Thompson, 2003).

By the late 1990s, immigration levels in this country reached 1.2 million per year, 800,000 of whom had proper documentation and 400,000 of whom were undocumented (Graham, 2002). Mexicans accounted for 54 percent (3.5 million) of all undocumented, followed by Salvadorians with the second largest percentage of 6 percent (Zhou, 2001a). Prior to 1980, Central America was not a major source of immigrants to this country, but this trend has changed since 1980, particularly in Los Angeles and Miami (Martin & Widgren, 2002). Further, Suarez-Orozco and Paez (2002b) note that the forces giving rise to Latino newcomers are quite powerful: "New data suggest that the immigration momentum we are currently witnessing cannot be easily contained by unilateral policy initiatives such as the various border control efforts and theatrics that have intensified over the last decade.... Transnational labor-recruiting networks, family reunification, and wage differentials continue to act as a powerful impetus to Latin American immigration to the United States" (p. 12).

Undocumented children entering the country have historically not been considered significant, but they are currently receiving greater attention (Thompson, 2003). Nearly 5,000 unaccompanied and undocumented children and youth are detained by the Immigration and Naturalization Service (INS) every year (*New York Times*, 2002a, 2002b, 2000c). This is twice the number for 1997. Over 30 percent of these children are held in custody in juvenile jails. The U.S. Border Patrol in Texas apprehended 20,704 children age 15 years or younger over a recent 12-month period (Schiller, 2002).

Children of undocumented immigrants in New York City constitute an increasingly large percentage of that city's child welfare system, making it arduous if not impossible to have them reunited with their parents (Cox, 2002). This dilemma, however, is not unique to New York City. The following case illustrates this challenge:

> In Queens Family Court, Morataya (an undocumented immigrant from Guatemala) admitted her part in the physical altercation and to having smoked marijuana. She resolved to do whatever the court mandated in order to get her children back. Morataya was told to find her own housing, to attend domestic violence and anger management classes, to undergo multiple psychiatric evaluations, to get monthly drug tests and to demonstrate that she could provide for her children (i.e., get a stable job), conditions difficult enough for the average single mother to meet. For an undocumented immigrant, fulfilling these conditions can be next to impossible. (Cox, 2002, p. 2)

In 2002, legislation was passed shifting the responsibility for unaccompanied immigrant children from the INS to the Department of Health and Education Services. This shift was in response to the need to increase access and services for this group of newcomers (*New York Times*, 2002d). The change in responsibility between departments increases the placement of immigrant children in least restrictive environments, and increases access to translators, education, and medical care.

The number of child-smuggling rings has proliferated to meet the demands of immigrant parents in this country who wish to have their children reunited with them (Hegstrom, 2002; Krikorian, Mena, & Miller, 2002; Thompson, 2002). Some of these children, unfortunately, never make it to their parents and instead are forced into prostitution or die in the process of making the journey (Maier & Paige, 1999; O'Connor, 2002).

The consequences of being caught and deported as an undocumented resident in this country are quite severe since Congress passed tough laws to counter the influx of immigrants without proper documentation and post–September 11th. Prior to passage of an immigration law in 1996, INS deported almost 150,000 immigrants per year; since 1996, the number has doubled to 300,000 per year (Ojito, 1998). Those awaiting deportation are incarcerated until the actual act of deportation (Anderson, 2000; Bailer, 1998; Kahn, 1996; Kerwin, 2001). Detainees are caught in a "Catch-22," since the INS is required by law to hold the detainees until they can be deported back to their country of origin, yet there is very little prospect of this happening within a reasonable period of time (Tebo, 2000).

Critics of the INS argue that this agency emphasizes law enforcement over its social service role (Hagan & Rodriguez, 2002; Hamm, 1995; Welch, 2000). There are over 900 county jails across the country housing detainees from INS, and some counties are dependent on detainees to maintain their facilities (Solomon, 2002; Welch, 2000). Since 1997, the average number of INS detainees nationwide has increased from 8,200 per year to almost 20,000 (*Associated Press State & Local Wire*, 2001). Incarcerated foreign nationals cost the United States over 1 billion dollars in fiscal year 1993–1994 (Wunder, 1995). Shenon (2002) raises a set of questions that strike at the heart of this nation's dilemma concerning immigration policy: "Should the government's immigration agencies focus on law enforcement—policing the borders to block the entry of illegal immigrants—or on services to welcome hardworking new immigrants to America's shores? Should the government's priority be keeping the bad guys out, or helping the good guys in?" (p. 4).

In 1996, the United States deported 67,000 immigrants, a 34 percent increase from 1995 (Spence, 1996). California alone deported 30,000 individuals in 1996, an increase of 50 percent from the previous year (Spence, 1996). An example of Cambodians who entered this country as refugees during the 1980s and 1990s (approximately 145,000) illustrates what can happen to those who do not seek citizenship and are convicted of aggravated felonies. In 2002, there were almost 1,400 Cambodians in the United States who awaited deportation after serving their prison sentences (Mydans, 2002). They went from refugees, to felons, to strangers in a land that was once home upon their return to Cambodia: "As the deportations continue in the months to come, the Cambodian government will find itself burdened with hundreds of people like this, lost, jobless, many of them unable to function in the Cambodian language, all with criminal records" (Mydans, 2002, p. A3).

Remittance and Gross National Product

The consequences of deportation back to countries of origins go far beyond the individual being deported, causing disruptions in two countries. Many times, these individuals worked in this country and were either the sole financial provider of their families back home or played an instrumental financial role (*Credit Union Journal*, 2003; Hernandez, 2003b; Meyers, 1998). Deportation often results in the country of origin having to reabsorb someone who cannot find suitable employment to support his or her family. Further, the loss of employment has economic implications for their families, communities, and the country as a whole.

Worldwide in 1999 it was estimated that $65 billion equivalent U.S. dollars were sent by "migrants" to their homes, an increase from $28 billion in 1988, $40 billion in 1994, and $54 billion in 1996 (Martin & Widgren, 2002). In 2000, $23 billion was sent back to family in the country of origin (Brazil, 2001). In that year, for example, remittances to the Caribbean and Latin America exceeded $20 billion for the first time in history (Fidler, 2001). In 2001, Mexico received over $9 billion in remittances alone (*Credit Union Journal*, 2003).

These payments are a significant portion of a country's foreign development investment. The payments, in addition, generally far exceed the funds these countries receive in foreign aid annually. In six countries it represents at least 10 percent of their gross national product: Haiti, 17 percent; Nicaragua, 14.4 percent; El Salvador, 12.6 percent; Jamaica, 11.7 percent; Dominican Republic, 10 percent; Ecuador, 10 percent.

In 1999, Mexico received the largest sum of money with $6.8 billion (or almost the equivalent of all tourism revenues), followed by Brazil ($1.9 billion), Dominican Republic ($1.75 billion), El Salvador ($1.58 billion), and Ecuador ($1.2 billion) (Brazil, 2001; Fidler, 2001). A 2002 estimate for El Salvador puts the figure at $2 billion (Rodriguez, 2002).

Undocumented youth and adults find themselves without basic identification documents because of their legal status in this country (Schiller, 2002). Efforts to facilitate banking by those who are undocumented are being explored. Undocumented Mexicans, for example, have no formal identification and as a result would have great difficulty banking in this country (Gori, 2002). In 2001, Mexico launched an identity card program that by 2003 had successfully issued over one million cards in the United States. Identity cards allow Mexican newcomers to open a bank account and, depending on the state, obtain a driver's license (Rodriguez, 2003). Mexicans can qualify for an identity card by providing a representative of the Mexican government with a birth certificate and a bill to establish proof of residence and, where appropriate, a driver's license.

Banking is one way of cutting the costs of remittance back to Mexico. Other efforts are also under way to cut the costs of wiring funds to countries of origin as a method of increasing the amount of money families actually receive. The costs of wiring funds are almost 20 percent or more of the money sent, making it possible to increase cash flow to Latin America, for example, by $4 billion per year by reducing costs of doing so (Brazil, 2001).

Telecommunication and Business Opportunities

Newcomers in the United States have created demands for more effective and efficient forms of communicating with relatives back home as well as business opportunities for meeting these needs. The selling of inexpensive phone cards is one example of how telecommunication has provided an effective communication means and a business opportunity. International telephone calling cards are a $2 billion a year business and were expected to continue to grow at a rate of 50 percent a year until 2004 (Sachs, 2002c).

Phone cards are ubiquitous in newcomer communities across the United States and provide newcomers with an inexpensive way of maintaining frequent connections with close relatives and friends back home.

> Eduardo Perez, a factory worker who moved to New York from the Dominican Republic 12 years ago, said he used to write letters to his mother back home. But that was the dark ages, before phone cards. Her expectations have changed radically. "My mom

expects a call at least once and really, a couple of times a week . . . she knows it's cheap and she knows it's easy, so if I don't call all the time, she cries." With phone cards, Mr. Perez added, there is no longer any excuse for tears. (Sachs, 2000c, p. 24)

The twenty-first century has provided newcomers with instant and inexpensive communication with their homeland, something that their counterparts in the twentieth century did not have.

California and Newcomers

Any discussion of newcomers to the United States can easily focus on a national scope without attention to implications for a particular state or region of the country. Broad overviews of statistics do serve important roles yet mask within- and between-state differences. There is probably no better state to highlight than California, since it has received a disproportionate number of newcomers over the past several decades (Baldassare, 2000; Fields, 2001; Hayes-Bautista, Schink, & Chapa, 1988; McCarthy & Vernez, 1997). Almost half of all Californians were either born in a foreign country or are the children of foreign-born parents (Marquez, 2002). In 1995, over 40 percent of this nation's undocumented immigrants lived in California, or 5 percent of the state's total population (Chapa, 2002; Population Resource Center, 1997; Zhou, 1997).

The characteristics and circumstances of their resettlement have influenced public perceptions, attitudes, and voter behavior (Barabak, 2001; Cornelius, 2002). Almost three-quarters of these newcomers are Latino (predominantly Mexican), Asian, and Pacific-Islanders (Fields, 2001). It would be a mistake, however, to think of population movements as only on an upward spiral. In the 1990s, Latinos not only settled in California but also left the state for other states, with an estimated 800,000 having left California for other states during the decade (Yeoman, 2000).

California's national political prominence is well understood historically and it has played a leading role in bringing many social issues to the national forefront. Many of these issues have been influenced by the changing demographics of the state's population (Calvan, 2003; Davis, 1995; Gandara, 2002; Gibbs & Bankhead, 2001; Unz, 1999). In 2000, California's population of color "officially" became a majority, although many observers would argue that this happened unofficially many years ago (Purdum, 2001; Wong, 1998). Although Hawaii and New Mexico achieved the status of majority of color designation previously, California became the first "major" state to do so. This watershed served as a lightning rod for national attention with implications for the nation's policies on immigration. A combination of factors caused the shift in the ethnic and racial composition of California—high Latino birthrates and low death rates, immigration, and a 43 percent increase in the state's Asian and Pacific Islander population.

California's percentage of foreign-born increased to 26.2 percent in 2000 (8,864,000) from 21.7 percent in 1990 (6,459,000) (U.S. Census Bureau 2002b). San Diego County's foreign-born population, for example, increased 41 percent during the 1990s, and has over 600,000 immigrants, or 20 percent of its total population (Weisberg & Sanchez, 2002). In the San Francisco Bay Area, the percent of foreign-born increased from 19.5 percent to 27 percent in the 1990s (Hendricks, 2002b). Importantly, 39 percent of the Bay Area's foreign-born population are naturalized citizens, an increase from 31 percent a decade earlier; in San Diego County, the percentage is even higher (41 percent) up from 36 percent in 1990 (Weisberg & Sanchez, 2002). The number of Californian children 5 years of age and older who spoke a language other than English also increased from 31.3 percent in 1990 to 39.5 percent in 2000.

Immigration has played a significant part in the dramatic increase among its Asian and Pacific Islander community when compared to other groups, particularly Latinos. Asian and Pacific-Islanders account for 3.9 million residents, or 12 percent of the state's total population, compared to 9 percent in 1990 (Purdum, 2001). Latinos increased by 2.7 million between 1990 and 2000; 20 percent of this total resulted from immigration. The Mexican population tripled in size between 1970 to 2000, from 760,000 to 8.8 million, accounting for 44 percent of California's newcomers during the 1990s (Fields, 2001). African Americans, however, declined by 3 percent to 2.3 million. Almost one-third of all Latinos residing in the United States reside in California (Purdum, 2001). Voter participation among Latinos and Asian and Pacific-Islanders increased during the 1990s in contrast to African American/Black registration and voting rates, which actually fell during the same period (Barabak, 2001).

California is 53 percent "of color" (primarily Latinos, African Americans, and Asian and Pacific Islanders). However, youth of color make up a larger percentage of the total youth population with 65.2 percent. White, non-Latino adults account for 46.7 percent of California's population but only 34.8 percent of the state's youth population (Heredia & Haddock, 2001). Unlike previous generations of newcomers who mostly settled in the Northeast, current newcomers have been disproportionately settling in the western part of the country. In 2000, the West Coast accounted for 28.8 percent (244,782) of all newcomers to the United States (U.S. Immigration and Naturalization Service, 2002). In 2000, California accounted for 25.6 percent (217,753) of all immigrants to this country, up from 21 percent in 1990 (Hendricks, 2002b; U.S. Immigration and Naturalization Service, 2002).

California as a primary destination for immigrants is not new; in fact, it has been the leading state of residence for new arrivals every year since 1976 (Population Resource Center, 1997; Singer, 1997). A total of 1.8 million immigrants entered California in the 1970s, surpassing immigration in all prior decades (McCarthy & Vernez, 1997). During the 1980s, immigration increased to 3.5 million, doubling the rate of the previous decade. The 1990s witnessed this continued trend (McCarthy & Vernez, 1997). In 2000, there were an estimated 8.7 million undocumented persons in the United States, 5.4 million (62 percent) were Latinos, with Mexicans numbering 3.9 million, or 45 percent, of the total (Population Resource Center, 2002).

In the latter part of 2001, the majority (50.6 percent) of babies born in California were Latino, marking a historic first in that state (Jablon, 2003; Murphy, 2003; Richardson & Fields, 2003). Asian or Pacific Islanders (11.7 percent) and African Americans/Black (6.1 percent), combined with Latinos, made up 67.7 percent, or more than two-thirds of all births. Southern California accounted for two-thirds of the Latino births (Jablon, 2003). The long-term implications of these baby births can be easily projected—Latinos will constitute the majority of children entering California's kinder-gartens by 2006 and the majority entering high school by 2014; they will be the majority of workers entering the labor force by 2017 and the majority of eligible voters by 2019 (Richardson & Fields, 2003; Sanchez, 2003).

Dr. Hayes-Bautista, a leading Latino demographer, summed up this demographic trend in Calfornia: "We can look at the future population of California by looking into the delivery room today" (Sanchez, 2003, p. 1). Another Latino scholar, Dr. Harry Pachon, noted: "We're seeing the inevitable demographic trend.... This is a demographic iceberg slowly moving through the California social structure" (Richardson & Fields, 2003, p. 1). Dramatically, births replaced immigration as the primary factor in Latino population growth in California. It is estimated that almost 85 percent of Latino growth since 1990 has been the result of births rather than immigration (Sanchez, 2003).

Urban Resettlement for Newcomers: Los Angeles, Miami, and New York City

It is impossible to talk about urban America without also discussing the presence of newcomers in this country, since the nation's cities have historically been the primary point of entry for newcomers (Cornelius, 2002; Phillips & Straussner, 2002). Cities have historically been refuge for many of this nation's unwanted people, including new-comers (Kazin, 2002). Although dispersal patterns to smaller towns is prevalent, almost 95 percent of all immigrants in this country in 2000 lived in metropolitan areas. Ten cities accounted for almost two-thirds of all immigrants in the United States (U.S. Census Bureau, 2000). Waldinger and Lee (2001) note: "As in the past, the newcomers to the United States head for the big cities and the surrounding areas. Compared to the native-born population, today's immigrants are more likely to live in metropolitan areas, with a still more marked propensity to reside in the 27 largest urban regions of the United States" (pp. 38–39).

The tendency of the world's population to be urban centered is a phenomenon that has continued unabated for the past 50 years. Familiarity with urban living conditions—combined with employment opportunities, existence of established social networks, and availability of resettlement services—all increase the likelihood of urban resettlement. In 1995, almost 45 percent of the world's population resided in cities. In 2000, that number increased to 50 percent and is projected to reach 65 percent by the year 2025 (Dow, 1997). As noted by the INS (2002), the top 10 major metropolitan areas attracting newcomers in 2000 were: (1) New York (85,867); (2) Los Angeles–Long Beach (70,644); (3) Miami (47,404); (4) Chicago (32,300); (5) Washington, DC, area (29,394); (6) Orange County, California (20,859); (7) Houston (17,429); (8) San Jose (16,874); (9) Boston-Lawrence-Lowell-Brockton, Massachusetts (16,469); and (10) Oakland (16,150).

Each of the areas has a history of attracting particular groups. Los Angeles–Long Beach attracts Chinese, Salvadorians, Koreans, and Mexicans. Miami attracts Cubans, Haitians, Jamaicans, Colombians, and Nicaraguans. New York attracts Dominicans, Chinese, Jamaicans, Haitians, and Indians. Chicago, in turn, primarily attracts Mexicans, Chinese, Indians, Poles, and Filipinos. Almost 80 percent of all newcomers to Chicago during the 1990s were Mexicans (Mendell, 2002). Chicago used to rank third in the country behind San Antonio and Houston prior to 2000.

Almost half (45 percent) of this nation's Asian and Pacific-Islanders live in Los Angeles, New York, or San Francisco (U.S. Census Bureau, 2002c). Asian and Pacific-Islanders in San Francisco, Oakland, and San Jose account for over 50 percent (50.8) of all foreign-born in those cities. San Francisco also attracts newcomers from countries other than Asian and Pacific-Island areas. Today, its foreign-born population accounts for 27.5 percent of its total population from 19.5 percent in 1990, increasing at a faster pace than that of California during the 1990s (Hendricks, 2002a, 2000b). Phoenix, Arizona, for example, is expected to have Latinos as the majority in the city, accounting for over 50 percent by 2007, up from 34 percent in 2003 (*Associated Press State & Local Wire*, 2003b). Immigrants largely fuel this increase. Hartford, Connecticut, has a Latino population accounting for over 40 percent, making it the largest concentration of Latinos among major cities in California, Texas, Colorado, and Florida (Zielbauer, 2003).

The presence of immigrants and refugees can be fully appreciated only when examined within the context in which they live (Blake, 2002; U.S. Immigration and Naturalization Service, 1997). Cities have historically played influential roles in the resettlement of immigrants and refugees in the nation's history, with New York City standing out as a prime entry point although not alone (Kotkin, 2002). In Chicago, for example, Latinos constituted 26 percent of the city's population in 2000 (Mendell, 2002). Interestingly, only Los Angeles had a larger Mexican American population than Chicago. Dispersal has followed the initial settlement, however, bringing newcomers to all parts of the country, rural as well as urban (Yeoman, 2000).

Los Angeles, New York City, and Miami represent three urban areas that have had tremendous changes in composition due to an influx of immigrants and refugees. If Houston's foreign-born population is added to those of Los Angeles, Miami, and New York, these four cities would have 9 million immigrants and refugees, with two-thirds (6 million) being noncitizen immigrants (Caring for Immigrants, 2001). Other cities, too, have witnessed prodigious changes (Hendricks, 2002b; Szanisklo, 2002). However, probably no three cities in this country have received more national publicity and are thus worthy of special attention in this chapter.

Los Angeles

The city of Los Angeles has a long history of welcoming newcomers to the United States (Laslett, 1996; Sabagh & Bozorgmehr, 1996; Waldinger, 2001a; Waldinger & Bozorgmehr, 1996). New York City is often mentioned as the gateway to the United States, and this holds true for certain ethnic and racial groups. However, Los Angeles' role in welcoming newcomers is of great importance in any discussion of immigrants and refugees in this country (Kotkin, 2002; Rieff, 1991; Sawhney, 2002).

The city's history of attracting newcomers to work in jobs at the bottom of the pay scale had much to do with Los Angeles' success in recruiting newcomers. This strategy fueled new waves of newcomers "but once a nucleus of newcomers had been in place, immigration became a self-feeding mechanism, with a momentum all its own.

The more immigrants moved to Los Angeles, the easier it was for the next batch to follow behind.... The contacts between veterans and newcomers as well as the institutions they founded (such as newspapers and churches) furthered movement into business" (Waldinger, 1996a, pp. 467–468).

The demographic composition of Los Angeles, like that of many major urban areas across the United States, has changed dramatically in the last 50 years, particularly since 1970 with the influx of Asian and Pacific Islanders, Central Americans, Mexicans, and Middle Easterners (Bozorgmehr, Der-Martirosian, & Sabagh, 1996; Hong & Yi, 2001; Laslett, 1996; Lopez, Popkin, & Telles, 1996; McGreevy, 2001; Sabagh & Bozorgmehr, 1996; Waldinger & Bozorgmehr, 1996).

Los Angeles' population in 2000 numbered 3,694,820, and its population profile showed that the city was predominantly of color with Latinos (47.0 percent), African Americans/Black (11.0 percent), and Asian and Pacific Islanders (9.8 percent) accounting for 57.8 percent of the population (Los Angeles City Department of Planning, 2001; U.S. Census Bureau, 2002). Between 1990 and 2000, Latinos (40 to 47 percent) made the greatest numerical increase followed by Asian and Pacific Islanders (9.0 to 9.8 percent), with African Americans/Blacks decreasing from 454,289 (13 percent) to 401,986 (11 percent) (Los Angeles City Department of Planning, 2001).

The Los Angeles metropolitan area has been the primary destination of many newcomers from Latin America, most notably Mexicans and Central Americans (Fulton, 2001; Vigil, 2002). Central Americans numbered 645,000 in 2000. Salvadorians were the most represented group (340,000) followed by Guatemalans with 186,500 (McDonnell, 2002). These figures represent those who are documented and undocumented. If only the latter are counted, the figure would be 437,000 in 2000.

In the Pico-Union neighborhood of Los Angeles, a predominantly Central American community, no one over the age of 14 years speaks English, which serves as an example of the impact of clustering newcomers within distinct geographical areas of a city (Marquez, 2002). Prior to the Rodney King riots, for example, South Central Los Angeles no longer consisted of a primarily African Americans/Blacks population (Morrison & Lowry, 1994; Wilson, 1993). However, people throughout the country watched television reports and got the impression that the typical profile of those who rioted were African American/Black, representing the majority of those who lived in South Central (Bobo, Zubrinsky, Johnson, & Oliver, 1994; Hayes-Bautista & Rodriguez, 1995; Petersilia & Abrahamse, 1994; Yemma, 1997).

The post-riot period witnessed an accelerated shift in South Central's racial/ethnic composition:

> It wasn't until the 1992 riots that anyone realized that Latinos made up the majority of what was once the heart of African American Los Angeles. The majority of Latinos in South Central are part of the wave of immigration into California that started in the 1970s and reached a crescendo in the 1980s. Contrary to many post-riot reports, South Central is not a major receiving area for the newest immigrants. A 1993 study of the riot-torn areas concluded that a "remarkably high percentage" of South Central Latinos have been residents of this counry for more than ten years. (Hayes-Bautista & Rodriguez, 1995, p. 202)

In 1970, African Americans/Blacks represented 72.6 percent of South Central's population, followed by Latinos with 12.8 percent and Asian and Pacific-Islanders with 3.2 percent. In 1980, African Americans/Blacks decreased to 67.6 percent and Asian and Pacific-Islanders decreased to 2.7 percent; Latinos, however, increased to 23.8 percent. In 1990, African Americans/Blacks were barely the in the majority (47.6 percent), with Latinos increasing to 45.2 percent and Asian and Pacific-Islanders not changing (2.6 percent). Estimates for 2000 have Latinos (foreign-born and native) increasing to 65 to 70 percent (Los Angeles City Department of Planning, 2001; McDonnell, 2002; Renwick, 1993).

Miami

Many people consider Miami to be the prototype of the city of the twenty-first century. Its global connections are unmistakable and so is its image in the media. It has a history of being the primary destination for newcomers from Latin America and the Caribbean (Didion, 1987; Rieff, 1999). In 1990, 59.7 percent of Miami's population was foreign-born, up from 53.7 percent in 1980. In 2000, the foreign-born percentage increased past 60 percent, not counting the children born to newcomers since they are counted as native to this country (Martin & Teitelbaum, 1998).

Miami is no longer composed of white, non-Latinos. In 2000, Florida's Latino population surpassed that of African Americans/Blacks for the first time, with 2.7 million versus 2.3 million (Riddle, 2001). In Miami-Dade County, including the City of Miami, Latinos represented 35.5 percent (338,330) during the 1990s (Farrington, 2001a, 2001b; Riddle, 2001). In 2000, 93 percent of the county's population was foreign-born, with Latinos numbering over 1 million, or 53 percent of the population. According to the 2000 U.S. Census, Miami had a population of 362,470. The vast majorities were Latinos (65.8 percent) followed by African Americans/Blacks with 24.2 percent, and Asian and Pacific Islanders accounting for 1.6 percent. Cubans (34.2 percent) numerically dominated the Latino community, in turn, with Puerto Ricans accounting for 2.8 percent, Mexicans representing 1 percent, and other Latino groups combined numbering over 100,000, or 27.8 percent of Miami's Latino community.

The period between 1960 and 2000 dramatically changed the ethnic and racial composition of Miami. In 1960, metropolitan Miami had approximately 1 million residents who were predominantly white, non-Latino (80 percent); 15 percent were African American/Black, and the remaining 5 percent were Latino. By 1990, metropolitan Miami had doubled in size to 2 million residents, with 30 percent being white, non-Latinos, 20 percent being African Americans, and Latinos accounting for 50 percent of the population (Martin & Teitelbaum, 1998). By 2000, the population had increased to 2.3 million and Latinos accounted for 57.3 percent of the county (Riddle, 2001). Cubans accounted for 49.4 percent (650,600), followed by Central Americans with 28.9 percent (129,000), South Americans with 6.8 percent (154,000), Puerto Ricans with 3.6 percent (80,000), Mexicans with 1.7 percent (38,000) and Dominicans at 1.6 percent (36,000).

Newcomers from the Caribbean, Central, and South America showed rapid growth during the 1990s (Benedick & Peltz, 2001; Stepick & Stepick, 2002). Nicaraguans decreased during this period from 74,000 to 69,000, still making them the fourth largest Latino group. Unofficially, they are said to number over 105,000 (Sharp, 2002). It is estimated that 41,000 Venezuelans live in or around Miami, or almost one-third (126,000) of their total in the United States. Miami-Dade County's population growth, largely fueled by Latinos, has continued into the twenty-first century. Between April 2000 and July 2001, the county lost 44,000 residents but gained 63,000 (Henderson, Epstein Nieves, & Bolstad, 2002). Demographic changes can be seen throughout Miami-Dade County. Little Havana, nationally known as a Cuban community, is no longer predominantly Cuban since they accounted for less than 25 percent of its Latino community in 2000 (Farrington, 2001a, 2001b; Ray, 2000; Sharp, 2002).

New York City

As late as 1970, New York City was home to approximately 25 percent of this nation's foreign-born population, with Los Angeles being second with close to 18 percent (Foner, 2000; Waldinger & Lee, 2001; Wright & Ellis, 2001). Los Angeles has since replaced New York City as the number-one destination of newcomers to the United States. This shift for Los Angeles has had considerable implications for that city, the state of California, and the nation as a whole.

In 2000, New York City topped 8 million residents for the first time in its illustrative history, or 6 percent of the total population (456,000) between 1990 and 2000 (Sachs, 2001). This increase is dramatic in light of slow growth between 1950 and 1990. It is estimated that over one million people left New York City during the 1990s, but new births and newcomers more than replaced those who left (Dao, 1998). In 2000, the white, non-Latino population accounted for 35 percent of the New York City's total. Latinos followed with 27 percent, African Americans/Blacks represented 25 percent, Asian and Pacific Islanders accounted for 10 percent, and multirace (3 percent) and other races (1 percent) completed the demographic picture.

The foreign-born population of New York City increased 38 percent, from 2.1 million in 1990 to 2.9 million in 2000, or 35.9 percent of the total population. In 1970, foreign-born were 18 percent of the city's population, the lowest percentage of the twentieth century (Foner, 2001a, 2001b). In 1980, the number increased to almost 25 percent (Kraly & Miyares, 2001); in 1998, it increased to 33 percent. In 2000, the percentage of foreign-born in New York City was the highest since 1910 (Foner, 2001b). One scholar has gone so far as to label New York City as "the nation's largest refugee camp" (Rosenberg, 1997). These newcomers have made New York City their home but still maintain an intense bond with their country of origin (Sachs, 2003; Sontag & Dugger, 1998).

Almost half of New York City's population age 5 and older (48 percent) spoke a language other than English in 2000, up from 41 percent in 1990 (Cheng, 2002). This increase of foreign-born is in part responsible for the drop in the city's median income during the 1990s (Scott, 2002). Proponents of using adjusted numbers in the census count argue that undercounting, particularly of undocumented persons, will cost New York City almost $700 million in federal aid (Smith, 2001a).

Between 1990 and 2000, New York City's ethnic and racial composition changed (Smith, 2001b). In 1990, 56.8 percent were of color, primarily African American/Black

(25.2 percent) and Latino (24.2 percent), followed by the Asian and Pacific Islander community with 6.7 percent (New York City Department of Planning, 2002). However, by 2000, the city's population of color increased by 65 percent, or 2.16 million. The Latino community, however, with 1.96 million people, surpassed the African American/Black population with 27.0 percent compared to 24.5 percent. The Asian and Pacific Islander population (primarily Chinese, Korean, and Filipino) increased to 9.8 percent (787,000), a 60 percent increase in one decade. In two affluent communities in Queens, the Asian (primarily Korean and Chinese) community doubled in size between 1990 and 2000 (Berger, 2003).

New York City also became more diverse during the decade of the 1990s. The early 1990s witnessed the immigration of 300,000 Soviet Jews (Orleck, 2001), and by the latter part of the decade there were 150,000 foreign-born Jamaicans (Vickerman, 2001) and 88,000 West Africans (Stoller, 2001), for example. However, nowhere is this more apparent than among the Latino and Asian and Pacific Islander communities (Lao-Montes, 2001; Min, 2001; Smith, 2001; Zhou, 2001b).

In 1990, Caribbean Latinos—such as Puerto Ricans (896,763) who are citizens of the United States, Dominicans (332,713) and Cubans (56,041)—accounted for 73.1 percent of all Latinos in New York City. By 2000, these groups accounted for only 57.2 percent of the Latino community. More specifically, Puerto Ricans (789,172) had declined in representation by 12 percent and Cubans (41,123) by 26.8 percent. Dominicans, however, increased by 22.3 percent (406,806). Central and South American groups increased numerically by a small sum (320,831 to 235,473) and represented 15.5 percent of the Latino community compared to 18.8 percent in 1990.

Mexicans increased between 1990 (61,722) and 2000 (186,872), by 202 percent, offsetting decreases among other Latino groups (Barry, 2003; Cox, 2002; New York City Department of Planning, 2002). The Mexican population increased so dramatically during the 1990s that Mexicans became the third largest Latino group in New York City behind Puerto Ricans and Dominicans. The establishment of institutions such as the Mariachi Academy is one consequence of this increase (Navarro, 2003a). It is estimated that in 2000 there were more Latinos in New York City than in 13 Latin American capitals (Scott, 2002). It is projected that Mexicans will be the largest Latino group on the East Coast within the next decade (Smith, 2001b). The increased presence of Mexicans has not been without conflict with more established Latino groups, most notably Puerto Ricans (Feuer, 2003).

The Latino community increased in diversity the past two decades (Jones-Correa, 1998; Lao-Montes & Davila, 2001; Levitt, 2001; Margolis, 1998; Waldinger, 1996b). Historically, the Latino community consisted primarily of Puerto Ricans. Since the early 1980s, other Latino groups have made New York City their home (Flores, 2002; Haslip-Viera & Baver, 1996; Pessar & Graham, 2001; Torres-Saillant & Hernandez, 1998). In 1980, Dominicans numbered 125,380. By 1990, they increased to 332,700 and to 495,000 in 1997. They are projected to surpass 700,000 in the early part of this century and shortly afterwards replace Puerto Ricans as the largest Latino group in the city (Dugger, 1996, 1997b; Firestone, 1995; Kaplan, 1997; Navarro, 2003b; Ojitio, 1997; Pessar, 1987, 1995). There are at least 800,000 Dominicans in New York and New Jersey (Kugel, 2002).

Asian and Pacific Islanders, too, have experienced significant increases and changes, particularly during the 1990s. Between 1990 and 2000, only one Asian and Pacific Islander group decreased numerically—Cambodians went from 2,565 to 1,701, down 31 percent (New York City Department of Planning, 2002). Every other group, however, increased, with Bangladeshi (286.4 percent), Sri Lankan (150.7 percent), Asian Indian (80.7 percent), and Chinese (51.3 percent) leading all other groups.

Conclusion

Social workers must become very familiar with demographics as they seek to position the profession strategically to address major social problems in this country. Nowhere are demographic trends more telling than in how the United States and its cities are undergoing changes in profile as newcomers increase numerically. The subject of newcomers is complex and ever changing and can best be understood when examined globally. Population upheavals are generally difficult to predict far enough into the future for countries to prepare themselves. Political strife and natural disasters play instrumental roles in causing population movements between countries, and so do severe economic and social deprivation. Demographic trends are just that—trends and projections into the future that are educated guesses. Yet, it is possible to develop an appreciation of an important subject for social work practice in this and other countries. Newcomers are not "new" to this country's social fabric, and some would argue are necessary for this nation to prosper in the twenty-first century.

The composition of the latest wave of newcomers is unlike that of any other period in the country's history and brings with it a host of challenges for policymakers. The social work profession is not exempt from feeling the consequences of these changes. The continued presence of newcomers in the United States, and particularly its major metropolitan centers, is expected to continue in the near future. The bringing together of newcomers of color with native residents of color in the nation's cities, for example, will prove challenging for government, education, and social service organizations.

If social work practice is to be effective in both the short and long run, the field must respond to the unique needs of the group being served (Potocky, 1996). The more knowledge providers have about the group they are helping, the higher the likelihood that services will achieve the goals they aspire to meet. Meeting the needs of newcomers, however, is not a static goal. Major social changes in this country in responding to the increase and nature of newcomers, as the reader will see in the following chapter, makes social workers' jobs that much harder to carry out, yet there are no shortcuts to this goal. Yes, there are resources available to address the challenges of helping newcomers to the United States. However, there are just not *enough* resources to make this process work for *all* newcomers.

3

Overview of Services

> *When today's immigrants look for work, a significant number have professional and technical skills, education, and even knowledge of the English language that would have been the envy of their predecessors a century ago. The range of human capital that contemporary arrivals bring with them is truly astounding.*
>
> —Foner, 2000, p. 71

Introduction

In order to have a better understanding of some of the challenges and barriers faced by immigrants and refugees, it is important to have an overview of services that they are entitled to upon resettlement in the United States. The services for refugees and immigrants are ever changing at both the federal and state levels. Every effort has been made to include in this chapter the latest changes regarding service eligibility, particularly at the federal level. However, it is possible that some of the information will be outdated by the time the book is published, and this reflects the dynamic nature of services to newcomers to the United States.

This chapter is not intended to provide the reader with great detail pertaining to the resources typically used to aid newcomers, because there are a number of excellent publications, some of which have been cited in this book, and local resources will undoubtedly differ according to state and region of the country. The overview presented in this chapter is intended to accomplish just that—an overview. We believe that this grounding makes it easier for the reader to better understand the nature of the needs and challenges that will be addressed in the next chapter, as well as possible resources that social workers and other helping professions can have at their disposal.

Legal Status and Entitlements

The status of the newcomer will play an influential role in the formal assistance he or she can expect while in the United States (Drachman, 1995). The federal government has divided the immigrants into different categories in terms of benefits eligibility. According to a chart published by the Massachusetts Immigrant and Refugee Coalition, the first category is *qualified immigrants*, which includes: (1) lawful permanent residents (green card holders); (2) refugees; (3) asylees; (4) persons granted withholding of deportation/removal, conditioned entry (in effect prior to April 1, 1980), or paroled into the United States for at least one year; (5) Amerasian immigrants; (6) Cuban/Haitian entrants; (7) some victims of domestic violence under the Violence against Women Act (VAWA) and victims of human trafficking; (8) veterans and their spouses, including Hmong/Lao and WWII Filipino; and (9) Native Americans born outside the United States.

The second category consists of *Permanently Residing Under Color of Law (PRUCOL)*, which means that the Bureau of Citizenship and Immigration Services (formerly INS) is aware of their presence in the United States, but has no plans to deport them. Immigrants who fall under PRUCOL status include, but are not limited to (1) applicants for permanent resident and asylee status, (2) individuals paroled into the United States for less than a year, and (3) immigrants with temporary protected status (TPS). It is important to point out that nonimmigrants, such as students or tourists, do not qualify as PRUCOLS. Further, it must be noted that not all "qualified" immigrants are necessarily eligible for all federal benefits. Eligibility depends on many factors, such as the person's date of entry or age at the time of arrival in the United States.

Personal Responsibility and Work Opportunity Reconciliation Act of 1996

The division of immigrants into two categories of qualified and not qualified was created as part of the 1996 welfare reform (Personal Responsibility and Work Opportunity Reconciliation Act of 1996 [PRWORA]). After the welfare reform in 1996, immigrants' access to many public benefits became restricted: "The PRWORA barred most 'qualified' immigrants who entered the U.S. on or after Aug. 22, 1996 from receiving 'federal means-tested public benefits' (i.e., Supplemental Security Income (SSI), food stamps, Temporary Assistance for Needy Families (TNAF), State Children's Health Insurance Program (SCHIP), and non-emergency Medicaid) during the first five years after they secure qualified immigrant status" (National Immigration Law Center, 2001).

Not only did welfare reform impose a five-year ban on immigrants who entered the United States on or after August 22, 1996, in terms of eligibility for federal services, but it subjected them to a process called *deeming*, where the income and other resources of the immigrants' sponsor would count toward the immigrants' own income to determine eligibility for any kind of assistance under the government's financial guidelines. As a result, thousands of lawful immigrants lost eligibility for benefits.

Broder and Wiley (2002) comment on the extent of the impact of these changes: "The 1996 welfare law was enacted in part to reduce the federal deficit, and 44 percent of the projected federal saving ($25 billion over the five years) stemmed from the immigration eligibility restrictions. But many in Congress and the general public did not realize that lawfully present immigrants (and the citizen family members) would bear the brunt of those budget cuts. Undocumented immigrants were already ineligible for most federal assistance programs" (p. 153).

According to the National Academy of Science, the average immigrant contributes $1,800 more in taxes than he or she receives in benefits and services provided by the government (including parks, public roads and all other state, local, and federal services and benefits, as well as the safety net benefits). The federal government receives the lion's share of those tax dollars (approximately two-thirds). However, states and localities provide the bulk of the services immigrants use, including health care and public assistance when needed (National Immigration Forum, 2003).

Also, after the 1996 welfare law reform, some states tried to design programs that could at least assist some of the immigrants who were "ineligible" for federal programs. According to the data published by the National Immigration Law Center (2002), 16 states provide state-funded food assistance to these immigrants, 26 provide medical assistance, 21 provide the State Children's Health Insurance Program (SCHIP), 23 provide Temporary Assistance for Needy Families (TANF), and 6 provide a state-funded Supplemental Security Income (SSI) replacement program.

Entitlements

For the purposes of this book, additional attention needs to be paid to the particular services to which refugees, asylees, and asylum seekers are entitled. As already explained, both refugees and asylees are considered "qualified" immigrants who are exempt from the five-year bar and are not subjected to "deeming" (even if they have relatives in the United States). Resettlement agencies are responsible for meeting the refugees upon their arrival to the United States and covering all their necessary expenses for the first 30 days. The resettlement agencies receive $400 per capita from the Department of State to cover the newly arrived refugees' expenses for the first month.

Since the reception and placement (R&P) money is given to the voluntary agencies by the federal government, the amount of money is the same across the board and does not differ from one state to another. This practice, however, does not bring into consideration the cost of living differences. For example, the R&P for a family of five would be $2,000 for the first month. In a state such as New York or Massachusetts where the housing market is very expensive, most of the R&P money will go toward the rent, whereas in other states such as Texas the money could cover the different necessary expenses the family might have upon arrival. In instances where the cost of renting an apartment and furnishing it exceeds the amount of funds provided by the Department of State, the voluntary (resettlement) agencies are responsible for securing their own funds elsewhere.

For an extensive overview of immigrant eligibility for federal programs and also state-funded replacement programs, the reader can refer to the *Guide to Immigrant Eligibility for Federal Programs* (2002), published by National Immigration Law Center.

In order to have a better understanding of how different factors may affect the well-being of refugees and asylees, it is first necessary to explain the process in which refugees are admitted to the United States. (Chapter 4 will discuss the connection between the resettlement process and refugees' economic stability upon resettlement in this country.)

Access and Entitlements

Each year, after consultation with Congress, the president decides on the number of refugee admissions and the allocation of these numbers by region of the world they are from. The president then submits a report known as the *consultation document* to the House of Representatives and the Senate containing the administration's proposed refugee ceiling and allocations for the upcoming fiscal year (Bruno & Bush, 2002, p. CRS-2).

Only those applications that are referred by the United Nations High Commissioner for Refugees (UNHCR) or a U.S. Embassy and those that meet other criteria defined in the Department of State's admissions policy will be considered for admission to the United States. According to Potocky-Tripodi's (2002) review of the literature, UNHCR has two main functions: to protect refugees and to seek durable solutions to their problems. Bruno and Bush (2003) go on to note: "The state department conducts overseas processing of refugees through a system of three priorities for admission . . . [this] priority assignment does reflect an assessment of the urgency with which such persons need to be resettled" (pp. CRS4–5).

The U.S. Department of State (2001) defines the priorities as follows:

> **Priority One:** UNHCR or U.S. Embassy identified cases: persons facing compelling security concerns in countries of first asylum; persons in need of legal protection because of the danger of refoulment; those in danger due to threats of armed attack in an area where they are located; persons who have experienced recent persecution because of their political, religious, or human rights activities (prisoners of conscience); women-at-risk; victims of torture or violence; physically or mentally disabled persons; persons in urgent need of medical treatment not available in the first asylum country; and persons for whom other durable solutions are not feasible. Priority One referrals must still establish a credible fear of persecution or history of persecution in the country from which they fled.

> **Priority Two:** Groups of special concern

> **Priority Three:** Spouses, unmarried sons and daughters, and parents of persons lawfully admitted to the United States as permanent resident aliens, refugees, asylees, conditional residents, and certain parolees; the over-21-year-old unmarried sons and daughters of U.S. citizens; and parents of U.S. citizens under 21 years of age. (Spouses and unmarried sons and daughters under 21 of U.S. citizens and the parents of U.S. citizens who are 21 or older are required by regulation to be admitted as immigrants rather than as refugees.) (pp. 1–2)

Those individuals who meet the criteria for application to the United States are then interviewed by the Bureau of Citizenship and Immigration Services (BCIS; formerly INS) officers who travel to the country of asylum to conduct the interviews. If the BCIS officer approves the refugee's application for U.S. resettlement, arrangements are made for the person's placement with a U.S. voluntary agency and his or her travel to the United States.

Information about all the approved cases is then sent to the Refugee Processing Center (PRC) in Arlington, VA. The center allocates those cases to the 10 voluntary agencies nationwide that are under contract with the Department of State to provide them with reception and placement services. "Several bureaucratic hurdles must be cleared before an approved allocated refugee can come to the United States. These steps—which take place concurrently and can take from two months to two years to complete—are needed to meet the requirements of the U.S. Public Health Services and INS. The U.S. Department of State also requires that refugees receive some basic preparation and assistance, in part, to ensure they become self-sufficient quickly" (U.S. Committee for Refugees, 2002, p. 2). All refugees have to receive medical clearance, security clearance, and cultural orientation prior to coming to the United States. It is worth mentioning that after the events on September 11th, and with the new regulations from the Homeland Security Department, refugees have been waiting for months to receive their security clearance. The security clearance process can take from several days to several months, depending on the level of clearance sought and the backlogs at the processing center. Since September 11, 2001, a higher level of security clearance is required for many applicants.

One of the authors of this book is aware of many cases that were approved to come to the United States (some people even had their tickets purchased through the International Organization for Migration [IOM]), but after September 11, 2001, refugee admission came to a halt and all applicants had to go through the second round of a security clearance process with new and tougher regulations.

A vast number of those cases are still waiting to hear the results of their security clearance. Consequently, only 27,000 of 70,000 refugees allowed for resettlement in the United States during 2002 actually arrived during that year. This problem has continued to exist, as evidenced by a report prepared by Immigration and Refugee Services of America (2003): "As of July 1, with three months remaining in FY 2003, Bureau of Population, Refugees and Migration (PRM) had admitted 17,415 refugees, 32,585 short of the 50,000 specified under regional ceiling to come to the United States. (The Administration authorized a ceiling of 70,000 but specified only 50,000 under regional ceiling and placed 20,000 in the unallocated reserve)" (p. 1).

Newcomers Awaiting Entrance into the Country

For the refugee individuals or families, this long unexpected period of waiting could drain their last resources and usually expose them to abuse, interrogation, extortion, and in many cases to imprisonment by the corrupted local authorities.

After a refugee is approved, the next step for voluntary agencies is assuring a case, which means that the agencies have to give assurance to the Department of State that they are prepared to receive the refugee case(s) that have been assigned to them. The assurance is a written guarantee that basic services outlined in the contract with the Department of State will be provided to refugees. The assurance process usually takes between four to eight weeks.

As a part of this process, a resettlement (voluntary) agency is contacted by its national sponsoring agency and is given biographic data of a potential case, including composition of the family, their names and ages, religion, level of education, level of English, and, most important, their medical condition. The next step for the voluntary agency is to do a calculation of the family's income based on the available information and compare the estimated income to the average cost of living in that particular state to find out if the family would be able to survive on the amount of assistance they receive from the government in their first few months before beginning employment.

If a resettlement agency assures a case, one of the main tasks would be finding an apartment and furnishing it so that it is ready to be occupied upon arrival of the refugees. Since the amount of financial assistance in most cases is barely enough to pay for the rent and utilities, the resettlement agencies have no choice but to look for housing in cheaper neighborhoods, where in most cases there is already a high concentration of low-income immigrant and nonimmigrant families.

Finding an apartment that will accommodate the number of expected people is a very challenging, time-consuming process for the resettlement agencies, particularly in some of the metropolitan areas where the housing market is very expensive. While the allocation of money varies in different states and different agencies, in most cases the resettlement agencies will pay for the first, and in some cases depending on the program refugees are enrolled in, up to four months of rent for a newly arrived refugee. It's the person's or family's responsibility to pay the rent after the period designated by the resettling agency. This can be a huge burden on a newly arrived family considering that in reality no one in a household is employed by the end of the first month. Chapter 4 will discuss in detail how service eligibility may have a direct effect on youth in terms of their future planning and education access.

The resettlement agencies are also responsible for assisting refugees with employment, English classes, medical care, school enrollment for children, and general orientation to public transportation systems, currency, shopping, and so on. The resettlement services for refugees are not over after the first 30 days. The agencies continue working with refugees closely for the first 90 days after their arrival and are also responsible for providing services for up to three years to refugees.

Since the cost of ticket(s) to the United States could be very high, particularly for larger families, the International Organization for Migration (IOM) covers the cost of the transporting individual(s) to the United States and is also responsible for collecting this travel loan later on. As an intergovernmental body, the IOM (http://www.oim.pt/body_mission.html) acts with its partners in the international community to (1) assist in meeting the operational challenges of migration, (2) deepen the understanding of migration issues, (3) encourage social and economic development through migration, and (4) uphold human dignity and the well-being of migrants.

Loan Payment

Refugees are generally expected to start paying back their interest-free loan after being in the United States for six months. However, for many families who are just beginning to be self-sufficient, making the payments can be very challenging. In most cases, each individual is required to pay $35 a month over the period of three years. If, for example, there are five people in a family, they need to pay $175 a month, which often creates a financial challenge for the family. In extreme cases, if a person or a family is unable to start making payments, an extension or smaller installments can be requested.

Asylees

In 2000, the Office of Refugee Resettlement (ORR), a federal agency that plans, develops, and directs implementation of the comprehensive domestic refugee resettlement programs (Potocky-Tripodi, 2002), announced that effective June 15, 2000, asylees are eligible for refugee assistance and services beginning on the date they are granted asylum. Under this policy, the date that an asylum seeker is granted asylum is considered that person's date of entry. The new law made asylees eligible to access refugee cash benefits, employment assistance, English classes, and medical assistance for eight months. The ORR also made it clear that no retroactive assistance will be given to those asylees whose eligibility period expired before June 15, 2002.

If an asylum seeker receives work authorization before a decision is made about his or her case, with it they also receive a social security number. However, if an asylum seeker does not receive work authorization and a social security number during the asylum process, he or she is eligible to apply for an unrestricted social security card upon receiving asylum.

In order to obtain asylum status in the United States, asylum seekers have to establish a well-founded fear of persecution or death if they were to return to their country of origin. Persons who intend to file for asylum in the United States have a one-year deadline from their date of entry. If a person misses the deadline, it becomes extremely difficult to file for asylum. Before filing for asylum, an asylum seeker is not entitled to receive any federal or state benefits. If a child of an asylum seeker is born in the United States, the American child of the asylum seeker would be eligible to receive cash assistance, food stamps, and health benefits. However, this does not qualify the asylum seeker or other family members to receive any benefits.

Only 150 days after a person has filed for asylum, he or she can apply for a work permit. After the application is sent, it can take between 30 to 90 days before the person receives a work permit.

Ineligibility for Services

Ineligibility for services places asylum seekers in a very vulnerable position. The majority of asylum seekers in the United States have either been primary victims or witnessed torture and atrocities done to their loved ones and co-patriots. Some of the asylum seekers come to the United States from war-torn countries, where they did not have access to proper health care, food, and other essential commodities. Their ineligibility to access services such as cash assistance, work authorization, health insurance, and proper housing during the asylum process has a very negative effect on their level of functioning and their emotional well-being.

In most cases, the housing choice for asylum seekers who have no means of supporting themselves or have no friends or family in the United States and are not eligible for any kind of assisted housing is a shelter. For those asylum seekers who have already fled their home or have witnessed their houses burn to the ground, and for those who have been subjected to torture and other types of trauma, being in such an environment can only be detrimental to their psychological health.

One of this book's authors recalls a case in which an asylum seeker who had just arrived from one of the African countries had to stay at a shelter. After calling all the shelters in the city, the only choice was to go to a shelter by 4:30 P.M. to see if the person could get a bed for the night. This individual, who was severely tortured in his home country and had left his family behind, spent his first night in the United States sharing a room with more than 50 other men, most of whom had substance abuse problems. In the middle of the night, the person who was sleeping next to this individual had a concussion and vomited on this individual.

That particular asylum seeker had to live in that condition for three months before an alternative housing arrangement could be made. Even under those poor circumstances, an individual is not guaranteed a bed for even a week. Every person must show up at the shelter every day by 4:30 P.M. to try to secure a bed for that night. During the day, all the guests must leave the shelter, with the assumption being that they have to go to work or look for a job. However, for an asylum seeker who is not authorized to work, a day has to be spent on the street, at a public library, or volunteering at a place if they can find one.

Another problem with shelters hosting individuals is that the guests are not given a locker in which to place their personal belongings, and in many instances people find that their valuables have been stolen from them while asleep. Asylum seekers often leave all their belongings behind in their homeland; if they were lucky, they managed to bring with them only a bag or a small suitcase. In many instances the individual asylum seekers had to carry their suitcases with them around the city all day so that they could save whatever they had managed to bring from home. Asylum seekers not only have to depend on charitable and human services organizations for their housing needs, they also have to rely on such institutions to meet other basic needs, such as food, clothing, and money for transportation. In many cases the drastic change in status, which brings one's dignity under question, can have a very negative and humiliating affect on asylum seekers.

Youth

The asylum process is dually complicated and much more difficult for children and youth who enter the United States unaccompanied. According to the World Refugee

Survey (U.S. Committee for Refugees, 2002), "Some 8,500 children seek asylum in the United States each year. Almost three-quarters of them are unaccompanied by an adult; approximately 5,000 are subjected to INS detention. No attorneys or legal guardians are appointed to represent children in immigration proceedings, and children with asylum claims often bear the burden of proving their claims in court without assistance. Many children are detained during their proceedings, either in private shelters, juvenile detention centers, or local jails" (p. 277).

Chapter 4 addresses the negative effects of detention on the emotional and psychological health of asylum seekers. Health care services are often delivered throughout local neighborhood health centers in cases where the newcomer does not have health insurance. These centers have increased in popularity, even when health insurance is available, because they provide services in a culturally validating manner (Clemetson, 2002).

Conclusion

Clearly, there are different worlds for the newcomers who are "eligible" versus "ineligible" for governmental assistance. The accessibility of resources to aid newcomers in their adjustment to this society is undeniable, yet very limited in scope. The availability of services and resources to aid immigrants and refugees in their adjustment within their new country, however, does not necessarily translate into actual of services and resources.

In summarizing the research on why some newcomers do not avail themselves of governmental benefit programs, Capps (2001) notes several causes:

> While there have been sharp declines in overall participation in benefits across the country, immigrants' participation has fallen faster than that of native-born citizens.... A growing body of evidence suggests that immigrants and their families are staying away from public assistance to a greater extent than citizens, even when they remain eligible for aid. In addition, many immigrants are concerned about the effects that using benefits will have on their ability to legalize, naturalize, sponsor relatives, and even reenter or remain in the country. Although most of these concerns are misplaced, they have nonetheless chilled immigrants' participation and caused immigrants to withdraw from public assistance and health services. (p. 1)

The inability or unwillingness of U.S. society to provide economic, educational, and social supports for newcomer families and their youth has prodigious consequences for the kind of problems and issues social workers will face in the coming decades. The next chapter provides the reader with an exhaustive account of the struggles of newcomers, and more specifically youth, and their goal of seeking to make a better life for themselves in this country.

4

Challenges Faced by Newcomer Youth

> *I watched these new refugee youth enter ... and witnessed the concern for their well-being. ... Yet with all the support and encouragement provided these students, it was clear that we were often unprepared for the challenges they faced ... each time a new refugee student arrived, we would once again find ourselves struggling to meet his or her unique needs.*
>
> —Kelen & Kelen, 2002, pp. 7–8

Introduction

This chapter provides a comprehensive overview of the key issues, including social-po-litical-economic-cultural-health-educational-religious/spiritual-emotional, that new-comer youth and their families face upon resettlement in the United States (Azima & Grizenko, 2002; Gavagan & Brodyaga, 1998; Kamya, 1997; Mirkin, 1998; Mohan, 1992; Pryor, 2001; Sisneros, 2002; Westermeyer & Wahmanhom, 1996). Youth must contend with multiple losses, often prolonged separation from parent(s) who first migrated, rap-idly changing family and gender roles, anti-immigrant sentiment, and racism (arguably understood and experienced differently than by U.S.-born youth of color).

The 1999 National Survey of America's Families (Capps, 2001) found that new-comer children, when compared to native children, experience greater hardships in meeting basic needs in nutrition, housing, and health care. Almost 25 percent of all immigrant children, compared to 16 percent for native children, live in economically poor families. Some 37 percent live in families that consistently worry about or experi-ence difficulties in purchasing food, compared to 27 percent of native children. Finally, 22 percent were uninsured, which is double the rate for native children.

Padilla (1997) notes that needs, in this case related to Latinos but also applicable to other groups, cover a wide span of arenas with direct implications for any form of social work practice: "Overall, the social work literature shows that to different degrees, immigrants face a series of stress-producing events that result in need for assistance and support; such events include separation from family and community, journeys of differ-ent duration and levels of danger, and relation problems associated with finding hous-ing and employment" (p. 595).

One of the most fundamental principles underlying the youth development par-adigm is that youth have rich assets and strengths, develop complex competencies, and prove strikingly resilient. Some might argue that this is particularly true of newcomer youth who, despite major disruptions and transitions in their lives, are succeeding in families, schools, and communities across the country. Although this is likely the reality for most, it is essential to recognize the challenges they must face, as well as to acknowl-edge that some do indeed struggle and need additional support and services.

This chapter summarizes the key issues, needs, and concerns of newcomer youth. It is important to acknowledge the incredible breadth and complexity of this topic. Not only are there myriad issues in multiple domains of newcomer youth's lives, but they are often inextricably intertwined. Further, there is tremendous diversity in their cul-tures, countries of origin, and actual migration experiences. Thus, there is critical inter-sectionality between the individual's unique traits and his or her culture, country of origin, family, migration process, life experiences, and current environment. The con-cept of *intersectionality* (Laird, 1998; Lum, 2003; Spencer, Lewis, & Gutierrez, 2000) underscores individuals' multiple group memberships and identities. As defined by Lum (2003), "Intersectionality is those multiple intersections and crossroads in our lives that are replete with multiple social group memberships that are interconnected and interrelated" (p. 42).

Intersectionality may be further broadened to include the intersection of various aspects of social identity with particular developmental stages and within specific socio-political contexts. Thus, if a newcomer youth is having difficulties, to what degree is he or she just dealing with "normal" adolescent development issues? In what ways might the youth reflect unique realities of being a refugee or immigrant—from a given culture and country, a specific family, at a particular point in his or her adaptation and accul-turation? How does one differentiate the impact of the wider environment from the ongoing personal legacies of migration? Obviously, these are all essential consider-ations in program design, outreach, and delivery of services to newcomer youth.

The authors begin with an overarching framework that outlines key "contextual variables" that are important when thinking about newcomer youth and their families. Then, potential issues and needs in 11 arenas are discussed: age/developmental stage, gender, family relationships, acculturation and ethnic identity formation, peer relation-ships, education, economics, health, mental health, spirituality/religion, and political realities.

Contextual Variables

There is growing literature that recognizes the need to understand newcomers within multiple contexts (Drachman, 1995; Mirkin, 1998; Padilla, 1997). These contexts are frequently organized in terms of the stages of migration: pre-migration, during migra-tion, and post-migration. Although this emphasis on temporal phases is helpful, the authors have chosen to think of contexts more broadly, recognizing possible continuities and overlapping as well as points of clear demarcation and change. Eight key contextual variables are thus noted: original culture, country of origin, pre-migration life, circumstances of migration, trauma experience, family fragmentation, legal status and resettlement process, and host community. Collectively, these variables help frame what Falicov (2003) describes as the "ecological niche" and each could clearly merit a chapter of its own. Although they are only briefly noted here, they are applied and integrated throughout the subsequent discussion of needs, issues, and concerns of newcomer youth.

Original Culture

Culture—as the shaper of values, beliefs, and norms, and the lens through which we see life and give meaning to events—has already been referenced many times in this book. However, it is useful to briefly revisit it here and remind ourselves how much it may influence all the domains of a newcomer youth's life and development, and thus the need to explore such questions as:

- What are the key values, norms, and religious beliefs of the youth/family's traditional culture?
- To what degree did the family embrace traditional culture and norms in their homeland?
- When they arrived in the United States, how consonant were their original cultural values and norms with U.S. mainstream culture?
- To what degree are differential rates of acculturation seen among family members? Are there varying preferences regarding the degree of cultural incorporation?
- Which cultural values and traditions may serve as significant "resources" to the newcomer family in the United States?

Country of Origin

All too often U.S. citizens hear newcomers described as coming from Asia or from Africa, without any specific statement regarding their actual country of origin. Cultures within continents vary tremendously, as do their historical legacies. Thus, it is useful to know:

- Is there a history of colonialism or occupation?
- Have there been prolonged periods of instability?
- What contemporary events/conditions (war, economics, politics) have contributed to the migration?
- What has been the role, if any, of the U.S. government in either historical or contemporary events?
- Has there been a history of conflict with neighboring countries, which are now also a source of migrants to the United States?

Pre-Migration Life

Life did not begin for newcomer youth and their families when they set foot upon U.S. soil. Thus, it is useful to know about their lives in their country of origin, and to consider the following:

- Urban or rural area
- Socioeconomic background (standard of living, class, status)
- Education (opportunities, highest level reached, significant interruptions, literacy)
- Employment
- Family structure, stability, level of functioning
- Member of majority or minority group
- Degree of exposure to western culture
- Degree to which "traditional" culture followed
- Experience, if any, with repression and discrimination
- Expectations and hopes for future (return to homeland?)

Circumstances of Migration

The most basic of questions here is whether the migration was forced or voluntary. As already noted, refugees and asylum seekers are considered victims of forced migration. Using the formal definition from the United Nations High Commissioner for Refugees, the individuals have a reasonable fear of persecution, based on religion, political beliefs, or membership in an ethnic or social group. More simply put, these people are in fear for their lives and flee their homeland to survive. Individuals who enter as immigrants are presumed to be voluntary migrants, coming for better economic opportunities and/or family reunification. However, it is important to note that many immigrants consider that they, too, are refugees, fleeing from repressive regimes and in danger, even though current U.S. immigrant policy may not officially recognize them as such (Nassar, 2002). It is essential to consider:

- Economic situation (standard of living, level of poverty, perceived opportunities)
- Political situation (degree of stability/instability, length and level of repression and violence, perceived risk and immediate danger)
- Decision to leave (made by whom, unanimous, dictated, or "assigned")
- Time table (planned for years, waiting for opportunity, spur of the moment)
- Opportunity for "leave taking"/good-byes (ample opportunity and no attached danger versus no opportunity and risk if plan revealed)
- Opportunity to take significant items with them
- Length of actual migration process (direct, in refugee camp for years)
- Opportunity to readily or ever return
- Single or multiple migrations

Trauma Experience

It is critical to recognize that for some newcomers traumas continue or are "retriggered" even after they reach the United States. Immigration policies that do not give equal priority to extended family members and thus force separations, or housing policies that restrict the number of residents who may live together may be experienced as new trauma. Similarly, violence in their new neighborhood, and/or news of continuing/renewed violence in their homeland may stir up traumatic memories and symptoms. It is essential, then, to consider:

- Pre-migration, during migration, post-migration
- Number, type, frequency, duration, and intensity of trauma experiences
- Natural disaster or caused by human(s)

Although the majority of documented "economic immigrants" may not have experienced trauma in their country of origin, refugees and asylum seekers without exception have—the question is how much, what kinds, and for how long? The trauma may include starvation, physical threats, beatings, imprisonment, torture, rape, seeing relatives killed, witnessing atrocities, being forced to violate one's moral code, and living for prolonged periods in fear for one's life. There is often additional or new trauma during the escape process itself, and indeed the violence may well continue even in refugee camps. A small percentage of documented immigrants may have experienced similar trauma if they have come from repressive regimes, even if they are not "official" refugees. It is likely that many undocumented immigrants, particularly those coming from Central America and Mexico, have also experienced some type of trauma during their dangerous trip to the United States. Such trauma can include physical attacks, rape, betrayal, and abandonment.

Even if the social worker's role in working with newcomer youth does not require or allow for any discussion of such trauma, it is critical to be aware of the degree of likelihood of traumas having occurred. Further, even if the youth themselves arrived at such a young age that they have no memory of the trauma, it is important to recognize that they may being parented by those who do, and indeed the trauma may be an integral part of the "family story."

Family Fragmentation

Although newcomer youth and their parents may appear to be an "intact" family, it is always useful to consider:

- Members left behind
- Members who may have been "lost" (died, killed, disappeared, fate unknown)
- Number and duration of previous family separations
- Number of family reunifications
- Pattern of migrations, if multiple
- Degree of contact with family members in country of origin; degree of continued influence of absent family members

Legal Status and Resettlement Process

Legal status and its implications for both needs and services will be discussed in detail later. However, when thinking about the basic contextual variables, key issues are:

- Actual legal status (refugee, asylum seeker, temporary protective status, documented immigrant, undocumented immigrant)
- Resettled through resettlement agency or sponsored by family member
- Unaccompanied minor, single adult, family group, or "family of convenience" (formed in camp)

Host Community

Whether the newcomer has been officially resettled by a resettlement agency, is joining a family member, or has arrived without official papers, the "host community" is a critical variable. Consider the following:

- Number/concentration of residents from homeland, same ethnic group
- Extent of ethnic organization/leadership/resources
- Educational and employment opportunities
- Availability of support services
- Perceived sense of security/safety; level of community violence
- Degree of racism, nativism, oppression

The contextual variables outlined here and summarized in Box 4.1 are undeniably critical in shaping the lives of newcomer youth, and their experiences are as unique and varied as the countries, cultures, and families from which they come. However, there are also certain common issues and needs that many newcomer youth and their families share. These include issues related to age/developmental stage, gender, family relationships, acculturation and ethnic identity formation, peer relationships, education, economics, health, mental health, spirituality/religion, and political realities. Although these are now discussed separately, they obviously are often experienced as intertwined.

Issues Related to Specific Age/Developmental Stage

The Young Child

The age of a child at the point of migration can have a significant impact on his or her subsequent development and acculturation, with potential advantages and disadvantages at each stage. If a child is quite young, conventional wisdom points to the opportunity to attend school regularly and the ability to quickly learn English and acculturate. In addition, given the needs of young children, care and proximity of parents is more likely assured, and as McGoldrick and Giodorno (1996) write, families with young children are "strengthened by having each other" (p. 17). However they, along with other

BOX 4.1 *Summary of Key Contextual Variables*

Cultural/National Contexts	Family Context	Refugee/Immigrant Experience	Losses/Trauma Experience

Cultural
Values and belief systems
Religion/philosophy
Patterns of interaction
Race—majority or minority
Ethnicity—majority or minority
Religion—majority or minority
 	
National
History
Colonial legacies
Political ideologies
Recent/current political, economic, social conditions
Conflicts w/ neighboring countries (which are also source of migrants)
	In Country of Origin
	Definition of family
	Structure
	Boundaries
	Roles
	Communication
	Decision-making
	Problem-solving
	Coping patterns
	Family loyalties/ obligations
	Family strengths
	
	In U.S.
	All the above
	Stage in family life cycle
	Expectation of family reunification
	"Future orientation"
	
	Individual Members
	Age, stage of life
	Gender
	Roles in family
	Education/employment
	Psychological profile
	Level of functioning
		Pre-Migration
		Rural/urban residence
		Class/status
		Education/employment
		Wars, oppression, economic conditions
		Impact of family unit, status, opportunities
		
		Escape/Migration
		Decision: when, how, by whom
		"Meaning" of migration
		Trip: length, conditions, trauma
		Camp: length, conditions, trauma
		
		Post-Migration
		Legal status
		Language capability
		Housing
		Health
		Education/employment
		Neighborhood
		Family fragmentation and reconfigurations
		Acculturation: differential choices and pace, conflict
		Ethnic community and degree of "connectedness"
		Racism/discrimination
			Losses
			Homeland, culture, language
			Family, friends
			Status, profession/work
			Trust
			Sense of self
			
			Trauma
			Who in family
			At what life stage
			Single or multiple incidents
			Experienced and/or witnessed
			What: beating, torture, rape, starvation
			Revealed or individual/ family secret
			Beliefs/assumptions shattered
			Continued traumatization in U.S.
			Symptoms of PTSD
			Impact on life:
			  Survivor guilt
			  Inability to trust
			  Learned helplessness
			  Immobilization
			  Isolation, withdrawal
			  Chronic maladaptive behaviors
			Degree to which trauma reinterpreted/ integrated; meaning and continuity of life restored
			Recognition/validation of "survivor strengths"

Source: Kay Jones, Boston University School of Social Work, 1991, revised 2003.

authors (Balcazar & Qian, 2000), also point out that those very same families, due to the children's rapid acculturation, may be most likely to have traditional hierarchies challenged during the ensuing years.

Another potential impact of arriving in the United States at a very young age relates to language development. In some families, the native language may not be successfully passed on to young children. Although some of these children may learn to speak their homeland language quite fluently, they remain unable to read or write it. Others may learn only the most rudimentary oral and reading skills. This inability to fully converse in their parents' first language may possibly contribute to communication and cultural barriers in the future. Another language-related issue is the ability of preverbal children to process traumatic experiences. Several authors (Pynoos, Steinberg, & Goenjian, 1996; Terr, 1991) suggest that refugee children who experienced severe trauma before they developed language skills may have a more difficult time in healing from this trauma.

Culturally specific child-rearing practices may also present issues for newcomer families (Bemak, Chung, & Bornemann, 1996; Korbin, 1991). The concept of formal daycare (entrusting one's children to strangers) may be alien, and the idea that outsiders (such as a child welfare agency) have the right to intervene in how one raises a child, may be incomprehensible (Masaki & Wong, 1997). Sleeping arrangements and disciplinary techniques may all create misunderstandings and conflict with external authorities.

The Middle School and Adolescent Youth

Children who arrive as preadolescents or adolescents are generally thought to bring fluency in their mother tongue and a sense of their own culture. However, one cannot always assume this. There are many refugee youth whose education has been significantly disrupted by years of war and political strife; they may arrive with limited language skills. Other refugee youth have essentially grown up in refugee camps, where traditional cultural institutions and norms are absent. Some newcomer youth who arrive as school-age children are described as the *1.5 generation*. Although potentially able to successfully blend the best of both cultures, not all youth experience this as their reality. Describing his experience as a member of the 1.5 generation, Ryu (1992, p. 50) writes of feeling anchored in neither culture. Though bilingual, he is also "bi-illiterate"; though bicultural, he also feels "biculturally deprived."

Finally, there is the adolescent developmental stage itself, which no matter what the cultural context, calls for some "stretching away from parents" and increased sense of independence. Further, the so-called norms of adolescence in the mainstream U.S. culture, with which the youth is bombarded through the media and by his or her peers, may be particularly dissonant with the traditional values and norms of his or her parents. This dissonance, combined with the inherent losses already sustained through migration, may well cause parents to experience this developmental stage as significantly more stressful than if it had occurred in the country of origin (Falicov, 2003). Also, as McGoldrick and Giordano (1996) note, families with adolescents may simply have fewer years together before these children move out, giving them less time to successfully negotiate the multiple transitions and adaptations required.

Issues Related to Gender

Gender can affect newcomer youth in multiple and diverse ways. At the most basic and physical sense, gender may place newcomer girls and young women at increased risk before (and even after) they arrive in the United States. Clearly, women and girls have always been particularly vulnerable during times of war, civil unrest, and escape/migration journeys. Thus, untold numbers of female immigrants and refugees have been threatened with, witnessed, and/or suffered sexual assaults or rapes. Indeed, some have been in conflict situations in which rape was actively used as a conscious tool of war (Freidman, 1992). Rape has essentially become an instrument of war and can no longer be seen simply as a consequence of war. Rape and sexual assaults are unquestionably traumatic for anyone, but for women and girls from certain cultures the consequences may be especially profound. If a culture places a very high value on female virginity, not only may the entire family be shamed, but the girl and even her sisters may be considered no longer worthy of marriage. In some instances, the threat of humiliation and community exclusion and stigmatization is so strong that the family may engage in a "conspiracy of silence" regarding the rape. Clearly, there are psychological costs and possible long-term consequences for such young women.

Since female virginity continues to be an important cultural/religious value and behavioral norm for many newcomers, parents may become increasingly concerned about their daughters as they approach adolescence. Indeed, Suarez-Orozco and Suarez-Orozco (2001, p. 78) assert that "in some immigrant communities, becoming 'Americanized' is synonymous with becoming sexually promiscuous." Predictably, then, in some families conflicts may quickly escalate, whereas in others the daughter may find herself caught between wanting to date like her American peers but also wishing to continue to be the "dutiful daughter." In addition to disagreements regarding dating and curfews, the age of marriage and the selection of a mate may also become issues. Among some Indian families in the United States, the parents may still expect to arrange their daughter's marriage; the daughters may or may not be willing to accept this (Grieger & Ponterotto, 1995). In the Hmong culture, marriages traditionally are arranged for daughters in their very early teens. This practice continues to some extent in the United States with mixed responses from daughters, the wider community, and school/youth providers (Westermeyer & Wahmanhom, 1996).

Many authors discuss the gender differences in role expectations in immigrant and refugee families. There is general agreement that most sons are allowed greater freedom and privileges. Daughters tend to be supervised more closely and their activities outside the home are more restricted. At the same time, they are frequently assigned more responsibilities within the home (Balcazar & Qian, 2000; Pettys & Balgopal, 1998; Suarez-Orozco & Suarez-Orozco, 2001). "Traditional" gender roles and expectations sometimes become more rigidified as the family seeks to adjust in their new homeland (Alaggia, Chau, & Tsang, 2001).

In terms of gendered educational expectations and performance, research reveals variable results reflecting both individual characteristics and cultural norms. Portes and Rumbaut (2001a) cite higher educational ambitions on the part of girls, and Suarez-Orozco and Suarez-Orozco (2001) conclude that, overall, immigrant girls have higher academic success. However, they also note the mitigating influences of both religion and culture. DeVoe (1994) cites examples of Afghani families where boys are encouraged to attend and achieve in schools, but "excuses" are found to keep the girls at home. In Ethiopian families, DeVoe notes that both girls and boys are encouraged to perform well at school. Among Lao students, girls tend to be more serious students and boys are more likely to exhibit behavior problems. However, DeVoe also cautions against making education-related assumptions based on either gender or culture, stating that multiple factors are involved.

Issues Related to Family Relationships

Although there are a few newcomer youth who arrive and/or reside on their own in the United States, most live with family members, who can be a great source of both strength and support. Family can nourish dreams for the future, while helping maintain connections and continuity with the past. Parrillo (1991) writes of the essential role of the immigrant family and its "emotional and moral encouragement to carry on" (p. 143). In discussing the negative impact of discrimination and racism on children, Falicov (2003) writes of the importance of the immigrant family's hope for the future, and their belief that they will somehow overcome the odds and achieve a better life. And indeed, the vast majority of newcomer families do see at least the beginnings of their dreams realized and are optimistic about the future for their children. Nonetheless, there are unique challenges these families face that must be considered in any discussion of newcomer youth development.

Family Composition: Losses, Separations, Reunions, and Reconfigurations

When newcomer families arrive, they have inevitably left someone important behind. This may be a parent or a sibling, or key extended family members such as grandparents, aunts, uncles, and cousins. For many refugee families, those left behind include some who have been killed and some whose fate is unknown. If the child or adolescent has been close to those left behind, clearly his or her loss can be felt in a painful way, complete with a sense of "survivor guilt" in some instances (Bemak, Chung, & Bornemann, 1996). Other children and adolescents may not particularly feel the absence of those left behind; however, the absence of these family members may well impact the parents' sense of support and thus their ability to parent.

Many newcomer families experience temporary separations. One parent may come to the United States in order to "get settled," leaving the other parent and children behind until they can be sent for. Or both parents may come, with children remaining behind in the care of other relatives. Usually, these separations are anticipated to be temporary and short; however, they may well turn into years. If and when reunions occur, the excitement is often tempered with pain, resentment, and misunderstandings. Canino and Spurlock (2000) describe the reaction of a 16-year-old boy reunited with his mother after a long separation: "He had come to the United States expecting his previously absent mother to be warm and available, as his grandparents in the West Indies had been. Instead, he met an overwhelmed working mother who had three other children and a full-time job" (p. 176).

Alvarez (1999) focuses on the "relational impasses" that may result from such separations. She discusses the depression some children experience when immigration separates them from their primary caregivers, the subsequent developmental delays that may occur, and the parents' guilt: "His mother had never before had the chance to voice her guilt feelings regarding her early separation from her son. Her guilt interfered with her ability to parent Tony effectively, since she saw him as a child 'damaged' beyond repair, which further exacerbated her guilt and made her become emotionally distant from and unavailable to her son" (p. 14).

Parents may also feel a sense of loss or "exclusion" because they have missed certain developmental stages or marker events, such as a first communion, in their children's lives (Alvarez, 1999). Children, upon rejoining their parent(s), may not only carry with them a sense of having been abandoned but also encounter new siblings born in the United States and/or a new stepparent. Alvarez describes the resulting sense of double displacement as "a sense of being strangers not only in the host country but in their families as well" (p. 17). Parents may still think of their child as the age/stage as when they left him or her, and thus find it harder to parent appropriately. If the child has reached adolescence at the time of the reunion, the transition may be especially difficult for both the youth and the parents. Parents, who often feel they have made great sacrifices to bring the family together again, may experience their children as ungrateful (Alvarez, 1999).

It is not just parents who may feel some disillusionment. One of this book's authors worked with a young adult who had arrived in the United States as a very young unaccompanied minor. Some 12 years later, having located her mother in her country of origin and worked tirelessly to arrange her immigration, her expectations of their reunion were enormous. Though there was joy, relief, and perhaps a greater sense of "wholeness" for both mother and daughter, there were also many painful disappointments. The daughter experienced a sense of being a stranger with her mother, while the mother could not comprehend the "hyphenated American" her daughter had become. There was no way the mother could make up all the "missed mothering" for the young woman, yet she quickly sought to reassert her parental authority, which the daughter resented. The mother felt disrespected and of course was also struggling to adapt to a very different culture. The daughter felt the mother did not appreciate all she had done to bring her to the United States. Periods of estrangement ensued.

In some newcomer families, there are multiple separations and reunions that may both confound and compound their impact. Many refugee youth experienced separations from their parents during political strife, as parents were jailed or lost during escape. Some were forcibly separated, as was the case during the Pol Pot regime in Cambodia. Reunions in such cases may be bittersweet, as unspoken accusations and/or untold trauma stories remain potent and poignant subtexts (Alvarez, 1999; Kuoch, Miller, & Scully, 1992). Subsequent separations may then reverberate off these earlier experiences with particular intensity and meaning.

In many immigrant families a parent may periodically return to the homeland to take care of family members or deal with business matters. In other families, children or youth who are perceived to be getting into trouble or becoming "too American" may be sent back to relatives in the homeland for a time. Yet another permutation of multiple separations and reunions is seen when families immigrate, but then one or both parents return to their country of origin for extended periods while their children remain to study. Alaggia, Chau, and Tsang (2001) describe these as "astronaut families" with "satellite" children. Whatever the cause or pattern, each new separation and reunion requires, at minimum, a "re-negotiation" of the family unit's boundaries, and may well significantly increase the stress for some family systems. Each separation and reunion has potential impact on a youth's relationship with his or her family and his or her personal development.

Finally, in some families there are significant reconfigurations of the family unit. For instance, a parent who immigrates may begin a second family; later, children from the family in the homeland may be sent for to enter into what becomes a "blended" family. In other families, older cousins or aunts and uncles already in the United States become surrogate parents to youth whose parents remain in their country of origin. Depending on the families involved, such reconfigurations may prove to be functional and reflect highly adaptive responses to the realities of migration. However, in other cases, such reconfigurations may present additional challenges for all involved, particularly for children and adolescents.

Family reconfigurations also occur among refugees when desperation or convenience sometimes forms a "family." One of the book's authors recalls a childless couple who fled their homeland, bringing with them the child of another relative who had decided she could not to leave. For resettlement purposes, the child was presented as their own, and the truth became a heavily guarded secret that permeated the family's lives. In other instances, unrelated individuals waiting in refugee camps sometimes form families of "convenience." Women whose husbands may be dead, imprisoned, or missing often flee with their children. However, there is a high level of violence in many refugee camps, and women are at particular risk (Freidman, 1992). Thus, some may feel the presence of a man is necessary in order to protect her and her children, and a new "family" is created (Kuoch, Miller, & Scully, 1992). Similarly, sometimes unrelated individuals present to immigration officials as a family because they believe this increases the chance of resettlement in the United States. Families born of desperation or convenience are clearly at higher risk once they are in the country, and youth within them may experience particular challenges to their development.

Changing Roles within the Family

Much has been written about the changing roles within newcomer families (Alaggia, Chau, & Tsang, 2001; Bemak, Chung, & Bornemann, 1996; Freidman, 1992; Gold, 1993; Lee, 1990; Pettys & Balgopal, 1998; Pipher, 2002; Westermeyer & Wahmanhom, 1996). At times, this is characterized somewhat simplistically as *role reversal*, with the children taking over adult responsibilities as they learn English and the American culture faster than their parents. However, the dynamics of changing roles needs to be considered in greater depth.

Certainly, language acquisition is a central theme in many newcomer families. Although generally discussed in terms of access to services in the new culture, it is also important to recognize that for some newcomers "learning a new language symbolizes leaving one's homeland and may be a catalyst for feelings of cultural identity loss" (Bemak, Chung, & Bornemann, 1996, p. 251). Bemak, Chung, and Bornemann (1996) recall a Cambodian adolescent whose dead mother appeared in her dreams angrily demanding, "Stop speaking English. You must speak Khmer! Remember you are Cambodian!" Canino and Spurlock (2000) describe elective mutism as a response in one 5-year-old girl, who, upon entering preschool, was required to speak English. In some families, particularly when children came to the United States when they were very young, language may eventually become both an emotional and communication barrier. If the children never really knew, forgot, or rejected their first language and if the parents are unable or choose not to learn English, the opportunity for real conversation and a sense of continued relational connectedness may well be seriously threatened: "Slowly, as our vocabularies grew, it became a bond between us [siblings], one that separated us from Tata and from Mami who watched us perplexed, [their] expression changing from pride, to envy to worry" (Esmeralda Santiago, as quoted in Suarez-Orozco & Suarez-Orozco, 2001, p. 74).

Perhaps the more common phenomenon seen is when parents who have limited opportunity to study and learn English are forced to depend on their children for interpretation and translation. This may well shift the power balance, with parents feeling their authority diminished (Fang & Wark, 1998). It is also frequently experienced as a significant burden by the youth (Alvarez, 1999):

> As a daughter of an immigrant mother who did not speak English, I was aware of the power I had to guide her through this country and through many agencies as her translator. Given that I was aware of my important role, I constantly pushed and tested my mother's power. However, . . . when I was a child. I also felt terrified many times about the responsibility of having translated something wrong that would have detrimental consequences for her well-being. (p. 26)

Serving as the parents' translator can also burden children if they are then exposed to "adult information" that, under normal circumstances, they would be protected from. This happens in hospital settings where children hear medical information and/or must interpret answers to deeply personal questions. One of the book's authors recalls a family in which a child was asked to translate a letter for the parent, and by doing so learned that the mother was living with a life-threatening, stigmatized illness; the mother had carefully sought to protect her child from this information.

For older youth, the burden that comes with being more fluent in English often goes well beyond simple translation. This may be particularly true in families where one parent is absent. In their study of "astronaut" Asian families in Canada, Alaggia, Chau, and Tsang (2001, pp. 300–302) cited themes of increased role responsibilities for both instrumental and affective tasks, and of premature independence.

Yes, I think my family is lacking something. For example, it used to be that my father would do the maintenance of the house. Now, as he was not here, I am the only male in the family. I needed to take up the job . . . sometimes I felt annoyed when there are so many things to do.

I don't feel angry about it but I just don't like the pressure to take care of my mother. Cause in Hong Kong she used to take care of us but now I have to take care of her.

I know she is just like a kid. She needs someone to take care of her, to love her, make her think she is valuable and important for the family.

I become independent and grow up. I have to grow up, but not that fast. What I have done is not suitable for my age. It is too fast for a 16-year-old.

Writing of a Cuban American youth, Canino and Spurlock (2000), underscore the psychological costs that are sometimes involved in prematurely taking on adult roles: "I skipped my own childhood. I started working at 13 to support my siblings. . . . I learned soon not to trust anybody" (p. 164).

Other authors emphasize the sense of shame that children may begin to feel about their parents' "deficiencies" (Landau-Stanton, 1990). Zephir (2001) notes:

I cannot say that I am ashamed of my mother. But sometimes, I have to say that I am not always happy with her, particularly when she asks me to go places with her because she cannot speak English. . . . I told her many times to go to English classes. But she would always say that she is too tired, and this and that. But she needs to realize that one has to speak English in order to survive here. This is a problem with her. (pp. 133–134)

Bemak, Chung, and Bornemann (1996) underscore some refugee children's decreasing confidence in their parents as they see them transformed from "previously autonomous and culturally competent caretakers to depressed, overwhelmed, and dependent individuals who are slow to acquire a new language and understand different customs" (p. 253). Suarez-Orozco and Suarez-Orozco (2001) quote a Vietnamese refugee, Lan Cao:

The dreadful truth was simply this: we were going through life in reverse, and I was the one who would help my mother through the hard scrutiny of ordinary suburban life. . . . Now, when we stepped into the exterior world, I was the one who told my mother what was acceptable and unacceptable behavior. . . . And even though I hesitated to take on the responsibility, I had no choice. It was not a simple process, the manner in which my mother relinquished motherhood. The shift in status occurred not just in the world but in the safety of our home as well. (pp. 75–76)

Certainly, it is appropriate in a book on newcomer youth to focus on the role changes for children vis-à-vis their parents, but it is also essential to at least briefly consider role changes that parents themselves may be undergoing. These changes may well impact their role as parents and indeed perhaps the whole family structure and functioning. Many newcomers come from cultures with hierarchical family structures in which gender roles are traditionally defined. However, after arriving in the United

States, women often secure employment outside the home, learn of women's legal rights, and begin to challenge these narrowly defined roles (Fang & Wark, 1998; Freidman, 1992; Bemak, Chung, & Bornemann, 1996). At the same time, many men find that they have lost status in this new land, and that their vocational skills or educational credentials are not transferable; thus, they may feel a loss in power. These shifts often place a great burden on the marital relationship, negatively impact the individual's self-esteem and sense of self-efficacy, and for some diminish their ability to be physically and/or emotionally available as parents (Zhou, 1997).

Intergenerational Conflicts

> He did not discuss his frustration and disappointment with his parents, believing they could not possibly understand and help. He insisted he still loved them, but did not respect them because they remained Russian, whereas he desperately wanted to become "American" as soon as possible. (Chazin, 1997, p. 161)

Despite widespread discussions of intergenerational conflicts, some authors such as Suarez-Orozco and Suarez-Orozco (1995) suggest there is probably less conflict between certain groups' (Mexican) immigrant parents and their children than there is among white U.S.-born families. Nonetheless, as both newcomer parents and children struggle with a different culture, a new language, and shifting roles, there are inevitably some problems (Chazin, 1997; Portes & Rumbaut, 2001a; Zephir, 2001). Although Rumbaut (1991) suggests these are more appropriately characterized as "adaptation lags," they are generally characterized as intergenerational conflicts. Most obviously, many parents feel that their inherent authority is challenged and that their children no longer automatically accept their decisions and rules, nor demonstrate proper respect for them. Conflict may also develop around discipline, since many newcomers hail from cultures in which judicious use of moderate physical punishment is perceived as part of being a good, caring parent. However, children new to the United States quickly learn that this is prohibited and may even threaten to report their parents to child welfare officials. Children often feel that their parents are overly protective (Chazin, 1997) and too concerned about what others will say (Zephir, 2001). There may well be disagreement around issues of dating and curfews:

> My parents are so different. They couldn't understand what homecoming is and my Dad would just like "No, you can't go." And I would ask why, why, and he would never answer. (Haibinh, from documentary film, *Five Girls*, 2001)

> In this country, kids start dating very early. . . . I am seventeen, but my parents would kill me if I were to tell them that I have a boyfriend. They do not realize this is something normal here. They still have that Haitian mentality, and they think that if I date I am going to get pregnant. (Zephir, 2001, p. 185)

> The greatest problem I have with my parents is when I need to be home. They are not able to understand that in this country high school kids are involved in a lot of activities that require them to come home late. (Zephir, 2001, p. 84)

Some adolescents feel enormous pressure to succeed at school and resent what seem to be unreasonable expectations on the part of their parents. Part-time employment can become a bone of contention (Zephir, 2001):

> My mother does not want me to work. She is afraid that I won't do well in school because I won't have time to study. I am kind of upset, you know. All my friends have after-school jobs, even some of the Haitians I know. My mother does not realize that in this country things are different than Haiti. (p. 83)

Pettys and Balgopal (1998), looking at the diverse multigenerational perspectives of adolescents, parents, and grandparents, describe six major conflicts areas: gender roles, respect versus assertiveness, power shifts, unique life cycle issues, triangulation between the three generations, and Westernization. Rumbaut (1996), in turn, discusses predictors of parent-child conflicts, with gender (female) and recent arrival being most significant. He identifies additional family features associated with intergenerational friction as including the following: mother is less educated; family economic status has declined; child has limited proficiency in native language and prefers English; child is experiencing educational difficulties; and youth has experienced significant racial discrimination.

Adaptive Family Responses

Losses, family separations, role changes, and intergenerational conflict have all been identified as significant challenges for newcomer families. However, before ending this discussion of family relationships, it is important to recognize the many creative and adaptive ways in which newcomer families successfully nurture and renegotiate their family relationships. Falicov (2003) challenges the traditional "deficit-oriented description" of immigrants as living between two worlds. Instead, she underscores "their capacity to find 'both/and' solutions rather than forcing an 'either/or' choice about incorporation of cultural change" (p. 280).

Falicov (2003) then describes immigrants' "dual visions of continuity and change": "By selectively and purposefully maintaining some aspects of cultural narratives while pruning others, resilient immigrant families are able to restore a sense of continuity and coherence to their lives. . . . A sense of coherence involves a global orientation to life as comprehensible, manageable, and meaningful, in spite of its many challenges" (pp. 284–285). Falicov goes on to specifically cite the role of children in helping "mix continuity with change in their language, values, and identities. Thus, they co-construct with the parents and with society the family's transformations" (p. 288).

Falicov (2003) also lists the myriad ways in which families may sustain daily "rituals" from the homeland, including meals, greetings, dress, prayers, and folk medicine, in addition to the continued celebration of special holidays and rites of passage. She also describes the evolution of new "rituals of connection" to family in the homeland, in the form of regular communication, visits, and remittances, which helps keeps them psychologically present even if physically absent. Such practices allow a sense of transnational or transcontinental family intactness.

In their study of multigenerational Indo-American families, Pettys and Balgopal (1998) documented the importance of continued contact with extended family. Regular communication via telephone calls, videos, email, and visits was reported to be "a great source of support throughout the family life cycle . . . [helping] the immigrant family maintain its family values, language, and religion" (p. 415). Indeed, they assert that recent technological advances in communication create a new chapter in the experiences of immigrant families. Alaggia, Chau, and Tsang (2001) similarly emphasize the potential benefits of long distance communication with family in the homeland.

A caveat is merited here, since both these studies are focused primarily on middle-class families with the resources to access technology and travel. In addition, the research is focused on immigrant families for whom visits back home are an assumed option, as opposed to refugee families for whom any form of communication with family in the homeland may be difficult. Nonetheless, each of these authors emphasize the rich ability of newcomer families not only to survive but also to adapt to changes in roles, learn new ways of relating and functioning, and develop viable ways of both sustaining their original culture and living within their adoptive one.

Other authors focus on ways in which newcomer families can be supported during this process. Szapocznik and Kurtines (1993) encourage practitioners to reframe intergenerational conflicts as "cultural differences." Mirkin (1998) states that family issues can only be understood "in multiple contexts"—the context of migration, social and economic environment, political climate, racism, and so on. Thus, she urges practitioners to "externalize" the problems when working with newcomer families—to help them recognize these external forces and not just blame each other.

Strier (1996) encourages practitioners to utilize the concept of the "adaptive adult" in their work. This concept is one's internalized, culturally influenced "map" of what it means to be a good, functioning adult and parents rely on it as they socialize their children. However, Strier notes that "clashes are most likely to ensue when the immigrant parents' 'adaptive adult' image differs from that of the host culture's" (p. 365). Recognizing and naming this concept can potentially help parents, children, and practitioners work more effectively to defuse tensions and move toward greater flexibility.

Landau-Stanton (1990) suggests using extended family members as "link therapists." In this model, the family itself selects the member they believe can be most helpful in resolving their issues. Usually, this is a member who is somewhat acculturated but not assimilated; thus, they can serve as a viable "link" between parents and children. Finally, many authors (Balcazar & Qian, 2000; Falicov, 2003; Zhou, 1997) cite the significance of "community"—of ethnic-specific institutions and activities—as providing important support to newcomer families.

Issues Related to Acculturation and Ethnic Identity Formation

The challenges of acculturation, and the tensions inherent when there are differential paces and choices regarding acculturation, are implicit in the preceding discussion of family relationships. We now examine these more specifically, as they relate to newcomer youth's "journey" of ethnic identity formation. First, it is helpful to consider recent shifts in acculturation theoretical frameworks. For much of the twentieth century, the adaptation of immigrants was discussed within the twin governing paradigms of assimilation and the melting pot. Acculturation, eventually leading to full cultural integration, was portrayed as if it were a naturally occurring, undeniably positive and linear process with predictable outcomes. Today, however, acculturation is better understood as richly complex, with multiple patterns and diverse outcomes.

Zhou (1997) presents the "pluralistic perspective" as a major alternative framework to that of assimilation—a perspective that perceives "ethnic or immigrant cultures as integral segments of American society" (p. 73). Portes and Zhou (1993) and Portes and Rumbaut (2001a) have proposed the model of "segmented assimilation" as more relevant for today's second generation, "where outcomes vary across immigrant minorities and where rapid integration and acceptance into the American mainstream represent just one possible alternative" (p. 45). They cite four critical variables that impact the process, direction, and end point: (1) immigration history of the parents, (2) pace of acculturation of both parents and children, (3) cultural and economic barriers faced by second-generation youth, and (4) family and community resources available.

Portes and Rumbaut (2001a, pp. 53–54) then identify three patterns of the acculturation process among families: (1) *dissonant acculturation*, in which children learn English and adapt to new culture faster than parents; (2) *consonant acculturation*, in which parents and children adapt at approximately the same pace and to the same degree, each giving up their native language and original cultures; and (3) *selective acculturation*, in which parents and children both retain aspects of their home language and cultural traditions.

Strier's (1996) seven-year qualitative study of immigrant families in Israel resulted in a somewhat similar typology. Using animal metaphors, because she found these helpful in parent education, she describes three coping strategies (which reflect three distinct acculturation processes). First, there is the *kangaroo or "uni-cultural"* strategy, in which parents seek to insulate children from the influence of the new culture and preserve their traditions. Second, there is the *cuckoo or "culturally disoriented"* style, in which parents essentially feel unable to serve as socializing agents in the new culture, turn their children over to schools, and witness a rapid assimilation of the children and the risk of disconnection with parents. Finally, there is the *chameleon or "bicultural"* style, in which parents definitely recognize the need to adapt to the new culture outside the home, though there may be varying degrees of acculturative change within the home.

Kelly and Schauffler analyzed survey data of 5,266 children of immigrants and in-depth interviews of a subsample of 120 children and their parents. They then created a label for each group "that captures a distinctive experience (Cubans as *Gainers*, Vietnamese as *Bystanders*, Haitians as *Strivers*, Mexicans as *Toilers*, and Nicaraguans as *Sliders*)" (p. 41). Although recognizing diversity within these groups, they cite five key variables that significantly shape the outcome of their migration experiences: "internal differentiation by class, type of reception, quality of resources, degree of spatial concentration, and length of time in area of destination."

Each of the preceding frameworks underscores the critical contexts and great diversity of experiences for newcomer families as they adapt to their new homeland, negotiate their way in the acculturation journey, and seek to determine where it is they wish to find themselves in the end. This is undeniably a challenge for adults and youth alike. However, for the latter, developmentally poised to "figure out who I am," it holds particular meaning and is frequently encapsulated in the question of What is my ethnic identity?

> To my parents, I am all American, and the sacrifices they made in leaving Korea...pale in comparison to the opportunities those sacrifices gave me. They do not see that I straddle two cultures, nor that I feel displaced in the only country I know.... As the child of immigrants, I'm torn between my parents' dreams and my own. (Hwang, 1998, p. 16)

> I have Vietnamese friends and American friends, but they don't mix. Sometimes it seems like having a dual personality. When I'm with Vietnamese people I act this way, and when I'm with American people I act another way. I like being both though, I don't want to give up one or the other. I'm not going to deny my heritage. (Haibinh, from documentary film, *Five Girls*, 2001)

More complicated is the identity juggling act of 17-year-old Jose Mendoza, a U.S.-born, Spanish-speaking Dominican who is not black enough for many African Americans, not light enough for most Hispanics, and is advised by his parents to "marry light." The way he figures it, "From the inside, we're Dominicans; from the outside we're black.... I'm still part Dominican. That's my nationality. If you become African American, you give your nationality away. That's like saying you're betraying your country" (quoted in Portes & Rumbaut, 2001, p. 150).

> For me personally, one cannot feel equally at ease in both cultures. Those who claim they can do so, I'll bet you, they are more American than Haitian. I am sure they do not speak Creole and do not really get involved in the Haitian community. For me they are paying lip service; they should simply say they are American. (Zephir, 2001, p. 65)

> When I'm at school and I sit with my black friends and, sometimes I'm ashamed to say this, but my accent changes. I learn all the words. I switch. Well, when I'm with my black friends, I say I'm black, black American. When I'm with my Haitian-American friends, I say I'm Haitian. (Waters, 1996b, p. 183)

These quotes only begin to capture the range and intensity of the ethnic identification experience. Rumbaut (1991), discussing Southeast Asian refugees, describes the particular challenges for 1.5 generation newcomer youth (those born elsewhere, but being primarily educated in the United States): "These refugee youth must cope with two crisis-producing and identity-defining life transitions: (1) adolescence and the task of managing the transitions from childhood to adulthood, and (2) acculturation and the task of managing the transition from one sociocultural environment to another.... In many ways they are marginal to both the old and the new worlds, and are fully part of neither of them" (p. 61).

Landau-Stanton (1990), in turn, writes of children caught in impossible double binds: "To please his parents, he had to achieve well at school, but to do this, he had to adapt to the new culture and make friends with his peers, thereby risking alienation from his parents. He had to choose between conflict with his grandparents, parents and sisters, or with his much admired older bother and peers" (p. 260).

Zephir (2001) writes about children leading "double lives," keeping "secrets," and going to great lengths to hide certain aspects of their lives (dress, nonethnic friends, dating, etc.) from their parents. However, some authors (Perez-Foster, 2001) and many practitioners also caution that acculturation in terms of dress, language, and social activities may not necessarily correlate with acculturation in the affective and cognitive domains of the individual. It is not difficult to think of multiple clients and colleagues who have a highly polished and effective "veneer of Americanization," but their hearts and souls remain essentially rooted in their cultures of origin.

Multiple studies, as well countless stories from the field, suggest that despite the great diversity among newcomer youth, their ethnic identification processes generally follow one of three or four distinct paths. Zephir (2001), who interviewed 125 Haitian second-generation youth and first-generation educators and parents, concluded there is a continuum of ethnic identity among Haitian youth, with three major manifestations: those with a strong sense of Haitianness, those with a lesser sense of Haitianness (bicultural), and those that go "undercover" (presenting selves as African American or as immigrants from another country). Waters (1996b), focusing on a somewhat broader West Indian population, found a similar pattern.

Portes and Rumbaut (2001a) use slightly different terminology in characterizing the patterns, citing four categories: "(1) foreign national-origin identity...; (2) a hyphenated American identity, explicitly recognizing a single foreign national origin...; (3) a plain American national identity; and (4) a panethnic minority-group identity" (p. 154). In their longitudinal study of 5,000-plus children of immigrants in schools in southern Florida and southern California, these authors initially found (in 1992) that 27.5 percent identified themselves by foreign national origin; 40.8 percent as hyphenated American, 12.6 percent as American, and 15.8 percent with a panethnic identity. However, four years later, as most were finishing high school, over half the youth reported a different ethnic self-definition, with an overall shift toward claiming either foreign national or panethnic identities.

What are the factors that push and pull newcomer youth down a particular pathway, toward his or her unique ethnic identity? The Portes and Rumbaut (2001) data are far too rich to discuss in detail here; however, their analysis broadly identifies three key factors that remained strong throughout this longitudinal study: (1) length of time in the United States and speaking English at home are strongly related to self-identification as a plain American; (2) children are more likely to define their identity in the same way they think their parents define themselves; and (3) regional location, school context, and discrimination may impact in multiple, diverse, and at times incongruous ways.

It is important to note that almost all newcomer youth and studies of them highlight the realities of discrimination. Zephir (2001) and Waters (1996b) both document that discrimination and racism are strong factors that can influence ethnic identity in either direction. Many Haitian youth describe the negative stereotypes of Haitians (HBO [Haitian Body Odor], boat people, AIDS carriers), and thus some seek to leave this ethnic marker behind and live as an American black. Other Haitian youth, having arrived with their own stereotypes about American blacks, seek to emphasize their Haitianness. These youth and their families often believe that being seen as a black immigrant will provide more opportunities in the future than being perceived as African American. Those Haitian youth described as bicultural appear more comfortable in accepting being a "minority" in the United States, and also in recognizing both the good and bad in the society. Zehpir (2001) also notes that there can be considerable conflict and resentment among Haitian youth who pursue different ethnic identifications; there may also be strong intragroup debate about whose physical attributes, language, and place of birth "qualify" them to claim the identity of Haitian. This will be further discussed in the upcoming section on peer relationships and competencies.

There can be special challenges related to ethnic identity development for refugee youth who have survived civil wars and/or genocide. Their associations to their original culture may be so negative that they choose to reject it outright. One of this book's authors recalls a Cambodian youth who remained so traumatized by the Killing Fields that she wanted absolutely nothing to do with her culture, the Cambodian community, or indeed even her own family. It was only after she had sufficiently healed herself that she was able to reembrace and reconnect with this part of herself; only then did she self-identify as Cambodian. Though somewhat less chilling, Zephir (2001) describes Haitian youth who reject their culture because they are embarrassed by Haiti's reputation as the poorest country in the Western hemisphere and by certain behaviors among Haitians in the United States.

One final perspective on the ethnic identification journey of newcomer youth is provided by Camino (1994). Focusing primarily on refugee youth, she first critiques their frequent characterization and treatment as "victims." She then posits that it is important to recognize that for newcomer youth there is "no single or static form of ethnicity," but rather "fluid conceptions of identity." She further asserts that these fluid identities need to be recognized and thus be tapped as sources of strength and differential cultural resources. Describing a community-based drop-in center program for refugees and undocumented youth from many different countries, Camino offers examples of contexts in which the youth identified as Salvadoran versus Dominican, Latino versus North American, and Latino Americano. The latter identification was actively supported through workshops that traced history and indigenous cultures in both the United States and the youth's homelands, with the goal of encouraging a "sense of oneness that sought to transcend regional, ethnic, geographic, and national categories" (p. 46). Finally, Camino notes the importance for these youth of a center that could simultaneously offer "respite from the stressors of 'total immersion,' or . . . opportunity to form cross-cutting associations" (p. 51).

The transition from childhood to adolescence presents challenges for all youth, as they seek to define who they are by weaving multiple and often disparate strands of themselves into a coherent sense of self. For youth of color, ethnic and racial identity is an inherently important part of this development process. However, newcomer youth face an even more complicated task, as they must simultaneously integrate their migration and national origin experience into their ethnic identity. It is a testament to their strength and resilience that they find many different and creative ways to do so. Nonetheless, many practitioners would stress the need for programs and environments that actively affirm newcomer youth's original ethnic identities, while also supporting their explorations of new self-translations and self-transformations.

Issues Related to Peer Relationships

As youth enter their adolescent years, peers become an increasingly important force in their lives and continued development. Indeed, many scholars and practitioners suggest that at this stage, peers have much greater influence in a teen's life than his or her parents (Elliott & Feldman, 1990). A recent study by Suarez-Orozco and Suarez-Orozco (1995), comparing lives, attitudes, and beliefs of four groups of students ("white Americans," Mexicans, Mexican immigrants, and second-generation Mexican Americans), challenges this. Their data suggest that peer groups are less important for Mexican immigrant youth than for any of the other groups: "The immigrant students seem to believe that work and parental authority are more important than play or peer group fun" (p. 152). When asked to whom they went for advice if they had a problem, 70 percent of the immigrant students identified their parents, compared to 43 percent of the "white Americans." Only 10 percent of the immigrants identified friends as their preferred source of advice, whereas 45 percent of "white Americans" did so.

Given the strong familism in many other cultures represented among newcomers, the relative importance of peers may also be somewhat less in other newcomer youth groups as well. Conversely, for certain newcomer youth, peer relationships may be particularly important: if their parents are working long hours and are physically unavailable, if their parents are struggling with the aftermath of past traumas and are emotionally unavailable, if the youth are acculturating so much faster than their parents that they begin to feel estranged, or if the youth came to the United States on their own.

Although the degree of importance of peers may vary, peer relationships are nonetheless an important domain in the lives of all newcomer youth and their families. Peers can offer emotional support, provide feedback and reflections as the adolescent seeks to develop his or her own sense of individual identity, and impact decisions and choices being made. Peer relationships also contribute to the development of social competencies (see Chapter 6). The majority of newcomer youth establish positive peer relationships and competencies, but it is noted that these are frequently developed with those of the same heritage.

In their 1992 study of over 5,000 Cuban, Nicaraguan, Haitian, Mexican, and Vietnamese children of immigrants (in Miami, Fort Lauderdale, and San Diego schools), Kelly and Schauffler (1996) found that "regardless of national origin, most children associate with members of their own group and a large number of their friends are foreign born" (p. 44). In addition, the Suarez-Orozco and Suarez-Orozco (1995) study documented that the attributes considered essential in a good friend significantly varied between their "white American" cohort and all the Latino groups. The white youths cited good communication as the most important, followed by "good personalities"/fun and trust. For the Latino youth mutual help was the most important, followed by good advice and good communication: "A good friend is someone who motivates me to study, she gives me good advice and helps me with my problems. She helps me with my homework. She supports me. She understands me" (p. 142).

Friendship patterns presumably reflect a natural "pull" toward shared cultures, languages, and migration experiences. However, they probably also reflect the struggles that newcomer youth may encounter with other peers. Conflict with fellow students is not unusual, and appears to stem from cultural differences, stereotyping, and racism.

> When people call me names, I ignore them, but inside of me I kind of get hurt. Right now they still call me names. They make fun of how I talk, they make fun of how I dress. (Hong Ly, age 11, Philippines/Vietnam, cited in Kelen & Kelen, 2002, p. 41)

> When I first came here . . . everyone started calling me names. My real name is Rounak. But they would call me *Groonak*, which means "shit" in Kurdish. (Rounak "Jasmine," age 13, Iran, cited in Kelen & Kelen, 2002, p. 43)

> The Americans put us down; they put Mexicans down. It is hard. They call us names. They don't understand our culture. (Suarez-Orozco & Suarez Orozco, 1995, p. 64)

The conflict may be between newcomers and U.S.- born youth, or between different newcomer groups themselves (Camino, 1994; Stepik, 1998). Sometimes the hostilities reflect historical conflict between groups which have been carried over from homelands or life in refugee camps (Westermeyer, 1991).

> The people who were in war against my people are here. My friend was beaten up by Bosnians, Muslim people. He had to go to the hospital. They beat him because of his religion (Nenad Suput, age 17, Serbia/Croatia, cited in Kelen & Kelen, 2002, p. 46)

Peer pressure may also present challenges for newcomer youth, as indeed it does with most adolescents. However, again there are added dimensions for refugee or immigrant youth. For example, Vietnamese refugee families have produced what is sometimes perceived as a disproportionate percentage of high academic achievers. One author of this book recalls the strong reactions of some Vietnamese students when newspapers announced that once again several of the city's valedictorians were Vietnamese. Although at some level there was pride, they also expressed a great sense of pressure and burden. Conversely, Stepik (1998) describes peer pressure to give up academic aspirations as a part of the assimilation process for some Haitian students attending inner city schools. Other forms of peer pressure that some newcomers will experience as they become more "Americanized" relate to dating, drinking, and drugs. If their parents are sustaining more traditional cultural beliefs, such pressure may create increased conflict at home.

Yet another arena in which peer pressure may possibly be experienced is gang activity. Gangs are often highly visible in the neighborhoods where newcomer families live and attend schools. As a result, for some immigrant and refugee adolescents peer relationships are developed primarily in the context of gangs. Although representing only a small percentage of newcomer youth, the issue is of growing concern to families, communities, police, teachers, social workers, and youth development staff across the country (De La Rosa, in press). In the general population, participation in gangs is usually attributed to poverty, family problems, lack of educational and employment opportunity, discrimination, and alienation from society. Gangs are also recognized as providing a sense of "belonging" and offering support and protection for members, and in that sense may be seen as an adaptive response (Huff, 1990).

Newcomer youth may be particularly susceptible to gang involvement because they frequently face the problems discussed in this chapter and they desperately seek to be accepted and "belong." In addition, their parents, who themselves may be struggling in this new culture, may be of little assistance as the youth strive to simultaneously deal with the challenges of acculturation and adolescent identity development. Finally, there may be very little cohesion or support within their own ethnic communities. In his study of Latino gangs, Vigil (1990) describes such youth as experiencing "multiple marginality," and termed the process of their alienation as *choloization*. Suarez-Orozco and Suarez-Orozco (2001) describe these youth as being unable to embrace their own cultural identity, and eventually constructing an "adversarial identity"—grounded in seeking to reject the mainstream society that rejects them. They poignantly summarize:

> They have been ostracized and humiliated by mainstream society; they have parents who are unable to guide them through the daunting obstacle course of adolescence; and they live in neighborhoods where there are no jobs and where gangs proliferate. They come to feel powerless and hopeless. During a vulnerable stage of development, gangs furnish the illusion of emotional, financial, and physical protection. (p. 112)

Although space constraints prohibit more detailed discussion of newcomers' involvement in gang activities, it is encouraging to note that there is expanding research and literature in this area (De La Rosa, in press; Kodluboy & Evinrude, 1993; Long, 1995; Vigil & Yun, 1990). There are also certain programs specifically targeting newcomer youth gang members or those "at risk" to join (ROCA, Greater Boston; Operation First Choice, Chicago).

Despite the challenges of a new language, a different culture, negative stereotyping, peer pressures, and "multiple marginality," the vast majority of newcomer youth nonetheless succeed in developing healthy peer relationships. For many, a part of this process involves becoming a role model to others and "giving back" to their peers and community. Suarez-Orozco and Suarez-Orozco (2001) describe 17-year-old Silvia from Central America, who articulates an explicit desire to help her community by tutoring other immigrant students and advocating on their behalf with school personnel. Fifteen-year-old Muna Ali from Somalia has multiple ideas of how she hopes to "give back":

> I would like to create a club particularly for the Somalian teens 'cause there is not a lot for us to do. We don't have a group or anything. . . . You know how [other] groups of kids have volunteers to help them out, or just go with them to play basketball, or do some activity. We don't have that, and I was just thinking we should have it. . . . And yesterday,

I was thinking . . . it would be good if we had our own website. We could tell people who we really are. I think we should get together and we should do something about it . . . we could even have a place that's like a community [chat room] and we can speak out—teens to teens. (Kelen & Kelen, 2002, p. 62)

Issues Related to Education

The challenges of school systems to meet the needs of newcomer youth applies to both urban and rural areas of the country (Midobuche, 2001). In 2000, it was estimated that almost 4.1 million students in schools had limited English language skills (Macias et al., 2000). Youth with limited English language skills require specialized teachers. Currently, there are 50,000 such teachers in the country and a projected need for an additional 290,000 (Zhou, 2002). The term *one-and-a-half generation* was coined by Rumbaut (1991) to refer to youth who straddle two worlds in their lives—the old world where they originated and the new world in the United States. The old world has limited meaning and reality, yet the new world may not be fully accepting of them (Mohan, 1992; Pierce & Elisme, 1997; Portes & Rumbaut, 2001a, 2001b).

In addition to these factors and needs, newcomer youth—depending on their age on arrival in this country—have to define their identity: "This process of identity transformation occurs in the context of the social structure in which immigrants find themselves. This social structure includes many of the traditional correlates of sociology such as education, income, availability of capital resources, racial attitudes and social class" (Waters, 1999, p. 7). An effort will be made to demonstrate the needs of these youth and their relationship to different social systems considering their particular situation in the United States.

> The role of formal education in the lives of newcomers and their children cannot be underestimated. The United States is being transformed by continually increasing levels of immigrants: No American institution has felt the effects of these flows more forcefully than the nation's public schools. And no set of American institution is arguably more critical to the future success of immigrant integration. . . . The limited attention and dollars dedicated to immigrant children reflect the continuing mismatch between the nation's comparatively generous legal immigration policies and its laissez-faire approach to integrating immigrants into the U.S. society following their arrival. (Ruiz-de-velasco, Fix & Clewell, 2000, p. vii-1)

The following statement is from an unaccompanied 18-year-old refugee: "I didn't know that I was supposed to work soon after coming to the United States. I thought I could finish high school first and get a good job after. I am working full time overnight and there are no GED classes in the afternoon. If I had known, I would have stayed in the refugee camp until I would finish high school" (personal interview).

Although the subject of refugee and immigrant education could be the topic of an entire book onto itself, this section will discuss some of the factors that have a great impact on refugees' and immigrants' educational opportunities. The text will focus on the following factors as they relate to immigrant youth education: (1) age, (2) access in terms of financial resources and people's eligibility, (3) cultural norms, (4) parental involvement, (5) parent(s)' degree of literacy, (6) availability of bicultural/bilingual teachers, (7) English for speakers of other languages (ESOL), (8) school environment and issues such as racism and hate crimes, (9) educational system pre-migration, and (10) number of years of schooling pre-migration.

Age is one of most important defining factors in terms of immigrants' and refugees' educational eligibility and access:

> Age at arrival may not only alter the amount of education, but it also affects the number of years of U.S.-specific education that an immigrant completes, and hence their economic mobility. . . .
>
> Age at arrival is an important determination of the educational attainment of immigrants from countries with traditionally low levels of education, such as Mexico and Latin America, as well as from countries whose immigrants tend to have relatively high levels of education, like Europe and Asia. Delayed entry not only results in lower overall education for certain immigrants, but also a lower percentage of U.S. specific education. (Gonzalez, 2002, pp. 2, 17)

Any person who resides in the United States is eligible to receive elementary and secondary education regardless of their immigration status. However, that does not mean that all immigrants are able to enroll in school upon arrival in the country. There are so many other factors affecting immigrants' access to education, such as economic stability, family expectations, and more. According to Gonzalez (2002): "It is increasingly recognized that age at arrival proxies for multiple factors related to socioeconomic outcomes among immigrants, such as earnings, English ability, and educational achievement" (p. 17).

One of this book's authors recalls many refugee families whose children were eligible by age to enroll in school but because of the family's financial situation the youth had to work along with their parents to meet their cost of living. The following example illustrates how a refugee family's financial challenges prevented one of their children from attending high school.

The family is composed of father, mother, and four children ages 4, 10, 15, and 19. Because of the minor children, the family would be eligible for Transitional Aid for Families with Dependent Children (TAFDC) upon arrival. (If the family did not have minor children, they would be eligible for either the Refugee Cash Assistance program or the Matching Grant program.) In Massachusetts, for example, the amount of cash assistance for this family would be $832 a month. This amount includes all the family members except the 19-year-old, who is considered an adult and thus eligible for Refugee Cash Assistance, which is $428 a month. The family is also eligible to receive food stamps from the Department of Transitional Assistance (DTA). However, in calculating the family's income for the amount of food stamps, the income of all family members who reside in the same household counts. Therefore, even though the 19-year-old is not eligible to receive any assistance from the DTA, her refugee cash assistance would count toward the family's income. As a result, the family would receive a lesser amount of food stamps. There are also other factors, such as the size of the family's apartment and the amount of money they pay for the utilities, that affect the amount of food stamps they receive. This family would be eligible for approximately $350 a month worth of food stamps. The following illustrates a comparison between the family's income and expenses upon arrival in the United States:

Income			*Expenses*		
TAFDC	$	832	Rent (average in MA)	$	1100
RCA	$	428	Food	$	400
Food stamps	$	350	Utilities (electricity, heat, phone)	$	250
	$	1610		$	1750

Without bringing into consideration other expenses, such as clothing, transportation, and so on, the expenses of this family exceed their income, which means that all the employable family members need to be employed as soon as possible. The father of the family had sustained major injuries during the war in the country of origin and was unable to work. He was eligible to apply for Supplemental Security Income (SSI), which would take about 4 to 6 months after arrival for the processing of the case. The mother was employable; however, finding child care for the 4-year-old was a major challenge, plus the mother did not speak any English and had never worked outside of home previously. According to public assistance law after the 1996 welfare reform, the family would be eligible to receive TAFDC for up to 24 months total. However, after the SSI payments for the father began, the amount of TAFDC would be reduced by $100 and the amount of food stamps would be recalculated.

Another problem this family faced was that if they still received TAFDC after two months and one of the family members was employed, the head(s) of the household had to perform 20 hours of community service per week; otherwise, their cash benefits would have been terminated. One of the major problems with community service was finding child care. In Massachusetts, for example, there is a long waiting list for low-income families who are in need of vouchers for daycare programs. (*Note:* If approved by the Senate, soon there will be even stricter work requirements for recipients of federal aid. "Legislation approved by the House of Representatives, in line with Bush's proposals, would expand work requirements for welfare recipients to 40 hours per week from 30 and allow 16 of those hours to be spent in related activities such as job training and substance abuse treatment" [*Metro:* Boston edition, 2003].

The 19-year-old daughter of the family had hoped to enroll in school upon arrival, never imagining that she would become the main breadwinner in the family. The mother eventually started to work, but by then the daughter was 21 years old and was no longer able to enroll in high school. Her only choice was to get her GED through an evening program.

According to Schwartz (1996) immigrant college-going is positively affected by a mother working outside of the home and negatively affected by the presence of three or more siblings. One of the potential outcomes of forced early employment for immigrant youth is weakening their motivation for acquiring higher education in the future. Because of the language barrier, most of the immigrants end up starting with low-paying jobs and gradually working their way up to higher-paying ones. But once they enter the job market and start earning money, they feel responsible for themselves and the family and perceive themselves as the breadwinner or at least one of several breadwinners in the family. As a result, youth may feel very guilty about the possibility of leaving their jobs or even reducing their hours in order to attend school. In some cases, however, youth will have an opposite reaction, resenting the fact that supporting their family was going to cost them their future goals and dreams.

On the other hand, early, forced employment may function as an incentive for newcomer youth to obtain higher education. Even though their salaries and the kinds of jobs they can find will improve over time, most immigrant youth realize that without higher education there are not many opportunities ahead in terms of advancing their career and upward mobility: "These youth [immigrant youth] will eventually enter a national economy that will demand more educated workers and fewer less-educated workers" (Vernez & Abrahamse, 1996, p. 1).

This could also be one of the reasons for the high rate of immigrants with post-secondary education in the United States. Schwartz (1996) notes that immigrants are more likely than natives to enroll in post-secondary education, attend college, and stay continuously through four years of college.

Not surprisingly, another important factor in terms of education eligibility is the legal status of an immigrant. Immigrants, regardless of legal status, are eligible for free primary and secondary education, but illegal or unauthorized immigrants are ineligible for federally funded higher education grants or loans: "The 1996 provision (sec. 505) instituted a restriction on states' residency requirements and in state tuition benefits for higher education, affecting an estimated 70,000 unauthorized immigrants students annually" (Morse, 2002, p. 1).

In 1996, the illegal immigration reform law included a provision that prohibited states from providing a post-secondary education benefit to an alien not lawfully present unless any citizen or national is eligible for such benefit. If an immigrant enters the United States as a refugee or a permanent resident (green card holder), that person is treated like an American citizen in terms of eligibility for financial aid and scholarships. On the other hand, asylum seekers are not eligible to enroll in any post-secondary educational institution unless they have obtained a social security number. Obtaining a social security number, however, is not an easy task. A person who intends to file for asylum in the United States has a deadline of one year after date of arrival.

Not every asylum seeker is aware of this law or is able to proceed on his or her own, and not every asylum seeker is able to secure a lawyer who would assist him or her through the process. According to a report published by the Human Rights Watch, as of March 18, 2003, a new policy, which is part of the Operation Liberty Shield by Homeland Security Department, requires the automatic and continued detention of all arriving asylum seekers from 34 countries through the entire asylum process. Under this policy, asylum seekers could face months and even years behind bars before the immigration bureaucracy finally makes a decision on their claim.

In 150 days after a person has filed for asylum, he or she becomes eligible to file for work authorization. After applying for work authorization, it usually takes up to three months before an asylum seeker receives his or her permit and obtains a social security number. Thus, if an asylum seeker files for asylum after being in the United States for 10 months and after 150 days from the filing date, applies for work authorization and waits 3 months to receive it, assuming that there were no complications with the case, that person has not been able to be employed or to be enrolled in any post-secondary educational institution for 19 months after arriving in the United States.

Obtaining a social security number is not the only hurdle asylum seekers face. Not being entitled to any kind of assistance through either the federal or state governments, the majority of asylum seekers face great difficulty meeting their very basic needs, such as shelter, food, and clothing. For the most part, they have to rely on charitable organizations, shelters, and individuals with goodwill to assist them through the process. Under such circumstances, it is almost impossible for an asylum seeker to enroll in an educational institution without receiving some financial assistance. On the other hand, asylum seekers are not eligible to receive any form of federal or state financial assistance unless they are granted asylum.

Even for those immigrants who enter the United States with a status and are eligible to enter into educational institutes at all levels, there are some other barriers, such as the financial situation of that individual or his or her family. Even though refugees who enter the United States are considered permanent residents (green card holders) and are eligible for financial assistance through the government, in many occasions the financial situation of the family is such that every eligible member of the family needs to work in order for the family to survive.

Aside from age and eligibility of individuals, cultural norms play an important role in education access for refugee and immigrant youth in the United States. Education can be perceived differently in various cultures and not all immigrant groups place an equal value on education for themselves and their children. Although education remains to be very important for many immigrants and even the cause of migration for some, other immigrant groups may place more emphasis on employment, and parents expect their children to be employed as soon as possible and support themselves and their family. The youth often get caught in the middle. On one hand, there is a desire to attend school, and on the other hand, the youth need to conform to the family's norms and values. For youth whose parents have mixed ideas about their education, it is more difficult to engage the parents with the education of their children, which can create more splitting within the family unit.

There are also other reasons that prevent immigrant parents from being involved with their children's education. Often, language is the greatest barrier to parental participation. Dealing with an educational institution makes it particularly difficult or even humiliating to communicate with teachers: "Many parents [study participants] noted that their children's English language ability was stronger than their own, and that they did not feel competent speaking with monolingual teachers or administrators about the child's schooling. As a result, they depended on their children to interpret for them and help them understand school norms and expectations" (Ruiz-de-velasco, Fix, & Clewell, 2000, p. 63).

Another significant factor is the cultural norms in different immigrant groups. In some cultures, it is not appropriate for the parents to get involved with their children's education because that might translate into questioning the teacher's authority and competence. According to Buetler, Briggs, Hornibrook-Hehr, and Warren-Sams (1998), "Many [immigrant] families come from cultures where teachers are accorded great authority and family involvement in schooling would be considered rude and disrespectful" (p. 12).

Trust is another key factor in involving immigrant parents with the education of their children. If newcomer students have come from war-torn countries and they or their parents have been subjected to persecution or torture, it would be very difficult to trust new people, particularly those who assume some kind of authority in a formal context. In addition, a parent's degree of formal education in the native language and their English proficiency have a great impact on their involvement with their children's education.

There is a great need for cultural competency within the educational system and different educational institutions in terms of recognizing and addressing the needs of immigrant students and their parents. Schools need to place a priority on having more bicultural/bilingual teachers—not only to be able to communicate with students and their parents but also to be available to other colleagues as a resource about a particular culture and the norms and expectations of that culture.

In addition to the need for teachers to educate themselves about their refugee and immigrant students, it is important for other students to be knowledgeable about where their classmates are from and, particularly with the refugees and asylum seekers, the kinds of living conditions they have been subjected to. Many refugee and immigrant children and youth face racism and hate crimes in and outside of school by their peers. Particularly after September 11th, many immigrant children and youth have been subjected to hate crimes in their schools and communities where they live. Their parents have not been an exception.

According to the Federal Bureau of Investigation's (FBI) statistics, there were 12,020 victims of hate crime in 2001. Of that total, 11,998 were victims of single-bias incidents. Of the 11,998 victims, 46.2 percent were victims of racial prejudice, 22.0 percent were victims of ethnicity or national origin bias, 17.7 percent were targets of religious intolerance, 13.9 percent were attacked because of sexual orientation, and 0.3 percent were victims of a disability bias. Ten of the hate crime victims were murdered in 2001. It must be noted that the number of hate crimes against immigrants, refugees, and asylum seekers remains underreported for reasons such as lack of knowledge about their rights and resources; fear of going to the police, particularly if they are in the asylum process; and having negative experiences with the police in their country of origin.

In a report published by American Civil Liberties Union (November 13, 2002), Dorothy Ehrlich, the executive director of ACLU of Northern California, says, "These stories [of 20 participants in the study] show that, more than a year after the attacks, the backlash is not over. It lingers on in the stores, schools and streets of Northern California, and it continues to touch the lives of people in our communities in varied, surprising, and often shocking ways."

Also related to their degree of success and pace of adaptation to the American education system is the education system immigrant and refugee children and youth were trained in before coming to the United States, as well as the number of years of schooling pre-migration. In many countries where refugees come from, the educational system is different from the American one.

In the U.S. system, children and youth are placed in schools based on their age, not the number of years of schooling. This practice, however, can be a major problem especially for refugee children and youth who in many instances were unable to attend school due to different reasons such as war and living in hiding or in refugee camps for an extended period of time. Such was the case of a 17-year-old refugee youth who had no formal education before coming to the United States and was placed in the tenth grade. At the time, the school did not have bilingual education or any bilingual/bicultural teachers familiar with the needs of the student. After a year of schooling in the United States, the student still did not have any friends, was ridiculed by classmates for not knowing anything and dressing in traditional attire, and had very low grades and a minimal amount of learning. There is a great need for more attention and structural organization to be focused on English as a second language (ESL) classes for limited English proficient (LEP) students.

According to Ruiz-de-velasco, Fix, and Clewell (2000), in the 1993–94 school year, almost two-thirds of LEP students were enrolled in English as a second language classes, bilingual classes, or both. Statistics show that a higher percentage of LEP students in primary school are more likely to be enrolled in ESL or bilingual classes. Among the findings of their study was the limited capacity of school staff to instruct LEP students: "At one level, this capacity issue is caused by a simple shortage of teachers specially trained to teach LEP/immigrant students. At another level, it is the result of the limited number of content teachers (i.e., math, science, or social studies) who can communicate effectively with LEP/immigrant children" (p. 13).

Another challenge facing immigrant and refugee youth is their lack of knowledge about the higher education system in the United States. For those refugee youth who finished their secondary school in the country of origin and are ready to enter college, there are very limited, if any, resources. These youth have questions ranging from taking the Test of English as a Foreign Language (TOEFL) to applying for financial aid. For youth who received their education in the United States, information and preparation for college is part of their education. However, for immigrant and refugee youth who come here with no prior knowledge of the system, navigating their way through the higher education system can be very challenging (Ruiz-de-velasco, Fix, & Clewell, 2000): "The challenges secondary schools faced were not confined to students whose language and other skills lagged. High achieving immigrant youth—that is, immigrant children who have age-appropriate literacy skills in either English or their native language—also faced barriers to realizing their full potential in school. These students and their parents were often unaware of the range of postsecondary opportunities available or the ways in which further study could be financed" (p. 4).

Issues Related to Economics

The economic well-being of immigrants and refugees has long been debated and studied among policymakers and researchers. However, in many instances, too much emphasis has been placed on immigrants being a burden on the U.S. economy and less emphasis placed on how immigrants' economic well-being can be enhanced (Potocky-Tripodi, 2002): "This concern focuses less on the economic well-being of the immigrants and refugees themselves, and more on their impact on the well-being of native-born population.... Nonetheless, these are two sides of the same coin, since the economic well-being of immigrants and refugees in turn influences the economic well-being of society as a whole" (p. 370).

The May 2001 edition of *The Review* reported that "the Federation for American Immigration Reform has been running ads in newspapers in the Midwest attacking immigrant workers. In the ads the organization claims the recent economic slowdown is due to immigrant workers holding jobs its members believe belong to American citizens." The myths about immigrants have, over time, resulted in anti-immigrant sentiment in some segments of the general public. As explained by Raymond Keating (2001): "Nonetheless, anti-immigration sentiments sometimes flare up in the nation of immigrants.... While opposition to immigration finds many sources, it seems that anti-immigration movements mainly spring from a grossly mistaken zero-sum view of the economy. In fact, the economy is not a pie of a certain limited size that needs to be divided among competing individuals and/or groups. Instead, the economy is capable of great dynamism and growth" (p. xx).

Contrary to the belief that immigrants are a drain to the U.S. economy, studies show that "immigrants and their children bring long-term economic benefits to the United States as a whole" (Immigration Forum, undated). Keating (2001), for example, goes on to note that the U.S. economy has benefited tremendously from newcomers, both documented and undocumented, because these newcomers have entered the country with a spirit to work hard and believed in the "American Dream." Thus, immigration has helped to contribute to the dynamics of this country's economy.

The Immigration Forum (undated) addresses the economic impact of newcomers to this country and uplifts the important role they play:

> In the most comprehensive study ever conducted on immigration, the National Research Council of the National Academy of Sciences (NRC) found that immigrants raise the incomes of U.S.-born workers at least $10 billion each year. This estimate is highly conservative because it does not include the impact of immigrant-owned businesses or the impact of highly skilled immigrants on overall productivity. Still, the NRC estimates that the typical immigrant and his or her children pay an estimate $80,000 more in taxes than they will receive in local, state, and federal benefits over their lifetime.... By conservative estimate, in 1997, immigrant households paid an estimated $133 billion in direct taxes to federal, state, and local governments.

The following statistics have been gathered from different sources by the National Immigration Law Center (2002) and demonstrate facts about immigrants and their effects on the U.S. economy.

- In 2000, the foreign-born population accounted for 12.4 percent of the total civilian labor force. Even though 7.1 percent of all workers are noncitizens, almost 20 percent of all low-wage workers who live in low-income families with children are noncitizens.

- Almost 43 percent of immigrants work at jobs paying less than $7.50 an hour, compared to 28 percent of all workers.
- Only 26 percent of immigrants have job-based health insurance.
- Children in immigrant families make up one-fifth of the low-income children in 20 states.
- Immigrants fill a growing number of low-skill jobs. "About 1.1 million new lower-skilled immigrants in the labor force have filled the gap since 1994 as the native-born population attracted to such jobs has declined from 9 million to 7.6 million" (Keating, 2001).
- Immigrants also help meet the growing demand for highly skilled managers, specialists, and professionals, with the number of foreign-born college graduates in the labor force rising by 43.8 percent since 1994 (Keating, 2001). Working-age immigrants who have been in the United States for more than 10 years are less likely to receive welfare than natives (Frosina, undated).

These statistics show that even though the U.S. economy is greatly enriched by immigrants of all different backgrounds, the children of immigrants are more likely to be disadvantaged than the children of natives. They are more likely to be poor (24 percent versus 16 percent); more likely to be uninsured (22 percent versus 10 percent); more likely to have no usual source of medical care (14 percent versus 4 percent); and more likely not to have a steady source of food (37 percent versus 27 percent) (National Immigration Law Center, undated).

In trying to develop a paradigm for youth development with newcomer youth, one must bring into consideration the particular needs and challenges facing refugee and immigrant youth. There are several factors affecting the economic well-being of immigrants and refugees. This section will address those that the authors believe have the greatest impact on newcomers' lives in the United States: (1) legal status, (2) degree of English literacy, (3) degree of literacy in native language, (4) transferability of skills, (5) loss of status, (6) underemployment, (7) socioeconomic class, (8) home ownership.

Once again, a distinction needs to be made between refugees, asylum seekers, and other immigrants because the legal status of those groups have a great impact on their economic well-being. As mentioned in Chapter 3, refugees are the only group of immigrants who are entitled to financial assistance from the government upon arrival in the United States. Refugees had to flee their homeland under extraordinary situations, ranging from war to political and religious persecutions. Also, having had to live in refugee camps for a number of years in many cases, the majority of refugees enter the Unites States lacking substantial financial assets.

They come to the United States—the land of opportunity—hoping for a safer and a better future: "[A] family's dreams and fears when migrating becomes part of its heritage. Parents' attitudes toward what came before and what lies ahead will have a profound impact on the expressed or tactic messages they transmit to children" (McGoldrick & Pearce, 1996, p. 13). Once refugees start to orient themselves to the new country and environment, they begin to face the reality of life for a newcomer in the United States. The following is an example of how different the perception of life in the United States is before and after resettlement from a refugee after being in the United States for four months:

> Before coming here, we were told that we would be entitled to free housing and a car. I wanted my children to start school right away. We had to be in hiding for four years and my children did not get any schooling during those years. Instead, they have to travel for 2 hours each way to work, so we can pay our rent at the end of the month. Sometimes, I feel it might have been better for all of us to have died during the war. That would have been only one moment. Now, I feel that I am dying gradually and the pain of losing my dignity is far worse than any war injuries.

The service eligibility for asylum seekers was discussed in detail in Chapter 3; however, it is worth mentioning again that asylum seekers are eligible for up to eight months of financial assistance upon receiving asylum, although in many instances asylees are not able to take full advantage of these services. For example, the eligibility date for asylee benefits begin with the date of asylum approval on their letter from the Bureau of Citizenship and Immigration Services (formerly the INS).

However, asylees always do not receive their approval letter immediately after the decision has been made. One of the authors of this book recalls many instances in which asylees received their approval letter one, two, or even five months after it was issued, which means that they lost five months of benefits. Keeping in mind that asylum seekers are not entitled to any benefits from the government during the asylum process, delay in service delivery after asylum approval further impedes the new aslyees' economic well-being.

In addition to these difficulties, asylees also face other challenges in securing economic stability in the United States. In many instances, asylum seekers have to flee their countries under extremely dangerous situations, and due to many reasons—such as safety concerns, lack of adequate time, and little or no financial resources—the entire family is unable to leave the country of origin simultaneously. Therefore, only the family member(s) who is in immediate danger flees first, hoping to reunite with the rest of the family in the country of asylum.

After a person receives asylee status, he or she is able to apply for family reunification. Under the current immigration law, family reunification for asylees includes only the immediate family members: spouse and minor, unmarried children. Family reunification for the majority of asylum seekers creates a great financial burden. Unlike refugees, asylees are not eligible to receive housing assistance as part of their benefit package upon receiving asylum. New asylees have had to depend on friends, charitable organizations, and shelters to meet their housing needs during the asylum process. Not only must they start looking for a place for themselves but they also need to think about the future, when their family will be reunited with them.

In many cases, asylees are unable to place their name on a waiting list for public housing due to the fact that they don't have a social security or alien number for those family members who are not in the United States. If asylees waited to apply for public housing once the entire family is present in the United States, it means that in most cases they at least have to wait for a year, and sometimes years, before they can get into any kind of public housing.

Another financial burden for asylees is supporting family members in the country of origin and eventually paying for the cost of travel to the United States. As complicated as the asylum laws are and as lengthy the asylum process is for the asylum seeker to go through, the issues become dually complicated for their families back in the country of origin and elsewhere (possibly in refugee camps). Often, the family who remained in the homeland expects the family member who is in the United States to work and send them money. One of the challenges faced by an asylum seeker is the explanation of the asylum process to the family and friends back home. There are many instances in which those family members and friends accuse asylum seekers of abandoning their children and not being a responsible parent, spouse, or child. The problem gets even more complicated after an asylum seeker is granted asylum. On the one hand, if they were staying with some family members or friends during the asylum process, they are expected to start contributing to the household expenses; on the other hand, the family member(s) in the country of origin are expecting to be reunited with the family member in the United States immediately.

However, there is at least one year of waiting for the applications to be processed. In some cases, when there is no proper documentation to prove the relationship between the family member in the United States and those waiting to come to the United States, the BCIS requires DNA testing from family members, which is a very costly procedure. This combination of different factors contributes to new asylees' economic instability.

The third category is other immigrants who are neither refugees nor asylum seekers, who, as mentioned in Chapter 3, are subjected to a five-year ban in terms of eligibility for financial or other kinds of federal or state services. Even though immigrants are those persons who leave their county voluntarily, it does not necessarily mean that their economic situation is better than that of refugees or asylees.

The reason for migration includes what the family was seeking (e.g., adventure or wealth) and what the family was leaving behind (e.g., religious or political persecution or poverty) (McGoldrick, Giordano, & Pearce, 1996). Immigration conjures up many images in the minds of newcomers: "Immigration to the United States has different meaning to different immigrants. It can mean increased economic opportunity, a chance to reunite with family members, or freedom from political or religious persecution. It sometimes means dealing with ethnic racial, or language biases still operating in the United States" (Northwest Regional Educational Laboratory, 2001, p. 1).

Regardless of the immigration status, there are several significant factors affecting the economic well-being of immigrants in the United States. English proficiency and degree of literacy in native language are two of the most important ones. A newcomer might be very educated in his or her native language but with very little or no knowledge of English. In such cases, it is very unlikely that the person can find a job related to his or her field of expertise. In such circumstances, a person has to go through a period of learning the language while working in jobs that, for the most part, are not related to his or her past educational or employment experiences.

In addition, since the person is not able to communicate in English, he or she will have to find jobs that require minimum level of communication, which in most instances are jobs that require heavy physical labor with minimum pay. For example, a person who used to be an engineer in his or her country of origin but is not literate in English could end up working for a supermarket or a freight company either placing items on the shelves or loading trucks. For refugees and immigrants, however, doing something that is so drastically different from what they used to do and who they used to be—in other words, the loss of social status—could have a very negative affect on their emotional and psychological well-being. One of the services refugees are entitled to upon resettlement is English classes. However, since the focus of resettlement programs is on early employment, if a refugee finds a job within two months after arrival, he or she will not be able to attend English classes (however, the person might be able to start an evening course).

Several studies have shown the direct effect of English proficiency on employment opportunities. A study by MassINC found that employed immigrants in Massachusetts who are fluent in English earn 33 percent more than immigrants with limited English speaking skills. Another study in Los Angeles by the Economic Roundtable found that former welfare recipients who were English proficient earned a higher wage than former welfare recipients who did not speak English or who were categorized as LEP (limited English proficient) (National Immigration Law Center, undated).

Also, in many cultures, *class* is of great importance, and the loss of it may have a very negative impact on refugees, asylum seekers, and other immigrants. One of the authors recalls many refugee families who identified themselves as middle or upper class and therefore expected to receive more extensive services or to be placed in more expensive areas of the state in which they were resettled. As this was the case in their native countries, they expected the same kind of treatment in the United States. Another problem that immigrants face is *transferability of skills*, meaning that an immigrant might have been a professional in his or her country of origin and literate in English, but is unable to transfer his or her credentials to the American system.

Loss of status, as noted by Potocky-Tripodi (2002) in a review of the literature, is an important factor in the lives of newcomers:

> Some immigrants and refugees, particularly in the early years after arrival, experience underemployment or 'status inconsistency.' This refers to having a job that is below one's level of education or abilities. This situation may be due to many factors, such as poor English proficiency; the nonrecognition of education, training, or licensure obtained in the country or region; or employment discrimination. Status inconsistency frequently leads to poor psychological well being and overall difficulty in the adaptation process. (p. 375)

A good example of this problem is immigrants with a background in the medical field, such as doctors and nurses. Any physician who migrates to the United States needs to pass the American board's exam in order to be able to practice medicine in the United States. There are several factors affecting such decisions, such as age at arrival time, financial resources, and degree of proficiency in academic and technical English.

For a person who comes to the United States as a refugee, according to the federal guidelines, the emphasis should be on early employment so that the individual or family can become self-sufficient as soon as possible. Under such circumstances, there is no immediate opportunity for the family members to look into different options they may have in terms of transferring their prior professional skills to the new system. Although this might become an option later on, in many immigrant families, the parents view themselves as a sacrifice, forgoing their chances of educational and career enhancement so the children may flourish and "become someone" in the new country.

On the other side of the coin, however, are the immigrants coming to the United States in the prime of their working years, having received their education in their country of origin. They are English proficient with transferable skills, which means that the United States does not have to spend any money for their education while it can benefit from their skills and knowledge. In this case, the immigrants boost the U.S. economy:

> The age profile of immigrants is one of the key characteristics that makes them a fiscal bargain for native-born U.S. taxpayers.... For example: More than 70 percent of immigrants are over the age of 18 when they arrive in the United States. That means that there are roughly 17.5 million immigrants in the United States today whose education and upbringing were paid for by the citizens of the sending country, not American taxpayers. The total discounted present value windfall to the United States of obtaining this human capital at no expense to American taxpayers is roughly $1.43 trillion. (Immigration forum, undated, pp. 2–3)

Another important factor in immigrants creating long-term economic benefits to the U.S. economy is their contributions to the social security and Medicare programs. According to the data published by the National Immigration Forum (undated), only 3 percent of immigrants are over age 65 when they come to the United States, compared with 12 percent among the American population. The study also found that the total net benefit (taxes paid over benefits received) to social security was almost $500 billion between 1998 and 2002 and will be approximately $2.0 trillion by 2072.

Home ownership plays an important role in economic well-being of refugees and immigrants. In many immigrant groups home ownership is viewed as a symbol of financial stability and thus the family focuses their effort and resources on buying a house. According to Potocky-Tripodi (2002), "Home ownership is an important indicator of economic well being since it helps individuals and families to increase their net worth through the accumulation of equity, it is a financial investment that yield gains, and it contributes to a community's growth and stability" (p. 376)

In some instances, a number of immigrant families decide to live together under difficult and sometimes substandard living conditions so that they are able to save enough money for buying their first home in the United States. This practice is often seen among refugees and immigrants from Southeast Asia, where up to three generations with some members of the extended family live in the same household. According to an American Banker report in Harvard University's State of the Nation's Housing Study (Albro, 1998), four million minority and immigrant households became homeowners between 1994 and 1997, surpassing the growth trend among Baby Boomers in the 1970s. In addition, 80 percent of all first-time home buyers in 2010 will be immigrants, according to William Schenck, chairman and chief executive of Fleet Mortgage Group. Still, the national homeownership rate is only 45.4 percent for Black Americans and 43.2 percent for Hispanic Americans, compared with a 72 percent homeownership rate among White households. Lenders are trying to meet the demands of the new market with multilingual loan officers, home buying education fairs, and new loans with low down payments.

Individual development accounts (IDA) programs are another means of supporting immigrants in achieving their financial goals, such as buying their first home, a car, or a computer. Although IDA programs can take different forms, they essentially consist of self-help programs designed to empower low-income families and individuals. These programs match the money saved by working refugees over the period of six months for up to two years, so that at the end of the assigned period the money may be used for a down payment on a house. After the events of September 11th, establishing financial stability has been increasingly difficult for immigrants and refugees. With a vast number of refugees losing their jobs, either as a result of an overall troubled economy or for reasons such as profiling and racism, immigrants and refugees have been taking the brunt of the economic upheaval.

It is important for the reader to keep in mind that newcomers should not only be looked at in terms of their contributions as taxpayers and how they might or might not be a burden to the U.S. economy. Immigrants, refugees, asylum seekers, and asylees are all individuals with a range of talents and potentials. The United States has benefited over time in many different ways from immigrants' contributions: "Immigrants contribute to America in many ways other than the size of their tax payments. Their enrichment of our culture and the overall vitality they bring to American society are not measured here—and in many cases are immeasurable—yet they are vital benefits to all Americans" (Immigration forum, undated, p. 4).

Issues Related to Health

Attention to physical health is an inherent part of the youth development paradigm, with a focus on the promotion of both good health habits and good high-risk management skills (Eccles & Gootman, 2002). However, it is also essential to consider the more fundamental issues related to health care. Newcomer youth and their families face the gamut of health care issues that so many in the United States do, particularly those who are poor, uninsured, and/or persons of color: inadequate service, inaccessible services, and systemic discrimination, racism, and disparities in treatments provided. In addition, some live in dangerous/unhealthy environmental conditions that increase their chances of developing certain health problems (e.g., asthma, lead poisoning). Also, many immigrants and refugees encounter specific challenges related to their newcomer status. These include language barriers, cultural barriers, eligibility issues, and special "situational" issues. Although space constraints prevent a detailed analysis of these, each is briefly discussed.

Language Barriers

The public health literature provides extensive documentation of the ways in which language barriers impact health care, be it preventive, ongoing, or emergency (Howard, Andrade, & Byrd, 2001; Lecca, Quervalu, Nunes, & Gonzales, 1998; Loue, 1998). These linguistic barriers can discourage newcomers from even trying to seek health care services, they can place children and youth in inappropriate roles as interpreters, and they can at times lead to serious, even life-threatening communication misunderstandings.

So common are language barriers that they have even found their way into comic strips. Witness the cartoon "Baldo," which appeared in the *El Paso Times on* May 18, 2000:

> A teenager has been designated to accompany a monolingual Spanish-speaking neighborhood woman to the hospital and serve as her interpreter. As Maria is being prepared for surgery, which is not why she came to the Hospital in the first place, the nurse says earnestly: "Tell her the surgeon is the best in his field and she'll get through this fine." The young interpreter valiantly attempts, "She say the doctor does best when he's in the field, and when it's over you'll have to pay a fine!" After another equally disastrous translation, Maria faints, and the nurse thinks she has been given anesthesia. (Howard, Andrade, & Byrd, 2001, pp. 39–40)

Although certainly humorous, the cartoon unfortunately reflects a sad and all too pervasive reality.

Even when medical staff and/or newcomers are somewhat bilingual, the complexity and subtlety of language may still present serious challenges. Howard, Andrade, and Byrd (2001) describe the couple who discontinued the use of contraceptive jelly because the man did not like the taste of it. Similarly, they describe the failure of a school nurse's family planning efforts with young Latinas, when "take the pill" *(tomar)* was mistranslated to *(llevar)*, meaning "carry them with you (and use as needed)." Obviously, health education is important for all adolescents as they consider sexual activity. However, it may be especially critical for newcomer youth who receive abstinence messages from parents but different messages from their peers and the larger society.

Cultural Barriers

Many newcomer youth and their families come from cultures that hold quite different understandings of the cause of illnesses. Instead of utilizing a Western model of disease, they may explain health problems in terms of disruption of harmony or balance, or blame "magical"/supernatural causes. They may also hold very different beliefs regarding appropriate healing practices and providers (Devore & Schlesinger, 1999; Howard, Andrade, & Byrd, 2001; Kleinman, Eisenberg, & Good, 1978; Lecca et al., 1998; O'Connor, 1998). For newcomer youth and their families, such cultural differences can lead to reluctance to seek health care, lack of trust in health care providers, and misunderstandings regarding diagnosis and treatment. For medical personnel, these cultural differences can lead to insufficient information, misdiagnosis, frustration, and labeling patients as "noncompliant."

Examples of cultural misunderstandings unfortunately abound in the literature, the reports of health care providers, and the feedback from newcomers themselves: the Haitian woman who did not really understand the significance of the lump in her breast, much less the resulting mastectomy (Devore & Schlesinger, 1999); the Chinese parent who was concerned with so many blood tests being carried out on her child and wondered if the hospital was selling it (personal communication); and the practitioner who patted a Southeast Asian child on the head, not realizing that the head is considered to be the site of the spirit and thus not to be touched, and then never saw the patient again (personal communication). Additional cultural misunderstandings may relate to newcomer patients' use of Western and "traditional" medicines simultaneously, without medical staff's awareness and/or approval of this (O'Connor, 1998). There are also many stories of bruises, which result from traditional "coin rubbing" or "cupping" treatments, being misdiagnosed as signs of abuse (Helm, 1991, Howard, Andrade, & Byrd, 2001; Korbin, 1991, Sue & Sue, 2003). Perhaps one of the most powerful and poignant accounts of how cultural misunderstandings impact health care is found in Anne Fadiman's (1997) book, *The Spirit Catches You and You Fall Down*. The book follows a Hmong family, with a child who has epilepsy, and their complex interactions with multiple health care providers; it eventually ends in tragedy.

Eligibility Issues

Far too many U.S.-born citizens do not have adequate access to health care services due to lack of insurance, ineligibility for Medicaid, and other reasons. However, newcomer youth and their parents can face additional eligibility hurdles. The 1996 Welfare Reform Act (Personal Responsibility and Work Opportunity Reconciliation Act, or PRWORA) created new restrictions on access to public assistance for legal immigrants during their first five years (Strug & Mason, 2002). Twelve states have opted to continue Medicaid coverage for all "legal" immigrants who meet the standard means testing requirements, and some local hospitals and clinics across the country continue to offer services. However, the National Health Law Program describes the resulting chaos as "a nearly incomprehensible patchwork of rules and restrictions that confuse even the most seasoned expert" (Porter, 2001). The guidelines are so complex that even if they are eligible for services, many newcomer families may not realize this, or may simply find the application process too cumbersome; others are ashamed to accept public assistance (Strug & Mason, 2002).

Special "Situational" Issues

The implications of PRWORA have been particularly harsh for undocumented youth and their families because the act essentially barred them from almost all federal and state benefits. Although most hospitals and some clinics still provide emergency care, many undocumented people are fearful that health care personnel will report them to immigration officials and they will be deported (Strug & Mason, 2002). In addition, some doctors observe that undocumented individuals are often sicker when they finally do come to the emergency room, and some have sustained serious injury while trying to cross the border into the United States (Galloro, 2001). The very practice of offering care to undocumented youth and families was challenged in Texas, with Attorney General John Cornyn's ruling (subsequently overturned) that public hospitals could not legally provide tax-supported preventive care to undocumented individuals (Associated Press, 2001). Finally, many health care facilities are citing the heavy financial burden of treating large numbers of undocumented patients, with certain hospitals stating that they face economic ruin unless they receive federal reimbursement (Canedy, 2002).

Migrant farm workers and families face additional barriers in accessing health care, not only frequently being without documentation but also working in rural areas far from health care facilities (Fuentes, 2001). Further, whether documented or undocumented, immigrant workers appear to be at higher risks of injury on the job—such as taking dangerous jobs for which they receive insufficient training. According to the 2000 U.S. Bureau of Labor Statistics, nationally 39 percent of all fatal occupational injuries involved immigrants; in New York City, the percentage was 67 percent (Maier, 2001). Associated Press writer Karen Matthews, discussing potential health hazards of the post–September 11th cleanup efforts, reported that "immigrant day laborers have performed thousands of hours of work removing debris . . . many without proper protective gear and most without health insurance" (Matthews, 2002).

One final issue related to health care issues for newcomer youth and their families is the reality that, coming from poorer nations with limited health care services, they may arrive with certain communicable diseases such as tuberculosis. Advocates emphasize that it is therefore not only humanitarian to provide health care but also in the interests of the greater public: "I call it enlightened self-interest," states Dr. Kenneth Castro, director of CDC's division of tuberculosis elimination in Atlanta (Doucette, 2001).

Adaptive Health Care Program Models and Strategies

Before leaving this discussion of health care issues faced by many newcomer youth and their families, it is encouraging to note the emergence of health care policies and programs that seek to more effectively reach out and meet the needs of newcomer youth and their families. In 2000, after a 10-year effort, advocates in Massachusetts were successful in passing legislation that *requires* hospitals to provide emergency room interpreter services. The Massachusetts Medical Interpreters Association has also been leading the nation in developing training curriculum and setting credentialing standards for medical interpreters.

New program models are also evolving, which reflect commitment to both cultural competency and greater flexibility in health care services for immigrants and refugees. One of this book's authors is personally familiar with the Metta Health Center, an innovative program of the Lowell Community Health Center in Massachusetts, which offers integrated Western and "traditional" health and mental health care to the large Southeast Asian population in Lowell. The center's waiting room incorporates Cambodian art, and most of its staff is bicultural. In addition to the regular staff of doctors, nurses, and social workers, a Buddhist monk, an herbalist, an acupuncturist, and a massage expert are also affiliated with the center.

The Pediatric Mobile Health Center in Hempstead, New York, is parked outside a family resource center two days a week and a public school three days a week, bringing health care to children who otherwise might only be seen in a hospital emergency room. Pediatrician Dr. Weiner states that "more than half of his patients are from Spanish-speaking [countries] and are recent immigrants." The staff includes a social worker, Damaris Daiz, "whose job is to provide counseling to parents and children who face, in addition to all the normal stresses of raising children or growing up, huge economic, cultural, language—and perhaps legal—barriers." As Dr. James Fagin, medical director of the mobile unit, says, "This is the antithesis of a bureaucratic facility. . . . We are particularly proud of the way people are treated here" (Ochs, 2001).

In Laredo, Texas, staff of a truck-turned-clinic has an explicit "don't ask (legal status), just treat" policy, and Sister Rosemary Welsh of the Mercy Regional Medical Center does outreach along the streets of the "colonias" (immigrant enclaves) along the border. "We're trying to train them not to use the emergency room as a clinic," she says. However, she also reports that the staff has had to learn, as well: "We were the barriers. . . . We were not nice, and we made people feel stupid. That was our biggest barrier" (Davis, 2001).

Finally, there are the "adaptive strategies" of the newcomers themselves. In addition to reliance on traditional medicines and healing practices, some report relying on family, friends, and community to help secure treatment and medicine (Strug & Mason, 2002): "If I need medicine but can't afford it, I usually ask a friend with health insurance to get a prescription from the doctor, get the medicine and then give it to me. I know this can be dangerous, but what can I do?" (p. 77). A Dominican man describes the "only other alternative": "[to] collect money from whoever, knock on doors, friends, relatives, anyone, go to a church and see if they will help out. And if I get sick and can't get medicine, I go to a family member to take care of me" (p. 77).

Issues Related to Mental Health

When speaking of the emotional and mental health of immigrants, refugees, and asylum seekers, one might automatically think about the hardship and trauma they might have endured prior to coming to the United States. Although this is true in most cases, it should not divert attention from the fact that the mental health of immigrants and refugees should be looked at in a multidimensional manner with each stage of the migration process entailing unique stressors. Based on Potocky-Tripodi's (2002) review of the literature, "the pre-migration and departure stage entails the loss of family members, friends, home, and familiar environment. Additionally, for refugees, this stage often involves traumatic experiences within their homeland, such as war, famine, violence, rape, imprisonment, torture, and witnessing violent death of family members, as well as discrimination, ostracization, and other forms of persecution" (p. 257).

The second stage is the actual migration process, during which individuals experience separation from family members, are exposed to dangerous situations during their escape, and fear the unknown future awaiting them. Also, depending on their circumstances, they might have to live in refugee camps or in hiding for sometime before they can travel to their final destination. The third stage, post-migration, entails new stressors, including adjustment and acculturation to the new country and environment. Also, it is during this period that refugees begin to come to terms with their losses and the trauma they endured.

Adolescent newcomers face a double challenge of having to integrate potential past trauma and a new identity that finds them between two distinctively different cultures (Rousseau, 1995). Each of the three stages of refugee trauma has its unique characteristics and challenges:

1. Emotional and psychological well-being prior to trauma
   a. Availability and kind(s) of care in the country of origin
   b. Access to services in the country of origin
2. Emotional and psychological well-being after traumatic experience(s)
   a. Availability of resources and services
   b. Time spent in refugee camps
3. Emotional and psychological well-being in the new country
   a. Mental health issues immigrants and refugees arrive with
   b. Issues of acculturation and assimilation
   c. Access to health services in the U.S.
   d. Availability of traditional healers or medicines
   e. Cultural norms about healing and treatment and acceptance of Western medicines
   f. High school clinics
   g. Availability of culturally competent mental health workers and physicians
   h. Availability of interpreters

A distinction, however, needs to be made between *availability and access* to general health care and one that is *psychological in nature*. In what appears to be far more countries than not, mental health is considered taboo and is not talked about openly. In many cultures, having emotional and psychological problems would be equal to "being crazy" and "losing one's mind." Thus, individuals themselves or the families of individuals prevent them from seeking professional help. In some cultures, people seek help from the religious leaders or traditional healers. The clinicians should be cognizant of clients' beliefs and their notions about healing and treatment. If a client believes in seeking help from a religious leader or a traditional and/or a spiritual healer, every effort should be made to find out if there are such existing systems in place and to explore the possibility of collaborating with them.

Even if there are mental health services available in countries from which immigrants and refugees come, the percentage of psychological help-seeking behavior among those populations is not very high. However, in working with immigrants, refugees, and asylum seekers, it is important to pay adequate attention to the history of mental health in these individuals before they were exposed to any kinds of trauma. A majority of refugees and asylum seekers have experienced different kinds of trauma, from losing loved ones, to losing one's home and belongings, fleeing one's home and country of origin, and being tortured through war or other circumstances such as one's affiliation with a particular political group, religion, race, or sex.

For those refugees and asylum seekers who come from war-torn countries, whether it be civil or with neighboring countries, very often there is highly limited or no access to mental health services. In the majority of those cases there is scarcity of resources and most often the medical services are focused on saving the lives of the injured and wounded. Another limitation with mental health services in countries where refugees and asylum seekers come from is that a number of American and other Western nongovernmental organizations providing mental health services in those countries are utilizing the Western model of diagnoses and treatment, which in most cases are not applicable to the cultures within which they are operating. An example of that would be the use of psychological testing for diagnosing depression or post-traumatic stress disorders.

The problem with this model is, first, the diagnosis is based on the *Diagnostic and Statistical Manual of Mental Disorders*, published by the American Psychiatric Association, and second, the tests that are being administered to assist in making such diagnosis have been written by a Western body of psychiatrists, psychologists, and other professionals. Thus, the validity of such tests can be very poor because they do not reflect the values and norms of the particular culture they operate within and thus could fail to measure what they have been designed to measure.

In some instances, foreign agencies train local people on some of the basic mental health concepts. However, due to factors such as lack of budget and workers, local providers do not receive comprehensive, extensive training on mental health issues. In a psychoeducational group conducted by one of this book's authors for a group of young men who had resided in a refugee camp for eight years, one of the participants started talking about having nightmares and being sad all the time. He was then teased by the rest of the group members, saying that he needed to see someone in the "crazy tent" to be given some food. After asking more questions, it became clear that the mental health services in the camp consisted of a tent with local staff. If a refugee in the camp accessed those services, he or she was often given food as a solution to his or her problem because food was something they did not have much of in the camp. Thus, the local staff thought that offering food would be the best way of addressing psychological and emotional concerns and challenges of the camp's residents.

Many refugees and asylum seekers arrive in the United States with emotional and psychological challenges. The issue in the new country might not be the availability of mainstream mental health resources; rather, the challenge is the scarcity of mental health professionals familiar with refugee trauma and the lack of adequate bicultural/bilingual providers.

It must be noted that not all refugees and asylum seekers develop mental health problems as a result of being exposed to trauma or as a part the migration process. Many refugees and immigrants demonstrate great resiliency in response to the traumatic events. The issues of *resiliency* and *major mental health problem* have been debated among the legal experts and clinicians working with asylum seekers. As explained earlier, asylum seekers must have a well-founded fear of persecution or death if they were to return to their country of origin, and many have been tortured and traumatized before coming to the United States. For those asylum seekers who are fortunate enough to secure an attorney and a mental health clinician, the attorney often requests psychological reports to accompany the legal affidavit prepared for the case.

Many attorneys, asylum officers, and immigration judges look for a "major mental health disorder" diagnosis for the person to prove that he or she has been exposed to trauma and that he or she does not have a false claim. Although many traumatized asylum seekers respond to traumatic experiences by exhibiting symptoms of post-traumatic stress disorder (PTSD) or depression, it is wrong to assume that all need to have a similar response. Also, the use of major mental health "disorder" does not seem very appropriate in relation to refugees' and asylum seekers' experiences. Exhibiting symptoms of PTSD, depression, or anxiety is their normal way of responding to very abnormal circumstances and experiences.

When speaking about the emotional and psychological problems that immigrants, refugees, and asylum seekers arrive with, it is of great importance to speak about those asylum seekers who get detained by the Bureau of Citizenship and Immigration Services (formerly INS) upon arrival. Although the U.S. government refers to them as *detainees* and not prisoners, these individuals are often kept in county jails among criminals. According to the findings of a study done by Bellevue/NYU Program for Survivors of Torture and Physicians for Human Rights, the Bureau of Citizenship and Immigration Services frequently detains asylum seekers in county jails and, while in there, they are kept in the same cells with convicted criminals, including violent offenders: "The INS moves detainees to other facilities without notice and often in the middle of the night. Several asylum seekers mentioned these surprise transfers as a source of distress, and a reminder of their profoundly disempowered status" (Physicians for Human Rights, 2003, p. 10). After being in detention for six months, one of the asylum seekers who participated in this study reported:

> The main problem is that we don't know what is going to happen. At least with a prison sentence you know you are lessening your time. But here, even after three years they may still send you back.... In my country I was in prison for five days and there were beatings, but then they released you after five days. But you get here to a democratic country, and it goes on and on with no release. It's another kind of torture—mental torture.... No one knows we're here. (Physicians for Human Rights, 2003, p. 5.1)

> When we think of refugees, we automatically think of the persecution and suffering inflicted in their home country. We rarely see the suffering endured when they come to this country for support. The very victims we feel so much sympathy for in the news reports become asylum seekers and we are tutored not to empathize but to distance ourselves and condemn. (Bracken, 2002, p. 1)

As mentioned before, many refugees and asylum seekers are forced to flee their countries under such dangerous situations that they are unable to bring with them any of their important documents, such as birth certificates, marriage licenses, educational documents, and so on. A common practice by BCIS for determining the age of the youth and minors who do not have any documentation or who are traveling with false documents is the use of dental x-rays. Despite the inaccuracy of this test, BCIS continues to utilize this method to determine whether the youth are over 18 years of age, and if the result is positive, they will be send to adult detention centers: "The practice of imprisoning asylum seekers who flee to America to escape torture and persecution in their own countries had damaging effects on the well-being of these individuals. Detention can induce fear, isolation, and hopelessness, and exacerbate the severe psychological distress frequently exhibited by asylum seekers who are already traumatized" (Physicians for Human Rights, 2003, p. 1).

The study by Bellevue/NYU Program for Survivors of Torture and Physicians for Human Rights focused on 70 asylum-seeker detainees. Results indicated that asylum seekers exhibited poor and worsening mental health while in detention, had limited access to mental and physical health services, were treated poorly by staff at detention centers, were denied legal representation, and were treated harshly with inadequate explanations about their rights and lack of interpreters at their port of entry.

The problem with inadequate access to professional interpreters is not limited to asylum seekers' port of entry and the detention centers. Medical and mental health providers often overlook this issue, and instead of arranging for trained interpreters, they utilize family members, including children. This practice, however, can create problems at many levels. It might be very difficult, for example, for a person to speak about his or her emotional and psychological problems in front of another family member. In many instances, the person might not be able to speak about his or her story of trauma if a family member is present. This particularly becomes an issue if the person has experienced sexual trauma, such as rape and female genital mutilation. For example, many times during a war, families scatter in different places and later reunite in a refugee camp. While on the run, women are sexually assaulted either by a rebel group or government soldiers. However, for a variety of reasons, such as the fear of consequences and the pain and shame associated with it, many decide not to share the incident(s) with their husbands and other family members. If a professional interpreter is not available, a therapist must be cognizant of issues such as this.

Also, using a family member and particularly a child for interpretation exposes the person to issues that might be inappropriate and damaging. Many times in the process of using untrained interpreters the actual issues do not get translated accurately to the therapist, which hinders the process of assessment and treatment.

As is often the case, children of immigrants are the ones who learn the language first and start navigating the system. Earlier, it was noted that there are role reversals in refugee and immigrant families. Asking children to accompany their parents to different places and appointments, be it a trip to the grocery store or an appointment with the therapist, places children and youth in an awkward situation and could have a negative effect on family dynamics.

The importance of using interpreters that are both trained professionally and are also familiar with the cultures where refugees and asylum seekers come from must be dually noted. There are many terms and expressions in different languages that require familiarity with that specific culture so that they won't be translated into "alarming signs" and abnormalities. For example, a foreign psychiatrist who had just started an internship in an American hospital saw a female patient. She started the session by complaining about the bad weather and that "it was raining cats and dogs." The psychiatrist, not being familiar with the American expression, thought that the client was hallucinating and was actually seeing cats and dogs falling from the sky. Reliance on untrained interpreters can cause tremendous harm:

> The harms of using family members or friends, and particularly minors, as interpreters are multifaceted. Research and anecdotal information reveal many problems that result from this practice. These include: (1) requiring children to take on additional burdens, adult decision-making and responsibilities; (2) causing friction and role reversal within the family structure, which can even lead to child abuse situations; (3) violating beneficiary confidentiality, which can lead to inadequate services or mistakes in the provisions of services; and (4) because family members and friends, particularly if they are minors, almost always are not competent to interpret, using them as interpreters often leads to serious negative consequences. (Health Law, undated, appendix, p. 1)

Also, in using family members as interpreters, careful attention must be paid to family dynamics and relationships between family members. For example, if a therapist is seeing a wife in a refugee family and has knowledge that the husband speaks good English, the therapist must make every attempt to arrange for an interpreter other than the husband, at least until he or she can rule out possible domestic violence in the family.

Probably the most influencing institution that immigrant children and youth come in contact with is the school. Since there are no designated child or youth services as part of the resettlement package for refugees, it is of extreme importance for the counselors and social workers in school clinics to familiarize themselves with the unique challenges faced by this population, as described by Gonzalez-Ramos and Sanchez-Nester (2001):

> The children in the family often are left to cope on their own, with the hope that they both learn English and acculturate as quickly as possible. The multiple losses the children and their families have gone through, the fears, confusion, sadness, and alienation they may feel often are left unattended. Yet it is these losses and changes that the children carry with them into their schools and that teachers, guidance counselors, and social workers are confronted with. (p. 3)

Issues Related to Spirituality/Religion

Issues related to spirituality and religion are rarely at the forefront of discussions when considering the needs of newcomer youth and their families. Nonetheless, it is important to briefly consider spirituality/religion, as they may serve as powerful resources as well as be arenas of potential conflict. As noted in Chapter 6, spirituality and religion are recognized as being different concepts; however, for the purpose of this discussion they are linked together as "spirituality/religion."

Multiple authors have noted both the diversity and the importance of spirituality/religion in Latino, Caribbean, African, and Asian cultures (Canda & Furman, 1999; Delgado, 1998; Devore & Schlesinger, 1999; Fukuyama & Sevig, 1999; Sue & Sue, 2003). Certainly for many newcomers, spirituality/religion continue as an important source of support and "meaning" in their lives even after migration. Johnson (1995) identifies spiritual support as one of ten key resiliency mechanisms for culturally diverse families, and describes the critical role of *family spiritualism:* "The family serves as a source of spiritual nurturance, honoring the family's connection to the metaphysical world and giving meaning to moral values and life transitions" (p. 324).

Chapter 6 highlights spirituality/religion as one of four critical "youth attitudes" that can help newcomer youth develop effective social navigational skills. Discussing how Latinos have "used religion as a survival mechanism," Gonzalez (2002) writes, "For many immigrants, religion served as a buffer against the toxic emotional effects of entrance into the United States" (p. 87). Stepick (1998) states that for Haitians, "religion provides a social matrix to support fellow immigrants" (p. 86), and Kamya (1997) notes the essential role of spirituality among African immigrants and its intimate connection with both individual and communal coping resources. Finally, it is important to remember that for some newcomers, the primary motivation for migration has been to find religious freedom:

> In my family, we are all Christian.... But in my country, we can't go to church. Here, my brother, sister and I go to a Lutheran Church every Sunday. (Mariel Kuay Diew, age 18, Sudan, cited in Kelen & Kelen, 2002, p. 47)

> For me, Izhevsk was fine.... But for my mom it was much harder.... the Communists didn't like Jews, so they wouldn't let her work. (Yegeniya Yushkova, age 17, Russia, cited in Kelen & Kelen, 2002, p. 26)

There is growing discussion of the role of spirituality/religion in refugee and immigrant literature. Canda and Phaobtong (1992) discuss Buddhism as an important support system for Southeast Asian refugees, outlining the broad range of services offered by monks and temples. These may include explicit religious ceremonies, healing rituals, life cycle transition ceremonies, organization of community holiday festivals, instruction in meditation techniques, and offering the temple as a place of retreat. Krulfeld (1994), studying Buddhism in the Lao refugee community, notes the ability of religious leaders to modify certain practices (e.g., the role of nuns) in order to sustain the religion in the new cultural context. Kinzie (2001) describes the healing role of Buddhism and involvement in the temple for some traumatized Cambodian refugees. Canda and Furman (1999) emphasize the need for helping professionals to recognize and respect the rich diversity of Hispanic/Latino and Caribbean expressions of spirituality, which "often combines...more conventional Christian teachings with African and Indigenous spiritual traditions"(p. 103), such as *cuandersimo, santiguando, espiritismo, santeria,* and *voudon.*

Within the past decade, not only have spirituality/religion become increasingly recognized as potential resources for newcomer individuals and families but practitioners are also more likely to be actively incorporating them into their work. Some counselors may encourage certain clients to seek out traditional healing methods to complement Western therapy (Amodeo, Robb, Peou, & Tran, 1996; DeMonchy, 1991), whereas others may integrate prayer into their work with immigrant families (Sue & Sue, 2003). Fukuyama and Sevig (1999) cite a Latina therapist who reports, "It is natural for [me] to pray with [my] religious Latino clients"(p. 151), and one of the book's authors has heard similar statements from some Haitian counselors. However, spirituality/religion are not just being incorporated into social and mental health services at the individual or family level; they are also being formally integrated into program models as illustrated in the following brief examples.

Project Sangkhim, a Massachusetts pilot substance abuse project for Southeast Asians, consciously recognized the importance of Buddhist philosophy and tenets to most Cambodians, and provided weekly trips to a local Buddhist temple as part of its program: "Reconnection with Buddhism and Buddhist practices was seen by the team as similar to utilization of Alcoholics Anonymous and other self-help groups" (Amodeo, Peou, Grigg-Saito, Berke, Pin-Riebe, & Jones, 1999, p. 12). *ROCA* (see Chapter 10), a Massachusetts-based youth development program serving primarily newcomers, utilizes a holistic approach that explicitly includes attention to spiritual development. This spiritual focus is reflected in a diverse range of activities, including community service, peacemaking circles, and collaboration with local clergy (*ROCA*, 2003). The Lowell (Massachusetts) Police Department, in response to escalating Asian gang violence, recently established a program in which Southeast Asian runaways are mandated to meet with the head monk at the local temple for counseling and instruction in the teachings of Buddhism (Ramirez, 2003). This same monk had previously been enlisted by a coalition of advocates developing an educational videotape in response to the growing domestic violence in the Cambodian community.

The video opens with shots of a Buddhist ceremony, and then the monk speaks to the camera, saying that domestic violence is not in accordance with Buddhist beliefs nor traditional Cambodian culture. Multiple Haitian churches have developed youth programs, specifically designed to reach out to Haitian youth, that are dealing with the challenges of acculturation (personal communication). Similarly, *al-Ummah: An Experience in Islamic Living* is a youth project described by its director, Dr. Fariyal Ross-Sheriff, as providing "an opportunity for Muslim boys and girls to link resources from the Islamic heritage with an understanding of what it means to grow up in America" (Nanji, 1993, p. 241).

Although the preceding discussion highlights the many ways in which spirituality/religion may serve as powerful resources for newcomer youth and their families, it is not always easy for newcomers to maintain their spiritual/religious practices. In the early days of resettlement of Southeast Asian refugees, when so many were sponsored by churches, occasional stories circulated of some newcomers "feeling the need" to convert to Christianity. It was often unclear whether this was due to subtle "messages" from church folk or out of sheer gratitude (personal communication).

In certain ethnic communities there may be a serious shortage of religious leaders (i.e., the majority of Cambodian monks were killed during the Pol Pot regime) or the total absence of the appropriate house of worship (e.g., a mosque or temple). Sometimes there are churches representing the familiar religion/denomination, but they lack a bicultural/bilingual priest or pastor and thus are not experienced or embraced as Haitian, Korean, or Ethiopian churches. Some spiritual practices may require "ingredients" that are not readily available or involve rituals that are perceived in negative, stereotypical ways (e.g., sacrifices associated with voudon). And alas, in the aftermath of

September 11th, it is painfully apparent that Muslim newcomers may suffer very real discrimination due to their religion and new barriers and/or risks as they seek to continue its practice.

Finally, it should be noted that although spirituality/religion is a powerful source of support for so many, they might also become a divisive issue in some immigrant and refugee families. As youth become more "Americanized," they may feel less connected to their parents' spiritual/religious belief systems and practices, which in turn can lead to further conflict between the generations. One Muslim teenager describes the "Friday problem": "Most of my friends go to parties on Friday evening, whereas Friday being the day of congregational prayer in Islam, I must make an effort to go with the family to the Mosque and then for religious education classes" (Nanji, 1993, p. 237). Ambivalence toward or rejection of parents' spiritual/religious traditions is certainly widespread among many U.S.-born youth, as well. However, given the multiple losses newcomer families have already experienced due to their migration, the "meaning" attached to children's negative attitudes regarding traditional spiritual/religious traditions may differ. Newcomer parents may well experience this as a more profound rejection and with a greater sense of loss—of both "self" and culture.

Issues Related to Political Realities

Earlier sections have discussed the effect of legal status on different aspects of immigrants' lives, such as educational and employment opportunities, economic well-being, and mental health. This section will demonstrate the relationship between immigrants' legal status and their political participation. Legal status of immigrants has a great impact on their degree of participation in political activities. It's only after an immigrant becomes a naturalized U.S. citizen that he or she obtains the right to vote. Be it refugees, asylees, or other types of "legal" immigrants, a large number of immigrants adhere to government regulations such as paying taxes like any citizen, yet they are still denied the right to vote—one thing that could make a great impact on their lives: "Why should an immigrant who pays taxes, is affected by local voting decisions, and even risks his or her life by serving in the U.S. military be denied a voice in the community? The U.S. Constitution leaves this question to local communities to answer; an increasing number of them are deciding that immigrants deserve a local voice" (Wucker, 2003, p. 3).

It is unjust to the immigrants and refugees who shape a considerable portion of the working class not to be able to have a voice and not to be able to be elected or vote for a person who would represent their ideas and advocate for their rights in important areas such as education. As explained by Wucker (2003), "The impact of immigrant workers goes beyond economics; it has political consequences for all workers. Because non-citizen immigrants can't vote, a large fraction of the working class ends up without a political voice, exploited by employers and resented by many native-born workers" (p. 1).

Giving such an important right to immigrants could be an incentive for them to participate and educate themselves more about the issues affecting them and others. Gaining such an important right can bring about a sense of belonging and empowerment: "The ability to have a say in the working of government, either as an elected official or as a voter, is a powerful empowerment tool" (Asian American Legal Defense and Education Fund [AALDEF] 2003, p. 1).

Becoming a naturalized citizen, however, is not an easy task and can be a very lengthy process. According to a paper published by the Asian American Legal Defense and Education Fund, 1.8 million applicants are stuck in the BCIS backlog. The process of becoming an American citizen is different in some aspects for refugees and asylees. Refugees can apply for their green card after being in the United States for a year, which usually takes between one to three years to obtain. Asylees are also entitled to apply for a green card one year after the date of their asylum approval. The difference, however, is that there is no limit on the number of refugee green card applications that are processed each year, but there is a 10,000-person limit on the number of green card applications processed for asylees. So, although there is no ceiling in terms of the number of applications that may be filed by asylees for green cards each year, there is a limited number of those applications that will be processed. For this reason, many asylees have to wait for up to five years to get their green cards.

According to the law, an eligible immigrant must be a permanent resident of the United States (green card holder) before he or she may apply to become a citizen (for those married to an American citizen, the number of years is reduced to three). For refugees, the clock starts to tick from the moment they enter the United States; for asylees, however, the time starts from the date they receive their green card and not the time of their asylum approval. As a result, an asylee who is required to abide by the laws of this country may go for as long as 10 years without having a voice and the right to vote.

Another challenge in newcomer communities is the newcomers' lack of knowledge about their rights and resources. Immigrants need to be educated about their rights and responsibilities. Many community organizations, such as human and legal services, have tried to educate immigrants about their rights by teaching them about the voting process or by sponsoring citizenship classes that assist immigrants in preparing for their citizenship exam.

Despite efforts by some community organizations, many immigrants decide not to participate in any kind of social or political activity organized by the institution. There are several reasons for lack of participation, some of which go back to ethnic or political factions even within a group of refugees from the same country. For example, some might have belonged to a pro-democracy group in the country of origin and some to another political rebel group. However, as it is the case with many newcomer groups, these differences remain a source of disunity and dissension within the community, even in the United States.

Also, many refugees and asylees are forced to flee their countries due to their political activities and subsequent torture, imprisonment, and threats to their lives. Having such traumatic experiences related to the political system in their country of origin could contribute to their fear and lack of interest in participating in any kind activity related to politics. In addition to the education and outreach that happens within the immigrant and refugee populations, there is a need for the general public and government officials to educate themselves about immigrants' and refugees' needs, to be a voice for them, and to help abolish the myths about them.

Whatever hat one wears, one must always remember the unique challenges faced by immigrant, refugee, asylum seeker, and asylee youth and adults and the barriers they face in voicing their problems and concerns. Ongoing education and advocacy is needed on behalf of these groups. Also, there is a need for a growing number of individuals from these communities to become the voices for their generation and the generations to come.

Conclusion

The key issues, needs, and concerns of newcomer youth are clearly complex and challenging. As noted in the introduction of this chapter, although the issues have been discussed here as separate entities, in reality they often not only coexist but they also dynamically interact with each other. These challenges clearly have implications for the youth and their families, and their future in this new land. They also hold implications for social workers, youth counselors, and other professionals who seek to understand these needs and their multiple contexts and to develop ways of effectively working with newcomers.

Finally, these challenges carry implications for the United States as a country. Newcomer youth and their families represent tremendous human assets for this nation and society, bringing rich diversity in culture and talents. Most also demonstrate a strong will to survive and adapt, the capacity to work hard, the dream of building a new life, and the desire to contribute to their new homeland. The challenge, then, is for Americans to gain the necessary knowledge, find the needed resources, and change policies and attitudes that present barriers so that these newest Americans may take root and thrive. As will be addressed in the following chapter, much has been learned about what constitutes the best practices in the field of social work regarding newcomer youth. These best practices inspire hope about how effective social work can not only meet the needs of newcomer youth but also serve as a model for other helping professions.

Major Elements and Building Blocks of Youth Development

Empowering youth helps ensure that . . . community-building is done with the community and not for the community. It also increases the extent to which sustainable change improves the capacities and life chances for all youth and families, helping to create a legacy of contributions to civil society that will enrich American life for generations to come.

—Gore, 2003, p. ix

5

Best Practice Principles with Newcomer Youth

In some respects, the children of immigrants . . . are quite similar to what one would find with a sample of non-immigrant, non-minority youth. But in others, they face complex circumstances that signally add to the stress of adolescence, and exhibit wide variations among national origin groups in their vulnerabilities and resources. Despite these added challenges—or perhaps because of them—the overall picture that emerges . . . is one of noteworthy achievement and resilient ambition.

—Rumbaut, 1998, p. 11

Introduction

Social work practice with any marginalized or undervalued group in U.S. society faces a series of challenges in finding balance between meeting the needs of the group and seeking reform at a societal level. Never is there the luxury of doing one without the other. First and foremost in these challenges is answering the question of the appropriateness and effectiveness of the service being provided. This takes on added importance when discussing newcomers, since the "baseline" knowledge on immigrant and refugee groups can only best be described as "evolving." Furthermore, the often-precarious conditions that newcomers face in this country are compounded by the limited options available to them in seeking assistance when required (as already noted in previous chapters).

There is no profession that does not affirm the importance of the service it provides as being the most up to date and effective. The embrace of *best practices* is an attempt by a profession to capture this position for the profession itself and the general public. The concept of "best practices" generally conjures up images of interventions based on the latest and most scientifically rigorous information. Although best practices do come from evidenced-based approaches, they evolve through systematic evaluation and purposeful change incorporating the latest findings. Thus, best practice principles represent the best of two worlds that often do not intersect (1) the academic and theoretical world and (2) the "real" world of practice on a daily basis. The intersection of these two worlds results in practice informing research and research informing practice.

This merging of theory and practice results in the establishment of a process for engaging in dialogue to ensure that best practices knowledge stays abreast of developments in the field. An inability to engage in this type of dialogue and partnerships between scholars and practitioners effectively limits the influence of each party on practice outcomes. This ultimately undermines the profession's "political capital" in seeking funding and establishing partnerships with other helping professions. In addition, it establishes a culture that effectively serves as a barrier—a divide between practitioners and scholars/researchers.

Any effort to arrive at best practice principles, however, requires greater attention being paid to specifics of population, problem-focus, and context. Ultimately, this increased attention requires reexamination of prior ways of serving population groups in need, a willingness to admit mistakes and ignorance, and a critical understanding of what is needed to better use existing resources. In essence, the search for best practices can best be conceptualized as a journey that necessitates being introspective and that exhibits a willingness on the part of a practitioner and a profession to do what is in the best interest of the person, group, or community being addressed. In many ways, it is also a journey without a final destination. Practice, being dynamic, is ever changing, requiring newer modifications to keep up with changing circumstances and new knowledge acquisition.

This chapter identifies the most promising intervention strategies used in the field as a way of guiding the reader toward practice with newcomer youth. Further, every effort is made to specify the group status (immigrant, refugee, asylum seeker), age group, and country of origin as a means of contextualizing the needs, concerns, and challenges facing newcomer youth. Field examples will be used to illustrate exciting and highly innovative services currently underway across the country. Unfortunately, the structure and delivery of social services to newcomers has historically not received the attention it deserves in the scholarly literature (Le-Doux & Stephens, 1992). The goal of this chapter is not to present a "laundry list" of all of the best practices. Instead, a select number of best practice principles have been identified because of the universal appeal they have in reaching and serving newcomer youth. These "core" best practices are translated into a set of principles that set the foundation from which practitioners can add or modify depending on local circumstances.

What Are Best Practices?

Social work practice with newcomer youth, their families, and their communities can not possibly be "business as usual" in the conventional sense of practice. Both the scholarly literature and practice wisdom indicate that practice with this population group must be highly contextualized. "Starting where the client is" is an axiom that few social workers, regardless of the method of practice, have not heard of before and embraced. However, starting where the client is when speaking about newcomer youth is greatly influenced by how long they have been in this country and when services actually begin. Further, services often necessitate innovative approaches and significant modifications to existing approaches. Consequently, before moving on to youth development practice, it is essential to pause and examine the principles of best practice with newcomer youth.

Interestingly, an extensive review of the literature and countless consultations from colleagues and practitioners across the country uncovered two significant themes regarding best practices with newcomer youth. First, the literature on best practices with immigrants, refugees, and asylees, regardless of age group, is sorely lacking in quantity, depth, and quality. Second, this observation is even more prevalent when discussing newcomer youth, with the possible exception of the subject of education (Castex, 1997). Nevertheless, the reader will be presented with an analysis of best practices with newcomer youth that weaves together material from a variety of sources, such as professional literature, newspaper articles, reports, personal communication with practitioners and academics, as well as conversations with newcomer youth themselves. Best practices with newcomer youth are best thought of as "evolving."

A definition of what is meant by best practices can be as simple or as complex as the reader wishes to make it and can easily be the subject of a multivolume set of books. Potocky-Tripodi (2002) for example, defines *best practices* concisely when noting that they are "practice activities that are grounded in . . . [an] empirically based practice paradigm" (p. 123). This definition may appear rather simple and straightforward. However, this simplicity is misleading because the subject matter is quite complex in nature and scope, and very much determined by sociocultural environmental considerations. Taking the necessary time to consider these factors may well be beyond the realm of most practitioners, however.

The process of synthesizing and consolidating research findings and scholarly conclusions, although a laborious task, often represents the initial and foundation building step in the development of best practices. This process, however, is very dependent on an extensive and systematic review of the literature and research findings on a particular population group, and the more specific the group, the better. When this literature and research do not exist, or if they exist in very limited quantity and scope because of historical neglect or because the population group is too new to this country to have been studied, then the challenge of deriving best practices becomes even more challenging and important for the field.

The process of deriving best social work practices is the responsibility of the entire social work profession, practitioners and scholars alike. In fact, this process can move forward only if scholars assume this task as part of their scholarly agenda. Scholars, after all, are paid to create and disseminate knowledge. This is not to say, however, that practitioners may not be undertaking innovative and highly effective practices. The profession as a whole needs to consolidate this practice wisdom and combine it with requisite research and scholarship for it to be labeled "best practices." The availability of funding to serve as a powerful motivator should never be underestimated. It takes funding as well as political will to come together for this goal to be realized.

The social work literature has in the last decade adopted the concept of best practices to uplift for analysis and utilization what are considered the most effective and efficient ways of providing services to population groups in need (Franklin, 2001; Franklin

& Corcoran, 2000; Howard & Jenson, 1999a, 1999b). The goal of advancing practice knowledge is fueled by the desire to arrive at what are the best practices in the field at that particular moment in time.

Some social work scholars would go so far as to take the position that failure of the profession to incorporate the latest research and thinking into practice constitutes a serious breach of ethics (Jayaratne, Croxton, & Mattison, 1997). Delgado (2003) goes so far as to say, "A profession that fails to stay up-to-date is a profession destined to remain stagnant and irrelevant" (p. 131). Thus, the movement toward best practices within the profession of social work is still in an embryonic stage.

The importance of best practices to the profession of social work has been noted by Franklin (2001) and captures the essence of the definition of best practices: "Use of the most effective practices is consonant with social work practice, our code of ethics, and professional goals for providing the highest quality of services to our clients" (p. 131). The concept of best practices is not unique to social work and can be found in a variety of professions, practice settings, and specific problem and population groups, such as school social work, child welfare, gerontology, substance abuse, to name but a few (Marotta, 2000). The origin of best practices has been traced to the medical model and mental health—two areas that have historically received considerable attention and requisite funding—and it has slowly moved into other professional spheres.

Best practice principles or guidelines represent a consensus of what experts (academics as well as practitioners) think is the preferred intervention approach for a specific population and situation. Best practice principles can be influenced by either or both expert consensus and empirically validated studies. These guidelines, in turn, are not cast in stone and are sufficiently flexible or dynamic, to take into account or be supplemented by practitioners' experiences with particular situations or cases. Best practice principles can be influenced by standards for care, empirically supported treatment manuals and protocols, expert consensus reviews, meta-analysis of professional literature reviews, and case reports.

The information distilled from these sources represents the best practice principles that should guide interventions, and do so by providing practitioners with knowledge on what interventions are the most effective, for whom they work best, and under what conditions or circumstances they maximize positive outcomes (Proctor, 2001). Best practice guidelines also serve to enhance professional reputation (Marotta, 2000): "Both critics and advocates of guideline development understand that the time is long past when practicing without guidelines is acceptable to both the public who use services and the professionals who provide such services. In addition, accountability in service provision is one way for a profession to grow in recognition" (p. 493). It can be safely said that best practices benefit all parties involved in providing services!

Clearly, best practices with newcomers do not rely on labels to capture a wide variety of human experiences that can only be properly understood with requisite contextualization. Koss-Chioino and Vargas (1999), although referring to Latino immigrant youth, address the consequences of such an approach: "From a contextual perspective, the objectification of problem behavior into a diagnosis that focuses exclusively on the individual ignores how such behavior is multidetermined as well as affected by reciprocal interactions between the youth and observers (parents, teachers, diagnosticians, and so on)" (p. 75). Culture-bound "syndromes" specific to newcomer groups may go totally unrecognized by practitioners (Kershaw, 2003). Post-traumatic stress disorder, conversely, may have no basis in non-Western cultures, and is often used to label newcomers with histories of witnessing or being the subject of violence in their countries of origins.

Summerfield (2000) observes that the psychiatric label of post-traumatic stress disorder (PTSD), one that incidentally is often used with newcomers coming out of conflict-ridden countries, may not adequately capture the essence of human response to conflict-related experiences. Furthermore, PTSD features can be epiphenomenal and not reflect what survivors seek assistance for or consider being important. In essence, a psychiatric label that does not contextualize presenting symptoms and needs is of limited use with newcomers who are survivors. Newcomer youth, even those who have suffered trauma due to armed conflict, share similar goals with their native counterparts in their new country of origin: "Not unexpectedly they expressed universal shared wishes—to have friends, play sports, do well in school, speak English and 'feel safe'" (Champassak, 2001, p. 20).

Key Elements of Best Practices

Best practice principles aid organizations and practitioners in viewing youth and families from a developmental rather than a problem or deficit perspective (Pittman & Zeldin, 1995). Any sincere effort to address best practices requires that a profession pay careful attention to three key elements: (1) attitudes, (2) knowledge, and ultimately (3) skills or competencies (Kelley & Enslein, 2001). It would be foolhardy to focus exclusively on best practices from a skills perspective, tempting as that may be for evaluation purposes. Best practices do not magically appear without being informed by attitudes and knowledge. Attitudes are influenced by a variety of factors, not the least of which are cultural values. As expected, the interplay of these three spheres is highly dynamic.

The fundamental belief that all human beings possess assets translates into a question of What are the assets? rather than Are there assets? This value necessitates the creation of techniques for identifying and enhancing. Another value may be that all human beings, regardless of the circumstances surrounding their arrival in this country, have an inalienable right to receive the best services based on the latest information and developments in the field. Their entrance or legal status in this country does not affect the quality of the services they receive. Best practices with newcomer youth, at least according to the authors of this book, cannot possibly exist without youth assets being systematically identified and mobilized in service to youth and their communities.

Challenges to Using Best Practices

Best practice principles, although of prodigious value to both practitioners and scholars alike, do not have universal acceptance in the field. In addition, due to the dynamic nature of the practice world and the ever-constant changing of population groups, best practices, like cultural competence, can best be thought of as a journey where one never fully arrives at a destination. Furthermore, best practices are never stagnant. In fact, what makes best practices is the ability of the practitioner to be ever vigilant for the latest information and research on a specific population group.

Goldberg (2000), for example, specifically examines best practice principles and multicultural social work practice and identifies three potential conflict domains for social workers, with particular reference to newcomers in this society:

1. *Respecting the contents of all cultures versus supporting basic human rights:* The tensions inherent in supporting cultural values when these values systematically deprive members of the group of basic rights, as in the case of children within particular newcomer groups, is not easy to reconcile (Fadiman, 1997). Moorthy (1996) addresses this very point when cultural practices view children as property or subject to the use of rituals and abuse as part of values within the culture. The subject of female genital mutilation is a case in point (IAC Fifth Regional Conference, 2001; Trueblood, 2000).

2. *Conflicts between needs and values of people from different cultural heritages versus mission of social work:* Newcomers enter this country with a set of values and beliefs that may well be counter to that advocated by the profession, thereby raising potential conflict between newcomer and worker. Furstenberg (1998), for example, notes that the subject of adolescent childbearing may not be considered a social problem in some cultures; inherent economic and kinship arrangements can encourage early onset births. This value is counter to that held by most social workers and social agencies.

3. *Conflict between a social worker's own ethnic preference versus his or her obligation to eliminate personal cultural bias and prejudice:* Stereotypes are not uncommon among professional workers, and eliminating them is a lifelong journey, particularly when they involve ethnic or racial groups with long histories of beliefs that are different from those of the worker.

Best practice principles must contend with the tensions of needing to be sufficiently broad to allow situation-specific factors to be taken into account but still having sufficient specificity to be of value to workers. When applied to populations such as newcomer youth, principles cannot be too broad or too specific because immigrant and refugee youth are not monolithic in composition and circumstances surrounding their departure from their country of origins. Best practice principles, as a result, should guide without restricting, inform without dictating, and suggest without demanding.

Finally, a practitioner having access to best practices, when they do exist, may also be a barrier. Procter (2001) notes that most knowledge about interventions is only available through scholarly sources such as books, journal articles, and reports. The lack of a centralized source for this information is a challenge, even when undertaken through use of electronic means. Once the source is located, the practitioner must then obtain it, which is a costly and time-consuming endeavor. Unfortunately, scholarly material, because of the review and publication process, can quickly become dated before it actually finds its way into print and widely disseminated to those who can best use this information.

Best Practices with Immigrant and Refugee Youth

The call for best practices with newcomers has been issued, particularly regarding the resettlement and reintegration of forced immigrants and international displaced persons (Potocky-Tripodi, 2002). It is estimated, for example, that 80 percent of all displaced population worldwide are women and children, making these newcomers particularly vulnerable. There are over 22 million people in the world who are refugees because of a well-founded fear of being persecuted and live outside of their country of origin as a result. The need for best practices, however, also applies to other newcomer subgroups. Best practice interventions with newcomer youth are best guided by a set of principles to inform assessment and services.

Following is a discussion of the six best practices with newcomer youth. It represents an effort to synthesize and consolidate material from research, scholarly, and practice sources. These catagories do not serve as a comprehensive list; however, they do represent that initial step or foundation presented earlier in this chapter. The authors hope that national organizations, such as the National Association of Social Work, the Council on Social Work Education, and the Society for the Advancement of Social Work Research, will move forward and systematically create a more comprehensive set of best practices with newcomer youth.

Enhancement of Adult Caring Relationships with Newcomer Youth

The professional literature on youth is quite explicit in identifying the value of caring relationships, particularly those involving adults, in enhancing youth self-esteem and competencies (Eccles & Gootman, 2002; Gilligan, 1999; Laursen, 2002; Rockwell, 1998). The youth development literature, too, emphasizes the need for programs to stress goals and activities that bring youth and adults into collaborative working relationships that place youth in positions of authority and having opportunities to utilize their assets (Nettles, Mucherah, & Jones, 2000; Rodriguez, 1997).

Youth leadership development, as a result, occurs within a context of adults rather than one exclusively consisting of youth. Adults and youth, however, must contend with the presence of insidious stereotypes of each other—stereotypes that have been reinforced by the popular press and entertainment media. Trust, an important component of any meaningful relationship, takes time to develop and prosper. Programming suffers when this element is taken for granted or not considered important.

Stanton-Salazar (1997), although making specific reference to working-class youth of color but no less applicable to newcomer youth, stresses the importance of a positive relationship between youth and adult institutional agents. These adult authority figures can assist youth in obtaining access to opportunities and resources and in acting as role models for brokering accessibility to institutions: "In sum, the development of social ties to institutional agents is essential to the social development and empowerment of ethnic minority children and youth precisely because these ties represent consistent and reliable sources from which they can learn the appropriate decoding skills and from which they can obtain other key forms of institutional support" (p. 11).

Practice seeking to enhance adult-youth relationships can place practitioners in excellent positions to model for newcomer parents. It can also place practitioners in difficult positions if both parents and youth alike do not fully understand or appreciate the goals of the practitioner. Nevertheless, practitioners cannot back away from assisting newcomer youth and parents in arriving at a "new" balance in child-parent relationships without seriously undermining important cultural norms pertaining to role expectations. Field-based examples of programs stressing adult caring relationships with youth are plentiful and highlight numerous possible interventions—for example, using mentorship as the central feature of the intervention. The Hispanic Committee of Virginia, through its school alliance program titled "Alianza Escolar," seeks to provide educational services that promote learning and encourage youth to stay in school while also assisting parents to participate in their children's education and expand their own potential. The program matches Latino children who attend targeted elementary and middle schools with adult volunteers for tutoring and other mentoring activities. The program works with students whose environment puts them at risk of dropping out of school. Teachers and counselors identify Latino students in the fourth through eighth grades for the program. After being selected, students are matched with a volunteer mentor. Throughout the school year, the students meet with their mentors one evening a week for one-hour sessions. The mentors help the students with their schoolwork, concentrate on verbal and math skills, and provide activities that promote the students' achievements.

The Oakland Asian Student Educational Services' (OASES) INSPIRE program addresses the general lack of guidance and support for Oakland high school students in pursuit of their educational goals. The INSPIRE Youth Mentorship Program, based at the University of California, Berkeley, seeks to provide motivation, support, guidance, and information to help Asian newcomer youth maximize their potential while in school. In addition, the program encourages Asian youth to get involved in their community. This program is in response to a perceived lack of support from the neighborhood, the family background, and the result of the poorly funded public school that the mentees attend. Most of the mentees live in neighborhoods where gang violence and drug dealing are prevalent. As a result, there are few role models to emulate. Many of the students' parents have not received a higher education and are hampered in offering assistance to their children in navigating this new world. Mentors guide their respective mentees, while team members learn valuable lessons in the operations of an organization.

Successful Brokering between Parental and Peer Influences

The importance of parents in the lives of *all* youth is well accepted in practice and research and not just in the youth development field (Marsiglia & Holleran, 1999). The same may be said for the influence of peers in the lives of adolescents (McMorris, Tyler, Whitbeck, & Hoyt, 2002). The tension between parental and peer influences takes on added significance in the case of newcomer youth who are in a propitious position to interact within the broader society (Castex, 1997). Mind you, tension is not limited to between parents and their children. Parents themselves may also experience tension between themselves, further straining their relationship with their children (Casanova, 1996).

Harris (1998) would go so far as to argue that peers and environments wield far greater influence in the life of youth than do parents, and makes a provocative observation to highlight the influence: "A child is better off living in a troubled family in a good neighborhood than living in a good family in a troubled neighborhood" (p. 60). Regardless of where the reader falls in this debate, suffice it to say that peers wield considerable influence in a youngster's life. Likewise, peers have a tremendous amount of influence on newcomer youth (Phinney, Romero, Nava, & Huang, 2001). This influence does not necessarily have to be negative, however.

The Planting Seeds Family Enrichment Program (PSFEP), based in eastern North Carolina, utilizes a series of five different types of workshops conducted over the course of one day (Anguiano, 2001). Latino families and youth participate in interactive exercises focused on the development of strong families, leadership skills, community development skills, and wellness. These workshops are conducted in Spanish and have been purposefully structured to engage Latinos. Setting aside one day makes it much easier for families to participate than extending the workshops over a period of weeks.

Having improved and supportive relationships between newcomer parents and their children represents a critical aspect of best practices. The brokering of relationships is not helped when newcomer youth have more responsibility than their native counterparts and far fewer freedoms (Abraham, 2003). Having language competencies that their parents do not have compounds role expectations, as noted by one director of refugee services: "Often the children become the head of household because they have the language capacity. They are taking on the adult role in that they act as translators. . . . However, when it comes to sticking with family values, oftentimes, it is still the parents [who are in charge]" (p. B6).

Practitioners are also faced with the challenge of differentiating between what can be considered "culturally normative" from "culturally dysfunctional." This assessment is further complicated when U.S. society's expectations of independence is entered into the discussion of what is "healthy" and "unhealthy" in the exercise of decision-making power. Mirsky and Prawer (1992) coined the term *sacrificial lambs syndrome* to capture the experiences of newcomer youth with pressures placed on them by their parents who tell them "We came to this country for you." Guilt is used as a powerful motivation to get newcomer youth to obey their parents. When guilt ceases to work as a technique, significant familial conflict can occur between youth and their elders.

The ability to help parents and youth negotiate potential conflictual roles in this society takes on added significance in circumstances where the cultural values held by the parents provides them with "absolute" authority over their children. Youth, in turn, quickly learn that they have "rights" in this country and are often encouraged to voice their concerns and demands. The effort of the parents to control, or influence, all facets of a youth's life invariably creates a tremendous amount of tension and conflict. The stress on independence, as a result, is valued in one social domain and discouraged in the other, where interdependence may be stressed, placing newcomer youth in an untenable position (Kim, 1994).

The following case study entitled "Why Can't I Wear Baggy Pants Like Everyone Else?" was developed by the University of Minnesota Extension Service (2001). It does a splendid job of illustrating tensions between newcomer parents and youth peers and the different perspectives between the "old" and "new" countries. The case involves a 15-year-old Cambodian male named Ra, who happens to be the oldest child in a family of seven. He is a student at a large urban school with a diverse student population with a significant number of students from Cambodia, Laos, and Vietnam. As noted in the title of the case study, wearing baggy pants is considered the "right" way to dress:

> [Ra states] "My Mom and Dad are really wigged out because I came home with a pair of these baggy pants that all the kids are wearing at school. It's no big deal or anything. Last time I went shopping with Mom, you should see what she wanted me to get—a white shirt, suit pants.... There is no way I could go to school in those clothes. I'm spending my own money on these clothes. Everyone else goes sagging and I don't see why I can't, too. It's not like I'm in a gang or anything. I'm just trying to look like the other kids." Ra's mother (Somaly) voices a number of concerns concerning Ra's baggy pants: "I'm so concerned about the clothes Ra wants to wear now. Every time I pick something out for him at the store he refuses to wear it. He only wants to wear baggy pants that come down to his knees—he looks like a gang member in those. His teachers must be offended by such clothes. He won't be accepted by the good kids. I'm afraid he'll get into trouble—maybe he'll start to be friends with gangsters, or even get picked up by the police. Others in our community will think we are terrible parents. I wish he would listen to me." (pp. 1–2)

> [There are multiple perspectives on Ra's attire.]

> *From a Cambodian perspective:* In Cambodian culture, conformity is [an instilled] value; it is important to follow the norms of the group. The opinions of the community are also important; the family may not be respected if the children dress inappropriately. Parents may also be unable to afford certain name-brand clothes. Parents have heard stories about certain clothes being associated with gangs, and fear for their children's safety. They fear that their children won't have "good" friends, will fall into the wrong crowd, or be picked up by the police if they are dressed inappropriately. The term *gangster* is often used generally to refer to any "bad" person or behavior, not only to actual gang members.
>
> *From an American perspective:* Disagreements over dress are also very common with American parents and teenagers. Teenage children have their own ideas about clothes, and are very susceptible to "peer pressure"—pressure to conform from friends. Styles also change quickly and clothes get outdated, so it is difficult and expensive to keep up. Some styles that could be called the "gang look" are not exclusive to gang members. Many parents decide not to make an issue out of their children's clothes, preferring instead to take a stand on other issues that are perhaps more important.

Sometimes the shift in roles youth experience can have both positive and unanticipated consequences that practitioners must be cognizant of, as in the case of Latino youth who assume broker roles for their family in this society:

> The parents arrive first in the United States, working to earn money so their children in Latin America can follow later. Once the children come, they are enrolled in school,

where they end up speaking better English than their parents. As they navigate the uncertain pathway through adolescence, the Latino youth become full-time interpreters for their elders. Seeking to conform to Americanized ways of dress and behavior, the young people also feel obligated to maintain family values from their native countries. For some Latino teens, the pressure to find a balance between two cultures may become overwhelming. Studies show that young Latinos are more likely to think about and attempt suicide than their white and black counterparts. (Forest, 2002, p. C1)

Based on their review of the literature on Southeast Asian refugees, Hyman, Vu, and Beiser (2001) conclude that little scholarly attention has been paid to the effects of migration on these youth. They found, not surprisingly, that family relations are an important source of both supports and stressors for newcomer youth. The ability of newcomer parents to change and accommodate to the norms of U.S. society is a major step in helping newcomer youth to be viewed as having rights within the family, encouraged to achieve regardless of their gender, and provided with greater latitudes in their behaviors (Ly-Phin, 1998). However, in the case of newcomer groups such as the Chinese and Vietnamese, this may threaten the core cultural values of discipline, loyalty, and family unity (Zhou & Bankston, 2000).

The need for sex education is another area where significant differences can exist between practitioner, parents, and youth. Sex education may not be addressed by parents within certain newcomer groups, such as Latinos and Asians (Community Association of Progressive Dominicans, 1999). The tendency of Asian cultures to emphasize propriety, social codes, and sexual behavior within the confines of marriage makes the obtainment of sexual and reproductive education from schools and programs arduous for youth to achieve without causing tension within the family (Okazaki, 2002).

Practitioners and teachers, in turn, may consider this an important subject and one that cannot be left uncovered in the course of education or intervention. Parents may be likely not to give permission for this subject matter to be addressed. Consequently, newcomer youth may find themselves learning about sex outside of the social domain of family and school (*Family Life Matters*, 1998).

Reinforcement of Language and Culture

It is important to acknowledge and reinforce the social decoding (assessing the situation correctly and responding accordingly) competencies of newcomer youth regarding their families, peers, and community. These competencies must be stressed in any intervention in order for newcomer youth to function effectively in social domains such as schools, workplaces, and external communities. Without question, language and culture play prominent roles in helping newcomer youth to decode social situations. Newcomer youth must be able to know and decode two separate and sometimes very disparate cultures with possible conflicting values, norms, rituals, and role expectations. This biculturality, so to speak, represents an important dimension in their lives (Do, 2002).

Having to learn a new language (i.e., English) can result in youth entering a state of depression or aggravating existing feelings of despondency from adjusting to a totally new living context. Isolation because of anxiety over speaking English or because it is spoken with an accent, for example, can further exacerbate a condition of depression with far-reaching implications for the family. Speaking with an accent in the United States brings with it a set of conditions and consequences that reach beyond an ability to communicate effectively. Depending on the accent, French and English (Great Britain) being two prominent exceptions, it can also cast the speaker into a social position of being "intellectually dull."

The example of Stephanie Ortiz shows the potential of young children having a mastery of two languages in a society that will slowly but surely require its citizens to be bilingual in the not so distant future. Stephanie Ortiz, 9 years old, was born in the United States to Mexican parents. She is cognizant of the value of being bilingual and bicultural and has been an interpreter since the first grade: "[Stephanie says] People say it's a very good thing when you know two languages. . . . And you'll get a good job when you grow up. You're lucky and stuff. And people ask me . . . 'How do you say that?' It's pretty cool" (Druley, 2002, p. 3).

Language competencies, however, are much more than verbal abilities. They also entail having nonverbal communication skills. Newcomer youths' abilities to converse in multiple languages as well as in English are important in the life of these youth. In fact, language competencies are closely related to cultural competencies. One of the major criticisms levied at the Internet is the almost total absence of material in languages other than English in this country and the nature of the content of the material having a strong tendency to reflect Western, Eurocentric values.

Druley's (2002) notes that children of newcomers experience tremendous differences in adjusting to U.S. culture, with a lack of mastery of the language being one of the key factors in impeding adjustment: "Some children of immigrants reject their native language and culture in hopes of fitting in. Parents are concerned that different generations in the family may not be able to speak to each other. They are left with a balancing act of preserving language, while joining the American melting pot" (p. 1).

The development of a greater understanding and meaning of cultural heritage and traditions fills a void newcomer youth and native youth of color face in school and society. Comas-Diaz (1999) sums up this point quite well regarding Latino youth but it is also applicable to other newcomer youth: "The Latino experience is a metaphor for our country's development. Latino youngsters transform their identities while remaining true to their roots. Don Quixote's words, 'I want to be someone else without ceasing to be myself,' seem to characterize Latino identity development" (p. ix).

Jensen (2002), however, raises a cautionary note regarding cultural identity: "There are gains and losses in forming a cultural identity. Maintaining a culture and adopting new traditions in a new culture are examples of positive facets of the formation of cultural identity. However, in a multicultural world, acculturation may also bring some sense of loss (giving up parents' traditions) or may be in conflict with the real world (i.e., adopting a cultural identity that has already changed in the homeland)" (p. 4). There is little question that growing up in the United States brings with it a host of rewards and challenges for newcomer youth. The key response to this question is How can social workers and others minimize the potential pitfalls and emphasize the potential benefits in the process of engaging these youth, family, and communities?

Having an understanding and appreciation of their historical roots serves to anchor youth when they are facing challenges to their identity in society. Rarely will they be exposed to or learn about their histories in school, television, or other media outlets youth favor. Helping newcomer youth develop identities that incorporate multicultural realities of living in U.S. society without losing their culture of origin identity is both a goal and a challenge in developing best practice interventions (Positive Youth Development Working Group, 2002).

The following story of Cheng does a wonderful job of illustrating the journey newcomer youth undergo in the United States. It also shows the tension that many of these youth feel between being proud and ashamed of who they are within the context of life in this country:

> Am I proud of being Chinese? Well, I'm proud of my ability to speak the Chinese language. However, I sometimes wonder why I am celebrating Moon Festival of Chinese New Year. Probably the only reason I go along with it is because I don't want to hurt my family and/or friends' feelings. I'm not exactly forcing myself to do this. It's kind of like lying to a fat person and telling them, "No, you're not fat." I mean no disrespect to the Chinese culture. The traditions just don't mean anything to me. That's why I see no reason to celebrate it. I am in between pride and shame, and I think that is a good thing; too much of either one can be a bad thing. Being ashamed is pretty much self-explanatory. As for pride, pride is a good thing. Being proud of who you are is a good thing, but is there such a thing as too much pride? I see a lot of this happening at school. The fine line between pride and racism is blurred when "we're so cool" suddenly changes to "we're the best." A clear example of this is a song I heard about two years ago. That song was called "Asian Pride," but after hearing it, I think it's more racism than pride. Being proud is one thing. Thinking you're better than others is something else. (KQED, 2002)

Any practice that reflects the importance of newcomer youth benefits youth, their family, and the community. Opportunities for self-actualization, in combination with a positive ethnic/racial sense of self, play a critical role in the development of an identity (Delgado, 2000a). The Latino Community Heritage Center in Washington, DC, developed an innovative project in collaboration with the Historical Society of Washington, DC, the Smithsonian Institution, and the Latino community. A community-wide exhibition was used as a central focus for workshops, lectures, and performances. The primary goals of this project were to instill in youth and the community knowledge of Latino culture and history, preserve cultural traditions, and create research skills among Latino residents.

The reader might well respond that learning about history could turn off newcomer youth. However, there are many creative ways of teaching history and cultural traditions through activities such as drama, dance, art, and music (Delgado, 2000a). Music, for example, is considered an important vehicle for transmission of culture and can be utilized as an activity to help newcomer youth learn more about their cultural heritage, as in the case of the Vietnamese: "Particularized by the Vietnamese and endowed with specifically Vietnamese messages that draw from an ideological and historical matrix, those songs recall a pre-1975 Vietnam, a culture that many former refugees believe must be conserved. . . . Through those means, these songs have been made repositories of Vietnamese history and culture as seen through refugees' eyes" (Reyes, 1999, p. 12). Music in this instance conveys a host of sentiments and emotions that can easily be overlooked by an outsider to the culture.

Reyes's (1999) analysis of Vietnamese music can also easily apply to other new-comer groups. There are probably few areas where the "disconnect" occurs to such a degree as in the case of music. Hip Hop, Rap, and other styles of music are totally alien to the parents of newcomer youth, and some would argue to practically any parent in this country. Newcomer youth, in turn, invariably view music from the "old country" as off-putting. Thus, a divide can exist that symbolizes much more than musical taste. Clothing style may be tied closely to preference in music, further accentuating differences between newcomer youth and their parents.

Needless to say, there is a great deal of room for innovation in the creation of intervention strategies for newcomer youth using activities, particularly when integrating cultural values, traditions, and rituals. The Portland Latino and Asia Pacific Program (LAAP) undertook the videotaping of their community's oral history as a means of helping newcomers better appreciate their community (Mejia & Prado, 2000). In New York City, for example, the use of *cuentos* (folktales) and modeling have been successfully used in assisting Puerto Rican children (ages 9 to 13 years old) to address a variety of emotional problems (Rogler, Malgady, & Rodriguez, 1989). *Cuentos* were modified to take into consideration the values and competencies widely believed to be necessary for successful coping in this society.

The use of photography by newcomer youth can be a valuable method of helping youth with their struggles with a wide range of issues such as inclusion/exclusion, valued/undervalued, pathfinders in a new land or traitors of the old country, and hope for or fear of the future (Buchbinder, 2002). The Columbia Heights West Teen Photo Project in Virginia has provided newcomer youth with the skills and supports to explore the meaning of the "New America," with newcomers being a significant part of the new demographic landscape in this country. Workshops and discussion groups provided youth with opportunities to share with others their thoughts, emotions, dreams, and creativity. Exhibitions of youth's photo essays, in turn, allowed them to share their vision with the external community.

Ho, an immigrant from Thailand, sums up the power of photography very well when she states, "Art helped me define who I am and find confidence in myself" (Buchbinder, 2002, p. 23). Endo, project leader, articulates a broader goal for use of photography with newcomer youth: "The seriousness with which they approach their work has improved the larger community's image of its youth, as well. People tend to be afraid of teenagers, especially foreigners, . . . but after they see this creative, well-crafted work . . . they realize how these young people contribute to the community" (Buchbinder, 2002, p. 20).

The youth development field is well aware of how activities can help youth reach personal goals in ways that are meaningful and exciting at the same time. Activities can be fun and provide newcomer youth with opportunities to stage events for their parents and community. These events serve not only to entertain but also to educate the community in the process. Use of activities to engage and work with youth is almost as old as the social work profession itself. Certainly, social group work has a long and distinguished history in this realm.

Interventions That Are Culturally Harmonious

Interventions must be culturally syntonic and respect the values, beliefs, and traditions held by newcomer family and youth. Although the merits of this best practice seem to be self-evident, it still must be uplifted for attention and influencing interventions of any kind. The term *culture shock* was first introduced in 1960 (Oberg, 1960) and captured the imagination of both public and professionals. Culture shock connoted feelings of anxiety caused by people encountering new and unexpected situations that rendered problem-solving ineffective.

The homeland of the newcomer remains an important aspect of any discussion of newcomer experience in this country, including the presence of culture shock in its various manifestations: "All migration sets up a tripartite relationship between the migrants, their homeland, and the host society. It is their relations with the homeland which migrants use as reference point when they present what they want to be understood as traditional in their new home" (Reyes, 1999, p. 211).

The past 20 to 30 years have witnessed incredible changes in how culture is identified and used in the planning and implementation of health and social services within the United States. This shift in thinking about the prominence of culture in the lives of people, particularly those who are newcomers to this country, has resulted in the emergence of the construct of cultural competence. Sam (2000) argues that the ability of newcomer youth to balance their cultural heritage and the culture of the host society will ultimately determine successful or unsuccessful adaptation.

The following three examples, one involving a Colombian/Chinese girl, another involving a Chinese male, and the last involving a Vietnamese youth, show how newcomer youth handle their journey through life in the United States. Here are the thoughts of Nancy Lee:

> Never in my life did I think about immigrating to another country. Even though I shared two cultures, I was assimilated to live in the same neighborhood, go to the same school for 10 years, hang out with the same friends. My life in Colombia was very exciting, I had a school, friends, family, a job, and my duties. I suffered a lot of discrimination because my background was Chinese, even though I felt that I didn't belong there, I believed it was God's wish. The Latino culture influenced me a lot, so much that I even became Catholic. My arrival in this country [the United States] was unexpected. My parents told me two weeks before my trip. When I arrived at the airport, I told my father that I was coming back soon, however we both knew that it was going to be long until we met again. Both my father and me wanted it to be a happy good-bye. But it wasn't like that. I was gone, and I didn't have the chance to say good-bye to my friends, teachers, neighbors, only to my two best friends. I felt that a lot of the things got postponed. In the airplane my thoughts wandered around. I always have been so tragic, but I thought that this was going to be a big step in my life, and I knew also that difficult times were yet to come, and I had to be strong to be able to continue, to be able to live. I had tons of goals, and I felt bad because I made promises to my friends that we all were going

to graduate in the same private school. I was sad that I broke the promise, but this was out of my hands. And I also thought that I wanted to be a little girl once again and live in a pink world. When I was in the line in order to enter legally to this country, I felt my heart beating fast. When I was through the line, I felt that my life was to begin, and it happened.

I started to live according to the Chinese culture, speak the language, and follow the traditions. It was a hard language, and I thought it was the hardest language on the planet. I started working in order to pay the rent, and even though I didn't have enough money, I felt content. I knew that this was a new country. It wasn't involved in a war, but it offered me more opportunities. I had to start again, but it didn't matter because it was a new goal. I know that it is time to grow, and take all the opportunities in front of me. Being here is a life goal and I'm not going to waste it. (KQED, 2002)

Gary Liang's story brings a different perspective on being Chinese in this country (KQED, 2002):

I'm Chinese, I was born in China. I do traditional Chinese stuff, I live in a Chinese district, I eat Chinese food, I have Chinese name, I look Chinese, and I speak Chinese. (KQED, 2002)

A Vietnamese male eleventh-grader states:

It took me a long time to learn that I am supposed to talk back [question] my teacher. My father got very angry with me for doing this, but I will not do well in school if I sit passively and do not ask questions. Most of the time I act like an American at school but don't tell my father. At home I follow Vietnamese customs. It makes it hard, but I am doing okay like that. (Rutledge, 1992, p. 92)

Zhou and Bankston (1994) use the sociological construct of *social capital* to develop an in-depth appreciation of how second-generation Vietnamese youth adapt to life in this country. Ethnic resources—such as strong family values, commitment to a work ethic, and high levels of participation-connectedness to community—were found to be strongly associated with successful adjustment to the United States. It should be noted, however, that the use of culture as a vehicle for outreaching, engaging, and ultimately serving youth is not without tension and controversy, as already noted in this chapter. This does not mean that practitioners must necessarily stay away from the subject of culture, but it does mean that practitioners need to be thoughtful and knowledgeable about the subject and how it can be used effectively to help newcomers. Gillock and Reyes (1999), for example, sound an alarming note about the validity of social supports offsetting stress among urban, low-income, Mexican American adolescents. Those authors found no gender differences in how stressors are perceived and reacted to by this Latino group. The findings are not generalizable beyond the sample of Mexican American high school sophomores in one urban school; however, it does raise a note of caution on the influence of social supports buffering or mitigating stressors.

Research on the topic of acculturation has certainly enjoyed a great appeal in a variety of professional and academic circles. Generally, the role of acculturation has been found to be have an indirect but positive relationship to risk-taking behavior on the part of newcomer youth (Dinh, Roosa, Tein, & Lopez, 2002). Thus, it becomes very challenging for the practitioner to actively seek to integrate newcomer youth into the broader society as a means of increasing the likelihood of their success. However, in the process of doing so, caution must be taken because integration into the broader society brings with it increased likelihood of risk-taking behaviors.

Koss-Chioino and Vargas (1999) highlight the inherent tensions that are associated with parents and youth when cultural heritage and traditions are used to hinder or facilitate the Americanization process:

> Many immigrant parents work very hard to raise their children according to how they remember their own upbringing, actively attempting to slow down the Americanization process that molds their children in ways they do not approve. . . . For children growing up in the United States, it is difficult enough to have their parents attempt to raise them within the traditions in which the parents were raised. It is almost intolerable to have their parents attempt to raise them according to an idealized cultural identity that does not even exist in the country of origin. (p. 9)

Interventions That Integrate

Interventions must not only be need driven from the perspective of the newcomer but they must also actively integrate newcomers within the broader community. Social workers must endeavor to develop a keen understanding of what needs newcomers wish to address. Are the presenting needs being addressed or are these needs being reconceptualized to what the organization can or is willing to provide? This is a provocative question that is not restricted to newcomer youth but that takes on added significance for this group. Chow (1999), in a study of centers serving Chinese American immigrant communities in Chicago, New York, and Los Angeles, finds that the importance of a holistic or comprehensive approach is often warranted in meeting the needs of this population. Many of the challenges Chinese immigrants face are not unique to them, however.

Some authors have raised concerns about having newcomer groups rely too heavily on kinship and other social supports, effectively limiting their motivation to seek contact and assistance beyond their immediate group. These actions, in turn, can be detrimental to newcomer groups establishing social relations beyond their immediate group (Menjivar, 1997). Practitioners need to seriously seek to strike a balance between helping newcomers maintain important cultural ties with their support network and helping them venture outside of this group for emotional, instrumental, and informational needs.

The absence of leisure time among newcomer parents is a reality because of their tendency to hold multiple jobs in the course of the work week (which can be seven days long) as well as a serious limitation in helping them adjust to life in this country (Stodolska, 1998). Parental ability to help their children gain wider exposure is also severely limited. Social workers will often find themselves in situations that necessitate negotiation between realistic and unrealistic options:

> For most immigrants, the United States offers opportunities unavailable to them in their homelands. In helping immigrant families benefit from these opportunities, interventions need to address both concrete resettlement issues ... and also clinical issues that focus on the social and emotional adjustments to a new society.... While life in the United States may have been presented unrealistically, as a sort of utopia, to the child, a realistic sense of hope can be defined, leading him or her in the direction of realizing some of these opportunities and the enjoyment of a full life. (Castex, 1997, p. 59)

The story of Crista Avila exemplifies the interrelationship between language skills and the broadening of a youth's immediate world that can transpire within school settings :

> When I go to the United States, I felt restrained and a sense of dread. I couldn't communicate or go shopping by myself because of my fear that I didn't speak English. I came to live with my sister in San Francisco in 1998. In the same year I went to Newcomer High School, where I learned a little bit of English. While I was there I felt comfortable because I was with youth who spoke Spanish. Once I got out from Newcomer, they sent me to a regular school where they spoke only English. I thought I got out to the real world because I had to depend on myself. With time I made friends from different parts of the world, and I told myself that I should start to make friends from different cultures and at the same time I would be practicing my English. Now I have diverse friends and I feel happy because now I can talk and show them the beauty of my culture. All this gives me more spirit to continue. It also motivates me to learn other languages so I can communicate with other people in their own language. Now I'm in a country that offers a lot opportunities and I have the advantage of being an American citizen. (KQED, 2002)

The construct of *belonging* takes on primal and symbolic importance for newcomer youth who have been uprooted from their original society and social networks (Pikes, Burrell, & Holliday, 1998). Kirova (2001), although specifically addressing the subject of immigrant children in Canada but also applicable in the United States, raises concerns about the deleterious impact of isolation and loneliness of newcomer children in the short and long run. It is not out of the ordinary to speak with newcomer youth and to discover that they are not accepted by natives or by their peers who may be much more highly acculturated, and therefore look down on the recently arrived youth to this country (Koss-Chioino & Vargas, 1999). The symbolic meaning attached to belonging, however, may have long-lasting ramifications in social, economic, and political arenas.

The case of Eduardo Jiminez, age 21, illustrates the key point of acceptance from an identity perspective involving adults from the same country of origin. Eduardo is the son of Mexican immigrants and was born in Oakland, California. He reflects on the importance of belonging, in this case to a group of Mexican men called the Tequila Luck Club—a Mexican and male version of the *Joy Luck Club* (elder Chinese women) made famous by Amy Tan:

> There is a group of old men who sit around in my backyard in Oakland, talking about world politics and economics.... They don't like it here in the United States, but they have families to feed, and my backyard is an oasis for them.... The Tequila Luck Club is a place where they're free to be men, drink hard, and discuss life with friends. They're

not academically schooled, but they're commonsense wise. None went higher than elementary school, but they know exactly what effects NAFTA will have on Mexico, how the Mexican government is failing them, and what separates a good tequila from a bad one. I used to sit in my room and look out the window, wishing I could be a part of the club. I was always too ashamed to go outside and join them, because I haven't worked a hard day in my life. My hands are soft from sitting behind a desk all day studying, while they are out constructing buildings and homes. More important, I felt I didn't belong because I am an American, not Mexican like they are. (Vang, Jiminez, & Ruukel, 1996, p. 11)

Eduardo's dilemma is not unusual for newcomer youth. They do not belong to the "old world" because they were either born or came to this country at a very early age and do not have shared experiences with the adults in their immediate circle. Yet they are not considered "American" because of their ethnic background and cultural values. This theme of acceptance radiates throughout virtually all newcomer youth groups. Kulynych (2001) suggests that citizenship be conceptualized from two perspectives: (1) citizenship as a right and (2) citizenship as an identity, both national and political. Citizenship as a right brings youth into conflict with adults who may view citizenship as a political identity. In the case of Eduardo, being an American citizen meant he was viewed from a national political perspective, effectively denying his Mexican cultural identity and heritage.

Not surprisingly, Gonzalez and Padilla (1997), in their study of academic resilience of Mexican American high school students, found that developing a sense of "belonging," and thus feeling welcomed, was a significant predictor of school achievement. The development of a sense of connectedness is indicative of the presence of many social factors, such as being valued for who they are, feeling respected, being self-confident, and knowing they are expected to contribute. Being marginalized by the dominant culture and peers who are much more acculturated places newcomer youth in an untenable situation, and may result in their desperate search to be accepted by any social group. This can lead to involvement with peers who, too, are "outcasts" and inclined to engage in risk-taking behaviors.

In a rare ethnographic study of 5- and 6-year-old South Asian girls, Connolly (2000) notes how race is perceived and acted on in determining peer-group relations in multiracial and ethnic gatherings. The forming of racism starts at a very early age and can dramatically alter social relations in schools that are multicultural. Practitioners and educators must be ever vigilant in identifying racist perceptions and endeavor to create situations whereby diverse groups come together and include goals for interventions that stress equality.

The New York Association for New Americans (NYANA) serves as an excellent example of how activities can be developed to broaden the worldview of newcomer youth and aid in the process of strengthening their literacy skills. The Family Heritage Documentary Project strengthens literacy skills among youth in New York City public schools and assists teachers and administrators in addressing the New York State and New York City standards in English Language Arts, the Arts, U.S. History, and Global History. The project teaches students to utilize photography and writing to document the history of their families and immigrant communities in New York. In doing so, newcomer students learn and improve documentation and critical reading and writing skills.

The project has focused on neighborhoods that have large immigrant populations to encourage immigrant youth to see themselves as part of a long historical process in which people from all parts of the world have come together to live and work side by side. Participants, for example, have photographed their neighborhoods and families, interviewed neighbors and family members, chronicled the experiences of their elders, and identified and recorded the sights and sounds of their communities.

In the process, students have deepened their understanding of how their personal and family backgrounds are connected to the history of their neighborhood and of New York City as a whole. In addition to looking more closely at their own heritage and family backgrounds, students explore the cultures of their fellow classmates, thereby increasing their awareness and understanding of other cultures and ethnic groups in this process of exploration.

Centro Ramano's (Chicago) Youth Learning and Leadership Project offers a diverse set of youth activities such as karate, computer classes, bowling, mural painting, social advocacy and empowerment workshops, community organizing, and tutoring. Such activities help Latino youth, most of whom are newcomers or children of immigrants, acquire skills and confidence to reach out beyond the world of their immediate community without losing sight of their heritage and the importance of their community.

Interventions That Empower

Interventions need to empower and address issues of racism and nativism through the use of advocacy and reforming existing laws that seek to limit or prohit newcomer youth from maximizing their potential within this society. This final best practice recommendation should probably not come as any great surprise to any social worker who practices with marginal groups in this society. However, it needs to be reemphasized that newcomer groups are very often placed in positions in U.S. society where they are easy targets for lawmakers, service providers, and employers (Castex, 1997). Consequently, they are often blamed for a community's ills even when they have no influence on these events.

Delgado (2002a) emphasizes the importance of advocacy and social change activities within youth development programs: "The expansion of intervention beyond a focus on the individual increases the potential of this paradigm to bring about social change. The potential—exciting and challenging as well as daunting and overwhelming—is to have positive impact not only on youths but also on their families, friends, and communities. The more spheres of influence targeted by youth development programs, the greater the likelihood that this will happen" (p. 123).

A word of caution is in order as the authors address this final recommendation. Social justice advocacy, as noted by Kiselica and Robinson (2001), although understood by professionals regardless of their discipline, is arduous to accomplish and can place those who seek social justice goals in conflict within their organizational settings. In addition, these types of actions can also have emotional consequences for advocates as they seek to bring about changes, particularly when they feel alone in their quest.

Effective practice with newcomer communities, as a result, necessitates that practitioners be prepared to address newcomers' needs at various levels, not just at the micro and mezzo levels, by speaking up and taking appropriate actions to address environmental concerns that impinge on the social rights of clients and their communities. Moorthy (1996) comments on the role of social work and child refugees are also applicable to newcomers in general in this society: "Social work responses to the plight of child refugees have been gaining momentum, and the awareness created by agencies and nongovernment organizations has had a significant impact on changing United States immigration policies that now recognize the special status of children. Social Workers, guided by the NASW Code of Ethics, must be vigilant in questioning the ethics of their dual roles as counselors and social advocates" (p. 5).

Strug and Mason (2002) and Martinez-Brawly and Zorita (2002), although making specific reference to Latino immigrants, nonetheless identify the importance of advocacy as a central core service need for newcomers. Strug and Mason note: "Social workers have an important role to play in helping Hispanic immigrants gain access to social services and overcome barriers to service delivery. By becoming active in advocacy groups they can work to encourage national, state, and local governments to spend more money for immigrant services, including the creation of community-based health care" (p. 84).

The story of Parteek Singh, a Sikh newcomer youth from India to Seattle, illustrates the struggles that both youth and their families face in this country, and the injustices that are often perpetrated upon them in seeking to establish a new violence-free life in this country:

> A cursory review of Parteek Singh's life in America fits the dream sequence laid out in his parents' minds. A love of basketball, reading books, performing well in school and tight family ties made up Parteek's seemingly happy life. The family went to community and religious events . . . where there is a gurdwara to which Sikh Americans come from all over the state. Parteek's internal life revealed another reality altogether. He kept a different world—one where he was forced to tolerate name-calling, teasing, pushing and punching by school peers—a secret to outsiders. When his family found out, they would try and move to a new area and hope the teasing would stop. It never did. The cause of this hostility towards Parteek? He wore a topknot of hair covered with a headwrap. . . . This is known as kesh; it represents one of the five sacred articles of the Sikh faith. . . . The family in an effort to prevent the teasing, cut Parteek's hair. (Kaur, 2003, p. 2)

This act, unfortunately, did not stop the teasing and eventually led to Partee's striking and hurting another youth, and involvement in the juvenile justice system. His family stopped taking him to community events and to the temple for fear of adverse reactions from the congregation. At a public hearing sponsored by Seattle's Hate Free Zone, 11-year-old Parteek made the following moving testimony:

> I wanted to tell you that I have take[n] a lot of abuse in my life in America. Ever since I have come to America, I haven't fought back to anybody. Sometimes, even though I was one of the best basketball players in school, I have been picked last and I haven't been able to play 'cause kids wouldn't let me play. Here in Auburn I tried to fit in. Then Sept.

11 happened and people started being mean to me again. Calling me Habib, towelhead, pepperhead. People call me Osama and Osama's son. And a lot of people did drugs so I was afraid that if I told anybody I might even get hurt bad.

It made me feel very bad when they called me diaperhead because I love my hair, it is part of my religion and I never want to cut my hair. I don't know why they just don't like different people. It hasn't gone away since Sept. 11 and people still call me those names. I wish kids who bully would just quit. Can't they see it hurts people? Even if they don't show it? I know teachers know it goes on in school and they just ignore it. Please don't ignore it. (Kaur, 2003, pp. 4–5)

The case of Parteek shows how a system and society looked the other way in providing leadership to an issue that is not unique to Parteek. Parteek's willingness to go before a public audience bodes well for his future in advocating for his rights. However, it is quite sad for an 11-year-old to have to do this. His parents were caught between two worlds and they made the painful decision to cut his hair even though it violated religious belief and marginalized them within their own community.

Empowerment is a powerful force in the lives of people, and youth are no exception. The following quote is from Bertha Rodriguez, a Colorado high school junior who is part of a student organization called Students 4 Justice. When asked what motivates her to be involved and stay involved, her reply typifies the multiple benefits youth derive from advocating for themselves: "You feel like you are doing something, like you are making a difference. It is good for students because we are actually doing something for ourselves. Everybody wants that feeling. Some of us have been in this longer than others, but we all feel it's time to step up and tell them about what needs to change" (Forum for Youth Development, 2002a, p. 4).

In Lowell, Massachusetts, a group of Khmer youth established the Khmer Youth Organizing Project to conduct youth-sponsored political campaigns and community activism. They have been very successful in advocating for Khmer language classes within their school. This project, supported by Youth Venture and the Coalition for Asian and Pacific American Youth in Lowell, illustrates the potential for change that newcomer youth possess.

Advocacy on behalf of newcomer communities must eventually lead to advocacy by newcomers themselves. Practitioners must not lose this shift in focus toward newcomers playing a greater and more significant role in determining the destiny of their communities. Advocacy efforts must, as a result, incorporate a significant teaching, mentoring, and consultation dimension, including the systematic inclusion of newcomers utilizing a developmental approach.

Empowerment can be operationalized through the provision of citizenship classes, voter registration, participation in public events, English as a second language (ESL) classes, and community organizing of newcomer communities (Chow, 1999). This political dimension toward empowerment must be short, intermediate, and long-term goals of community-based organizations with large or total constituencies of newcomers. Empowerment in newcomer communities can probably best be considered an investment in the future of the community, and this means adults as well as youth embracing the power and potential behind this construct. The advent of the Internet has created opportunities to empower newcomer youth. San Francisco's Korean Community Center of the East Bay (SKCCEB) developed a youth program that utilizes a web magazine focused on addressing issues of social justice in the Korean, Asian, and broader community: "Our goal with this website is to get the voices of Corean Americans out. Instead of the buttered up Media from the American News Papers, and important issues put in a little corner of the newspaper, we want to give the issue to you straight out. No BS, and no cover up just straight up facts and opinions from the Corean American Youth."

One recent issue of the web magazine focused on Korean American identity and politics of the Bay Area. The magazine also included an in-depth interview with Korean American filmmaker and adoptee Deann Borshay-Liem. In addition, there were featured stories about the Alameda County Juvenile Hall expansion, as well as Korean American history articles, forums, and stereotype articles. The May 2002 issue commemorated the tenth anniversary of the Los Angeles civil unrest of 1992.

The use of a conference format allows communities to develop coalitions and reach an audience beyond one specific newcomer group, as in the case of the Asian American Youth Leadership Conference. This conference is an annual event sponsored by the Refugee and Immigrant Coordination Program in Portland, Oregon—a coalition of organizations, community leaders, and schools. It has three guiding goals: (1) impart leadership skills, (2) provide career guidance and opportunities, and (3) foster a strong sense of culture and self-pride among student participants. The conference targets Asian students (Cambodian, Chinese, Filipino, Iranian, Japanese, Korean, Laotian, Pakistani, Thai, and Vietnamese, among others) from refugee and first-generation immigrant families: "These students struggle to overcome language, cultural barriers and prejudice in order to excel in school and become more active members of their communities. What this conference aims to do is instill participants with the value and importance of discipline, self-confidence, self-esteem and the overall rewards of achievement" (Refugee and Immigrant Coordination Program, 2002, p. 1).

Conclusion

Social work's search for best practices with newcomer youth is part of a broader movement seeking to increase the effectiveness and efficiency of services to people in need, regardless of their social and economic circumstances. This quest has raised a series of questions that must be successfully answered in any form of intervention, be it youth development centered or otherwise. However, this search has also raised a series of challenges that social work and other helping professions must struggle with in the hopes of arriving at the destination called "best practices." This journey, although worthwhile and rewarding, has its share of hurdles and obstacles.

Readers of this book will undoubtedly have many "best practices" that they would argue that need to be on any list. Local circumstances regarding agencies, communities, and newcomer groups dictate what is the most relevant form of practice and how it should be carried out. The best practices identified in this chapter are not the *only* best practices that exist in the field. Nevertheless, these practices not only strike at the heart of what is needed by newcomer youth but also what should be the "core" of any form of intervention targeting this group. Best practices can never afford to be static; they must evolve as more is learned about newcomer youth's needs and the "best" way of addressing their circumstances. These practices, in turn, must also endeavor to build on the assets that newcomers bring with them to this country.

Although the best practices addressed in this chapter specifically target social workers, they clearly are not restricted to that profession. Some human service practitioners may well argue that best practice is not possible without interdisciplinary relationships. The authors see great value in that perspective. Nevertheless, each profession must ultimately arrive at its own set of best practices, and where they overlap with social work, there is ample opportunities for meaningful partnerships; where they differ, then professions may go their separate ways.

Social work best practices with newcomer youth embody the importance of embracing an ecological perspective that emphasizes the significance of social and economic justice values. Further, having newcomer youth play a decision-making, and thus empowering, role in helping to shape interventions strikes at the heart of what many practitioners believe to be the essence of "good" social work practice. As addressed in Chapter 6, social navigational skills and community assets represent perspectives and approaches that help shape how an ecological viewpoint and integration of social and economic justice values can be carried out in daily interactions and practice.

6

Social Navigational Skills and Community Assets

Momentum has developed to concentrate professional practice on coping rather than risk, on opportunity rather than on fatalism, on wellness and self-repair rather than illness and disability. In other words, a change from a medical damage model that focuses on curing illness to a health model that concentrates on promoting health.

—Norman, 2000b, p. 1

Introduction

The emergence of new paradigms that systematically eschew a focus on deficits found a home in many of the helping professions and academic disciplines such as anthropology, psychology, and sociology during the 1980s and 1990s. The turn of the twenty-first century witnessed this continued trend and an effort to broaden these paradigms beyond traditional emphasis on at-risk groups in urban areas of the country. In many ways this book is an example of this thrust toward applying asset-related paradigms to new population groups. These types of paradigms have an inherent belief in the power of human beings to change the course of history, and this can only be accomplished when society recognizes assets in people and communities.

The social work field has played a significant role in advancing constructs and strategies that systematically identify and build on the competencies of the population served by social workers (Phillips & Straussner, 2002). Strengths, resiliency, coping, protective factors, and community assets, for example, have found prominence within the field in the last decade (Delgado, 2000a, 2002b; Fraser, 1997; Norman, 2000a; Saleebey, 1992, 1996). This is also true for the cultural competency paradigm that has been in existence since the late 1980s and early 1990s, as addressed in Chapter 7. All of these constructs have served to advance practice, particularly for those who are not valued in this society. These constructs, in turn, very often overlap with each other and it is not unusual to see them interchanged in the professional literature. Applying constructs such as these to interventions focused on immigrant and refugee youth brings an added perspective to social work practice.

This chapter will focus on a relatively new way of viewing newcomer youth in the United States—namely, using the organizing constructs of social death and social navigational skills to develop an understanding of what newcomer youth encounter in this society and what they need to succeed. The professional literature provides many labels to focus on why youth, newcomer or native, are not successful upon reaching adulthood, and yet, labels addressing why they succeed are rare. It is the authors' hope that the concept of social navigation serves to redress the paucity of material on newcomer youth and their competencies to navigate themselves toward success.

Quest for a Paradigm

There is little dispute concerning the need for a paradigm that can help explain why certain newcomer youth fail and others succeed within this society. An ability to succeed, however, must be viewed from broad historical and ecological perspectives. It would be a serious mistake, however, to overlook the many assets newcomer youth and their parents bring with them to this country and the collective assets commonly found in their communities (Barwick, Beiser, & Edwards, 2002; Dugger, 1998; McCubbin, Thompson, Thompson, & Fromer, 1998; Rousseau, Gagne, & Bibeau, 1998; Scheinfeld, Wallach, & Langendorf, 1997). Further, it would be irresponsible to conceptualize these assets as having a history beginning with the arrival of immigrants and refugees to this country. The fact that they "survived," sometimes at great personal costs, to make it to the United States speaks to the presence of extraordinary strengths or coping mechanisms.

Those subscribing to a resiliency approach, for example, would argue that every child entering this country as an immigrant or refugee can rightly be considered resilient. This stance necessitates the search for elements that make newcomer youth not only capable of surviving a transition to a new country but also thriving in the process of doing so. The value of practitioners having knowledge of these elements can prove immensely valuable in the development of newcomer youth-specific interventions. Practitioners are in excellent positions to make important and lasting contributions to the field. Scholars, in turn, must endeavor to tap and disseminate this expertise through journal articles, books, and presentations at professional conferences.

The professional literature on immigrants and refugees, with some exceptions, has largely ignored their assets, but even when addressed, it has neglected to put these constructs within a historical context dating back to the newcomers' homelands. The social support network of newcomers can be quite extensive, surprising the most experienced practitioner. The concept of *social navigational skills* will be used to organize the content of this chapter. Success, not surprisingly, is defined by environmental circumstances or context and consists of instrumental (concrete possessions), expressive (emotional well-being), and informational (knowledge of when and where to seek assistance when needed) dimensions. How immigrant and refugee youth socially navigate their way through life in a new country and when and how they seek assistance is critical information for practitioners to have in the development of services, youth development focused or otherwise (Sum, Fogg, & Mangum, 2001).

Grinberg and Grinberg (1989) coined the term *inner equilibrium* to capture the abilities of immigrants to adjust gradually and positively to their new environment. Achieving this equilibrium is a process fraught with anxiety, especially for immigrant youth because of their newcomer status. The immigrant "ceases to belong to the world left behind, and does not yet belong to the world in which one has newly arrived" (p. 23). The search for a broad and encompassing construct to help identify, explain, and use key factors in guiding interventions with newcomer youth is a challenge for the field of social work.

The *strengths perspective* popularized by Saleebey (1992, 1996) builds on the work of numerous scholars, and is a widely accepted paradigm within the social work profession. However, the use of a strengths perspective, although extremely popular with social work, is too narrow for use with newcomer youth. Fogey (2000) comments on the limitations of a strengths perspective:

> The strengths perspective in social work education places social workers in the proper framework for utilizing resiliency factors. However, the strengths perspective is primarily used in clinical situations when a problem has already been recognized and resiliency factors or strengths are seen as a way of ameliorating the existing problem. The strengths perspective needs to be expanded conceptually within social work practice for use in developing strategies to prevent the onset of problems. (p. 223)

The search for a paradigm that incorporates strengths but is not reactive is in order for better reaching and serving newcomer youth. A youth development paradigm fills this void.

A *youth development paradigm* has a tremendous potential to contribute to any helping profession addressing newcomer youth in U.S. society. The wide recognition and acceptance of this paradigm is beyond dispute. This perspective, unlike the strengths perspective, is not predicated on addressing problems and needs. Instead, it focuses on enhancing youth assets and the assets of their community. However, the authors want to reframe a youth development paradigm into a "new perspective" that relies on many of the elements associated with youth development but frames this content in a manner that lends itself for use with newcomer youth who come from a multitude of different backgrounds and circumstances.

Highlighting social navigation stresses the need to be an effective map reader (social domains) and brings into the foreground the interplay of a variety of skills (communication and action) that assist the navigator to arrive at his or her destination with minimal distractions and consequences. Social navigation also serves to broaden the parameters, such that providers must consistently be cognizant of its existence and address it in their interventions.

The spirit of youth development is alive and well in the overarching construct the authors propose—namely, the use of social navigational skills as a way of identifying youth assets and the challenges they face in achieving optimal success in this society. This construct uses an ecological set of principles that takes into account multiple social arenas, and also seeks to capture the dynamic process of stresses and adaptation newcomer youth encounter. Social navigational skills introduce the reader to terms such as *social death, navigation, sanctuaries, hassles, survival pride,* and *discourse,* all of which serve to conceptualize and operationalize a view of newcomer youth as possessing competencies. However, when integrated into the broader construct of social navigation, they take on even greater significance in their interplay with each other.

Social navigational skills, nevertheless, must be grounded within a community context to be more fully understood and appreciated. As a result, this chapter also addresses the presence and role of community assets in the lives of newcomer youth and their families. The interplay of community assets, such as self-help traditions, nontraditional settings, and sanctuaries, for example, are dynamically linked to youth; furthermore, this interrelationship plays a prominent role in how social navigational skills are conceptualized and carried out on a daily basis. Community assets will be approached through a multifaceted focus on self-help traditions, nontraditional settings, and youth as assets themselves.

Social Death

Social death may be a totally new concept to some readers. Use of the term, when used with newcomer youth, runs the risk that it may elicit incredibly painful experiences in the cases where youth have witnessed murder prior to their uprootment to this country. The term *social death* may work well in discussions with colleagues, but it will not work when addressing newcomer youth and their parents. Thus, the reader may wish to substitute another term, such as *loss of hope, social discomfort,* or *social awkwardness.* However, having acknowledged this potential conflict, the authors will use the construct of social death in the treatment of the material in this chapter because it serves to highlight a state of being with tremendous implications for the future of newcomer youth in this society.

Before providing a definition of what is meant by social death, it is necessary to pose a question. Rumbaut (1998) raises a provocative and potentially troubling question when addressing the social consequences of newcomer youth not succeeding in this society: "There is a final consideration on the horizon. Given the modest family origins and material resources of many of these children [newcomers], their aspirations and expectations may be at odds with what many will be able to achieve; it remains an empirical question of what will happen to these youth if their aspirations are frustrated, and what the consequences may be if they are, not just for the students themselves, but for the nation as a whole" (p. 13). Failure of these youth to succeed can easily be tabulated by a range of statistical indices such as prison rates, dropout rates, drug use patterns, and the like. When reported by the media, these indices are well recognized by the general public.

Rumbaut (1998), reporting on the findings of two (1995 and 1997) National Children of Immigrants Longitudinal Studies (CILS), made important observations pertaining to newcomer youth ability to thrive:

1. The children of immigrants have embraced the English language (speak, read, and write) with fluency and prefer it to their parents' native language.
2. These youth have assumed more of a nationalistic identity (Cuban, Filipino, Jamaican) or pan-ethnic minority group identity (Hispanic, Latino, Chicano, Asian, Black). This has occurred despite or because of an increased reporting of experiences with racial discrimination in this country.
3. Children of immigrants are ambitious and place high value on obtaining a good education.
4. Children of immigrants have a greater tendency to stay in school and outperform their native-born cohorts in grade-point average.

The 1999 CILS results found that immigrant children possessed additional strengths. This study noted that these children, when compared to native children, are more likely to live in two-parent families (Reardon-Anderson, Capps, & Fix, 2002). Newcomer families, in addition, have a higher likelihood of having full-time workers than nonimmigrant families with comparable incomes. Viewing newcomer youth from an asset perspective is not such a stretch. However, this shift does necessitate the development of constructs and appropriate language to help capture newcomer youth assets.

The profile that emerges from the CILS is one that places immigrant youth into a "positive" rather than an "alarming" category. Although newcomer youth have social and educational needs, and some will ultimately fail to achieve "success" in this society (as evidenced in Chapter 4), their status has more in common with a resilient-asset perspective than a risk-deficit perspective. This perspective ultimately changes how society should view them and their parents, how practitioners assess the appropriateness of intervention strategies, and how researchers/scholars approach newcomer status in this country.

The consequences of newcomer youth not developing the requisite social navigational skills for success can be labeled in numerous ways, depending on academic discipline and premises used to conceptualize difficulties in youth making a transition to adulthood. However, the emphasis of *social* in social navigational skills necessitates that consequences of failure be framed in this manner. Social death may well capture these consequences.

The term *social death* may conjure up in the mind of the reader a wide variety of negative images. The use of the term captures what many newcomer youth fear most. McLaughlin and Heath (1993) are widely credited for popularizing the term *social death* to describe the lives of youth who have disengaged from pursuits and behaviors sanctioned by the wider society.

The term *social death* first appeared in the professional social science literature on youth first in the 1980s, although it wasn't until the early 1990s that it started to receive recognition. The definition provided by Ifill (1996) defines *social death* as the destruction of important innate characteristics of human kind that are required for a person or group to progress in society. Delgado (2002a) notes that social death "refers to the perceptions of marginalized youths that their lives are devoid of meaningful employment and social mobility and that they have low self-confidence and belief in themselves. This social death can result in youth joining gangs, having children, dropping out of school, and turning to drugs. They disconnect from the positive elements of their social domains because they believe that the 'cards are stacked against them' and that sustained efforts to progress are futile" (p. 139).

Terms such as *at risk, lost generation, reawakening motivation, reclaiming youth at risk, discouraged youth, disconnected youth*, and *throw-away kids* are some of the more popular ones that approach the condition of social death (Bendtro, Brokenleg, & Van Bockern, 2002; Besharov, 1999; Mendler, 2000; National Research Council, 1993). All of these terms attempt to capture a social condition that finds youth in a prolonged, and in some cases a permanent, marginalized state within this society and reflect the seriousness of this condition. These terms, however, generally place the onus on the youth themselves, and possibly society, for not succeeding in reaching the youth. Biehl (2001) and Hecht (1998) use the concept of social death to capture the dire consequences of life in the streets of Brazil for homeless youth. In so doing, however, they also point out the many positive qualities these youth possess—qualities that are often overlooked or undervalued by society. The use of a construct such as social death does not mean that one totally disregards youth assets.

The popular literature has also started to embrace the concept of social death. However, with minor exceptions, researchers have grounded the concept into a social-relations realm with an emphasis on socioeconomic class and social conduct, and have emphasized the consequences of stigmatization and exclusion:

> It's social death to be seen without one of these little objects. (O'Brien, 1998, p. 2)

> Cocktails, like fashion, change with the seasons and drinking the wrong concoction could mean social death in some circles. (Harden, 2001, p. 44)

> Philippa Kennedy meets a viscountess who is teaching ladies to avoid social death. (Kennedy, 1998, p. 1)

> The social death suffered by political prisoners... (*Jakarta Post*, 1998, p. 1)

> At a Labour conference, where proximity to power, access to it and the illusion of it, is more important that power itself, it is social death to be seen alone and idle: waiting or thinking. (*Guardian*, 1999, p. 13)

> A prominently displayed Tretchikoff can be a social death if seen by the wrong circles. (Gillilan, 2000, p. 10)

> Lily inhabits a narrow, stifling society where a stare held an extra beat in a drawing room could amount to a social death sentence. (Carr, 2001, p. D1)

> Young people are taking the mobile phones given to them by their parents for personal safety and using them to protect themselves against social death. (*Daily Telegraph*, 2001, p. 10)

> It's social death to clap between movements, but everyone enjoys a good cough during the quiet times. (Johnson, 2000, p. 14)

The term *social death* can take on a richer and multifaceted description of a phenomenon that is serious and that can have profound consequences, particularly for newcomer youth who must either totally unlearn previous social navigational skills or reconcile the need for new ones with those used by their parents (*Newsday*, 2000). The consequences of not avoiding social death can be far reaching. Its implications for programming and social policy development with newcomer youth is captured in the following statement: "A child who cannot read, write, relate or 'compute' is sentenced to an economic and social death in our knowledge-based and global economy" (*Buffalo News*, 1999, p. 3H). English language acquisition skills play a vital role in helping newcomers, youth as well as adults, negotiate hostile environments in this country (Koss-Chioino & Vargas, 1999).

Some may well posit that the term *social death* can be substituted for other more common terms, such as *high risk* and *disconnection*. However, the appeal of using *social death*, in this case with newcomer youth, is its emphasis on the importance of these youth being able to navigate socially in their new world. Besharov (1999) defines *disconnected youth* as "not being enrolled in school (either having dropped out or not continuing after graduation), not employed, not in the military, and not married to someone who met at least one of the criteria—for 26 weeks or more out of any calendar year" (p. 4). Besharov's definition provides only one perspective on the consequences of failure; the social dimension is missing, although implicit. The need to make the social consequences explicit is impressive and is best captured by the term *social death*.

Besharov's (1999) definition, for example, does not capture those youth who may be attending school but have no hope for a bright future after graduation. They may even attend school while taking various kinds of prescribed and illicit drugs. Their grades may reflect a low grade-point average and reflect that they are clearly "not college material," yet there is no meaningful and fulfilling alternative. Youth who because of their dark skin color or because they speak English with a strong accent may not be viewed as "college material"; even though they possess the potential to succeed in college, they are not given the proper support and opportunities. Social death best captures what are newcomer youth's greatest fears in this country—the tensions that are associated with navigating two distinct and very different worlds, one belonging to their parents and the past, and the other belonging to peers and their future.

The parents' world may involve a language other than English, traditions, attire, religious practices, roles for youth, gender expectations, and values such as interdependence and cooperation. This worldview could both be appealing and oppressive concomitantly for newcomer youth. Such a worldview can also clash with the new world represented by life in the United States. The value of interdependence or collectivism, where youth never leave their parents until they are married, and when they do get married, are expected to live close to their parents, may prevail within the culture. Independence as a value in U.S. society means that youth leave home upon achieving adulthood or sooner, as is promoted by enrolling in higher education that requires them to live away from home or by enlisting in the military after high school graduation.

Reconciling two cultural expectations is stressful and arduous under most circumstances. However, it takes on added stress and challenges during a crisis, such as when youth "come out" about their homosexuality (Merighi & Grimes, 2000). For example, in discussing their study of African American, European American, Mexican American, and Vietnamese American gay males aged 18 to 24 years old, Merighi and Grimes note how culture often hampers the process of disclosure. In this context, culture relates to family, particularly the importance of preserving and upholding family relations. Merighi and Grimes go on to note the need to understand how the level of acculturation can impact the understanding of what factors support or hinder sexual orientation disclosure for newcomer youth.

Social Navigational Skills

Social navigational skills have been used in professional practice and literature as an organizing construct for analyzing how urban youth are able to avoid, or "navigate," life's challenging situations inherent in living between two separate worlds—immediate community and external community. Mathews (1995) stresses the importance of environment and culture on youth's abilities to negotiate their space and understanding. Social navigational skills incorporate culture and social contexts while stressing competencies in both spheres. Both contexts are of critical importance but can be contradictory in values and goals for youth.

The construct of *cognitive mapping* has emerged in the professional literature but it must not be confused with social navigation. Cognitive mapping is a broad construct that seeks to capture and measure mental representations that can encode knowledge and information (Golledge, 1999; Harrell, Bowlby, & Hall-Hoffarth, 2000; Mar, 1998). These image representations have generally focused on psychological issues, needs, and problem-solving psychological states. The emphasis on the individual rather than social context makes social navigational skills differ from the more prominent cognitive mapping approach in a variety of ways.

The emphasis of social navigational skills is on the *social* dimensions of youth negotiating multiple social arenas in their lives. These arenas very often are based on different cultural traditions and belief systems and have specific expectations of behavior and conduct. Negotiating or brokering differences between social arenas allows youth—in this case, those who are newcomers to this country—to grow emotionally and intellectually. Burton (2001), having been raised in a low-income and high-crime Los Angeles neighborhood, advocates for the importance of a navigational construct and the need for both practitioners and researchers to help youth understand how these skills are critical in their lives.

A number of scholars have embraced a social navigational perspective in helping to explain "success" within their native neighborhoods. Elijah Anderson (1999), in his widely acclaimed book entitled *Code of the Streets: Decency, Violence, and the Moral Life of the Inner City*, brings attention to a host of behavioral factors such as attire, language, proximity, eye contact, and manner of walk that ultimately determine the likelihood of youth obtaining and maintaining respect and safety within inner-city communities: "There is also a great deal of 'code-switching': [people have] an ability to code-switch. They share many of the middle-class values of the wider white society but know that the open display of such values carries little weight on the street; it doesn't provide the emblem that says, 'I can take care of myself.' Hence, such people develop a repertoire of behaviors that do provide that security" (p. 37). Anderson goes on to note that those who are more oriented to street life may not have the competencies to code-switch within the broader community because of a lack of exposure to this world or an unwillingness to try to do so.

Richard Majors, a psychologist at the University of Wisconsin, in a newspaper article interview (Coleman, 1992) coined the phrase *cool pose* to describe the actions of young African American males in their efforts to maintain a sense of pride and identity within a hostile society. However, this same pose can also result in isolation and misunderstanding by the outside world that effectively further marginalizes them.

A youth's chance of surviving and thriving, as a result, is very much determined by his or her ability to possess this knowledge and be able to "switch codes" according to social situation. In other words, a youth's ability to socially navigate within his or her own community can determine whether someone lives or dies. Although the distinction between these two outcomes may seem dramatic, it is nonetheless a reality.

According to Connell, Aber, and Walker (1999) the differences in social navigational skills between "advantaged" and "disadvantaged" youth highlight the importance of adaptation of skills to context:

> Learning to navigate is relatively easy for youth who grow up in advantaged neighborhoods, where they daily witness adults who practice their roles and procedures. But many poor youth do not grow up where adults practice their mainstream roles and procedures; instead, these youth learn different kinds of navigational skills, aimed at surviving on the streets. In some ways the skills they learn are similar to combat skills in their challenges and the seriousness of their consequences—and also in their low applicability and transferability to mainstream life. This inability to navigate in mainstream circumstances puts many poor youth at a serious disadvantage in joining mainstream life, even when they have the will and opportunity. (p. 8)

Connell, Aber, and Walker (1999) emphasize the advantages of high socioeconomic status of native youth. However, their observations are also highly applicable to youth who come from countries of origin that are significantly different from the United States and find themselves trying to understand what is expected of them in this country. The inability to successfully socially navigate can result in discomfort, embarrassment, shame, and, depending on circumstances, failure and permanent marginalization. The importance of social navigational skills will have life-long significance.

There are probably very few readers of this book who have not found themselves in situations where their social navigational skills, like that of a compass, have gone awry, losing all meaning. This may well happen when traveling overseas and visiting a country where the social norms related to conduct are unlike those one is accustomed to, or being raised in a middle- to upper–middle-class community and finding oneself working with poor or working-class clients or communities. There is a tremendous amount of anxiety that results from this disorientation. The enhancement of social navigational skills effectively allows newcomer youth to function within their own community and in the external community at the same time (Anderson, 1999). However, identifying and adapting to these skills require the aid of a guide who can be instructive and supportive during the difficult transition period.

In their study of Latino immigrant youth, Gonzalez-Ramos and Sanchez-Newster (2001) find that having a sense of being lost, confused, and embarrassed at not knowing the new language and culture are common themes in the lives of these youth. One provider articulated this point quite well (although referring to Latino newcomer youth, the message is applicable to other groups as well): "It's really common to see Latino kids who are so completely isolated and alienated. . . . There are a lot of issues of displacement. Adapting to the culture themselves, parents often can't help children navigate the social environment" (Forest, 2002, p. C1).

The anxiety associated with the absence of social navigational skills plays a prominent role in the lives of newcomer youth. Gonzalez-Ramos and Sanchez-Newster (2001, p. 49) capture these themes quite well in the stories youth shared with them:

Back home I knew the language, I knew how to dress, and I had friends, here I am lost.

My religion is the only thing that has stayed the same from back home, everything else is new and I don't know what to do.

I hate it when other kids make fun of my accent, so I don't say anything.

My home was surrounded by trees, we were near the beach, we had a backyard. Now all I see are dark, tall buildings. At first when I got here I used to run, thinking that these brick buildings would fall on me.

My teachers don't ask about my culture, about my home. I have no one to talk to.

Newcomer youth are ever vigilant about their place among peers and society, and are cognizant of how they are "different" from others and are desperate to be "accepted" by others.

Avoiding social death situations (incidents that severely embarrass, demoralize, and ultimately severely limit social mobility) is one of the primary goals of someone who is adept at social navigation. *Social navigational skills*, in essence, refer to a set of competencies necessary to negotiate life's trials and tribulations (everyday and major event hassles) to maintain and enhance self-esteem and to achieve success in U.S. society. These trials and tribulations have been conceptualized in a variety of forms. However, the most promising from a youth perspective is using the perceived "hassles" construct to capture the frustrations in negotiating transactions within social arenas (Hee-og, 2000; Samainego & Gonzales, 1999; Seidman et al., 1995). Kanner, Coyne, Schaefer, and Lazarus (1981) define *hassles* as "irritating, frustrating, distressing demands that to some degree characterize everyday transactions with the environment" (p. 31).

Perceived hassles refer to the stress associated with navigating successfully through daily or major life events and the distress that occurs as a result for youth having to do so. The behavior resulting from these transactions represents the social and emotional price paid by reacting to these stresses. The everyday interactions youth have with their immediate family, friends, peers, schools, and community constitute an important ecological set of mediating processes (Bronfenbrenner, 1979; Seidman et al., 1995). Each of these social arenas will necessitate youth behaving in different roles and responding to different sets of expectations.

Seidman and colleagues (1995) divide perceived daily hassles within families into two distinct categories that have relevance for other social arenas: (1) family conflict and (2) conflict due to lack of instrumental resources. Perceived hassles may also be specific to a setting (e.g., school) but may also be thematic in a youth's life—an inability to speak English well, for example. The navigation of all social arenas outside of the immediate family, peers, and communities is affected (Vinokurov, Trickett, & Birman, 2002). This takes on added significance when newcomer youth with limited English-speaking abilities are thrust into roles acting as interpreters for family members, brokers of human services, and other situations where they have immense responsibilities if they fail in their mission.

Perceived hassles for newcomer youth go far beyond what may be typically encountered and meant for a "typical" American adolescent. Perceived hassles and the social navigational skills required take on new meaning within an ecological perspective for newcomer youth. The use of perceived (everyday and major event) hassles, in turn, provides a language through which negative experiences and feelings can be better understood. Beauvais and Oetting (1999), for example, conceptualize *youth resilience* as youth possessing attitudes and skills fostering resistance to environmental risks. The same observations can be applied to the use of social navigational skills to eschew hassles.

A social navigational construct allows for a variety of disciplinary perspectives to be integrated into this worldview. An ecological broad view is able to cast a wide net on refugee and immigrant assets. Reyes (1999), for example, in a study of music and musical boundaries among Vietnamese refugees in refugee camps, uses the concept of *signposts* to distinguish between social arenas. She identified the use of music as a public and private act; the former is used during celebrations of special events that may well involve non-Vietnamese participants, and the latter refers to music that is sad or that touches on love sentiments and therefore private for Vietnamese ears only.

Social navigational skills will be addressed through examination of two dimensions: (1) attitudinal and (2) competencies. The close interrelationship between these two spheres makes their separation as distinct entities artificial. However, doing so makes it easier to present information on the subject. These dimensions build on the resiliency attributes identified by Benard (1991, 1997)—social competence, problem-solving skills, autonomy, and sense of purpose and future. These attributes are considered to be present in every youth member but may vary according to degree, depending on the role of protective factors and life circumstances. This variability in degree, in turn, determines the likelihood of youth having success in socially navigating in society.

These two dimensions of social navigational skills can incorporate a large number of asset-related constructs, such as resilience, strengths, protective factors, coping mechanisms, and adaptation, for example. This broad conceptualization of social navigation skills, however, is both a strength and a limitation in furthering its wider acceptance within the field of youth services. The inclusiveness of the construct provides scholars and practitioners with ample opportunities to integrate their particular perspectives on youth assets. Nevertheless, this same inclusiveness makes the empirical assessment of social navigational skills that much more challenging and, critics may argue, impossible.

The process of social navigation among newcomers starts prior to their resettlement in the United States. In the case of refugees, it commences in refugee camps, with the Vietnamese being a case in point:

> Prior to arriving in the U.S., most Vietnamese refugees had gone through the process of painfully learning routines totally alien and almost incomprehensible to most of them as they passed from one camp to another. Each move meant severance from support systems that seemed to grow increasingly fragile with each step. In the United States under a policy of dispersed resettlement, many were sent to live in assigned locations where they may or may not be co-nationals to ease adaptation. For many, the search for a new home would not be over until they had found the wherewithal to settle down in a place of their own choice. (Reyes, 1999, p. 11)

The challenge of using a social navigational construct, and the same applies to resiliency, is in large part the result of this construct consisting of more than one construct worthy of study as a discrete entity unto itself (Gordon & Song, 1994). These challenges, however, do not limit the appeal and value of using social navigational skills for bridging professions and academic disciplines in search of better interventions for reaching youth, newcomer youth notwithstanding. Thus, the flexibility of social navigational skills allows for the incorporation of a wide variety of constructs that attempt to tap into youth competencies and aspirations.

Youth Attitudes

Hope for a Better Future.   The fundamental belief that life will only get better in the future represents a critical element in any effort to enhance social navigational skills for newcomer youth. Newcomer youth have dreams and aspirations, but adults in positions of authority frequently do not capture them. Kurth-Sehai (1998) notes that youth "possess an unparalleled potential to catalyze positive social change through the development and expression of diverse, exploratory, and optimistic images of future societies" (p. 120). Having a profound sense of hope for a better future brings with it a need to postpone or delay gratification.

This type of hope, although it is arduous to measure, is nonetheless present in youth who have surmounted incredible odds to succeed. Helping professions have almost totally disregarded the role and value of hope for a better future in the life of youth, and this has seriously limited its incorporation into preventive interventions (Masten, 1999). Kumpfer (1999), however, notes that this may be the result of a reliance on risk processes: "A paradigm shift appears to be occurring towards an increasing emphasis on optimism and hope as opposed to the frustration and despair that can occur from an emphasis on risk processes" (p. 179). Thus, a shift in paradigms from deficits to assets requires the creation of a different language to capture the processes and elements that enhance a youth's ability to succeed. Hope is a direct manifestation of this paradigm shift.

The ability or will to dream of a better future and to create a mission of higher purpose in life have been identified as qualities or characteristics of resilient youth (Bandura, 1989; Kumpfer, 1999; Quinton, Pickles, Maughan, & Rutter, 1993; Rutter & Quinton, 1984). Dreams and fantasies about the future are not differentiated for the purposes of use in social navigational skills of newcomer youth. The work of Werner and Smith (1982, 1992) has played an instrumental role in uncovering the importance of resilient youth having a strong sense of direction or purpose in life. This sense of mission translates into an embrace of responsibility toward others, or "required help-fulness." Providing newcomer youth with opportunities to serve their community not only means they perform a public service but service learning also results in an acquisition of new knowledge and skill sets.

A social purpose for newcomer youth, such as making the life of other newcomer youth more fulfilling in the future, can be a direct manifestation of a dream or mission for a better life for themselves and their significant others. Hovey's (2000) observations, although based on a study of psychosocial predictors of acculturative stress in adult Mexican immigrants, support the findings that feelings of hopefulness about the future serve as a supportive factor in the adjustment process. The response of a 22-year-old Mexican woman illustrates this theme: "My future will be much better than how I am now. And for my family, their future will also be better, since I will put all of my being toward that. You have to always think positively. Youth, we are the future of the world" (p. 497).

Hope for a better future, however, must be combined with an equally important embrace that the future cannot be left to chance and that strategic actions taken in the present will shape future outcomes. In essence, hope, although an important element in any success at social navigation, requires action on the part of youth to help shape outcomes. Consequently, hope is but one part of an equation, with action being the second part. This action, when applied to newcomer youth, can take on a variety of manifestations, including furthering their education, volunteering or working outside of school, developing a peer network sharing similar aspirations, participating in community programs that keep them safe (physically and psychologically), and exposure to a broader world beyond the immediate neighborhood.

Pride in Cultural Heritage. The term *cultural pride* emerged during the 1960s and took on greater significance in the 1970s. This term eventually encompassed ethnic, racial, and heritage dimensions during this evolution. The emergence of the construct of culture within human service programs and professional literature during the past 30 years is unprecedented, and will play an influential role in shaping interventions. Culture went from being of sole interest to anthropologists and sociologists, to being of interest to the world of social work. It seems as if no aspect of practice escaped the influence of culture. One aspect, however, has taken on greater prominence with youth—namely, cultural heritage and ethnic identity, and how they influence self-esteem.

The following two youth stories bring a dimension to this discussion that exemplifies the reality faced by newcomer youth and the tensions inherent in making complicated decisions about who they are. Elaine Wong, an American-Born Chinese (ABC) shares her story of being caught between two worlds—Chinese and American—and how cultural heritage can serve as a tremendous onus in the life of a newcomer youth:

> Being an ABC... was pretty hard for me when I was younger, since I was often judged and criticized by my relatives and close friends because I was too "Americanized" or "white-washed." I dreaded visiting relatives over the New Year because of my constant fear of being looked down upon. I can remember the nervousness I would feel when going to meet them. I would... [be] careful not to make eye contact with anyone.... I would just sit there quietly and avoid making conversation, because I knew that my Chinese was really bad, and did not want to embarrass my parents or myself. It was torture... waiting until it was over, just so I could go home and continue watching Saturday cartoons. (KQED, 2002)

Warren Cheng shares a perspective on citizenship and shows the multifaceted meanings it has for newcomer youth:

> I identify myself as Chinese American, but more American than Chinese. I was born in America and have been Americanized. If it weren't for my parents, I would've lost my Chinese identity, and language. I guess the most important thing to remember is that American is a nationality, not a race. (KQED, 2002)

The phenomenon of hyphenated identity such as Mexican-American, Vietnamese-American, Peruvian-American, Jamaican-American is referred to as *diasporic nationalism*. Diasporic nationalism captures the sentiments of newcomer youth losing or having lost their connectedness to their homeland, but still residing in communities that consist primarily of one newcomer group (Tambiah, 2000). Hyphenated identities address the concerns and politics inherent in accommodation, acculturation, integration, and assimilation, and having newcomer groups achieving equal rights with natives.

The field of social work is well versed in the use of many concepts that seek to capture negative experiences, and practice with newcomer populations is no exception. The concept of *cultural bereavement* has been used to describe Cambodian refugees in the United States who still experience guilt over their abandonment of their homeland and unfulfilled cultural obligations to their dead (Eisenbrunch, 1991). These sentiments, however, are not unique to Cambodians. Some practitioners may well argue that some element of cultural bereavement will always be a part of the newcomer experience and family legacy, helping to explain the popularity of ethnic festivals and parades.

Another concept has slowly emerged to capture a different perspective of the newcomer experience. The importance of having a sense of *pride in one's cultural heritage* may seem obvious to anyone who has taught or worked with marginalized youth in this society, particularly those who come from countries commonly labeled as "developing." The popularity of Alex Haley's book *Roots* sparked a national movement for ethnic and racial pride and development of an awareness of one's cultural roots prior to emigration to the United States. Although Haley's book focused on African Americans, it did resonate for many other Americans. The role of ethnic pride in promoting positive self-esteem is one aspect of youth possessing effective social navigational skills.

The construct of self-efficacy can translate into a resilient youth having feelings of self-worth (self-esteem), and control over their environment (locus of control) can easily be incorporated into a construct of cultural pride. Newcomer youth, particularly those coming from cultural heritages that are misunderstood or actively frowned upon in U.S. society, can be made to feel embarrassed or ashamed of their ethnic/racial background and are at a distinct disadvantage in navigating social situations where they find themselves to be in the "minority." The authors of this book believe that self-efficacy cannot be separated from self-esteem; self-esteem, in turn, cannot be separated from cultural pride (Bandura, 1995).

Stressful situations are not uncommon with newcomer youth who venture outside of their immediate family and peer network: "No one lives in a vacuum. Our environment—especially the people we interact with—can amplify and help to construct whatever resiliency we are capable of" (Norman, 2000b, p. 8). Thus, the testing of a youth's social navigational skills can occur only after he or she leaves the protective environment of family, peers, and community. It is not until then that newcomer youth can accurately assess their competencies and integrate new knowledge and experiences into their "navigational kit." These new experiences will undoubtedly be enriching, rewarding, and painful. Lessons can and should be learned from both successes and failures. Having someone who can serve as a guide to help them interpret these experiences can be of immense importance in the life of youth.

Survival Pride. The identification and mobilization of survival pride in interventions among newcomers has only started to receive attention in the field. The ability to convert a negative experience into a positive force is not unheard of in social work and other helping professions. However, the pride that develops as a result has generally been overlooked in the professional literature if not the practice field. It does not take the experienced practitioner very long to realize that refugee and immigrant youth and their families have generally been through tremendous ordeals in the course of their journey to this country. This journey invariably has necessitated that sacrifices be made that may well involve leaving loved ones behind in circumstances that can best be described as precarious for existence. The decision to leave their homeland is never made without serious considerations of the benefits and challenges of uprooting to a new land (Harker, 2001).

The process of getting newcomer youth to identify and exemplify their strengths is critical in any intervention guided by a youth development paradigm. The ability to survive—and in many cases, thrive—cannot be readily dismissed in the development of any form of intervention, youth development driven or otherwise. *Survival skills* can easily be substituted for *social navigational skills.* However, social navigation becomes an umbrella for a set of competencies without the sensational association that the term *survival* can engender among program participants and the general public.

There are a variety of ways to label this survival experience within an asset identification perspective. Wolin and Wolin (1998) have labeled this process as deriving a *survivor's pride.* They define *survivor's pride*

> as the well-deserved feeling of accomplishment that results from withstanding the pressures of hardship and prevailing in ways both large and small. It is a bittersweet mix of pain and triumph that is usually under the surface, but sometimes readily visible, in many children and adults struggling with the troubles in their lives. This pride, developed over

time in the course of a struggle, typically goes unnoticed in professional and lay circles that are more apt to document the deficits in children than their strengths. (p. 61)

Development of an awareness of pride can transform this awareness into action.

Spirituality/Religion.   The subject of spirituality and religion has only recently received prominence within the social work and other helping professions (Canda & Furman, 1999). There has been a tendency to combine these two subjects and use them interchangeably. However, although there can be a degree of overlap depending on how they are conceptualized, using *spirituality* and *religion* interchangeably does a disservice to this important subject.

Religion can be defined as an "organized system of experiences, beliefs, values, and adaptational and transformative strategies that are shared by a community, with reference to concerns vested with a sense of ultimacy, sacredness, or spiritual status" (Canda & Furman, 1999, p. 54). *Spirituality*, in turn, according to Cervantes and Ramirez (1992) is defined as "a transcendent level of consciousness that allows for existential purpose and mission, the search for harmony and wholeness, and a fundamental belief in the existence of a greater, all-loving presence in the universe" (p. 104).

Youth workers in an interfaith study conducted in 1995 identified 10 common goals across faith traditions that lend themselves for use in social navigational skill and youth development-focused programs (Search Institute, 1995):

1. Help youth apply faith to daily decisions.
2. Nurture in youth a lifelong faith commitment.
3. Provide a safe and caring place.
4. Develop youth values and skills.
5. Keep youth involved in congregation.
6. Help youth build caring relationships with other youth.
7. Encourage self-respect and personal dignity.
8. Provide positive activities.
9. Reach out to serve youth at risk.
10. Help youth build caring relationships with adults.

These cross-cutting goals serve to prepare newcomer youth for a wide variety of situations in the future that can dramatically alter their life course.

Gordon and Song (1994) find that religion plays a critical role in the lives of African Americans: "A belief system seems to provide anchorage and stability in the face of faith-challenging experiences. When questioned about religion, most of the subjects expressed the sense of community, direction, and fellowship typically associated with African Americans, and a traditional affiliation of religiosity" (p. 38). Organized religion not only plays significant roles in helping communities cope and aspire but, through formal mechanisms, it also provides a wide range of educational and social services.

In their study of the "ethnic church" in helping Vietnamese adolescents adjust to life in the United States, Bankston and Zhou (1996) have found that church attendance is consistently a significant positive influence on ethnic identity through the use of such services as education within the house of worship. This institution, in turn, can best be conceptualized as part of an ethnic network that actively seeks to help youth adjust in their transition to this society. Chrispin (1998), too, has found that church-affiliated Haitian immigrant youth benefit from their participation within this institution.

Yeh and Inose's (2002) study of mental health concerns and coping strategies in Chinese, Japanese, and Korean immigrant junior high school students shows that they often encounter a variety of stressors, such as stereotyping, racial discrimination, language and cultural barriers, and intergroup conflicts and tensions within their school. However, reliance on social supports, such as religion, aids in their successful coping by providing a space where they may share these experiences and feel validated in the process.

According to Higgerson (1998), religion helps newcomer youth with their development of an ethic identity in this society and provides avenues for youth to become contributing members of their community in the process. Chrispin (1999) writes that the church provides newcomer Haitian youth with a climate that fosters the development of optimism and hope, which form the building block of any successful effort at developing social navigational skills. Kim (1990) also relates that cultural programs offered through houses of worship play influential roles in helping newcomer youth adjust to their new world. These programs stress the cultural, social, and religious goals and help youth find their place in U.S. society while adjusting. In essence, houses of worship very often represent one of the few constants in the lives of youth and represent a haven for them and their families.

A number of studies identify spirituality as a significant predictor of resiliency and later positive life adaptation (Dunn, 1994; Kumpfer, 1999; Walker, 1995). Masten (1994), in focusing on religious faith or affiliation, says that it is an important individual resiliency factor. Chrispin (1998) agrees, finding church participation to be positively associated with academic and emotional resilience for Haitian youth.

Perseverance. The ability to thrive under difficult circumstances is a quality most human beings would like to have. However, this ability takes on greater meaning when applied to youth. Lopez, Nerenberg, and Valdez (2000) state that Latino migrant adolescents are extremely resilient and resourceful in surviving in new environments and surmounting obstacles. Wolin and Wolin (1999) acknowledge the importance of viewing resilience as a process rather than an endpoint: "We do not equate resilience with final endpoints of success such as graduation from high school or college with a high grade point average or total recovery from an eating disorder or an alcohol or drug problem, or full disengagement from a destructive friendship. We see resilience as the process of struggling with hardship. The process progresses by accumulating small successes that occur side by side with failures, setbacks, and disappointments" (p. 3).

It is important to emphasize that youth assets do not fully protect youth—and in this case, newcomer youth—from setbacks and disappointments. Life, after all, would not be "life" without disappointments and a lack of total success. However, the will and ability of youth to persevere against odds is a quality that can rightly be conceptualized as an asset. Further, it would be artificial to conceptualize these assets as strictly personal without regard for ecological forces, such as social support networks. The ecology of assets stresses the importance of interplay between internal and external factors.

The ability to "bounce back" and continue to progress forward is a quality much admired in this society. Much more can be learned about a person's character by observing how the person handles adversity and failure than by how he or she handles success. Apfel and Simon (1996), for example, have focused their research on children of war and how to identify and enhance resilient qualities, and have shown how even when a part of horrid experiences, children still show remarkable resilience.

Youth Competencies

A social navigational construct with an emphasis on skills complements the general thrust of best practices on the part of helping professions. These skills must traverse with the individual as he or she moves within the social environment; a focus on one without regard for the other will achieve limited success at best. Huebner (2003) identifies two important elements of positive youth development: positive and sustained relationships with adults and opportunities to develop competencies. Garbarino (1985) defines *competencies* as "a set of skills, attitudes, motives, and abilities needed to master the principal setting that individuals can reasonably expect to encounter in the social environment of which they are a part, while at the same time maximizing their sense of well-being and enhancing future development" (p. 80).

The five competencies addressed in this section necessitate that newcomer youth assess, converse, and move into action. These competencies, it can be effectively argued, play instrumental roles in facilitating learning and furthering youth development (Huebner, 2003).

Discourse.   A key element of social navigational skills is the use of language in the engagement of discourse across age groups and social situations. Culture, in turn, influences the nature and scope of discourse (Moon, 1996). Discourse is a construct that seeks to capture "acceptable" ways of using language and engaging in communicative behavior (Gee, 1989; Stanton-Salazar, 1997). It is greatly influenced by the social arenas within which it occurs. Gee (1989), for example, differentiates between *primary discourse* (that used at home, with peers, and in the community) and *secondary discourse* (that used in contexts that allocate social goods such as finances, status, and prestige). Hodge (2002) specifically uses the construct of discourse in addressing the state of Muslim youth in the United States. Discourse becomes the vehicle for social workers to use in identifying significant Islamic values and beliefs and how they have the potential to create value-based conflicts with "dominant secular discourse."

This "identity kit" of discourse influences a whole set of behaviors—such as body language, vocabulary, proximity, and loudness—that reinforces a role within a particular context or arena. Being able to decode a particular situation and reacting accordingly increases the likelihood that youth, and in this case, those who are newcomers, will be willing to explore new surroundings and circumstances beyond their immediate world. Such ventures, when properly backed with requisite skills and confidence, will increase their likelihood of success in transcending geographical, psychological, and cultural boundaries.

The successful psychological adaptation of immigrant youth is expectedly a complex and multifaceted phenomenon. In analyzing the common attributes of three prominent perspectives on adaptation and immigrant youth, Sam (2000) noted: "The perspective of social group identity, acculturation strategies, and family values—share a common core.... An emphasis on 'old' and 'new' cultures and, to a degree, the need to find a balance between the two cultures for a successful adaptation outcome are common to these three perspectives" (p. 6). Although each of these perspectives shares commonalties with the others, each has a unique approach toward how it is used in intervention.

Newcomer youth need to engage in discourse with their immediate family. This necessitates that they develop the "appropriate" language and use of rituals and symbols to convey to their parents and immediate relatives who may subscribe to values originating in the "old country." An ability to minimize or avoid tension is one of the immediate benefits of discourse within a social navigational perspective with family. However, discourse within the family will take on elements that are significantly different from those involving peers and adult figures of authority in other social arenas. Each of these social arenas requires youth to engage in a distinct type of discourse.

Problem Solving. Researchers and scholars have identified problem-solving skills as important elements in youth achieving a degree of success in this society. Problem-solving skills have been labeled in a variety of ways, such as *social and behavorial competence, effective functioning,* and *street smarts* (Antony, 1987; Garmezy & Masten, 1986; Kumpfer, 1999; Neiger, 1991; Rutter & Quinton, 1994). Norman (2000b), in reviewing the literature on strengths and resiliency, states that problem-solving skills reinforce a youth's sense of self-esteem, sense of competency, and sense of mastery. The integration of problem-solving skills in prevention programming has been advocated by a number of prevention researchers since the 1980s (Botvin, Baker, Renick, & Filazzola, 1984; Elickson, 1984; Pentz, Dwyer, Mackinnon, Flay et al., 1989).

Kumpfer (1999) identifies six key elements associated with effective youth problem-solving skills:

1. A proclivity for addressing problems through use of a cognitive-affective-behavioral response set
2. A realistic assessment of presenting problems
3. A generation of contingency solutions
4. A systematical consideration of possible outcomes for each option
5. Selection of the best strategy
6. Implementation and evaluation of outcomes, including identification of lessons learned for future use.

Each of these elements could not be effective on its own without the interplay of the others. In essence, these elements need to be conceptualized as a "package deal" in problem solving.

Carroll (1996) finds in a study of Hmong children growing up in Fresno, California, that having a resilient past played a prominent role in helping these children navigate conflicting worldviews. This is particularly the case in how they solve tensions arising from conflicting expectations between family, peers, school, and the broader community. These children's ability to recognize and mobilize their assets served them well in adjusting to life in the United States.

Social Assessment.   The ability of newcomer youth to accurately assess the social context in which they interact highlights much of what has been stated in this chapter, but it is still worthy of specific attention. A youth's ability to assess social situations within the family, peers, schools, work (when applicable), community functions, and functions within the broader community is a test of their competencies. However, when the youth is a newcomer to this country, it is a test that many people could consider unfair. Each of these social situations places newcomer youth in positions where expectations of their behavior will differ.

The construct of *manners* best captures the importance and elusiveness of social assessment. Manners, or the conduct of expected behaviors, are not constant across social situations. The social assessment of what behavior is expected, tolerated or not tolerated is a challenging process because of the interplay of key factors, such as socio-economic class and culture. "Proper" behavior at a dining table, for example, can prove quite challenging to assess. How one sits, what utensils to use and the order in which to use them, and the use of one's hands and body language are very much dictated by the social climate in which the meal occurs. Assessing this climate is arduous because the social situation is dynamic, requiring a wide range of social skills and self-confidence.

Newcomer youth face the challenge of having to assess numerous social situations in the course of a typical day and week in their lives. Social assessment requires youth to detect social cues and to react accordingly. Possessing social assessment skills, as a result, means being "socially aware," being able to problem-solve new social situations, and trusting one's intuition about how to behave when in doubt. Social assessment competencies can apply to behaviors in the street (otherwise known as "street-smarts") as well as social situations at as parties, formal celebrations, academic settings, and houses of worship, for example. Misreading a social situation can result in newcomer youth being made fun of and being socially isolated.

Social Relational.   Probably very few themes in the literature stand out more prominently than the critical role of social relational skills. The ability to establish and maintain relationships is a skill that is essential in any form of endeavor, for any age group. Nevertheless, these skills play such a vital role with youth in helping them develop and maintain their social network. Social relational skills, as it will be noted in Chapter 8, have started to receive attention from researchers and practitioners, particularly the development of activities (educational and experiential) to assist youth in assessing their abilities and acquiring necessary relationship-building skills.

Social relational skills are closely tied to a youth's age and developmental stages. However, regardless of age developmental stage, youth development activities usually stress collaboration, listening, communication, and the role of social cues in informing interactions (Erwin, 1994; O'Donnell, Hawkins, Catalano, Abbott, & Day, 1995; Strodl, 1993; Westby, 1997). There are no youth development interventions that do not necessitate positive social relationships to achieve youth development goals. An awareness of how youth see themselves, their apprehensions in establishing close relationships, and how they generally go about assessing and establishing relationships—all play critical roles in achievement of significant life goals.

The impact of sociodemographic factors—such as gender, race/ethnicity, age, native/newcomer status, income level, sexual orientation, and physical and cognitive abilities—play influential roles in dictating the nature of social relationships for youth. Clearly, a comfort level and the ability to establish social relationships across diverse groups bodes well for their future as adults and citizens in an increasingly multicultural society.

Use of Sanctuaries.   The popular use of the term *urban sanctuary* can be traced back to the work of McLaughlin, Irby, and Langman (1994). *Sanctuaries* are places within a community that fulfill formal or informal roles in the lives of community youth. These places can take the shape of a community-based organization with active youth programming or an institution without a specific social mission, such as a library or a house of worship. The authors take the position that there are no communities in the United States, regardless of how economically and sociologically distressed, that are considered to not have some form of community sanctuary for youth and adults alike.

Connell, Aber, and Walker (1999) coined the term *supportive sanctuaries* to capture the role of neighborhood networks of competent adults with shared values and norms. Supportive sanctuaries may or may not involve adults in organized programs or working in community-based organizations. These individuals may be neighbors, community leaders, and distant relatives, or they may fulfill other roles that bring them into contact with youth. When this contact does occur, it is supportive and respectful of youth.

A sanctuary takes on added significance in the lives of youth who, because of a troubled home life or troubled community, need a place where they can go and be physically and emotionally safe. This climate, in turn, provides them with the opportunity to grow intellectually and socially. The professional literature has largely ignored the role that nontraditional community settings have and continue to play in the lives of youth. When specifically addressing newcomers, these sanctuaries are places where youth can learn new knowledge and skills that will ultimately aid them in adjusting to life in the United States. These settings can also be of help to their families.

Community Assets

Self-Help Traditions.   The concepts of caring and helping can be viewed both from an individual and a communitywide perspective. However, regardless of perspective, self-help efforts grow out of a group's plight and the belief that common concerns can best be addressed through people assisting each other (Weber, 1982). The interplay of beliefs in helping oneself intersects with the availability or lack thereof of resources and service external to the community. Self-help cultural traditions, as a result, can be manifested as well-conceptualized and coordinated efforts that are transmitted through cultural values and belief systems. Carney and Gedajlovic's (2002) study of how Southeast Asian families create family businesses (FBGs), for example, shows that cultural values of interdependence, path dependence, and system openness facilitates member access to capital, labor pools, and markets.

The role of culture in helping to shape help-seeking and help-giving is well accepted in the social sciences and in the helping professions. Menjivar (1997), in comparing Vietnamese, Salvadorans, and Mexican immigrant kinship networks, states that kinship support plays a prominent role in helping immigrants through all facets of the immigrant experience. However, it takes on added significance when the host government does not "officially" recognize the presence of the newcomer group. The options for assistance in these cases makes reliance on kinship that much more necessary than in situations where the newcomer group can also rely on "formal" assistance from governmental entities.

The professional literature is rich in examples of how mutual aid associations have played instrumental roles in society, particularly in helping newcomer communities help themselves (Banks, 1997; Williams & Windebank, 2000). These associations are usually staffed by members of the communities and provide economic, social, recreational, advocacy, and educational services. Their existence within newcomer communities are often thought of as indicators of a community's stabilization and growth within urban areas, and they signify a potential indigenous institution that can offer other community-based organizations collaborative opportunities. Summerfield (2000) goes so far as to advocate the position that the major protective factor in the lives of refugees is the presence of a community to provide mutual support and to "nurture problem-solving strategies."

Contrary to common assumptions about mutual aid associations, these institutions can consist of a wide range of age groups, including youth. The mutual aid associations that have expanded their membership and staffing to include youth are often in the most propitious positions to play leadership roles within their respective communities and broker resources for use in the community. Newcomer communities are made up of assorted age groups and these organizations have recognized this point quite well. The extent to which youth play leadership roles within these organizations, however, requires further research. It is the authors' impression that it is rare to find youth on boards of directors and fulfilling important staffing roles. However, this may change as mutual aid associations evolve in the near future.

There have been a number of exciting developments in the field specifically focused on identifying and enhancing indigenous newcomer community assets. In Pennsylvania, the Multi-Ethnic Community Resources Project has a vision for establishing collaborative initiatives in immigrant communities too small in size to have their own independent community organizations. The goals of the project are as follows:

- Help emerging refugee communities identify their own assets and resources in order to strengthen their communities.
- Assist refugee communities in organizing themselves into effective self-help groups.
- Encourage refugee communities to participate in collaborative efforts through a shared vision of the capacities and assets of the broader refugee and immigrant communities.
- Increase refugees' access to resources and services by building and maintaining bridges to other communities and mainstream local resources and organizations. (Institute for Cultural Partnership, 1999, p. 1)

Nontraditional Settings.   As noted earlier, immigrant and refugee groups come to the United States with rich and lengthy traditions of self-help, including the establishment of enterprises. These efforts not only seek to meet community needs for services or products but also serve to hire local residents who would have a difficult time working outside of their communities because of linguistic and cultural backgrounds. In addition, these enterprises very often fulfill roles as *nontraditional settings* by providing a wide range of social services in addition to the selling of a product or service, such as hairstyling, manicures, and so on (Delgado, 1999).

Nontraditional settings, particularly those well grounded within the community they serve, can be expected to provide any or all of the following services: credit, assistance in job search, companionship, interpreter services, translation of formal documents from English into the language of the patron, advocacy, dissemination of news from the homeland, assistance in finding housing, and problem-solving of many kinds. Consequently, nontraditional settings fulfill critical roles within their respective communities.

The nature of nontraditional settings may be unique to specific newcomer groups, although a core set of settings can be found throughout newcomer communities across the country. Botanical shops, for example, can be found in most newcomer communities but will be called by different names. Grocery stores, too, fall into this category, as well as convenience stores. Some of these settings lend themselves more to providing services to consumers than other types of establishments. Restaurants, for example, necessitate that patrons sit and spend an extended period of time. This window of opportunity facilitates the establishment of relationships, an exchange of information, and the provision of other types of services.

Youth as Assets.   It is important not to lose sight of youth as assets in their own right in any discussion of newcomer community assets. The possibility that youth can be considered community assets, especially in the case of those who are newcomers to this country, is not a foreign concept when discussing youth services, particularly those subscribing to youth development principles. There is a tendency to view community assets from an adult perspective, which can seriously limit any in-depth understanding of the multiple ways youth can help each other, adults, and the community.

Upon closer examination, newcomer youth can fulfill a variety of helper roles within their respective communities. Delgado (1998), for example, has used Latino youth as key resources in the undertaking of community needs and asset assessments. Latino youth, according to Delgado, have intimate knowledge of their community, high levels of energy, commitment, creativity, and requisite competencies to undertake research with the proper support. They also have the potential for assuming leadership roles in their community and in society.

Paulino and Burgos-Servido (1997) and Strug and Mason (2002) advocate for social workers to assume roles as cultural brokers between community-based organizations and newcomers. The term *cultural broker* has historically been used to describe the role of key members of the community in helping to mitigate the tension that emerges from cultural clashes between newcomer and native-born groups (Cooper, Denner, & Lopez, 1999). Cultural brokers can perform a variety of tasks in carrying out this role, such as providing information, advocating, encouraging, advising, and anticipating and breaking down potential barriers. The term, however, has recently been applied to newcomer youth who, because of various competencies, have been thrust into this role at a relatively young age. This term serves to counterbalance the term *refugee syndrome* that is commonly used to capture a state of being where newcomers find themselves helpless, incapable of helping themselves and others, and being in tremendous need for a variety of mental and social services.

Orellana (2001), for example, writes that Mexican and Chicano American immigrant children play important helper roles within their schools and communities. Their knowledge of English also plays an important role in serving as interpreters for their families and neighborhoods and brokering their search for resources. These youths are perceived to be assets to their families, schools, and communities. However, if adults in positions of authority within schools are not inclined to recognize newcomer youth as helpers, these actions will essentially go totally unrecognized in the lives of these youth.

Conclusion

Communities, in this case those that are urban based and consisting of high numbers of newcomer residents, may have limited social capital because of uprootment from country of origins. The process or journey of leaving one country and moving to another is never easy, even for the most privileged and capable. This process becomes an incredible challenge for those who have limited formal education, English language skills, and access to financial capital. Youth can play influential roles in helping to restore trust, creating support networks, and acting as a bridge between society's major institutions and the communities themselves (Hart, Atkins, & Ford, 1998).

The early part of the twenty-first century promises to be an exciting era for developments in interventions using youth assets as the basis for engaging youth. This chapter has hopefully provided the reader with exciting and emerging new ways of viewing immigrant and refugee youth as community assets. The use of a social navigational skill frame lends itself to incorporation of numerous constructs that are currently used in the field of social work and other helping professions and in academic discipline research and practice. This elicits the potential of multidisciplinary collaborative partnerships, and ultimately increases the efficient use of resources targeting youth.

The relatively recent emergence of the construct of social death brings with it great potential for use with newcomer youth in aiding them to conceptualize their journey in this society. The concept of social death captures the realistic fear newcomer youth experience in their quest for acceptance and success in this society. Success is complex and multidimensional, and dependent on the interplay of numerous factors. Identification of what it means for an individual newcomer youth is but the first step in the development of a social navigational kit that he or she can use to enhance personal competencies. This initial step serves to outline the process and goals youth will engage in and embrace in navigating their way through life.

The reader may well ask, If a construct is so elusive to identify and study, why does it continue not only to exist but thrive? Ultimately, the intrinsic value of a construct determines its validity regardless of the challenges scholars and researchers face in determining boundaries and elements. The construct of social navigational skills develops broad appeal across professions and academic disciplines for use in practice and research with newcomer youth. Like all constructs, it will evolve and take on many different shapes, depending on the context in which it is operationalized. Nevertheless, the intrinsic value of social navigational skills for use with newcomer youth must withstand the test of time; obscurity will be the consequence of the lack of relevance for the field of practice.

There are so many different ways that the social work profession can ground social navigational skills and social death in work with newcomer youth. However, using a culturally competent set of lenses, as addressed in the following chapter, is probably the most feasible way. Cultural competence, as the reader will see, has a long and distinguished history within the profession, and this perspective has flexibility in incorporating new methods and techniques such as those identified in this chapter.

7

Culturally Competent Practice

> *Within the last couple of decades, social work, as well as other professional disciplines, has been concerned with the cultural appropriateness and effectiveness of services offered to ethnically diverse clients. It is important that social workers, operating from an empowerment, strengths, and ecological framework, provide services, conduct assessments, and implement interventions that are reflective of the clients' cultural values and norms, congruent with their natural help-seeking behaviors, and inclusive of existing indigenous solutions.*
>
> —Fong, 2001, p. 1

Introduction

The role of culture in shaping interventions, be they at the micro, mezzo, or macro level, is prominent. Culturally competent practice, as a result, must systematically build on this historical context to be successful. This chapter identifies and details the strengths and community assets held by refugee and immigrant youth, with a particular rationale for incorporation within youth development programming.

What Is Cultural Competence?

Before examining what is meant by *cultural competence*, it is necessary to pause and provide an operational definition of *culture*. Locke's (1992) definition was selected because of the emphasis it places on navigational skills: "Culture is the body of learned beliefs, traditions, principles, and guides for behavior that are commonly shared among members of a particular group. Culture serves as a road map for both perceiving and interacting with the world" (p. 10).

The concept of cultural competence has been in the human service field for well over 30 years. As to be expected, it is defined in a variety of ways, depending on the author. Cultural competency has also found its way to practice with newcomers. Malik and Velazquez (2002) point out the rewards and challenges of culturally competent practice with newcomers. Cultural competence serves to ensure that the backgrounds of the youth are not lost in the process of assessing their assets, needs, and goals, and it serves as a basis from which to implement youth development guided interventions (Williams, 2001). Although youth development has been promoted based on the implicit understanding of culturally based practice, this needs to be explicitly stated.

The theory of youth development provides a rich framework for a strengths-oriented, multidimensional approach to practice with newcomer youth and their families. Equally critical is the concept of cultural competence and the resulting framework for culturally competent practice.

Themes related to culture and diversity are woven throughout this book, and multiple examples have already been offered that powerfully illustrate how culture is particularly salient when working with newcomer children/youth and their families. Given this saliency, the concept of cultural competence is now examined more formally. This chapter begins with a brief overview of the historical roots of the concept and the major paradigm shift it reflected. Core components of cultural competence are then outlined, as well as additional evolving perspectives that further enrich the framework. Current critiques of the concept are also noted. Finally, certain key elements of cultural competence, which are particularly important in work with newcomer youth and their families, are highlighted.

Historical Roots of the Culturally Competent Framework

As individuals who have professionally and personally been invested in issues of culture and diversity for many decades, the authors are greatly encouraged by the recent exponential growth of literature and research during the past 20 years on the relevance of culture in social work and related helping professions. Although a detailed examination of the historical evolution of this focus and the current emphasis on cultural competence is beyond the scope of this book, a brief overview is merited.

Spencer, Lewis, and Gutierrez (2000) offer a particularly helpful historical analysis of the development of the multicultural perspective, beginning with a summary of this major paradigm shift: "This shift has moved from a view that encourages practice that is culture-free and universal to one that seriously considers the role that gender, culture, sexual orientation, race and other social identities play in the experiences, problems, and solutions of the communities with which we work" (p. 131). Spencer, Lewis, and Gutierrez then outline five "waves" of development in this process. Describing pre-1965 as a period reflecting ethnocentrism and a naïve belief in so-called color-blind practice/research, they identify Wave 1 (1965-1974) as the period during which a focus on race and ethnicity first emerged. During Wave 2 (1975–1984), gender became an additional point of interest, as was an increased focus on social justice issues. During Wave 3 (1985–1995), sexual orientation joined the cultural roster, and there was also greater recognition of multiple social group memberships. Finally, Wave 4 (1995–?) included physical/mental ability and class in the "multicultural perspective," as well as the concept of "intersectionality."

This chronological framework clearly reflects that today the term *culture* is used in the broadest of senses, and that practitioners seek cultural competence in working not only with those who may be racially or ethnically different from themselves but also across differences of gender, sexual orientation, class, ability, and more. Nonetheless, given our focus, this chapter will primarily discuss cultural competence as it relates to race, ethnicity, and national origin, beginning by highlighting a few seminal publications. Obviously, countless practitioners and many authors have contributed to the gradual evolution of the cultural competence framework—far too many to comprehensively acknowledge. Those highlighted here are selected not only as representative but also as reflecting certain landmarks in the development of the literature and in the paradigm shift.

Culture began to emerge as a focus of discussion in social work/mental health literature in the 1950s. However, up until the mid 1960s this discussion reflected primarily a cultural deficit model (Spencer, Lewis, & Gutierrez, 2000; Tsang & George, 1998), in which individuals who varied from the mainstream norms were seen as deprived or deviant. By the late sixties, paralleling the Civil Rights movement, a *minority perspective* was emerging and the focus shifted from individual "deficiencies" to the impact of societal oppression on minorities (Chau, 1991). Although clearer recognition of the results of racism and discrimination was an essential step, the literature generally represented minorities as powerless, passive victims.

A somewhat broader focus on culture was introduced in the Council of Social Work Education's 1978 publication, *The Dual Perspective: Inclusion of Ethnic Minority Content in the Social Work Curriculum.* Author Dolores Norton (1978) introduced the concept of *dual perspective*, defined as "the conscious and systematic process of perceiving, understanding, and comparing simultaneously the values, attitudes and behavior of the larger societal system with those of the client's immediate family and community system" (p. 3). This concept was seen as particularly important in work with minorities, whom she recognized as existing/operating not only in their own cultural world but also in the mainstream dominant culture. Norton highlighted the considerable incongruence often experienced, and the resulting stress involved. She and her contributing authors further challenged social work educators to teach social work students to incorporate this dual perspective in their work. The dual perspective concept was further elaborated by Diana de Anda (1984) in her discussion of *bicultural socialization*. She more clearly articulated this process, identifying significant variables and a range of outcomes.

Devore and Schlesinger's 1981 book, *Ethnic-Sensitive Social Work Practice*, represented a major milestone in the social work literature. As they note in the preface of their fifth edition (Devore & Schlesinger, 1999), they sought to "integrate understanding of the impact of ethnicity, social class, and minority status with the principles and strategies of social work" (p. xv). They called for attention to ethnicity in all aspects of practice, stressed that minorities must be seen in total context (historical, political, and economic context), and specifically urged practitioners to recognize the strengths of minority groups and cultures. Similarly, Green (1982) called for awareness and acceptance of cultural differences and recognition of cultural resources.

Ethnicity and Family Therapy, by McGoldrick, Pearce, and Giordano (1982), brought another major contribution, as it sought to integrate the growing focus on culture into the field of family therapy and family-centered practice. It also reflected a significant step in expanding what had primarily been a focus on African Americans to a wider discussion of multiple racial/ethnic groups. It is interesting to note that McGoldrick (as quoted in Markowitz, 1994) now describes some of the book as "a little naïve," recognizing that "we didn't include any discussion of power or the politics of race" (p. 23).

In *Understanding Race, Ethnicity, and Power* (1989), Elaine Pinderhughes addressed this gap by explicitly discussing issues of *power*, and how power differentials may impact both practitioner and clients, and their interactions. She also added to the existing literature by focusing on the need for professionals to develop cultural sensitivity, by underscoring the intersection of ethnicity and class and by stressing the role of race.

Finally, Peggy McIntosh's 1989 brief but powerful article, "White Privilege: Unpacking the Invisible Knapsack," helped many whites to examine themselves and their lives in new ways. For many readers, it sparked not only greater racial self-awareness but also an increased understanding of racism in U.S. society and in the lives of people of color.

Collectively, then, these authors, along with many others, helped expand the prevailing paradigm from one that had been ethnocentric and monocultural to one that began to recognize multiple and intersecting cultures. They also helped the move from a rather "decontextualized" approach to one with increasing recognition of social contexts, particularly of oppression. Thus, the stage was well set for the next major shift: the emergence of the concept of cultural competence.

Emergence of the Culturally Competent Framework

Although each of the various authors just discussed made tremendous contributions to the evolution of the current emphasis on culture in the social work field, Terry Cross, executive director of the National Indian Child Welfare Association, is often referred to as the "father of the cultural competence movement" (Lum, 2003, p. xvii). In their groundbreaking monograph *Toward a Culturally Competent System of Care*, Cross, Bazron, Dennis, and Issacs (1989) offered what is probably the first formal definition of *cultural competence:*

> The cultural competence model . . . is defined as a set of congruent behaviors, attitudes, and policies that come together in a system, agency, or amongst professionals and enables that system, agency, or those professionals to work effectively in cross-cultural situations. . . . A culturally competent system of care acknowledges and incorporates—at all levels—the importance of culture, the assessment of cross-cultural relations, vigilance towards the dynamics that result from cultural differences, the expansion of cultural knowledge, and the adaptation of services to meet culturally-unique needs. (pp. iv–v)

The monograph (Cross et al., 1989, p. v) stressed that becoming culturally competent is a developmental process and, whether pursued by the individual practitioner or the institution/agency, involves five essential elements:

1. Valuing of diversity
2. The capacity for cultural self-assessment
3. Consciousness of the dynamics inherent when cultures interact
4. The institutionalization of cultural knowledge
5. The development of adaptations to diversity

An important aspect of Cross and colleagues' (1989) seminal work is that they discussed cultural competence not only for the individual practitioner but for organizations. They argued that in order for there to be movement toward institutional cultural competency, there must be a commitment and change at every level of the organization. They outlined a continuum of cultural competence within an organization: cultural destructiveness, cultural incapacity, cultural blindness, culturally open, culturally competent, and culturally proficient. The importance of change at this level is reflected in Sue's (2001) pithy pronouncement: "It does little good to train culturally competent helping professionals when the very organizations that employ them are monocultural and discourage or even punish psychologists for using their culturally competent knowledge and skills" (p. 803).

Cross and colleagues' (1989) basic framework has since been elaborated on by multiple authors (Fong & Furuto, 2001; Lecca, Quervalu, Nunes, & Gonzales, 1998; Lum, 2003; Sue, 2001; Sue, Arredondo, & McDavis, 1992; Sue & Sue, 1999, 2003), with each adding new and/or more specific detail. Today, most discussions of cultural competence identify competencies in three key domains: awareness of beliefs and values, acquisition of knowledge, and development of skills. Box 7.1 presents a brief summary "composite list" of core competencies in each of these domains (drawing on the authors' experience, as well as many of the authors noted above).

Elaborations of the Culturally Competent Framework

This general cultural competence framework is widely accepted today. Indeed, specific reference to cultural competence is now included in most human services and health and mental health professional and institutional standards (the 1999 National Association of Social Work Code of Ethics, the 2001 NASW Standards for Cultural Competence in Social Work Practice, the Council on Social Work Education 2002 Educational Policy and Accreditation Standards, the 2000 Standards on Culturally and Linguistically Appropriate Health Care, Office of Minority Health, U.S. Department of Health and Human Services). Not surprisingly, however, this framework also continues to be expanded and enriched, with selected additions or newly emphasized dimensions. These are briefly highlighted here.

BOX 7.1 • *Cultural Competence Framework*

Awareness of One's Assumptions, Values, Beliefs, and Biases
- Awareness of own cultural background and its influence on attitudes, values, worldview
- Awareness of own ignorance, stereotypes, biases, prejudices, and discrimination
- Comfort with and respect for "differences"
- Valuing of diversity and multiculturalism
- Commitment to ongoing introspection and learning

Acquisition of Knowledge
- General knowledge about role of culture in values, relationships, communication style, family structure, communities, and access and utilization of services
- Knowledge of history of oppressed groups and contemporary sociopolitical realities
- Recognition of strengths, resilience, and cultural assets of diverse populations
- Culture-specific knowledge related to client, consumer, community being served, and with attention to the diversity within all cultural groups
- Commitment to ongoing active learning regarding specific cultures, with an understanding of where and how to access "key informants"

Development of Skills
- Ability to relate to those who are culturally different, with flexible use of self and expanded verbal/nonverbal responses
- Active search for clients'/consumers' definition of problem or need, their understanding of its origin, meaning, relative importance, desired outcomes, and possible solutions and resources
- Recognition of limitations or "mismatches" of helping style with client/consumers, and ability to modify approach, redesign services, utilize bicultural/bilingual staff, and/or refer to other professional
- Ability to access assets and resources within culture (beliefs, values, and traditions) and community (elders, informal leaders, traditional healers, and religious leaders)
- Ability and commitment to challenge institutional barriers and policies that impede or deny clients'/groups' access to culturally appropriate services

Exposure, Interaction, and Experiential Learning

Multiple authors (Campinha-Bacote, 1991; Weaver, 2003) have argued that in addition to values, knowledge, and skill, a fourth domain is essential for cultural competence—the need for "exposure" and interaction with those who are culturally different. Becoming aware of one's own cultural values and lens, valuing difference, and acquiring culture-specific knowledge and intervention skills are all necessary, but these authors argue that such learning cannot be accomplished and truly integrated without actual sustained exposure (outside the classroom) and interaction with those who are culturally different. Even in the early 1980s, Lappin (1983) recognized this need: "To paraphrase Salvador Minuchin, one must 'taste the soup' to know it. Very literally, a culturally aware therapist must do just that. Go out into the community; meet people; go to the stores; eat what the people eat; make home visits" (p. 134). Sue (2001, p. 805) stresses that practitioners must seek a "balanced picture" of any new culture, which requires spending significant time interacting with "healthy and strong" people of the culture. Toward this end, some educators (Boyle, Nackerud, & Kilpatrick, 1999; Gallegos, Bondavalli, & Chandler, 2000; Jones & Lane, 2000) are advocating cultural immersion via international social work placements and/or study trips.

Social Justice Issues and Personal Responsibility

Another emerging dimension of cultural competence that is receiving greater recognition is the inherent responsibility for attention to social justice issues. Spencer, Lewis, and Gutierrez (2000) specifically draw attention to issues of "pluralism and/or assimilation, allocation of resources and power" (p. 138). Sue (2001) focuses more on personal responsibility for action: "Personal cultural competence requires accepting responsibility for any action or inaction that may directly or indirectly perpetuate injustice. . . . [It] means one can no longer escape personal responsibility for change" (pp. 803–804). Van Soest (2003) states that cultural competence "includes as a requirement a commitment to promote social justice. . . . Ultimately, the goal of culturally competent practice is to transform oppressive and unjust systems into nonoppressive and just alternatives" (p. 347). This dimension of cultural competence is perhaps most strikingly exemplified by the Just Therapy program at the Family Centre in Greater Wellington, New Zealand, where staff simultaneously do both therapy and community development work (Dulwich Centre, 1990). Markowitz (1994) writes: "No one pushes the outside of the multicultural envelop farther than the Just Therapy Team. . . . According to their approach, therapy and community building are almost synonymous. The Family Centre staff has helped clients create tenants' unions and unemployed workers' unions; they have been at the forefront of policy battles to get better housing and welfare laws in place" (p. 24).

Ethical Issues in Culturally Competent Practice

Both practitioners and educators alike are increasingly cognizant of the additional and unique ethical dilemmas that can arise when working cross-culturally. Pedersen (1995) states, "Ethical principles generated in one cultural context cannot be applied to other substantially different cultural contexts without modifications" (p. 34). Thus, everything from institutional policies, agency procedures, "standard" assessment protocols, group models, community capacity development, and specific interventions to research designs may at some point raise ethical issues. Goldberg (2000) offers a powerful example of conflicting principles in multicultural social work, describing a case in which cultural norms allowed a father to fondle a young daughter's genitalia, yet predictably local child protective services became involved and the social worker grappled with the "best interests of the child." Gray (1998), utilizing a complex Cambodian family case example, raises the question of whether clients are required to achieve certain levels of acculturation in order to get services, and whether this is ethical. Gray observes: "Many Eurocentric values are congruent with the values of the agency, such as: individualistic focus, independence, and success/performance/achievement orientation. The ethical dilemma then becomes: honoring culturally specific family structures and life orientations versus following agency program and policies" (p. 140).

Pedersen (1995) focuses his critique on the psychology profession itself (and presumably other closely related ones): "By neglecting cultural variables in the ethical guidelines, by defining culture narrowly to exclude social/political/economic factors, and by marginalizing the importance of culture in the teaching of psychology, the profession of counseling psychology has failed in its ethical obligation" (p. 48). A quick review of recent ethics texts (Congress, 1999; Manning, 2003; Parsons, 2001; Reamer, 1999) suggests that there is some increasing recognition of the additional ethical issues that may be raised in multicultural practice, and at least a beginning effort to better prepare practitioners.

Measurement Instruments of Cultural Competence

Numerous measurement instruments have been developed to ascertain the degree of cultural competence of both the individual practitioner and agencies/institutions (Boyle & Springer, 2001; Jackson & Holvino, 1988; Leung & Cheung, 2001; Lum, 2003; Ramsey, 1994; Switzer, Scholle, Johnson, & Kelleher, 1998). Although these are certainly helpful tools, encouraging individuals and institutions to more formally assess their progress in the development of cultural competence, some of the above authors, as well as others (Ridley, Baker, & Hill, 2001; Suzuki, McRae, & Short, 2001), raise cautionary questions regarding validity and reliability.

Multiculturally and Culturally Competent Research

There has been increasing attention to the challenges and ethical issues involved in research of "minority" or ethnic-specific groups over the past 30 years, as well as publicity about some of the worst abuses by researchers (e.g., Tuskegee experiment and the Colville Indian Reservation Study) (Sue & Sue, 2003). Most contemporary articles and books on cultural competence stress the need for more multicultural research, and some (Skaff, Chesla, Mycue, & Fisher, 2002; Sue, 1998) offer specific cautions regarding design, access, training of staff, translation of instruments, data collection, and interpretation.

There is also growing recognition of the particular advantages of qualitative research or "inductive social research" (Lum, 2003) and community-based or participatory action research models, particularly when working with culturally diverse groups (De La Rosa, Segal, & Lopez, 1999; Lee & Ramirez, 2000; Spencer, Lewis, & Gutierrez, 2000). Also emerging is an increasingly strong call for more systematic research on the effectiveness of cross-cultural practice and the cultural competence model itself (Lum, 2003; Ridley, Baker, & Hill, 2001; Sue, 2001; Sue, 1998; Tsang & George, 1998).

Critiques of the Culturally Competent Framework

Despite the widespread acceptance and continued elaboration of the cultural competence framework, there are nonetheless significant critiques of the model that are important to acknowledge. Suzuki, McRae, and Short (2001) observe that although the definition of cultural competence is comprehensive, its operationalization is much less so, and indeed suggest that "cultural competence may look different for each individual clinician" (p. 845). They do note, however, that the framework offers the potential to "think outside the box of racial groupings" (p. 848). Ridley, Baker, and Hill (2001) raise the more basic question of what is cultural competence, and suggest a solid definition is still lacking. They also are concerned that the prevailing model of cultural competence appears to be only "descriptive," not "prescriptive," leaving practitioners unclear on how to actually operationalize cultural competence. Further, they express reservations that the predominant model seemingly focuses almost exclusively on a race-based group perspective, rather than a more multidimensional perspective that recognizes intersectionality.

Tsang and George (1998) posit that most models of cross-cultural practice have a "cultural literacy" approach that assumes the practitioner is the "expert" and that utilizes culture-specific techniques. However, they assert that such an approach can lead to dangerous stereotyping and overgeneralization. They argue that effective cross-cultural practitioners must utilize an "experiential-phenomenological model," presenting themselves as curious learners and seeing each client as a unique individual.

Dean (2001) raises a much more profound critique of cross-cultural competence, labeling it a "myth." Instead, she proposes a model in which the goal is to be aware of one's lack of competence. Drawing on post-modernism, Dean suggests that practitioners need to operate from a position of "not-knowing" and that the client is to be seen as the expert while the clinician is seeking knowledge and understanding: "I am proposing that we distrust the experience of 'competence' and replace it with a state of mind in which we are interested, and open but always tentative about what we understand" (p. 629).

Dean's (2000) emphasis on the practitioner's responsibility to learn, particularly from clients themselves, is certainly critical, as well as her call for clearer recognition of the sociopolitical contexts of oppression and social injustice. She also offers an excellent clinical vignette to illustrate these points. Some proponents of cultural competence might, however, suggest that seeing the client/consumer as expert, maintaining a sense of "cultural humility," being committed to active ongoing learning, and the acute awareness that the journey toward competence is never done have always been an integral part of the cultural competence framework.

Cultural Competence and Newcomer Populations

Having presented a broad summary overview of the cultural competence framework, the authors now turn more explicitly to its relevance and application to work with newcomer youth and their families. Certainly the core competencies outlined in the framework are essential in effectively working with this population. In addition, there are several specific concepts that the authors find particularly salient.

Cultural Encapsulation and Monocultural Tunnel Vision

Several authors (Pedersen, 1994; Pedersen, Draguns, Lonner, & Trimble, 1989; Wrenn, 1985) discuss the dangers of *cultural encapsulation*—when the individual counselor (and perhaps his or her profession) exists in a cocoon of stereotypes and is unable to see the realities of the world or the cultural variations among clients. Corey, Corey, and Callanan (2003) use the term *monocultural tunnel vision* to describe students who have "limited cultural experiences, and in many cases . . . unwittingly impose their values on unsuspecting clients, assuming that everyone share these values" (p. 112). Even though an increasing percentage of practitioners have worked with "traditional minorities," there are many who have yet to practice with newcomers. The risk of cultural encapsulation and monocultural tunnel vision thus remains.

Sociocultural Dissonance

Chau (1989) spoke of *sociocultural dissonance*, cautioning practitioners to be aware of the degree to which a client's cultural values and norms are consonant or dissonant with so-called mainstream values. He posits that the greater the degree of dissonance, the harder a client's adaptation process will be. A similar caution would be that the greater the dissonance, the bigger the challenge may be for the practitioner to establish trust, understand worldviews, and work effectively.

Even if practitioners have rich experience with newcomers from one part of the world, it is certainly possible that they may experience a sense of sociocultural dissonance with another group. One author of this book, having worked for many years with Southeast Asians, still recalls the initial sense of "dissonance" when she began working with populations from the Caribbean.

Cultural Romanticism and Cultural Blindness

The concepts of cultural romanticism and cultural blindness probably originated in the field of anthropology. However, they are now commonly invoked in discussions of multicultural practice (Campinha-Bacote, 1991; Gross, 2000, McGoldrick, 2003), with focus on the dangers of each. In the former, the practitioner is likely to explain all symptoms or unusual behaviors as "just culture," and thus may overlook serious family problems or mental health issues. Conversely, if the practitioner believes in or simply is "culturally blind," then he or she may well overpathologize a client's behavior. The risks of cultural romanticism or blindness may be especially high when one first starts working with newcomers and/or if they come from a culture that is radically different/dissonant from the "mainstream" U.S. culture.

Historical Trauma and Healthy Paranoia

Maria Yellow Horse Brave Heart (2001), writing about Native Americans, describes *historical trauma* response as "a constellation of features associated with massive cumulative group trauma across generations and within the current lifespan" (p. 166). Pinderhughes (1990) writes similarly about the traumatic legacy of slavery. The concept of historical trauma is equally relevant to some groups of newcomers—for instance, Cambodians and Salvadorans—who experienced war, oppression, and even "cultural genocide" for many years. Thus, although they may now be "safe" in the United States, the legacies of past trauma are felt not only by individuals but also collectively within the community. Indeed, they may also be a strong part of the "family story" and passed down to children born in the United States.

Clearly related to the concept of historical trauma is that of *healthy paranoia*. Groups who have historically been oppressed, and whose members continue to experience discrimination, are likely to be quite wary of authorities and those in power. In the past this was all too frequently diagnosed as paranoia by clinicians; today, it is more readily recognized as an adaptive response. Indeed, for many newcomers, healthy paranoia helped them survive in their homelands and continues to be a predictable part of their survival strategy in the United States. Therefore, practitioners working with newcomer youth and their families need to be acutely aware of the historical legacies of past trauma and also be respectful of healthy paranoia.

Secondary Traumatization/Stress

The trauma that many newcomers have experienced in their homelands and during their escapes has already been underscored at multiple points in this book. The dramatic expansion of trauma theory and research over the past 30 years allows all practitioners working with newcomer youth and their families to be more aware of trauma, its aftermath, and its potential treatment. Perhaps equally important is the related concept of secondary or vicarious trauma/stress, which has become more widely recognized only during the past 10 years. This concept is particularly salient for practitioners working with newcomers who are refugees or asylum seekers, and consequently may hear heart-wrenching stories and descriptions of unbelievably inhuman acts.

Multiple authors (Catherall, 1995; Danieli, 1996; Kinzie, 1994, 2001; Munroe, Shay, Fisher, Makary, Rapperport, & Zimering, 1995; Yassen, 1995) caution helping professionals to be aware of their own responses on both the personal and professional levels. Many of the above authors also point out that preventing secondary traumatization involves not only individual self-care but also workplace supports. Practitioners who have long worked with traumatized newcomers may be skilled in recognizing signs of vicarious trauma (such as apathy, burnout, emotional numbness, or anger). However, for individuals and agencies just beginning to work with this population, there is an urgent need to understand and seek to prevent this common yet very troubling response.

Cultural Borderlands

The concept of *cultural borderlands* (Falicov, 1995), or "overlapping zones of differences and similarities within and between cultures" (Imber-Black, 1997, p. 609), is a more recent concept that underscores the complexity of the acculturation process. Acculturation is no longer seen as linear nor uniformly sought, developed, or "fixed" across all aspects of an individual's life. Instead, as Falicov (2003) writes, newcomers live in multiple social contexts and have dual visions—"ways of maintaining contact with familiar cultural practices while making new spaces manageable. . . . Behavior is readily, flexibly alternated according to the need at hand. The result is a sense of fit or partial belonging in more than one cultural and language context" (p. 285).

Recognition of cultural borderlands, and the intersectionality of such dimensions as gender, generation, class, race, ethnicity, geographic location, and so on is critical to practitioners working with newcomer youth and families. Indeed, explicitly introducing the concept of cultural borderlands may be useful in helping bridge the familial cultural and generational conflicts discussed in Chapter 4. The shifting realities of cultural borderlands also need to be recognized and respected when designing youth development programs.

Special Aspects of Culturally Competent Practice with Newcomers

Due to their particular backgrounds and life experiences, there can be some unique aspects and challenges in applying the cultural competence framework in work with newcomers. The authors thus conclude this chapter with just a few examples of ways in which culturally competent practice may look somewhat different when working with newcomer youth and their families.

Most obviously, working with newcomers requires practitioners to learn about widely disparate and perhaps hitherto "unknown" ethnic and national groups. Early research on cultural competence spoke primarily of learning about African Americans, Latino Americans, and Asian Americans, but practitioners today may be called on to learn about people from countries and cultures from around the world. Beliefs, worldviews, and life experiences of some of these newcomers may prove to be dramatically different from anything the U.S.-born practitioner has ever encountered, or indeed perhaps even imagined.

Further, information about the group may be limited and/or inaccessible. Thus, there can be significant additional challenges in all three key domains of cultural competence—beliefs, knowledge, and skills. For some practitioners, it is possible, at least initially, that the degree of difference with such newcomers may seem so great that their shared commonalities are hard to find.

Another example of the special aspects of culturally competent practice with newcomers relates to the concept of *empowerment*. Empowerment is often stressed in social work and in youth development activities. Historically, this term has suggested assertiveness and independence on the individual level, and the ability to organize, speak out, and advocate/confront at the community level. However, an empowered young Cambodian or Somali woman may not necessarily present as an outspoken, "independent" individual. Similarly, a Vietnamese or Sudanese community group may be quite effective and empowered but will rarely "confront" authorities or organize rallies. In other words, the attributes of empowerment, as well as the style and methods that operationalize empowerment, may be different within the cultures of certain newcomers.

Community collaboration and involvement is another long established emphasis in youth development and social work, and both may present special challenges with newcomer groups. Perhaps most obviously, when refugees (and certain immigrants) first arrive, they may be so geographically scattered and too few in number to be able to form any sense of community. Even once there is a "critical mass," sheer survival needs may be so overwhelming that there is no energy left to connect with those from the same region or country. Further, among some groups there are continuing political and/or ethnic factions that prevent the easy emergence of a "community." Thus, there may or may not be any identifiable, accessible, organized community with which to collaborate.

Conversely, there may be multiple organizations and touted leaders within a new-comer community. In that case, the challenge for the social worker or youth counselor is to identify those with which they can optimally collaborate. Quite often, human service agencies and professionals tend to gravitate toward those leaders who are most "syntonic" with their own personal, institutional, and cultural values. They therefore collaborate with individuals who are more acculturated and have greater English language fluency, and with organizations that value strategic planning, have clear program protocols, meet report deadlines, and the like. However, these individuals and groups may or may not be most representative of the community.

A similar phenomenon can arise when an agency seeks to hire bicultural/bilingual staff to work with a particular newcomer population. Frequently, the selection committee may be drawn to a younger individual from this group who has been primarily educated in the United States, speaks fluent English, and is readily comfortable in the agency/professional culture. Again, such an individual may or may not be well positioned to reach out and serve his or her own community. Indeed, the very attributes that make him or her attractive to the agency may actually lessen the agency's credibility and effectiveness within the broader community.

At the same time, it is essential that agencies and practitioners recognize that newcomer communities are not static. Particularly within those groups, such as the Vietnamese and Cambodians, that have now been in the United States for several decades, there has been significant acculturation among many of the adults, and a whole new generation has grown up in the United States. Thus, the community leaders/groups and perhaps the bicultural staff that were most credible and effective in the past may no longer be the only important "gatekeepers"; indeed, some may no longer be key players at all.

Finally, there is always, at some point and in some way, the issue of *boundaries* in culturally competent practice with newcomer populations. Social workers' professional training has historically emphasized the need for clearly defined boundaries between the worker and his or her client or consumer, and the potential dangers of ineffective, unprofessional, or even unethical practice if these boundaries become blurred or are crossed.

The need for professional boundaries, to protect against exploitation of or "dual relationships" with clients, is indisputable. However, the increasing focus on multicultural populations, as well as the recently renewed emphasis on home-based practice, has already suggested that a degree of flexibility may be needed in defining these boundaries. Some newcomers may challenge social workers to rethink professional boundaries even further.

If, for instance, the newcomer family has come from a culture where there are no formally organized social services, they are likely to have relied on extended family, elders, religious leaders, and/or natural healers for help. The qualities sought in such "helpers" were not formal credentials but good individual character and a respected reputation in the community, and probably there was little "divide" between their personal and helping/advisory roles. Transferring this same paradigm to the United States, some newcomers may well wish to know about the "character" of their social worker or youth counselor and may indeed ask quite personal questions.

If trust develops and a positive relationship forms, the family may assume that the worker can then help them with most any kind of problem at any time. They may also naturally invite the worker to eat with them and join in family and even community celebrations. Most professionals who work with newcomers can recall multiple times when their preexisting assumptions regarding "correct" professional boundaries have been challenged. There are no clear cut, ready-made answers here, and each worker must grapple with how to be both professional and culturally competent.

Conclusion

The use of a cultural competence construct to guide interventions is widespread, although it is only in recent times that it has been specifically used with newcomer populations within the United States. This construct is dynamic and its ultimate success in informing practice rests with its ability to incorporate changes in population groups and take into consideration their circumstances within this country.

The cultural competence framework continues to be expanded and enhanced. There may be calls for clearer guidelines for its operationalization and a demand for research that can measure its effectiveness, but few question the need for such a framework. As practitioners seek to better serve this country's increasingly diverse population, the awareness of one's own values/beliefs, the acquisition of cultural knowledge, and the development of culturally appropriate skills is essential. However, it also worth noting that the development of cultural competence is a life-long journey; practitioners may become more aware, knowledgeable, and skilled along the way, but there is always more to learn.

It is encouraging to see that vignettes of immigrant and refugee clients/consumers are increasingly included in publications related to cultural competence. There is also a growing body of literature (articles, texts, and journals) specifically focused on practice with this population, and most appear to reflect a cultural competence perspective. Nonetheless, to date, this framework has not been widely discussed as it applies specifically to newcomer youth and their families. It is hoped that this brief overview of the cultural competence framework, and the many examples offered throughout this book, underscore the value of this perspective when working with refugee and immigrant youth. This perspective, when combined with the youth development paradigm that follows in the next chapter, can prove quite powerful and useful in social work practice with newcomer youth.

Part III

Youth Development Paradigm
Elements and Practice

One of the most significant findings is that recent developments in the sphere of international migration, including both voluntary and forced movements, do not provide evidence of a "crisis" and that holds well for realistic proection in the near future.

—Zolberg, 2001, p. 1

8

Youth Development Paradigm

In many quarters, educators, preventionists, clinicians, and policymakers are decrying the drawbacks of an "at-risk" label for talking about and categorizing youth. However, one source of resistance to dropping the label and all the other negative terminology associated with it is that a useful and widely accepted vocabulary of strengths has not been developed to take its place.

—Wolin & Wolin, 1998, p. 64

Introduction

This chapter seeks to accomplish an ambitious goal—to capture the essence of a youth development paradigm and discuss the challenges in a relatively short amount of space and draw implications for social work. This field of youth development is expanding dramatically to broaden its scope and incorporate the latest research findings from a host of disciplines and fields. Thus, the authors' task is to provide the reader with an awareness of definitions, core elements, multifaceted domains, strategies, and factors influencing how youth development gets operationalized in service to youth. Each section of this chapter utilizes numerous scholarly and newspaper citations as a means of further directing the reader to other sources of interests.

The importance of youth to a country's future is well accepted in the United States. The measure of their worth is incalculable in social, economic, and political terms. It seems that very few people would argue against the belief that youth are the future of any country, not just the United States. However, embracing this perspective has historically not translated into policies and resources that effectively prepare youth for the important role of shaping and leading a country in the twenty-first century (Tienda & Wilson, 2002). In many ways *Youth are our future* has taken on the same status as *It takes a village to raise a child*. At best, both statements, although accurate, can be considered clichés empty of commitments. Creating a caring culture, many would argue, is the first critical step in attaching meaning to these statements (Rauner, 2000). Social workers—because of their values, history, and competencies—are in excellent positions not only to make important contributions to this social paradigm but also to help shape it in particular reference for use with newcomer youth and their communities.

A set of values must serve as a foundation for guiding the development of programs and services to ensure that youth achieve health (psychologically, physically, and spiritually), experience motivation, and acquire the necessary competencies to successfully transition from youth to adulthood within an ever changing and highly diverse society. With this set of values comes a vocabulary that helps translate a vision into everyday reality, and a commitment to ensure that policies are developed and resources are committed.

Paradigms have often been referred to as "maps of the mind" that influence people's perceptions of the world around them and guide their actions and reactions (Covey, 1989). Paradigms also implicitly and explicitly embrace a set of values. The quest for a paradigm that best conceptually bridges values and programs is no small feat, since it must serve the needs of scholarly, practice, and consumer constituencies. A youth development paradigm is specifically geared to accomplishing the important goal of bringing youth, practitioners, and social work scholars together. This paradigm has a language and terms that lend themselves for communicating across constituencies, facilitating the establishment of broad-based coalitions for change.

The shift from a deficit to a strength-based approach focused on positive developments is much needed in the field of social work practice, although the field has a distinguished history in this area (Gilliam & Scott, 1998). However, the need for this paradigm shift is not restricted to social work and the helping professions (Northwest Regional Educational Laboratory, 1999): "Building on the strengths of city kids, rather than tallying up their weaknesses, takes a fundamental shift in thinking about urban education. But it's a shift that makes sense to researchers, classroom teachers, and administrators who already know plenty about the challenges facing the children of America's cities" (p. 1). One of the paradigm's central features is that it can be used in all social arenas youth function within, and can also be adapted to the institutions entrusted to serve them.

Zeldin, Kimball, and Price (1995) have concluded, on the basis of their extensive review of the literature, that opportunities and social supports benefit youth irrespective of who provides them or where they exist: "Legitimate opportunities and supports can exist in each of the primary settings where the young person lives—homes, schools, peer groups—and can have a positive impact on development. Moreover, beneficial supports and opportunities exist in additional settings—extended families, social networks, youth organizations and religious organizations" (p. 37). Not all of these settings can or will provide necessary opportunities and supports. This increases the importance of community-based programs that address existing gaps in the lives of youth, newcomer and otherwise, and necessitates the development of collaborative partnerships between programs whenever possible. Resources are always limited and no one setting can possibly be expected to be sufficiently comprehensive to meet all the needs of youth across all ages.

Collaborative partnerships, although time consuming and arduous to establish, are the most prudent strategy for community-based organizations interested in youth. The field of youth development has embraced the virtues of collaborative partnerships as a key component of any intervention strategy. These partnerships can take on a variety of forms and goals from fiscal collaboration between organizations to actual programming.

Definition of Youth Development

Arriving at a comprehensive and consensus definition of *youth development* is not possible at this time. This is not necessarily something that should raise an alarm of concern, however. The dynamic nature of youth development brings with it inherent tensions at deriving a definition that has sufficient broad appeal to a wide audience since no paradigm enjoys a universal definition and acceptance. There are too many factors at work to make this goal achievable in the early part of the twenty-first century. This does not mean that the authors of this book will not provide the reader with their definition. Admittedly, however, any definition is at best a work in progress.

First, it is impossible to fully grasp a definition of a youth development paradigm without examining what society means when it uses the label of *youth* to describe an age group and the expectations it has for the group (Aitken, 2001; Scheer, 1999). Shaklee (2000) notes that this country's definitions of *childhood* and *adolescence* have changed greatly over the past 200 years to take into account major demographic, political, economic, and technological changes. The importance of people achieving a high standard of living is directly tied to achievement of educational credentials beyond a high school diploma and development of work habits that further this goal. As a result, youth have benefited from society viewing their transition to adulthood from a more holistic perspective, but one still greatly influenced by earnings potential.

Delgado (2000a) notes that there is a qualified difference in viewing youth as "adults-in-waiting" and taking into account their immediate needs. Providers must plan for the future without losing sight of the present; one without the other does a disservice to youth. Fortunately, such a goal is within the reach of any youth-focused activity if it is carefully planned.

The field of youth development has witnessed unprecedented growth in programming, training, and scholarship over the past decade (Witt, 2002). Not surprisingly, its definition, too, has evolved and taken on various manifestations. Terms such as *youth development, positive youth development*, and *community youth development* reflect how this paradigm has expanded its scope of influence to reach broader audiences (Baines & Selta, 1999; Guest, 1995; Hahn & Raley, 1999; Halper, Cusack, Raley, O'Brien, & Wills, 1995; Hughes, 2000; Hughes & Nichols, 1995; Lawrence, 1998). This evolution is indicative of a paradigm that is not only alive and well but also thriving and vibrant.

It is important to pause, however, and highlight Gould's (1994) very provocative observation concerning the so-called scientific method: "I would reject any claim that personal preference . . . does not play a key role in science. . . . [O]ur ways of learning about the world are strongly influenced by the social preconceptions and biased modes of thinking that each scientist must apply to any problem. The stereotype of a fully rational and objective 'scientific method' . . . is self-serving mythology" (p. 14). Youth development scholars advocate for the development of an epistemology for the field that continuously defines this paradigm and its essential components with particular attention being paid to precursors, contextual issues, and outcomes (Positive Youth Development Working Group, 2002).

Youth development is defined using Delgado's (2002a) operational conceptualization, which is informed based on extensive research in "traditional" youth development programs and "new frontier," or nontraditional, youth development programs:

> Youth development views youth both as partners and central figures in interventions. These interventions systematically seek to identify and utilize youth capacities and meet youth's needs. They actively seek to involve youth as decision makers and tap their creativity, energy, and drive; and they also acknowledge that youth are not superhuman— that they therefore have needs that require a marshaling of resources targeted at youth and at changing environmental circumstances (family and community). Positively changing environments that are toxic and antithetical to youth capacity enhancement requires the use of a wide range of strategies—tailored to fit local circumstances—ranging from advocacy to consciousness raising and political mobilization. (p. 48)

Youth development has ambitious goals that go far beyond a narrow definition of youth needs and competencies.

Clearly, "local circumstances" refers to the ecological place refugee and immigrant youth find themselves within and the need to tailor youth development to take these circumstances into account in the development of programming activities. Benard (1999), a prominent pioneer in the research of resiliency, advocates for a broader identification and assessment of environmental factors' influence on youth:

> Resilience research creates a new paradigm for both researcher and clinicians alike. It situates risk in the broader social context of racism, war, and poverty—not in individuals, families and communities—and asks how is it that youth successfully develop in the face of such stressors. Resilience research provides a powerful rationale for moving our focus in the social and behavioral sciences from a concern with individual deficits and pathology to an examination of individual and community strengths. (p. 269)

When discussing newcomer youth, "local circumstances" can be any, all, or a combination of the following factors—length of time specific to a newcomer group; relative size/concentration, degree to which the group is "organized" and has its own recognized leadership, general levels of acculturation, legal status, degree of "welcome" by the community and society at large, and age composition of the newcomer community. These circumstances are just a few of a wide range that can play influential roles. Thus, a youth development paradigm must be sufficiently flexible to have viability with many different populations across the United States.

Newcomer youth's geographical location within this country, level of social support systems within their community, and level and extent of formal services specifically geared to their unique backgrounds and current situations, for example, all also contribute to what is referred to as local circumstances. In essence, "one size does not fit all" when applying a youth development paradigm to newcomer population groups. Efforts to generalize programming must be tempered with the need to respond to the uniqueness of the group. This goal of balancing overall versus specific youth needs has historically caused tension in youth-centered programs.

The ever-broadening reach of youth development in the early part of the twenty-first century is both a cause for celebration and alarm. As noted by Delgado (2000a), youth development, by being all things to all people, encompasses a wealth of constructs, social arenas, and interventions. This broadening base lends itself to multidisciplinary collaboration and the creation of a multitude of intervention strategies. However, by being so encompassing, this paradigm is everything and nothing at the same time. How does one effectively identify what is uniquely youth development and evaluate?

Regardless of the expansiveness of the paradigm, there is general agreement on what are the essential elements, or climate, for this paradigm to achieve its potential (Rahman, 1999):

> Youth development means the development for the youth and by the youth. For this purpose, young people are to be empowered. They are empowered when they feel that they have or can create choices in life, are aware of the implications of those choices, make an informed decision freely, take action based on that decision and accept responsibility for the consequences of that action. Empowering young people means creating and supporting the enabling conditions under which young people are empowered. (p. 4)

Empowerment of youth, as a result, necessitates a holistic or comprehensive perspective—one that requires a social, economic, and political foundation that is supportive of this goal.

The paradigm of youth development has been in existence in various forms since the early 1970s. However, it remained largely "undiscovered" until the early 1990s. Since that time, it has grown in popularity both within the practice and scholarly arenas. Like any paradigm preceding it, it has evolved to broaden its reach beyond just youth to include family and community. This evolution has brought with it a series of tensions on how best to define and operationalize youth development for practice and research. This development is not only to be expected but also considered "healthy" for those who advocate its adoption in the field.

The field of youth development, many would argue, has its roots in prevention programs during the 1980s and 1990s (Witt, 2002). Staff and policymaker dissatisfaction with a very limited focus of prevention programs—such as teen pregnancy, drug abuse, smoking, and violence, for example—led to the search for a field of practice and research that was less reactive and more holistic in how it viewed youth. Witt (2002), however, argues against an either-or proposition when viewing problem-specific prevention and youth development-focused programs. Quinn (1999) has conceptualized *youth development* at one end of a continuum and *social control and incarceration* at the opposite end. *Prevention* is the stage just before youth development.

The concept of *at risk* has been very much a part of the lexicon of youth-focused services and is a response to negative youth behaviors during the 1980s when crime, drugs, and unwanted adolescent pregnancies received increased national attention. "Because stopping or decreasing negative behaviors was deemed necessary by the public and politicians, agencies requesting funds promised that their programs would decrease unwanted behaviors and prevent youths from undertaking these behaviors in the first place. To label youth as 'at-risk' was politically useful, if not necessary, and helped agencies define their niche and purpose, and get funding" (Witt, 2002, p. 58). Indicators that were considered useful in defining success include impact on crime rates, adolescent pregnancies, and drug and alcohol consumption.

Society and the programs and services that target youth often utilize a vocabulary that is all too willing to focus on youth as a threat and an economic drain on society, shaping much of the debate on the "best" way of addressing youth. The National Assembly and the National Collaboration for Youth (2000) state: "When we talk about our youth, we too often use negative terms: what we would like them to stop doing. We want them to stop using drugs, stop drinking, stop dropping out of school, stop having sex, stop getting pregnant, stop being violent, and stop committing other delinquent acts. In short, we would like them to stop having problems—and stop being problems. When we focus only on youth problems, we may begin to think of youth only as problems" (p. 1).

Youth development scholars and practitioners do not consider youth as individuals waiting to have an accident or being "at risk." Youth represent individuals who have many assets and incredible potential for achieving good in society. Unfortunately, categorically funded programs took too narrow of a view of youth, effectively losing sight of the dynamic nature of their lives and the challenges they face on a daily basis. Youth are not perfect; neither are adults. However, adults invariably are more willing to emphasize youth needs, problems, and issues and to neglect the many virtues that they possess.

Historical Roots of Youth Development

Tracing the etiology of any paradigm is difficult under the best of circumstances and should always be considered an adventure. However, in the case of youth development it takes on an added challenge. Invariably the year of the emergence of a paradigm in the professional literature marks its "birth year." Much thought, discussion, and debate proceeds this wide acceptance: "The etiology of a paradigm can rarely be traced to the work of one individual, organization or a particular year. Paradigms, by their very nature, owe their creation to many people, practitioners as well as scholars. However, there is general agreement in the youth development field that the work of Werner and his colleagues stands out in its early influence on the movement" (Delgado, 2002a, p. 29). The work of Werner and associates dates from the late 1970s to the early 1990s (Werner, 1989, 1990; Werner & Smith, 1977, 1982, 1992). The actual use of the term, however, has been traced to 1971 when the National Technical Information Service issued a report entitled "Youth Development Program Models."

Youth Assets

The past decade has witnessed a tremendous increase in the research and literature on a variety of constructs that can be categorized under the term *youth assets*. Constructs such as strengths, hardiness, competence, coping mechanisms, ego resilience, ego strengths, protective factors, adaptation, social buffers, and resilience, for example, have all started from a basic premise that youth are much more than just problems or individuals in need (Tarter & Vanyukov, 1999). Scales and Leffert (1999) use the term *developmental assets* to capture a wide range of factors, such as positive relationships, opportunities, competencies, values, and self-perceptions, that youth need in order to succeed in U.S. society.

Society can either view youth as problems to be managed or resources to be developed (Roth, Brooks-Gunn, Murray, & Foster, 1998). Placing youth within a broader perspective that goes beyond needs, problems, and issues, and instead views them as having potentials, gifts, and competencies has caused a tremendous wave of excitement in fields focused on youth. This excitement has resulted in bold and innovative approaches toward involving youth in decision-making and leadership roles within organizations. Youth involvement in these meaningful roles is a trademark of youth development-inspired programs (Huber, Frommeyer, Weissenbach, & Sazama, 2003).

This shift in thinking is quite profound and yet arduous to accomplish in practice:

> The *at-risk* mindset can easily shape work with youth into a search for problems. Its hallmarks are diagnoses, labels, and "fix-it" interventions. Dwelling on the negative, it induces despair and burnout in staff, biases their understanding of the youth they serve, and promotes low expectations. For youth, the at-risk mindset also has negative consequences. Regarded as clients or victims rather than as resources in their own lives, youth can experience services guided by the at-risk mindset as uncaring, disrespectful, and even threatening. (Wolin & Wolin, 1999, p. 1)

Youth seeing themselves as assets rather than as victims, or victims in the making, requires that program staff be patient in waiting for this transformation to occur. Workers need to remember that youth are rarely told, and sincerely so, that they possess assets in addition to needs. Newcomer youth, for example, may come out of cultural backgrounds where they are viewed as "property" by their parents and must behave as such. Many youth have essentially spent their entire lives being cast into at-risk roles. Therefore, being told that they possess assets will not transform their way of thinking about themselves instantaneously simply because someone in a position of authority said so.

Youth possess assets that serve to help them and their community and that can be mobilized through a variety of actions that are influenced by the context in which they live. Youth can be viewed as possessing competencies that effectively help them negotiate their way through life's many challenges. This premise is a fundamental building block for any interventions utilizing youth development principles. However, as already noted in the case of youth who act as interpreters for their families and neighbors, the stressors associated with a helping role can be quite emotionally draining for them.

A youth awards ceremony honoring San Francisco students for helping others brings this very point to life. The second annual (2002) Youth Recognition Day honored six San Francisco students, three of whom were newcomers to this country:

> Among the honorees . . . [were] Helen Qi, a junior at Newcomer High School who recently immigrated from China and impressed her teachers with her extra effort on homework and assistance of other classmates. Victor Lim, a senior at Galileo High School, was honored for his involvement in a Chinese literacy education program, through which he learned three dialects, and for helping form his school's Recycling Club. Laura Melgarejo, a senior at International Studies Academy and a Mexican immigrant, was recognized for her work on behalf of immigrant youths and for helping educate immigrant families about college benefits (KQED, 2002, p. 2)

Newcomer youth helping others and communities can be found in any area of the country.

The recasting of a negative experience into positive lessons for life has been advocated by a number of scholars. Seligman (1991), the individual who coined the term *learned helplessness*, has since developed the concept of *learned optimism*, which can result in life-long positive actions. O'Leary (1998) also recognizes the need and importance of turning adversity into survival and thriving attitudes and behaviors. Wholey (1992) postulates that suffering and major hardships are part of everyone's life and the will to conquer and benefit from these experiences can turn victims into inspiring role models. These experiences mature the individuals, but also provide them with competencies and self-confidence that can be of immense aid to them in their immediate and future social circles.

Finally, McMillen (1999), a social worker, developed a series of theoretical pathways by which benefit can occur and positively influence adjustment and coping: (1) "Stress Inoculation, or 'What Doesn't Kill You Makes You Stronger'"; (2) "Health Enhancing Changes in Life Structure, or 'Heeding the Wake-up Call'"; (3) "Changed Views of Others: 'People Aren't So Bad After All' and 'A Kinder and Gentler People'" and (4) "Transformation through Interpretation: Finding Meaning." These pathways, or ways of looking at life, provide youth with a frame or perspective through which to categorize their experiences, thus aiding them in social navigation through difficult circumstances in their future.

Various professions and academic disciplines—such as social work, education, psychiatry, counseling, recreation, psychology, anthropology, and sociology, to name a select group—have played instrumental roles in bringing forth terms that are related to assets and have functional equivalents of each other. In so doing, the field of youth development has both benefited from this attention and inherited a set of challenges in the process. The emergence and acceptance of a resiliency construct is one example of how the field has benefited and been challenged at the same time.

A resiliency construct is arguably the most prevalent construct in the field of youth development: "Over the last four decades increasingly a new vocabulary was adopted by behavioral scientists interested in explaining more or less benign/malignant outcomes of the development process. . . . Arguably, the most provocative among these constructs is resilience. When a concept such as resilience captures the imagination of a large group of scholars we should perhaps be grateful" (Kaplan, 1999, pp. 17–18). Resiliency, it must be added, has also captured the attention and imagination of practitioners and policymakers, making the "currency" of this construct more powerful than any one group embracing it. In essence, resiliency has very strong intuitive appeal (Glantz & Sloboda, 1999).

In their summary of the literature on youth resiliency, Chaukin and Gonzalez (2000) identify five significant protective factors in three prominent social arenas (families, schools, and communities):

1. The importance of supportive relationships, especially those involving school personnel and other key adults
2. Individual characteristics such as self-esteem, motivation, and a willingness to accept responsibility
3. Family factors related to parental supervision, concern, and support
4. Community factors related to after-school programming
5. School factors such as prosocial skills training and academic success

Wolin and Wolin (1999), in turn, describe resilience as consisting of seven qualities that interact to strengthen each other:

1. Insight (willingness to ask tough questions and give honest answers)
2. Independence (pulling back from sources of emotional and physical troubles)
3. Relationships (initiating and maintaining meaningful relationships with others)
4. Initiative (not being afraid of taking charge of problems)
5. Creativity (use of imagination and expression of oneself in art forms)
6. Humor (finding the comic in a tragic situation)
7. Morality (informed conscience dictating behavior)

Although the construct of resiliency is widely accepted, it has its share of critics. The vast array of professions and academic disciplines embracing this construct can be judged as both good and bad. This embrace has made the process of researching youth assets both easier and harder. This attention has advanced knowledge and practice in incorporating youth assets, although each profession and discipline conceptualizes these assets slightly differently from each other, even when addressing the same construct, as in the case of resiliency. Kaplan (1999) identifies four primary reasons for variability in use of the construct of resiliency beyond profession and academic discipline:

1. The distinction between resiliency and outcome
2. Variation in outcomes
3. Variation in defining characteristics of resilience
4. Variability in outcomes and their attributed causes relying on terms such as *risk factors* that are also highly variable

Glantz and Sloboda (1999) argue that the concept of resilience is too heavily laden with subjectivity, rendering it as having very limited conceptual and empirical viability.

They advance a reconceptualization of resilience that goes beyond a temporal or cultural state, and focuses instead on specific identification of stressors: "It is important for research and theory on resilience to recognize that multiplicity of positive influences and of the ways in which people adopt to problems, and for the most part this is accepted by the field" (p. 119). Kumpfer (1999) points to the elusiveness of studying resilience, primarily because of the broadness of the construct. Johnson (1999) notes that resilience is not just one construct but a combination of constructs that are dynamic over a period of time. Resilience may well be present in a youth's life but invisible in any attempt to be identified and systematically studied, raising important questions about its possible use in programs.

Regardless of where one stands on this debate, there is no arguing for the importance of developing a better understanding of how youth faced with incredible odds against them, like many newcomer youth, still manage not only to persevere but thrive in this country. Whether the reader prefers the use of a particular construct other than resilience, the ultimate goal remains the same—namely, how to mitigate the consequences of a less than hospitable environment through social intervention and how to mobilize youth assets in service to themselves, their families, and their communities.

Vision and Goals of Youth Development

The authors' vision of youth development places youth in positions of not only making a successful transition to adulthood but in the process of doing so makes them valuable members of their community and society. This vision seeks to achieve goals that are immediate and futuristic at the same time and that need to be accomplished while making participation meaningful and fun—quite a challenge for any organization. The field of youth development has essentially focused its attention on ensuring that youth can make a successful transition to adulthood status. There is very little or no disagreement with this goal. However, what the field means by "successful adult" leaves much room for debate and interpretation.

Essentially, successfully functioning as an adult can be defined along narrow or broad parameters. Narrowly, it can mean being able to engage in a career and fulfill family roles. This definition, however, does not place adults within a broader social frame—namely, their civic role within their communities and society. The authors' vision and goal for youth development is one that prepares youth to assume important roles as adults. This means that youth are not only welcoming but also capable of assuming significant civic roles in helping their communities and society at the present time rather than waiting until they officially become adults.

To be successful in achieving their vision, youth development programs must be inclusive of all groups within this society. This will not be easy because many of the groups with which practitioners work and plan are not valued in this society and are consequently very often stigmatized. Nevertheless, the vision is that youth development programs will prepare youth to function well within a multicultural society, in addition to fulfill key economic and familiar roles. This translates into having a youth development paradigm being inclusive of youth from differing economic, ethnic and racial, sexual orientation, gender, and physical and cognitive abilities. Communities are never monolithic in structure and characteristics, nor is society. The dynamic nature of urban communities, more specifically, means that they are virtually always changing in composition, making demands on youth programs to do the same to maintain relevancy (Scheer, 1999).

A paradigm such as youth development must strive to articulate and address issues of social and economic justice in addition to better preparing youth to undertake careers. The authors stress careers rather than jobs because the former entails serious thought, consideration, and preparation (Delgado, in press). The latter, however, does not necessarily do so. The former assumes that after youth become adults, they can engage in employment activities that tap and enhance their potential for significant contributions. The latter places too much emphasis on wages and income and not enough on potential for growth and advancement.

The reader has undoubtedly come to the realization that a great deal is expected from a youth development paradigm, and this may be considered unfair of any paradigm, even one that has such lofty ambitions. However, to settle for anything less is to do a disservice to youth and to indirectly jeopardize their contributions to society and the world. The popularity of youth development makes it easier for scholars and practitioners to "push the envelope," so to speak, because policymakers and private foundations usually respond only to those advocates who are enthusiastic about their cause.

Efforts to integrate youth into decision-making roles is not restricted to the field of youth development, however. The field of literacy, for example, has made significant strides in embracing paradigms that explicitly or implicitly state the belief that the power and potential of literacy campaigns can be fully achieved only if youth play an active and meaningful role in shaping the contents, strategies, and tactics used in these interventions (Moje, 2002).

Youth Social Characteristics and Youth Development

One of the many appealing aspects of a youth development paradigm is its expansiveness in reaching out to all youth regardless of their social characteristics and circumstances (Onaga, Carolan, Maddalena, & Villarruel, 2003). All youth can benefit from this paradigm, from the most privileged to the most marginalized. However, the paradigm's potential is best maximized when it seeks to reach youth that are marginal in this society. These youth are marginal because of their race, ethnicity, sexual orientation, disabilities, income, and gender, for example (Lerner, Taylor, & Eye, 2002; Watkins & Iverson, 1998). They, in turn, face considerable social and economic challenges in having their voices heard and their dreams and aspirations realized in this society. Their opinions, as a result, are rarely solicited or taken seriously in the course of their participation in school and youth-centered programs.

The concept of *youth* within the paradigm of youth development is too broad to have great significance in guiding intervention strategies. The age of participants plays an important role in how all of the elements of youth development get conceptualized and carried out on a daily basis. The field of youth development, as a result, has made significant strides in identifying the key social characteristics of youth they are trying to reach and making necessary modifications in intervention strategies to take these factors into account.

Roehlkepartain (2001) makes a strong case for the importance of gender being a key factor in any form of youth development programming—in this case, advocating for a concerted effort at programming for boys. Although boys and men are in a privileged position in U.S. society, they still make up a disproportionate share of those individuals who are incarcerated, killed, and the victims of other types of violence; they are also more likely to abuse alcohol and other drugs, drop out of school, and have a series of chronic, debilitating conditions. All of these indices point to the importance of gender-specific programming for males.

Girls, on the other hand, are also in need of gender-specific programming (Denner & Griffin, 2003). These authors briefly review the literature on gender expectations and mentoring, and note that girls' expectations of a mentor generally focus on supportive relationships, allowing for trusted exchange; boys, in turn, may prefer mentors who are more experienced, or worldly, and can thus provide support and knowledge.

Finally, the authors realize the challenge of translating a vision into theory and then into practice. In addressing supports and opportunities for professional success of youth workers, Walker (2003) identifies the challenges academics face in influencing the youth development field, although there is a significant role that can be played by this group:

> In the interviews, youth workers voiced a general distrust of academic theory. Some expressed the belief that theories are often put forward to challenge or repudiate the wisdom of experience in unwarranted ways. Some felt that theory is only used by people who have never been in the trenches, making comments such as the following: "You learn more in 40 hours on the job that you do in one hour of training." "If you go strictly on book knowledge and what you read in textbooks, you will be lost in the world of young people." "You can read articles or books, but you really don't have a clue until you are there with the kids." (p. 378)

Nevertheless, this challenge must be acknowledged and actively addressed through establishment of collaborative partnerships between youth, practitioners, and academics. The field of youth development cannot broaden its legitimacy without this collaborative relationship based on mutual trust and understanding!

Core Elements

The complexity of successful transition from youth to adulthood is underscored by the interplay of various core elements. *Core elements* can be defined as essential characteristics that must be tapped in the development of any intervention using a youth development paradigm. No core element is all encompassing enough to dictate success for youth. The literature on youth development has identified numerous core elements.

Delgado (2002a) categorized them into six major primary types: (1) social, (2) emotional, (3) cognitive, (4) physical, (5) moral, and (6) spiritual. Youth development is not possible by relying on only one or two of these core elements. In fact, the authors would go so far as to argue that maximum potential can be achieved only when all six core elements are systematically addressed in an intervention. All six may not be of equal weight or strength, and this status may change over a developmental period.

Some youth may be particularly strong in some of these core elements and in need of further developing others. Strengths and areas for enhancement may also shift through different developmental stages in the life of youth. Consequently, youth development programs must endeavor to assess the competencies of youth in each of these core elements, tap their strengths, address those in need of enhancement, and be ever aware of changes brought about by developmental stages and environmental conditions. In essence, core elements should be thought of as dynamic.

Social Relationships

The role of social relationships in the lives of youth is well recognized in the professional literature and practice field. These social relationships need to span multiple age groups, from youth to adults, if youth are to be able to make a smooth transition to adulthood (Huebner, 2003). A multigenerational perspective on these relationship skills helps youth be better prepared to interact with age groups other than their own, but it brings with it a set of inherent challenges revolving around youth-adult relations. An inability to establish and maintain social relationships severely limits the abilities of youth to fulfill meaningful roles in this society at the moment and in the future.

Research has shown that preschool children who are able to establish positive peer relationships, compared to those who are unable to do so, are more likely to maintain these positive peer relationships in grade school (Ladd, 1990; Ladd & Price, 1987; Ladd, Price, & Hart, 1988; Mize & Abell, 1996). According to Damico and Damico (1993) youth from culturally and linguistically diverse backgrounds, native and newcomer, generally achieve higher levels of acculturation through such skills as language decoding, handling conversational discontinuities, and the ability to save face. Cartledge (1996) and Rivera and Rogers-Atkinson (1997), in turn, tie cultural influences to social behaviors and the importance of developing and implementing social skills training programs for both youth and parents.

The complexity of isolating a social relationship construct should not come as any great surprise to practitioners and scholars. Welsh (1998), for example, incorporates multiple core elements in the construction of social competence. The elements of emotion and cognition are stressed because of their particular importance. Possession of a wide range of social relationship skills to complement increased social awareness translates into socially competent youth. The importance of social competence in resilient youth has also been identified by a number of researchers and scholars (Benard, 1997, 1999).

Wolin and Wolin (1999) go on to point to the importance of a caring relationship between youth and adults in helping youth gain a sense of connection and confidence.

These qualities can then translate into increasing youth motivation to aspire for achievement. This desire, in turn, serves to attract the positive attention and support of adults. Youth who succeed in surmounting incalculable odds do so in large part through the power of positive relationships with adults. The role of mentoring has received considerable attention in the field of youth development because it is a vehicle through which multiple goals can be incorporated (Barron-McKeagney, Woody, & D'souza, 2000; Evans & Ave, 2000; Rhodes, 2000a, 2000b; Taylor & Bressler, 2000).

Laursen (2002), in reviewing the literature on strength-based practice with youth, notes the importance of social relationships in fostering youth competencies: "The strength-based perspective assumes that positive development is best supported by relationships in which youth feel that they are respected, that they have knowledge about what benefits them, and that they have strengths which enable them to make a difference in their own lives" (p. 10). The meanings derived through mutual relationships are a critical source for personal validation for youth in general, regardless of their nationality, with the concepts of meaning and validation being also closely linked to cultural and social definitions (Genero, 1995).

Most scholars would agree that peers are a vital source of this personal validation. Peers can be facilitating forces in helping youth to navigate their way through a world dominated by adults by providing advice, listening to concerns, helping to problem solve, and showing mutual respect and mutuality. However, the peer network can also serve as a significant barrier, alienating youth from their parents and society. It seems that the negative role peers play in the life of youth has received undue attention (Delgado, 2002). A balanced perspective on peer relations and influence is needed in order for practitioners to develop a better understanding of the role and extent of peer influences in the lives of youth.

Emotional

The construct of emotional development has received increased attention when applied to youth within a youth development paradigm (Eccles & Gootman, 2002). Emotional health signifies a youth's ability to "respond affirmatively and cope with positive and adverse situations, to reflect on one's emotions and surroundings, and to engage in leisure and fun" (Huebner, 2003, p. 347). Central to an emotional core element is youth having positive self-regard or self-esteem. This translates into youth possessing self-regulation skills, coping skills, and social navigational skills. These emotional-related competencies, in turn, play influential roles in better preparing youth for setbacks as well as the handling of success in life.

Like all the other core constructs addressed in this chapter, an emotional core element can be conceptualized in a variety of ways and can include a multitude of elements. Delgado (2002a) notes that this core element invariably is operationalized in the field of youth development as possibly consisting of any one or a combination of the following nine factors: (1) feeling empathetic, (2) displaying appropriate emotions, (3) controlling anger, (4) identifying and labeling feelings, (5) motivating oneself, (6) inspiring hope in oneself and others, (7) delaying gratification, (8) establishing and maintaining relationships, and (9) tolerating frustration. As the reader can see from these factors, an emotional core element can be quite encompassing and critical to the ultimate accomplishment of making a successful transition to adulthood.

The capabilities of youth in addressing periods of uncertainty and upheavals, such as the case of uprootment from one country to another, plays an influential role in helping them develop confidence in their ability to surmount arduous times. These positive experiences, in turn, serve as historical signposts that can be effectively used in helping them surmount future emotionally laden situations. It would be unreasonable, for example, for newcomer youth to uncover these "hidden talents" on their own. They need to engage in a journey of discovery focused on how they managed to cope and survive under adverse circumstances.

Cognitive

Cognition, or what some scholars refer to as *intellectual health*, captures a range of skills that go far beyond innate intellectual abilities. Huebner (2003) defines *intellectual competence* as "the ability to learn in school and in other settings; to gain the basic knowledge to graduate from high school; to use critical thinking, creative, problem-solving, and expressive skills; and to conduct independent study" (p. 348). The Center for Youth Development and Policy Research (1995) includes a number of items under the term *cognition*, such as academic knowledge, critical thinking, problem solving, expressive skills, ability to initiate independent study, and motivation to learn.

Scales and Leffert (1999) tie cognitive development to decision making—a set of competencies that help youth identify and define problems, search for viable alternative solutions, select solutions with the highest probability of success, and exhibit an ability to assess/evaluate the outcome of their decisions. Cognition, as a result, cannot be viewed from a narrow perspective. A broader viewpoint facilitates the development of goals and activities specifically targeting one of several subcomponents of cognition, allowing programs to target their resources accordingly.

Koss-Chiono and Vargas (1999) bring ethnic identification into a cognitive developmental process with social-environmental factors (culture being a key one) playing an increasingly significant role. This approach toward cognition effectively integrates an important aspect of newcomer youth life—namely, how they identify themselves vis-à-vis their cultural heritage. Having the cognitive ability to inquire into their cultural heritage, problem-solve sources for this information, and develop insights that highlight how their ethnic identity influences their perceptions of the world around them, all combine to make cognition a key social element. Chapter 4 is replete with numerous examples of how the process and success newcomer youth have in establishing positive identities is so critical in their lives. A positive embrace of an identity that incorporates their ethnic origins bodes well for their future success in this country; a rejection, however, has serious consequences.

Physical

The ever-changing physical makeup of youth brings with it a need for a paradigm to take these changes into consideration in how interventions are planned within a variety of settings (Perry, Kelder, & Komro, 1993). A developmental understanding of how physical development changes over the life span within a cultural context is instrumental in helping youth development programs better measure progress on achieving physical core goals for youth (Earls, 1993). The physically healthy development of youth, like its emotional counterpart, requires the field of youth development to better assess and enhance this core element (Huebner, 2003). Generally, the field has viewed physical health from two complementary perspectives: good health habits and good high-risk management skills (Eccles & Gootman, 2002).

Each of these perspectives emphasizes a set of behavioral goals that lead to youth achieving optimum health. Although each stresses certain goals, youth may or may not embrace some goals over others. However, each of these health-related spheres has a wide variety of professions charged in addressing them. Needless to say, it would be artificial to emphasize one over the other, or to totally disregard one in favor of the other. Both approaches are of critical importance in the life of youth.

The role of proper nutrition, exercise, and development of competencies to ward off sexual, drug, alcohol, and tobacco experimentation has been well established in the field of prevention over the past two decades (Evans, 1998; Frank, 1998; Grimmett, 1998). Risk taking, however, is considered to be a part of life of any youth. The consequences of risk-taking behaviors, however, differ considerably according to a youth's political status in this country, socioeconomic status, gender, and level of formal education (Klerman, 1993). This should not come as any great surprise to any practitioner. The youth perspective on how they define health and the priority they place on having "good" health is essential (Millstein, 1993). An adult's view of "health" invariably is not shared by youth!

Hellison, Cutforth, Kallusky, Martinek, Parker, and Stiehl (2000) have specifically tied youth development to physical activities, and the potential of these activities to help form positive relationships between adults and youth, as well as among youth. Ewing (1997) advocates for the use of sports as a mechanism for promoting social and moral development. Sports, both organized and unorganized, provide youth with ample opportunities to develop physically. They also provide opportunities for them to develop social skills and establish a set of "rules" governing their behaviors, such as fairness and sportsmanship. Thus, sports can serve a wide range of goals, depending on the programs.

The field of youth development has expanded the core element of health from an exclusive focus on the individual to encompass families and communities (Galambos & Ehrenberg, 1997). There is a greater recognition of how the health of youth is closely associated with the health of families; the health of families, in turn, is tied to the health of the broader community. The latter observation reflects the exposure to diseases and illnesses and the types of access to quality health care. Thus, from a programmatic perspective, to be effective in addressing youth health, needs must be viewed from an ecological viewpoint. Health promotion activities, for example, lend themselves to addressing youth, families, and community. Health promotion, however, must be keenly attuned to cultural beliefs of the groups being targeted.

Moral

The construct of morality is increasingly becoming a popular subject in this society and in professional helping and educational circles (Nucci, 2002). Pace (2003) notes that moral development is probably the longest explored core element within a youth development paradigm. Public outcry about the moral decline of society, and more specifically its youth, has led to an acknowledgment of the importance of this core element.

A consensus definition of *morality* does not exist and a search for one is beyond the scope of this book. For our purposes, morality can be defined as "a system of beliefs and conduct based on accepted principles of what is considered right, virtuous, or just" (Rich & DeVitis, 1994). This definition highlights a multiplicity of elements and the importance of contextualizing this core element (Lerner, Brentano, Dowling, & Anderson, 2002).

It is important, however, to separate morality from religion. Morality can be addressed from both secular and religious perspectives (Huitt, 2000; Nucci, 1989). Further, as noted by Shelton (1991), morality must also take into account youth developmental stages, as in the case of adolescence: "Adolescent morality can be defined as the adolescent's personal striving, in the midst of his or her own developmental struggles, to internalize and commit the self to ideals within a situational context that incorporates the interplay of the developmental level, the concrete situation, and environmental factors, and which in turn leads to self-maintaining and consistent thoughts, attitudes, and actions" (p. 24).

The field of youth development and youth services has taken the goals of moral development and operationalized them in the form of either character or moral education (Huitt, 2000; Olsen & Pace, 2002; Nucci, 2002). Character is judged by an individual's conduct (Huitt, 2000). Thus, character is often discussed and defined in the form of desirable traits. Character education is usually conceptualized as a process of learning common attitudes, beliefs, and actions that are widely considered important for people to possess as responsible citizens (Olsen & Pace, 2002). Olsen and Pace (2002) identified six key factors, or pillars, of character: (1) trustworthiness, (2) respect, (3) responsibility, (4) fairness, (5) caring, and (6) citizenship.

In addressing moral identity in adolescence within an urban context, Hart, Atkins, and Ford (1998) argue that morality, defined as one's sense of self in promoting the welfare of others, cannot be simply defined as moral reasoning or a personality trait, and can be considered a resilient quality: "There is considerable evidence that involvement in prosocial activities... has a protective effect on individual development. ... To the extent that moral identity helps support such actions [service to community], then it behooves society to attend to moral identity as one facet of personal reliance." Providing youth with opportunities to serve their communities and indirectly make contributions to society is an effective strategy for maximizing this core element.

Youniss, McLellan, and Yates (1997), too, have used a civic perspective on moral development. Their research findings highlight the importance of youth being provided with meaningful opportunities to serve their communities. The experience translates into adults who are not only willing to get involved in civic-related projects but are also more likely to vote in elections, unlike their counterparts who did not engage in serving their community in their youth.

Flanagan and Horn (2003) issue a powerful charge to society and the field of youth development regarding youth having a moral stance: "If the community youth development approach is to realize its full potential for nurturing the next generation of local and national leaders—of engaged, committed citizens—we need to take seriously the need for greater innovation in the development of new youth institutions that respond to and build on the wealth of assets of our increasingly diverse population of young people" (p. 291).

If it is possible to identify one central key element that is part of any scholar's definition of moral, it could be argued that an ability to express empathy or caring is such an element (Rauner, 2000). The role of empathy is a crucial component of moral development (Kehret, 2001). Empathy serves to instill in a person the need to treat others with respect and kindness, which can be operationalized through a variety of individual and collective actions, such as community service. When empathy is applied to newcomer youth, it highlights their experiences and knowledge of what it means to be uprooted. Community service activities stressing their work with newcomers, youth, and adults makes it relatively easy for programs to operationalize a more core element in youth development programming.

Spiritual

The youth development field, like its human service counterparts, has only recently sought to address aspects of spirituality within programming. However, Pace (2003) notes that "a deep respect and spiritual connection to the larger community and to the earth are important aspects of community youth development" (p. 259). The topic of spirituality has been embraced by a number of major youth development national organizations such as the National Assembly, Networks for Youth Development, National Youth Development Information Center, and the National Collaboration for Youth. Nevertheless, the reader may still experience discomfort in venturing out to embrace this core element, and quite frankly she or he is not alone.

A number of scholars have specifically addressed the importance of spirituality in communities of color within a youth development context. Olive (2003), for example, comments that African American children and youth are constantly questioning the presence of the "spiritual realm" in their lives. Rodriguez, Morrobel, and Villarruel (2003), in turn, address the importance of spirituality within Latino cultures and observe the support role it can play in the lives of Latinos struggling to adjust to life in the United States.

Probably better than anyone in the field of youth development, Shear (2000) has articulated the concerns that practitioners, policymakers, and funders may have about the systematic effort to incorporate spirituality into programming: "How do we as youth workers reclaim the sacred in youth work without stepping into the murky quicksand of dogma of spirituality and spiritual development? To create a metacontextual design that supports the discovery of new meaning. To design an appropriate learning system that demonstrates the spiritual development and discovery process. To layout a roadmap that practitioners can follow" (pp. 24–25).

Benson (2002) specifically addresses the need for the field of youth development to think of a new line of scientific inquiry that places spiritual development on the same level of importance as cognitive development. Research in the area of spiritual development will go a long way toward helping the field of youth development broaden its reach of influence and practice, and will play an important role in the eventual success of youth development among newcomer youth and their communities.

Social Arenas

The ecology of youth is best divided into several units to facilitate analysis and intervention. The field of youth development has conceptualized this world as falling into four social arenas: family, peers, school, and community. Each of these four social arenas overlap with each other yet maintain a distinctive identity and influence over the lives of youth. Each of these social arenas, in addition, is worthy of extensive research unto themselves and their interactions with the other social arenas. For the purposes of this chapter, a brief overview of each of these social arenas is provided. Each of these domains has or will receive extensive attention in other parts of the book. However, their importance necessitates that they be discussed within this chapter.

Family

The role and importance of family in the life of youth can never be underestimated. The family is very often the primary organization that engages in youth development, and this is often overlooked in the field of youth services. Nevertheless, families can also be in positions to do a great deal of harm to youth. Second-generation youth often face the onus of keeping "family secrets" that have been transmitted across generations, as noted by Wolf (1997) in family research on Filipino youth.

However, it is very important to have a broad definition of what is meant by family—one that may well go far beyond conventional definitions such as nuclear. How youth define their family must play a central role in how to operationalize a youth development paradigm addressing the social arena of family. A broad and highly fluid definition of family will go counter to the prevailing definition of family widely accepted in this country —namely, the nuclear family.

Hughes (2002) articulates a vision that particularly focuses on the interdependency of family within a youth development paradigm:

> The truth is, young people will lead us into change whether we like it or not. When we move to this new understanding of youth, family, and community interdependence, when we embrace the high rich gifts young people can bring to our families and communities as partners with adults, we will learn much more about the workings of the world, and how to address them. We will, as a result, gain generations of community leaders who have deep roots in healthy, vibrant families. (p. 55)

Thus, there is little dispute that youth development and the construct of family are closely intertwined and no where more so than when discussing newcomer youth in the United States.

Peers

The research and scholarly literature on peer influence has generally taken a negative tone with a focus on how peers wield tremendous power in getting youth to take risks of various kinds. However, peers can also have positive influences in assisting youth to develop and maintain relationships, have fun, receive encouragement to develop interests in education, and take positive risks that will lead to growth (Zeldin, Kimball, & Price, 1995).

The influence of peers on newcomer youth involvement with alcohol and other drugs has received increased attention in the professional literature in the past decade. Tani, Chavez, and Deffenbacher (2001) have found that peers do play an influential role in determining drug use. Mexican American adolescents who had drug-using peers, like their white, non-Latino counterparts, had a higher likelihood of also using drugs. A Massachusetts study of immigrant youth focusing on recency of immigration (six years of less), substance use, and sexual behavior, found that they were more likely to have reported lower lifetime use of alcohol and marijuana than those who had been in this country for a longer period of time (Blake, Ledsky, Goodenow, & O'Donnell, 2001). There were no differences between groups, however, for rates of sexual intercourse. Interestingly, recent newcomer youth reported greater peer pressures to engage in and less parental support to avoid risk-taking behaviors.

School

The role and importance of school as a social arena in the life of youth is well understood, although how this system is carrying out its mission is hotly debated. However, regardless of where one stands on this issue, there is universal agreement that schools are capable of being more effective in reaching students (Pianta, Stubbman, & Hamre, 2002). Advocates for youth, and newcomers in particular, stress the need for schools to play more active and meaningful roles in getting newcomer parents involved in their children's education; schools, through their teachers, administrators, and other personnel, need to reach out to newcomer communities. Newcomer parents may be reluctant to get involved in schools because of limited language skills and fear of being disrespectful to teachers: "Poorly educated parents, including many Hispanic immigrants, have an added disadvantage if they give teachers undue deference. Such parents not only don't know what to ask but may think that questioning teachers is disrespectful" (Rothstein, 2002, p. A16).

Advocates of newcomers argue that for this group to assume a position of self-confident citizens, with all corresponding rights and privileges, schools will have to collaborate with parents and youth. In essence, schools in largely newcomer communities cannot take a narrow view of their responsibilities to society. Failure to educate and prepare youth for their future role within a multicultural society essentially disenfranchises them, and relegates them to a life of marginality. The responsibilities of schools in the lives of newcomer youth are much more significant than in the lives of native youth.

Much national attention has focused on how to get schools to better prepare youth for the world of work or career. Unfortunately, most of this attention has been negative and has focused on how this key institution is failing society. Youth spend a significant portion of their lives in schools of various kinds, and when not in school, they are usually undertaking work assigned by schools. "Free time," some critics argue, has largely disappeared.

In their review of the literature on resilience research, Benard and Constantine (2000) summarize the following key findings:

> These longitudinal developmental studies of resilience provide several lessons to schools. First, they have consistently documented that most youth can—and do—"make it."...Second, most of these youth succeeded because somewhere in their families, schools, and communities they experienced three major protective factors, the critical developmental supports and opportunities that shifted their life from risk to resilience. These protective factors are consistently described as caring relationships, high expectations, and opportunities for participation and contribution....A third lesson...is that teachers and schools are more often than not identified as the turnaround people and places who tip the scale from risk to resilience for challenged youth. (pp. 1–2)

However, much of the literature on youth development and schools is generally quick to point out that the potential of schools to transform youth within the paradigm is limited, at best (Delgado, 2002a). It is necessary, however, to separate schools from after-school programs. The former rarely engage in a comprehensive approach toward using a youth development paradigm, although elements can be found in many schools, such as the use of peers in various leadership activities. The latter engage in a comprehensive effort at institutionalizing youth development principles.

Benard and Constantine (2000) make a poignant observation that rarely gets mentioned by both schools and the field of youth development: "A key point documented in the research literature is that positive youth development and successful learning are not competing goals. Rather, it is through meeting developmental needs that every person's capacity for learning can be motivated, supported, and enhanced. When schools provide students with caring relationships, high expectations, and opportunities for participation and contribution, students naturally learn more effectively" (p. 3).

Schools can engage youth through the development of a variety of approaches, allowing local goals and circumstances to dictate the nature and scope of programming activities: (1) mentoring, (2) adventure learning, (3) service learning, (4) the arts, (5) school-family-community partnerships, (6) professional culture and wellness, (7) supportive school structures, (8) peer support, (9) safe and respectful environments, and (10) school-to-work approaches (Benard & Constantine, 2000). Each of these approaches offers students a wealth of opportunities to pursue individual and group goals that not only benefit themselves but also the community.

Community

Community as a context, place, and target for youth development programs has garnered its share of supporters and advocates. The evolution of youth development from an almost exclusive focus on youth themselves to community has occurred rapidly over the past decade. This shift in focus has been the source of considerable discussion and debate because as the field of social work has expanded, some critics have argued that the field has "bitten off more than it can chew." Namely, the focus on youth cannot be lost as greater challenges involving family and community are undertaken.

Pittman (1996), one of the field's earliest and most ardent supporters, argues the case that youth development within a community context is a natural perspective that has been too long overlooked. The institutions entrusted to serve youth can be treated as separate entities. However, when viewed within a community context, it serves to unify disparate organizations, formal and informal, that can best be organized to collaborate when viewed through the lenses of a community.

A youth development paradigm draws on ecological principles to guide how interventions are best conceptualized to enhance the likelihood of successful youth transition to adult. Community plays an instrumental role in an ecological perspective. It would be foolhardy and of very limited vision to conceptualize youth development as influencing only the lives of youth fortunate enough to be a part of an organized program. Viewing youth development from a process and output perspective effectively takes youth out of the communities in which they live. Youth participating in youth development programs have siblings, friends, next-door neighbors, and are part of schools where youth who have not directly participated in organized programs come into contact with those who have (Anonymous, 2002; Scheer, 1999). In essence, it is wise to think of youth contributing to communities, and communities contributing to youth (Forum on Youth Investment, 2002a, 2000b).

Interventions

Intervention strategies systematically build on the goals and core elements covered earlier in this chapter. The social arenas they target, in turn, influence how these strategies get carried out on a daily basis. Youth development strategies can consist of a variety of approaches, techniques, goals, and staffing configurations. Staff, particularly when they not only possess knowledge and skills but also have what Yohalem (2003) calls "job skills"—optimism, consistency and passion—are particularly well suited for work with youth.

The youth development field, not surprisingly, utilizes program activities that are not mutually exclusive of each other (Roth, Murray, Brooks-Gunn, & Foster, 1998, 1999). This allows for a tremendous amount of flexibility in how youth development interventions can be conceptualized and modified to take into account local circumstances. However, Perkins and Borden (2003) stress the need to intentionally create places and spaces that nurture the development of youth. No one program can effectively provide all opportunities for youth to grow and increase their competencies.

The goals of community-driven youth development programs can be conceptualized in a multitude of ways. Villarruel and Lerner (1994), for example, identify four overarching goals for youth:

1. Promotion of social competence
2. Development of problem-solving skills
3. Creation of a sense of autonomy
4. Development of a sense of purpose and future orientation

Each of these goals places youth within the broader context of community-focused benefits; the two are inseparable.

Interventions utilizing a youth development paradigm must endeavor to identify and enhance youth assets and involve youth in the decision-making process. In summarizing the current thinking on youth assets within the field, Eccles and Gootman (2002) provide a solid foundation from which programming can occur:

> Individuals do not necessarily need the entire range of assets to thrive; in fact, various combinations of assets across domains reflect equally positive adolescent development. Having more assets is better than having few. Although strong assets in one category can offset weak assets in another category, life is easier to manage if one has assets in all ... domains. Continued exposure to positive experience, settings, and people, as well as opportunities to gain and refine life skills, supports young people in the acquisition and growth of these assets. (pp. 6–7)

Not surprisingly, the field of youth development has devoted considerable attention and resources to better understand what makes an effective youth development paradigm. Eccles and Gootman (2002), for example, identy eight key features of effective youth development organizations and programs:

1. Physical and psychological safety
2. Developmentally specific structure
3. Emotional moral supportive relationships
4. Opportunities for positive relationships between youth and adults creating a sense of belonging
5. Positive social norms
6. Support for efficacy and mastery
7. Opportunities for skill building through service to community
8. Establishment and integration of strong links between family, school, and the broader community

Each of these features involves numerous youth and adult relationships, in addition to youth-to-youth and youth-to-community relationships.

Youth development activities can be categorized into a variety of types, none of which are mutually exclusive: mentoring, community service, sports, communication, leadership development, visual arts, performing arts, advocacy/community change, biographic, and research and evaluation. The reader has no doubt quickly grasped the range of possibilities for youth development interventions based on these 10 categories. Each of these types of activities can incorporate many of the elements of each other to take into account program goals, characteristics of youth, types of settings, and local circumstances.

Mentoring

The art of mentoring, in many ways, is intuitively appealing and relatively easy to grasp for the average person or professional (Rhodes, 2000a). This type of activity within youth development programs is exciting because of the variety of ways it can be carried out with multiple labels, one of which is *mentoring*. Terms such as *coaching, facilitator, consultant*, and *guide* are just a few of the labels that can be assigned to mentoring. The mentoring label invariably has adults as mentors, and youth as mentees. When mentoring transpires within a youth development paradigm, it takes on new forms. This flexibility, in turn, facilitates the use of this activity within youth groups and between youth and adults in a variety of settings.

A number of scholars have advocated for the use of mentoring as the preferred activities in helping youth enhance moral development (Parks, 2000; Shelton, 1991). Mentoring, however, can also be used to address enhancement of the other core elements that form the foundation for youth development interventions (Roffman, Suarez-Orozco, & Rhodes, 2003). Rhodes (2002a, 2000b), however, although extolling the virtues of mentoring, cautions the reader not to think of it as a panacea for all of society's ills.

The primacy of adults within a youth development paradigm is well accepted within the field; adults play significant roles in helping youth navigate their way through many of life's obstacles (Taylor & Bressler, 2000; Witt, 2002). Youth, in turn, can assume positions of leadership with the proper guidance and support from adults (Witt, 2002): "Don't focus on the primacy of the activity over the process of participants interacting with meaningful adults. Adults can serve as leaders, coaches or teachers. Whatever the role, adults have the potential to guide and influence youth as they move along the pathways to adulthood. No one setting offers the richness and variety of experiences" (p. 56). Vygotsky's (1978) concept of proximal development stresses the importance of quality of contact and duration of contact, and places adults in central and advantageous roles for helping youth learn new roles and tasks, as well as challenging themselves in the process. Penuel (1995) notes that adults subscribing to youth development principles must not only respect youth but also be ready to assume a nontraditional stance whereby adults are not dominant or view youth as redemption projects.

It is important to emphasize that both adults and youth benefit from mentoring relationships and that the advantages indirectly affect the siblings and peers of the mentee: "Mentoring is a win-win situation when adequate preparation is given to mentoring programs and practices. The picture of youth does become a positive one.... Young people win; adult volunteers win. In the end, society at large is the real winner" (Saito & Roehlkepartain, 1992, p. 6). All too often, evaluation efforts can take a narrow perspective on the benefits of a mentoring relationship focusing almost exclusively on youth. However, an expansive view of benefits will quickly identify how the mentor is enriched by the experience. The mentees' siblings and peers benefit from the experiences, particularly in situations that newcomer youth often find themselves in—namely, exposure to life outside of the community.

Saito and Roehlkepartain (1992), in their review of programs using mentoring as a central strategy for reaching youth, uncovered five primary types of mentoring programs:

1. *Traditional programs:* Usually an adult is paired with a youth and a schedule and a contract is made for meetings, activities, and long-term commitment.
2. *Long-term, focused activity:* These types of mentoring programs have a focus on a particular set of goals that are usually school and career related and involve tutoring and remedial activities.
3. *Short-term, focused activity:* These mentoring programs are very similar in nature to their long-term counterparts but have a limited contract period of about six months.
4. *Team mentoring:* More than one mentor is assigned to work with a youth member over an extended period of time lasting more than one year.
5. *Group mentoring:* One adult group member is assigned a small group of mentees.

This typology generally places one or more adults with one or more youth. Time commitment and focus vary across each type. Interestingly, the model of youth being mentors to other youth is generally unexplored yet has tremendous potential for the field. This model can be used when younger youth have mentors who may be five or six years older than they are, and the mentors are in college or have been in the workforce for several years.

The perspective that these mentors bring with them, when combined with a shared cultural heritage, can be quite powerful in helping mentees develop hope and acquire necessary social navigational skills to help them achieve. Cooper, Denner, and Lopez (1999), for example, put forth the idea of having older siblings be conceived as potential mentors to their young siblings, and programs should seriously consider them in this role. They not only bring an intimate understanding of their mentees but they also share cultural heritage.

Intergenerational mentoring involving elders and youth also has endless possibilities, as illustrated in the following two examples, one involving youth as mentors and the other involving elders in this role. Extended Support for Elementary School ESL Students (ESEE) is based in Poway, California:

> Hana, age seventeen, launched ESEE as a mentoring program for English as a Second Language (ESL) elementary students. With the help of Trinh and Annette, Hana hopes to alleviate the hardships of immigrant children who struggle in isolation and misunderstanding due to language barriers. ESEE aims to facilitate a positive cultural transition for immigrant students. By providing support and individual attention to new students, ESEE works to improve English and academic proficiency. Moreover, in hopes of more

effectively engaging students, ESEE provides instruction through the use of songs, children's books, videos, and conversation. A native of Pusan, Korea, Hana understands firsthand the difficulties associated with immigration. She thus wants to provide new immigrant youth with positive learning experiences as they assimilate to their new schools and communities. The purpose of this venture ... is to help alleviate emotional hardships of the immigrated children and narrow the gaps in the community. By helping kids understand and become a part of the new environment easier and quicker, the venture will create a more positive atmosphere in the community. (*Youth Venture*, 2002, p. 11)

The following program, based in Montgomery County, Maryland, unlike ESEE that utilizes youth as mentors, instead relies on elders as mentors. Bridges Intergenerational Mentoring was established in 1990 as an attempt to meet the growing needs of new, mostly economically poor, immigrant families. The program has since expanded from 8 to 40 elder mentors (age 55 and older) who serve elementary school children from Cambodia, El Salvador, Nicaragua, Vietnam, Ethiopia, and Jamaica who have been in this country less than three years. Mentors provide mentees with support on acculturation, improving communication skills, and personal development.

A word of caution is in order concerning the activity of mentoring: The forging of a relationship based on mutual trust and benefits is never easy to establish and maintain over an extended period of time. Freedman (1993), for example, argues for the need to minimize the cultural, ethnic, and racial barriers between mentees and mentors as a means of increasing the likelihood of success using this form of intervention. Mentoring by itself, although important, cannot be expected to turn around the life of youth facing numerous daily challenges. It needs to complement other activities that stress attitudinal changes and acquisition of knowledge and skills.

Community Service

The popularity of community service, otherwise known as *service learning*, has increased by leaps and bounds and is no longer restricted to colleges and universities. Service learning, it should be noted, is open to all youth age groups (Kielsmeir & Klopp, 2002). The past 10 to 15 years have witnessed this form of intervention becoming an integral part of youth education across the country. Melchior (2002) notes that community service within school settings is "a teaching and learning process that involves young people in service to their communities in conjunction with a structured learning process or curriculum. In a school-based setting, service-learning is a method of teaching that integrates regular academic curriculum" (p. xx).

The role of students in service-learning activities is empowering—they plan, implement, and integrate academic subjects in the process. Rapport (2002) effectively captures the meaning of service learning and how different it really is from schooling as usual: "Effective service-learning isn't based on giving students the 'right answers' to questions they don't see any reason to pose in the first place. Effective service-learning addresses authentic issues raised by young people after first-hand exposure, linking students to real 'players' and meaningful activities" (p. 28).

Many advocates of service learning believe that this form of youth development activity, probably more than any other type, lends itself to use within schools. When service learning integrates academic subjects within a curriculum, youth not only learn but provide benefits to both communities and schools. Service learning serves to break down barriers between schools and communities. This is particularly significant when addressing newcomer youth who have histories of deference to teachers and schools, which results in minimal or lack of participation in school-centered activities. McCabe (2002) argues that service learning can be effectively tied to sustainable community goals, integrating civic action in the process.

Community service can be tailored to any age group (Shine, Shoup, & Harrington, 1981). Instilling in young children the virtues, honor, and benefits to community, family, and self bodes well for future service as children become youth and youth become adults. Service to community benefits all parties (Smith & Jucovy, 1996). The following example, based in San Gabriel, California, illustrates the potential of service learning to newcomer youth:

> Minh, age seventeen, launched Tutoring for Immigrant Children, a tutoring and mentoring program aimed at the high population of immigrant children in his community. After reading Robert Coles' *The Call of Service*, Minh recalled his own immigration to America as a young child, and remembered particularly both his bewilderment and his inability to communicate in English. Determined to help newly arrived immigrant children assimilate into American society, Minh and team member James created their venture to provide these youth with support, mentoring, and guidance throughout their transition. The team provides homework assistance through tutoring sessions, and hosts a supplementary English as a Second Language (ESL) curriculum weekly to accelerate students' progress toward English mastery. The team also provides 'mentoring afternoons' each Friday. Minh and his team are committed to helping newly immigrated youth develop healthy, vibrant lives. Recognizing the influence of local Asian and Hispanic gangs on newly immigrated youth, the team believes that through effective mentoring and guidance, they can help these young people lead productive, successful lives in America. (*Youth Venture*, 2002, p. 32)

The long-range implications of having youth actively involved in providing community services is only now starting to receive the attention it deserves. The benefits of youth involvement in service go beyond the community being helped: "Youth action is a gateway to future civic action. Young people who participate in community service experiences as part of voluntary youth groups are more likely to vote and to join community organizations fifteen years down the road than adults who did not participate in such experiences during high school" (Forum for Youth Development, 2002b, p. 7).

The example of Bust-A-Move (North Carolina) shows the multiple beneficiaries of community service:

> The purpose of this community service project is to involve and provide support to the North Carolina Children's Hospital, the only nonprofit hospital in North Carolina. To do this, the Bust-A-Move team, Katie, Ben, Micah, Sarah, and Rob, will implement a dance marathon to raise money for the hospital at North Carolina State University. This

dance marathon, scheduled to take place for an entire twenty-four hours in Spring 2003, will include dancers, people to motivate the dancers, volunteers and staff, and the guests of honor—the children and families from the hospital who will receive the funds raised. In addition to Dance Marathon, Bust-A-Move will hold fundraisers throughout the year and also organize social events to spend quality time with the children in the hospital. (*Youth Venture*, 2002, p. 7)

Sports

Any one who has worked with youth will quickly recognize the magic that sports have in attracting them to programs (Beedy & Zierk, 2000; Gerzon-Kessler, 2000). However, not all youth are interested or perceive themselves as athletic, contrary to the impression one gets from watching sporting events on television. Historically, any mention of sports as a programming activity meant that the program was geared toward males. The past 20 years have witnessed the emergence of female sporting events for all ages.

The following three examples involve youth playing leadership roles in establishing sports programs, in this case, playing basketball. However, each program brings to this activity a particular perspective and set of goals.

Young Savants, Inc.:
This not-for-profit organization began as a basketball league and tournament for Boston's inner-city youth and was developed to serve as a "substitute for the streets." Today this group of young people, led by Challenge, Chris, and Destiny, has expanded its organization to provide five coed programs, including: The Escape Dribble Savants Basketball Program; Drills n Skills 4 Life; S.E.N.T. 4 Life; an after-school academic program; and Savants*Savant, a program that forms community based partnerships, outreach, and collaborations. (*Youth Venture*, 2002, p. 35)

RUA Baller Tournament:
The RUA Baller Tournament is a basketball tournament to help keep kids off the street. Most of the profits from the tournament will support the Angel Wish Foundation helping children and babies with AIDS. This idea was formed because many teens love to play basketball and would support the objective of raising money for children with AIDS. To participate in this tournament we are requiring students to have a minimum GPA of 3.8. Students will be encouraged to do well in school and be rewarded by participating in this tournament. (*Youth Venture*, 2002, p. 22)

Finally, the Baller's Late-Night Basketball, Birmingham, Alabama, is a sporting activity that brings youth and adults together in pursuit of common goals.

Baller's Late-Night Basketball:
Henry launched Baller's Late-Night Basketball to provide a late night gym for teens and young adults. Henry created Baller's in order to "provide a positive refuge for teens and young adults." Henry hopes that Baller's will provide young people with a safe and healthy environment and hopes that offering the youth in his community the option to play basketball late at night will steer them away from participating in unhealthy or harmful activities. Henry is hosting his Late-Night basketball league in the local YMCA and will be open from 8:00 P.M. to 12:00 A.M. on the weekends. Henry encourages all young people ages fourteen and up to become involved in the opportunity. When asked

why he decided to create Baller's, Henry replied, "I came up with this idea over the summer when some friends of mine were looking for somewhere to play basketball late night. I figured that since the YMCA closes at 8:00 P.M., why not open the gym that continues past that time." (*Youth Venture*, 2002, p. 5)

Communication

Communication-related youth development activities, probably more than any other type of activity, lend themselves to incorporating multiple team members with communication goals targeting youth and adults. Communication activities can consist of any of the following types: newsletters, videos, contributions of articles to local newspapers, web-page design, radio programming, workshops on youth issues for local audiences, poetry, and public speaking at local events as well as at state and national conferences. Fortunately, the field of youth development has numerous examples of the role and importance of communication. Here are two examples that utilize video as the mechanism.

Youth Vision, in New York City, uses video within a community context:

Youth Vision:
Venturers Kellon and Kenneth are leading a team that creates youth videos that focus on community issues. They have already begun hosting public screenings in the community, where viewers learn about the issue following the video presentation. Kellon and Kenneth have recently held viewings at the Smithsonian National Museum of the American Indian in New York, and are focusing on gaining more opportunities for public viewings and public discussions of the issues. (*Youth Venture*, 2002, p. 36)

Youth Vision Television, based in Boston, developed a cable show specifically focused on youth:

Irvel and Ike, 17 and 18, respectively, of Boston, Massachusetts, are the creators of a new teen cable TV show called *Youth Vision Television.* This show by teens for teens will air weekly television segments about teen issues and will engage Boston youth in a variety of fun and educational community building activities. Irvel and Ike plan to help Boston youth find places to obtain jobs, receive academic help, and research colleges, while also providing a safe and effective venue for kids to get engaged and find something productive to do. They hope this informational resource will enable kids to help build and improve their Boston communities. (*Youth Venture*, 2002, p. 36)

In California, another program seeks to reach out to youth through a website. Teen Advice Center.net is based in Los Altos:

Ian launched this website to create a safe, confidential, easily accessible place for teens to get advice from their peers. Ian got the idea to start this website after visiting a similar site and finding it helpful, as well as experiencing the loss of a friend who committed suicide. Says Ian, "I thought that she probably just needed someone to listen to her and be there for her. I think about my friends now and realize that they are all going through so many things in their lives, and a site where they can just talk and be understood and listened to is very important." (*Youth Venture*, 2002, p. 28)

The example of Girl to Girl, Richmond, Virginia, utilizes a mechanism for helping youth that has a long and distinguished history:

> Girl to Girl [was] created . . . by a sixteen year-old lead Venturer, Shannon. Girl to Girl aims to provide a journal for young women, written by young women, which addresses issues ranging from peer-pressure and relationships, to family issues and school. Shannon and her team created Girl to Girl to provide an outlet for girls to express themselves, and to provide a venue for them to talk about their problems and to meet other young women who may be experiencing similar issues. . . . "The name of the journal will be 'Ask Keysa.' We came up with this idea after a brainstorming session about how we could address the needs of young women in our community similar to the needs and problems we have had to deal with." . . . As the team produces its first journal, they will simultaneously launch their website, which provides an online forum for young women to chat about their problems, or to seek advice from other teenage girls who have gone through similar issues. (*Youth Venture*, 2002, pp. 12–13)

Finally, the last program brings together the subjects of disabilities and the visual arts. E.X.P.R.E.S.S.I.O.N.S., based in New York City, does a fine job of illustrating how youth can effectively communicate when they are encouraged and supported to do so:

> Brandon started his organization to impart the knowledge he has gained about expressing one's feelings through art. Born 90 percent deaf, Brandon grew up with a speech impediment that deterred him from communicating with others. Brandon was introduced to photography and poetry, and discovered that he could effectively communicate his feelings through these art forms, thereby enabling him to better communicate with others. Now an avid photographer and poet, Brandon founded E.X.P.R.E.S.S.I.O.N.S. to teach younger children in his Brooklyn community how to express themselves through these mediums. He holds after-school classes weekly at a local elementary school, where students learn photography and poetry basics and hear guest lectures from professionals in the field. Brandon also plans to start teaching another class devoted to helping young people resolve their conflicts through photography. (*Youth Venture*, 2002, p. 10)

These examples illustrate how communication as an activity can be brought to fruition and how such activities can fulfill important community services in the process.

Leadership Development

Youth development programs, with few exceptions, are widely expected to engage in youth leadership development as part of their mission. Helping to prepare youth for roles as adults often involves some level of effort on the part of programs to acquire leadership skills. However, leadership development within the field has taken on definitions and dimensions that have generally avoided the common public perception of what is a "leader."

The field has avoided taking the definition of *leader* as one who possesses all of the qualities necessary to command attention and a following. Instead, the field has identified a number of leadership qualities that leadership requires, but no one individual is expected to possess. The example of Helping Hands shows how leadership can take many forms beyond what is conventionally thought of as "leadership":

> Helping Hands was created by Johnny Williams in February 2002. Johnny aims to involve youth volunteers by providing positive activities for children in elementary school. The activities, such as games and arts and crafts, will be offered twice a month after school. Gradually, Johnny plans to encourage the children to take on increasing responsibilities within the group to help improve and build their self-esteem and leadership skills. Johnny has already been very active with the Youth Venture community, having attended the Youth Venture NY Regional Community Council meeting held last January and additionally accompanying Youth Venture on "Dream It. Do It" presentations to inspire young people to take advantage of the Youth Venture opportunity. (*Youth Venture*, 2002, p. 15)

Visual Arts

The purposes of visual arts are often quite ambitious and can consist of numerous activities in seeking to address public concerns of marginalized urban youth. Breitbart (1998) states:

> In the context of difficult life experiences and often hostile environments, public art, design work and other forms of local environmental intervention have enabled some young people to see possibilities in urban settings that otherwise form only neutral or constraining backdrops for their activity. The many benefits that derive from this involvement nevertheless raise the question of how such creative youth driven work fits within a larger movement for social change. (p. 319)

Do It Your Dame Self Video and Film Festival, Cambridge, Massachusetts, brings together youth using multiple media and exhibitions to educate youth:

Do It Your Dame Self Video and Film Festival:
Paulina, Saquora, and Tania, teenagers at the Community Arts Center of Cambridge, developed a Boston-wide festival to present teen videos on social issues. The festival, the first of its kind in Boston, showcased the talents, capabilities, and interests of inner-city teens in video production, and encouraged them to use those talents to improve their communities. The first festival received 55 entries and recruited over 20 teens to help in reviewing and selecting the best 12 videos to show at the festival. The second and third festivals received increased attention, recognition, and submissions. Other teens have now taken the place of the original festival founders, who have since graduated from high school, and in each subsequent year, these successors have continued a tradition of excellence by hosting the now critically acclaimed annual festival, with the number of submissions growing to over 350 entries. (*Youth Venture*, 2002, p. 9)

Performing Arts

Ball and Heath (1993) note that the performing arts—in this case, dance—fulfill a multitude of very important goals in helping youth, particularly those who are marginal in this society. Performances require youth to maintain high standards, engage in a discovery process that actively ties the past and the present, create group cohesion, and allow for the expression of an ethnic self and political commentary to occur.

The program Live to Dance, Dance to Live, in Junction City, Wisconsin, integrates dance with knowledge and skill acquisition for youth to lead more healthy lives:

> Tyler launched Live to Dance, Dance to Live, a venture created to hold two dances a year that focus on and promote healthy choices—no smoking, no drinking, no sex. The first dance that Tyler has planned will have a Roman theme. Admission for the dances will be discounted if the young person brings non-perishable food to donate to Operation Boot Strap. During the dances Tyler plans to spend a few minutes each hour speaking about healthy choices. He aims to provide factual information to the teens, making [them] informed enough to make healthy and smart choices in their lives. Tyler believes that the dances will not only serve to provide the teens with a safe and positive activity, but will serve to educate them about the negative effects of drugs, drinking, and sex. (*Youth Venture*, 2002, p. 18)

The second example is the Guernica Project, which seeks to achieve a major environmental change—the revitalization of a community:

> The purpose of this project is to revitalize downtown Raleigh through murals and artwork that can boost community involvement in addition to having government officials recognize and endorse the efforts of citizens. Team members Billy, David and Christina, from North Carolina State University, will involve community artists of all ages to beautify downtown Raleigh with urban artwork. The team will advertise in local artistic groups and in elementary, middle, and high school art classes, and recruit painters and muralists in order to express Raleigh's culture in a diversity of styles and age groups. (*Youth Venture*, 2002, pp. 30–31)

Advocacy/Community Change

As noted earlier in Chapter 5, practitioners do not enjoy the luxury of not engaging in advocacy and system change efforts, regardless of the primary method of intervention practiced. The same can be said for newcomer youth involved in youth development programs. Advocacy/community change initiatives can consist of many different types and targets for change. Activism can embrace numerous goals. Martin (2002), for example, ties environmental education, service learning, and civic action in seeking environmental justice. Change efforts can also involve different time periods for commitment by youth. These change efforts, however, always involve a group of young people, sometimes started by one but never the sole activist in the long run.

The following two programs are examples of such flexibility. The Imani Players present for discussion the importance of social action in the lives of youth. SANE Expansion Project, in turn, represents an environmental focus for activism.

Imani Players:
Team leaders Jessica, Crystal, Dawn, and Adrian and the Imani Players perform plays to educate the Irvington, NJ, community and elementary school children about social issues such as racism, violence, drugs, homelessness, and alcohol prevention. Through their performances, the Imani Players teach community youngsters about these important issues and help youth understand their role as community leaders. (*Youth Venture,* 2002, p. 15).

SANE Expansion Project:
Westfield, Massachusetts–based Melissa, age seventeen, created the SANE Expansion Project. The purpose of Melissa's venture is to expand her current environmental club, increase involvement in local conservation projects, further engage the community, and solicit new members. Fueled by her activism and interest in environmental issues, Melissa is committed to preserving the natural world. SANE aims to increase awareness about local and global environmental problems through a variety of projects including a local presentation and cleanup campaign. SANE also provides a monthly newsletter to the school community. Through its work, the team not only serves to educate youth about environmental and global responsibilities, but also to provide instruction on volunteer recruitment, environmental research, and social responsibility. (*Youth Venture,* 2002, p. 23).

McCabe (2002) developed a six-stage continuum of civic action to better ground activism from a developmental perspective: (1) sporadic volunteering, (2) sustainable service, (3) service learning, (4) civic engagement/policy building, (5) long-term service, and (6) nonprofit career/social entrepreneurship. This continuum shows how the journey toward activism can evolve over a period of time, progressively involving more time, expertise, and commitment.

Biographic

The journey of self-discovery, which represents a central element of any youth development activity, can take many different forms. However, the use of biographical activities is one of the most common. These activities usually seek to commit youth to share their stories with others. This process necessitates conducting interviews with relatives, as well as engaging in thought-provoking discussions with peers and other members of the community.

The stories, in turn, can and often involve multimedia methods, such as video, poetry, photography, music, and art (Rees, 1998). Biographic activities take on added importance in the lives of youth of color and those who are newcomers to this country, since their stories and the stories of their groups rarely get the attention they deserve in schools and the media.

Students United for Racial Equity, Palo Alto, California, is a fine example of a biographic project:

In February 2002, Palo Alto–based twenty-year-old Nina Sung created Students United for Racial Equity (SURE). Growing up as one of the only minority students in her high school, Nina became motivated to create race dialogue sessions after she participated in one herself. Explains Nina: "My goal is to provide a forum for local high school juniors and seniors to explore the significance of race as it is reflected in psychological, social, and economic well-being." As part of her venture, Nina created a fourteen-session seminar, in which students meet every other week for two hours to discuss pre-assigned readings and assignments. Nina constructed a syllabus, which provides readings, discussion topics, recommended videos, projects, and activities for each session. "SURE is designed to give young people an opportunity to discuss the meaning of race as it presents itself in today's society; through academic readers and individual research projects, students will explore a more inclusive curriculum," she explains. Nina is working with five different high schools in her community, two of which serve as initial pilot sites. Though launching modestly and strategically, Nina's ultimate goal is to leverage her initial dialogue sessions as a model for replication in schools nationwide. (*Youth Venture*, 2002, p. 27)

Research/Evaluation

Over the past five years the field has witnessed exciting developments involving youth in research and program evaluation efforts. This period has resulted in numerous case examples and models for training youth to be researchers, although efforts to use youth in research roles can be traced back to the 1970s (Bloom & Padilla, 1979; Delgado, 1979). The process of research and evaluation has, as a result, been energized through the active participation of youth within their organizations and respective communities, and opened up a new arena for youth development-focused initiatives.

The emergence of empowerment evaluation in the late 1990s and early part of the twenty-first century, although not singling out youth, nevertheless applied to youth-led research (Fetterman, 2001). Giving voice to the ultimate beneficiaries of programs and research can take on many forms. One objective is to involve youth in sharing their stories with researchers who may not share similar histories and backgrounds with them. Another objective seeks the voices of youth by involving them in conceptualizing, planning, and implementing research. When this approach is applied to youth, it entails having them play influential roles throughout the research process. Youth-led research aspires to elicit youth voices by actively using youth to share with peers.

Youth participation in program evaluation, from an organization perspective, is not arduous to achieve (Checkoway & Richards-Schuster, 2002; Fetterman, 2001; Horsch, Little, Smith, Goodyear, & Harris, 2002; London, 2002). Community-based research, in turn, although more challenging from a logistical point of view, is nonetheless within the grasp of any community-based organization and community (Checkoway & Richards-Schuster, 2002; Delgado, 1979, 1981, 1998; Horsch et al., 2002).

The goals common to most youth-led research initiatives fall into three major categories (Horsch et al., 2002):

1. They seek to enhance individual development (social-emotional-cognitive-moral) of participating youth and encourage their active involvement in the decisions that affect their lives.
2. Their participation results in benefits to sponsoring organizations and capacity enhancement.

3. These initiatives provide youth with a mechanism and goal to create significant and sustainable community change efforts.

Clearly, youth-led research projects benefit all participating parties. However, youth are by far the major beneficiaries of these efforts (Delgado, 1998).

Adults do play roles in youth-led research; however, these roles can best be thought of as collaborators, facilitators, and consultants. Expert knowledge is provided when solicited and not freely offered otherwise. The democratization of knowledge, and in this case that which is research related, is one of the primary goals of youth-involved research initiatives. This goal can be considered "labor intensive" to achieve but well worth the investment of time, energy, and finances, if conceptualized as community capacity enhancement—an investment in the development of the future leaders in the community and the nation.

Youth-involved research can also be easily conceptualized as community service or service learning. Venturing out into the community to undertake research offers youth an opportunity not only to ultimately provide a service but also to better understand the context of their own community. This awareness and the contacts developed in the process of undertaking research will lend themselves to other spheres in their lives, such as school and career.

Inherent Challenges in Using a Youth Development Paradigm with Newcomer Youth

This section identifies and addresses the key conceptual and practice challenges of using existing variations of a youth development paradigm. Although refugee and immigrant youth may share similar ages with U.S. marginalized youth, they bring with them a range of factors that mitigate against using a youth development paradigm without substantial modifications. Thus, it is necessary to make requisite changes to a youth development paradigm, as is practiced in this country, for it to have the potential for youth and community transformation in newcomer communities: "Those committed to the field of youth development must walk a thin line between being 'realistic' and being 'visionaries.' We must continue to dream the impossible dream while keeping our feet firmly on the ground. We need to inspire youth and each other to maintain a steadfast devotion for a better world, yet understand that setbacks are a natural occurrence in this line of work" (Delgado, 2002a, p. 16).

The preceding quote encourages practitioners to pursue their quest to bring the principles of youth development to fruition. However, the quote ends on a cautionary note—namely, setbacks are a natural occurrence in this line of work. Setbacks are unavoidable, but their consequences can be minimized with forethought. An understanding of the conceptual limitations inherent in a youth development paradigm goes a long way toward the development of contingencies. It also sounds a warning to practitioners and academics alike to pause and be prepared to accept the "good" with the "bad," in applying a social paradigm to diverse population groups, newcomers being one of them.

It would be rare for a social paradigm to be able to be translated effortlessly into practice without it undergoing some form of modification in the process and the uplifting of potential contradictions or problem areas. Flexibility to take into account local circumstances and mediating factors increases the attractiveness of a paradigm for actual use in practice. Practitioners, after all, have often used the saying, "This is real life out here," as a way of letting scholars know that what is being proposed is either not possible or totally misses the mark. In the case of youth development, the ability to transcend the circumstances leading to youth and their family uprootment from their native countries, and their political status in this country, are two significant considerations in assessing the validity of a youth development paradigm for use with newcomer youth.

Successful application of a youth development paradigm to newcomer youth specifically requires practitioners to examine how youth development values, core elements (cognition, emotion, physical health, morality, social, and spiritual), and social domains (families, peer groups, schools, and community) need to be modified to take into account the backgrounds and living situations of immigrant and refugee groups. Values, core elements, and social domains influence the nature of activities used to achieve youth development goals. Whenever possible, specific national origins will need to be noted to avoid overgeneralization.

Value Conflicts

There are probably few topics that can bring agreement on the part of practitioners, academics, youth, and parents like the importance of values. Values form the cornerstone of much of human behavior and perspectives or ways of looking at life and the future. Consequently, it is only appropriate to start with values when identifying potential conflict areas between youth development and newcomer youth.

Flanagan and Horn (2003) note that achieving equality as a goal is difficult to accomplish, although egalitarian relationships are a basic tenet of any democratic society, including that of the United States. However, when equality is not the norm within a group, the ethnic/cultural heritage of a newcomer group compounds achievement of this lofty but widely embraced goal in this society. Denner and Griffin (2003) outline ways that youth development can support gender equality. They are in strong support of staff role modeling equality between genders and using mentoring and service-learning activities. However, Denner and Griffin do not discuss how equality between genders can and should be addressed when deep cultural traditions and values support males being more worthy of decision making than females.

Newcomer groups very often bring with them a set of values that have historically served them well in their country of origin but act as significant barriers to achieving success within this country (Lynch, 1991; Sue & Sue, 1999). These values have probably been passed from one generation to the other so many times that youth and their parents accept them as "truths." One of the major inherent challenges in using a youth development paradigm without modifications to take into account youth cultural backgrounds and ecological circumstances is the stress placed on youth to make a successful transition to adulthood and go from a state of dependence to independence.

Pan (1998), for example, touches on one value that is widely accepted within youth development programs (equality between the sexes) and shows how Chinese immigrants have had to adjust as a result of this value perspective. In addition, Pan (1998) goes on to address how other values—such as discipline, loyalty, and the family unit, bedrocks of Chinese culture—have been challenged. Chinese youth involved in youth development programs, as a result, have had to balance two worldviews.

The value of collectivism or interdependence, as already noted, is one that places youth in a position of being closely tied to their family of origin regardless of their age and marital status. Thus, the goal of independence that a youth development paradigm embraces will not be widely understood or encouraged within some, if not many, newcomer groups. Among some newcomer groups it may represent one of the primary values that sets their worldview apart from that typically found in this country. Cooperation as a value very often can be considered the opposite of competition. This society, many would argue, is known worldwide for the value it places on competition rather than cooperation (Mishra, 1994). Hierarchical relationships versus equality of relationships represents another potential value conflict for many newcomer youth.

Mixed versus Single-Gender Programs

The subject of how best to undertake youth development programming involving gender considerations is not a new question in the field and it certainly has implications for newcomer youth (Denner & Griffin, 2003; Rodriguez, Morrobel, & Villarruel, 2003). Delgado (2000a) addresses this very point when stating: "There is clearly much to be gained from undertaking programming combining males and females. If programming activities are to provide youths with experiences that will better prepare them for living in this society, then learning how to interact with the opposite sex is a worthwhile goal. This form of programming provides staff with a golden opportunity to help shape gender relations" (p. 250).

Although youth development never loses sight of the individual, group activities play significant roles in activity selection. Groups provide youth with a chance to interact and develop social skills. However, when these groups involve both genders, an added dimension to the experience emerges—namely, how males and females work effectively together in an egalitarian manner. What happens when youth embrace cultural traditions and values that effectively separate the sexes from working together as a team? What if the youth are willing to engage in gender-integrated activities but their parents forbid it? The answers to these questions will have a profound impact on the very essence of youth development programming.

Mixed versus Group-Specific Programs

One of the many appealing aspects of a youth development paradigm is its embrace of ideals integrating youth from various ethnic and racial backgrounds in pursuit of common goals. American society consists of many different ethnic and racial groups, thereby making pursuit of this goal very attractive. However, when this approach and goal are applied to newcomer youth it becomes quite challenging. Some newcomer youth come from cultural backgrounds with a long history of antagonism toward other groups, and upon their arrival in this country, their histories do not go away but are revisited.

Mixing youths from different backgrounds brings with it a host of challenges for providers in developing activities that meet the needs of all program participants and not just a small group. From a programming standpoint, single-group activity makes programming that much easier and cost effective. Recruitment, for example, can be targeted. Mixed-group programming from a recruitment perspective, particularly if staff need to meet with the parents of participants individually, can prove very labor intensive. Some advocates of this approach also point out that it is much easier when single groups are targeted to develop activities and put prerequisite supports in place to maximize the time youth spend in the programs.

Critics of single-group focused programming, on the other hand, argue that this type of programming may be easier for staff, but it further isolates the group being served from other groups. In addition, it wastes an excellent opportunity to help influence the dynamics and relationships between groups, particularly ones that have an extensive history of conflict between each other. The breaking down of between-group differences and values is predicated on inclusive principles. This noble goal is often an integral part of any youth development-inspired program. However, single-group programming misses an opportunity to create climates of understanding and acceptance.

Is Empowerment a Realistic Goal?

Empowerment as a goal, appealing as it may be for use with newcomer youth and youth in general, has numerous barriers to overcome to achieve its potential (Huber, Frommeyer, Weisenbach, & Sazama, 2003). Although the social work profession has played an influential role in the use of this construct within service delivery (Gutierrez & Lewis, 1999; Lee, 1994; Simon, 1994; Solomon, 1970), and other professions have embraced this construct, its applicability for use with newcomer youth is still largely unexplored. Empowerment must not be conceptualized along narrow dimensions such as a focus on individuals. Empowerment can be far reaching if thought about in a broad manner (Power, 1996). In the case of communities with high concentrations of newcomers, an individual act of empowerment, when placed within a specific age group as in the case of youth, can bring about significant communitywide ramifications. These ramifications can be both positive and negative, however.

The experience of the senior author of this book in addressing empowerment among newcomer youth in Miami illustrates the potential issues youth face if they exercise this newfound power. I was contracted by a substance abuse prevention program in Miami to train the trainers for working with Latino youth. One of the key constructs to be addressed was how empowerment of these youth was to take place. After a short period of time presenting how empowerment usually gets conceptualized and implemented with youth programs, one of the trainees raised a question that took me aback. Her question was, How do we empower undocumented Latino youth when, if the authorities find out that they are undocumented, they and their families face deportation back to their countries of origin?

The moment these youth organized to bring about badly needed changes within their schools or communities, they would become very vulnerable to a political backlash that would then result in the Immigration and Naturalization Service being called. The process of empowering these youth meant that ensuring their protection was critical. Empowerment as practiced with native youth who have rights protected by the Constitution is operationalized quite differently from that of "undocumented" youth who have very limited rights in this country.

Should Parents Be Involved?

The field of youth development, as already noted, has evolved and broadened its reach to include the communities where youth reside. This evolution has brought with it a set of questions or challenges pertaining to the involvement of parents in programs. One study, specifically focused on investigating the influence of socio-demographics, family, and peer effects on adolescent illicit drug initiation, found that family bonding began to decline after age 18 and peer influences increased after age 15 (Guo, Hill, Hawkins, Catalano, & Abbott, 2002). The authors advocate for prevention programs involving both parents and youth with the goals of reducing negative peer influences for engagement in antisocial activities and increasing parental supervision and communication.

The field of youth development has slowly moved toward integrating parents in various activities, such as ESL, computer training, citizenship classes, and assistance with job referrals. There is explicit acknowledgment that youth are part of a wider social system that includes the family and community, and this has necessitated that programs also reach out to parents. Any efforts to stabilize and assist families will translate into a stable and functioning household for youth.

This outreach to parents, however, has raised serious questions, particularly on the part of youth and staff about the appropriateness of this move. There are situations where parents may well be playing harmful roles in the lives of youth; and involving them in programs where their youth are also participating may undermine the sanctuary role of programs. It is important to point out that it takes an exceptional staff member to be competent in working with both youth and adults. On the surface, the reader may argue that the competencies of working with youth are easily transferable to work with adults. The authors of this book, however, do not share this perspective. It takes many years of learning, practice, and possessing the "right" attitudes to effectively engage and work with youth, newcomer or otherwise.

Paradigms are of critical importance in helping scholars and practitioners navigate through the many ambiguities associated with practice in the "real world." Critics may argue that paradigms are developed by scholars for scholars. The authors disagree with this statement. Practice without use of a paradigm can best be thought of as random acts of kindness. However, it would be foolish for scholars and practitioners to think that any paradigm can escape enormous challenges in bringing its goals to life through practice. A youth development paradigm has a set of inherent challenges when used to reach newcomer youth. The challenges to using a youth development paradigm with newcomer youth are quite formidable, and this must be acknowledged. Nevertheless, there is a tremendous potential for this paradigm in achieving significant changes in the lives of newcomer youth and their communities.

As noted in this chapter, it is possible to modify some of the key elements of youth development as it is practiced today to take into account the unique set of circumstances newcomer youth find themselves within in this society. A paradigm that does not lend itself to modifications as circumstance change is of very limited utility in social work practice. In short, there is no need to "throw out the baby with the wash water." However, we may have to change the water on occasion. This is one of those occasions.

Conclusion

The youth development field is dynamic and expanding in influence in practice, policy, and academic circles, and it has not reached its full potential for assisting youth to achieve significant and positive transformation. Many of the key concepts and terms addressed in this chapter are no doubt not new to social workers. Nevertheless, youth development's potential for positive change is only matched by the challenges the field faces in harnessing the energy of youth in bringing to life a youth development paradigm. The importance of the field is too great for it not to be willing to meet its challenges. Policymakers, scholars, practitioners, and youth alike must share this goal. In essence, adults play central roles within a youth development paradigm. How they carry out their roles, however, will require a dramatic shift in attitudes. The youth development field cannot do it alone without the aid and partnerships of other social institutions that play influential roles in shaping the life of youth. Adults lead these institutions without exception!

This chapter has outlined a multifaceted perspective on definitions, boundaries of this paradigm, and the core elements of this paradigm. Each of the paradigm's core elements, social arenas, and interventions are worthy of a book unto themselves. The ever-expanding knowledge base of these aspects of youth development makes it challenging for practitioners and scholars to keep abreast of the changes and the thinking about them. Further, the introduction of newcomer groups brings with it corresponding challenges for making this paradigm relevant to them. However, it is only fair to state that the social paradigms cannot remain static and must change as the knowledge base deepens through increased research and scholarship; youth development is not an exception to this point.

There is still considerable debate about the influence of many of the key elements addressed in this chapter and their ultimate influence within a youth development paradigm. The authors believe that this is a healthy indicator of a paradigm's vitality, and its importance is reflected in how well the field of youth services has embraced it. The evolving nature of the field of youth development has broadened its reach beyond youth themselves to also encompass schools and communities. These are indicators that a youth development paradigm will continue to wield considerable influence in education and human service-related professions. The youth development field, it is important to note, is not only expanding in this and other industrialized countries, but throughout the world.

The challenges identified in this chapter are just that—challenges. Not one of them is insurmountable. Furthermore, these challenges have a history that precedes adaptation of a youth development paradigm to newcomer youth. The challenges that have been raised, nevertheless, require considerable attention—dialogue, debate, research, and scholarship. In many ways they strike at the heart of what youth development is in this country. How well the field addresses them, however, will ultimately influence how successful the field will be in the twenty-first century, and its international appeal. Society does not have the luxury of ignoring these challenges! These challenges must not be conceived of as having adults finding solutions for youth without youth actively involved in that process. Adults will need to plan *with* youth rather than plan *for* youth.

Chapter 9 will provide the reader with an opportunity to witness both the rewards and challenges associated with using a youth development paradigm with newcomers in an urban area. The case study that is used, however, also raises important and disturbing questions for social workers. A youth development paradigm may be the "answer" to these types of questions.

Part IV

Reflections from the Field of Practice

> *There are a variety of settings in which adolescents can experience the opportunities needed for positive development. Young people need continuous exposure to positive experiences, settings, and people, as well as abundant opportunities to refine their life skills so that they have the means to move into productive jobs and other roles that build fulfilling relationships.*
>
> —Eccles & Gootman, 2002, p. 43

9

Case Illustration

> *The application of theory to practice is a challenge in any helping profession. Consequently, the facilitation of this application to real-life examples must be stressed in any book that professes to be practice-directed. Case studies provide readers with the rare opportunity to see how practice occurs in otherwise inaccessible settings.*
>
> —Delgado, 2002, p. 233

Introduction

This case study of Reaching Out to Chelsea Adolescents (ROCA) in Chelsea, Massachusetts, will consist of seven sections: (1) Rationale for Case Selection; (2) Setting the Context; (3) Mission, Descriptions of Program Components, and Funding; (4) Evaluation Commitment; (5) Peacemaking Circles; (6) Best Practices; and (7) Role of Social Workers in ROCA. Although each of these subject areas will be addressed as a separate unit, it will become obvious that they are integrally related. Part of this case study provides the reader with a description of various elements as a means of providing requisite background information for the analysis that follows.

Case Study: ROCA, Inc., Chelsea, Massachusetts

Rationale for Case Selection

Case studies have historically played a critical role in the teaching of skills and knowledge related to helping professions, and social work is certainly no exception to this method and approach. Ideally, case studies provide the reader with a unique vantage-point from which to witness the application of theory to real-life situations. A case study's ability to perform this function ultimately dictates the degree to which the reader can take what he or she has read in a book and transfer these lessons to actual events that take into account the unique set of factors and circumstances that the reader faces.

Case studies take on added significance in situations where social interventions that are being proposed advance new paradigms or apply these paradigms to new situations. In this book, the authors are advancing the use of youth development with newcomer youth with particular attention to how best practices manifest themselves in adapting this paradigm to a relatively new type of youth group within this country. This case study pays careful attention to how newcomer youth are integrated into the everyday workings of an organization that embraces a youth development paradigm, and how an organization responds to the dynamic nature of population changes within its geographical area.

Obviously, there are numerous decisions and considerations that are made in the selection of case studies, particularly when only one will be highlighted because of space limitations. Students from Boston University School of Social Work have had a long tradition of having field placements at Reaching Out to Chelsea Adolescents, and current colleagues are still active in working with this organization. Accessibility to a program or organization is always one that is at the top of any list of considerations; location and costs associated with travel to the site are others. However, most important of all is that the case provides the potential, although there are never any guarantees, that it will reflect many of the key points raised throughout the book for the reader to develop an in-depth appreciation of the excitement, challenges, and rewards associated with practice.

Many times, the decision-making process entails authors having to travel long distances and spending considerable time and financial resources to find the ideal site for a case study. Fortunately, such a site was located in the authors' own backyard so to speak. Chelsea, Massachusetts, is located but a few miles from Boston University, thus allowing the authors a tremendous amount of time and freedom to write the case study of ROCA, Inc. The authors of this book are very familiar with the city of Chelsea because of many years of involvement in a variety of professional capacities with social service organizations dating back to the early 1970s, further facilitating the development of a case study. Unfortunately, the role of social work within this organization has been very limited, as the reader will find out toward the end of this case study. This lack of impact on the part of the profession reflects what the authors think to be a broader trend across the country and has serious implications for the future of social work in addressing newcomer youth through a youth development paradigm.

Reaching Out to Chelsea Adolescents is a unique organization because of its emphasis on urban youth and their families, particularly newcomers to this country, its embrace of a youth development paradigm that actively positions youth in decision-making roles within the organization, and the multitude of programs that are offered to youth and the community. This broad reach brings with it a determination to make a difference in the lives of youth through making a difference in the life of a community and taking a holistic perspective on their needs.

This organization has been able to succeed in reaching newcomer youth and finding staff of similar backgrounds to serve this community, and has done so in a context that many other organizations would argue that has been particularly challenging for social-political reasons. The staff not only shares many similarities with the youth that they serve but also bring important qualities that are often never mentioned in job descriptions—caring, trusting, generosity, openness, and availability. Staff members seek to instill in youth a "sense of *belonging* so they see the world as a place where they and all others can chart a positive and personally fulfilling course for themselves, and a sense of purpose and an understanding of their own worth by building and acting on *generosity*" (organization document).

To say that ROCA's accomplishments have won it national if not international recognition would be a serious understatement, as evidenced by the following awards— selected as one of 100 programs included in the first Catalogue for Philanthropy, the New American Appreciation Award by the Massachusetts Office of Refugees and Immigrants Program, and Massachusetts Ten Point Coalition for outstanding work with youth. These awards have made ROCA's mission easier to accomplish, although the program is not without its share of challenges that persist to this moment. Nevertheless, the ultimate and most satisfying award is that of youth participants and their claim to belonging to this organization.

Setting the Context

As evidenced throughout this book, for social work practice to be effective and meaningful, it must be contextualized to take into account local circumstances that may have many elements unique to that area. This section seeks to ground the reader in a variety of subject areas as a means of creating a better understanding of ROCA, its history, and the city of Chelsea. Careful attention will be paid not to overburden the reader with details that can be considered extraneous to the central purpose of this case study. However, in all honesty there very often is a thin line between too much information on a particular subject and just the right amount.

Historical Overview of Chelsea, Massachusetts.   Like many towns and cities throughout Massachusetts, Chelsea has enjoyed a long existence, particularly when compared to cities in other parts of the United States. Chelsea was initially settled in 1624 and was formed as a town in 1839. It was eventually incorporated as a city in 1857 and currently covers 1.8 square miles. Chelsea was named after the famous district in London, England. It is located next to Boston Harbor.

The city has since undergone a series of significant transformations over that time. Initially, it was a trading post during the early colonial period; later, it changed to "manorial estates" and then to an agricultural community. It proceeded to have a history as a ferry landing, a summer retreat, a residential suburb, and finally an industrial city. These periods of transformation also witnessed significant changes in resident composition.

Demographic Profile of Chelsea, Massachusets.   The city of Chelsea has a long and distinguished history in Massachusetts, and the evolutionary process it has undergone very much parallels the process that the state and, for that matter, the country has undergone during its history. The current diversity of the city is reflected in the more than 21 languages that are spoken there. The demographic profile over the past, the current, and the projected speaks to a city that has long been a stopping off point for newcomers to the United States who have stayed long enough to make an imprint before dispersing to all sectors of the country.

Between 1980 and 1990, the total Latino population of Chelsea increased significantly (154 percent) from 3,551 to 9,018, or 14 percent of the total population. The influx of Puerto Ricans (who numbered 4,581) and other Latino groups (4,002) largely fueled this increase in Latinos. The decade of the 1990s witnessed Chelsea experiencing a 22 percent increase in population that was also largely fueled by the arrival of immigrants, mostly from Latino backgrounds. However, this time non-Puerto Rican Latino groups were responsible for the increase.

According to the 2000 U.S. Census Bureau, Chelsea's population numbered approximately 35,000. Latinos, numbering 16,984, or 48.2 percent, represent the largest ethnic group. Puerto Ricans, in turn, are still the largest single subgroups of Latinos, with 5,363, representing 15.3 percent of the total population and 31.6 percent of the Latino community. Other Latino groups from Central and South America numbered 10,734 for 30.6 percent of the city's total population, or 63.2 percent of the Latino community. Almost 30 percent (28.9) were foreign-born, not U.S. citizens, representing a far higher percentage than in the state (6.9 percent) and the nation as a whole (6.6 percent).

The age distribution of Chelsea's population points to a very young population, with 23.4 percent at the age of 15 or younger. This percentage is higher than that of the state (19.8 percent) and the nation (21.4 percent). According to the U.S. Census Bureau count of 2000, there were 9,727 youth enrolled in schools, with 13.2 percent enrolled in preschool and kindergarten, 68.9 percent in grades 1–12, and 17.9 percent in college.

In summary, Chelsea has continued to evolve over its history and has maintained its reputation as being a haven for newcomers to the United States. The historical migration periods experienced by the United States is reflected in the influx and composition of numerous newcomer groups. In the early part of the twenty-first century, Latinos are the most visible in this city. However, what the future holds about other newcomer groups no one can predict.

History of ROCA, Inc.   The name ROCA has taken on the Spanish reference to "rock" or "foundation" to symbolize its importance within the lives of youth (Saposnick, 2003). ROCA, Inc., was established in 1988 as part of the North Suffolk Mental Health Association and had an expressed commitment to reaching youth, families, and the communities within Chelsea. Its origins can be traced to a coalition established to address teen pregnancy in Boston, as noted by its founder and executive director, Molly Baldwin: "Soon after we got together, we realized there were several looming issues in our community but no organization in place to address them." ROCA was created to fill this need. Since its inception, the program has grown into a highly established and respected youth organization that has enjoyed national attention because of its innovative empowerment approach toward reaching and engaging youth within an urban context. In 1991, ROCA expanded to provide services to other Boston neighborhoods (East Boston and Charlestown) and three additional cities in Massachusetts (Lynn, Revere, and Winthrop), and eventually incorporated into its current entity as a nonprofit organization in 1995.

Situated in a converted two-story building that initially housed a car dealership, ROCA is geographically well accessible to the entire Chelsea community. The building houses a recreation center, a basketball court, a dance studio, a daycare center, computer labs, and a host of classrooms. Mr. Pallin, a Jewish Russian immigrant who moved to Chelsea when he was 1 year old, donated this building in 1993. Pallin noted, "I think these young people today deserve the same opportunity to work their butts off that I had. . . . I came here as an immigrant in an impoverished family of nine children—but this country offered me the opportunity to succeed."

It would be a mistake to view ROCA's ascent into the world of youth services without acknowledging its uphill struggle to gain acceptance of adults:

> Despite ROCA's successes, the organization's efforts were unpopular with many adults in the community. Especially early on, when the staff initiated conversations around the hard questions—dealing with gang violence and drugs, healing the post-traumatic stress disorder that plagued the Cambodian community, supporting youth development programs, and celebrating diversity—many residents refused to engage with them, calling them communists or cult leaders and attacking their core values of justice and peacemaking. (Saposnick, 2003, p. 2)

Not surprisingly, the youth were eager to engage in dialogue and be part of an organization that not only welcomed their participation and input but also placed them in decision-making roles within the organization. Over time, adults within the community slowly embraced ROCA's view of empowerment and participation and did not view it as a threat to the community. ROCA serves approximately 15,000 community members annually. Its philosophy on youth involvement is well articulated by Baldwin: "Our theory of change is that, if young people feel that they matter in the world, they'll take care of the important things; they'll make healthier and safer decisions and be more considerate of others" (Saposnick, 2003, p. 2).

Mission, Descriptions of Program Components, and Funding

Mission. An organization's mission statement is often considered the first step in better understanding its primary purpose for existence. In essence, it represents the genetic blueprint for the establishment of programs and services and sets a context from which to examine its shared values and priorities. Further, it provides the community with an important anchor from which to connect it to the broader fabric of the community as represented through other formal and nontraditional settings. Thus, it makes sense to start a description and analysis of ROCA by noting its mission statement: "to promote justice by creating opportunities with youth and families to lead happy and healthy lives."

This mission statement is derived from a vision that stresses meaningful participation of young people and their families thriving and leading social change. ROCA, according to Baldwin, seeks to "provide a safe haven for neighborhood youth, where they gain the skills and knowledge to lead healthier, more successful lives in a safe, caring environment."

Although its mission is simple in definition, it is quite profound in complexity when it is operationalized, as noted in how it is portrayed in the following examples that speak to an organizational climate that is both validating and empowering:

- A place where young people thrive and lead change
- A place where newcomer families can gather and find support
- A place that asks hard questions about violence, race, schools, community involvement and leadership
- A place where peace is promoted in our community and in our country
- A place where police, clergy, school administrators and elected officials train together in Peacemaking Circles
- A place of safety and celebration
- A place where young people learn and practice leadership skills
- A place where immigrants can take ESL classes and where young Latinos lead dance classes
- A place where members of the Cambodian community meet and talk with the mayor
- A place where participatory democracy is alive and is promoted daily
- A place where all are welcomed and all people feel like they belong
- A place where parents and their children come to learn, to grow and to succeed. (organization document)

Program Components.   An organization's abilities to respond to changes in the environment are often cited as key factors in determining its success in surviving through difficult times. This necessitates having a youth-serving organization that is able to modify existing programs or even create new programs that respond to new needs but can be complementary to existing programs. Developing an array of important yet disparate programs can effectively undermine the mission of an organization and seriously alter its direction to the point that it eventually loses sight of the vision that led to its creation.

At the time of this case study, there were six major programs operating at ROCA: (1) Coalition for Youth and Families and Community Building Team; (2) Healthy Families Program; (3) Lynn Project (another city located north of Boston); (4) Project Victory; (5) Youth STAR Program; and (6) VIA Project. These programs are described here to provide a better appreciation of the multitude of services provided to Chelsea and neighboring city residents who are youth.

The Coalition for Youth and Families and Community Building Team is an outgrowth of a coalition established in 1988 and that coalition is widely credited with providing the impetus to establish ROCA. The present-day coalition has expanded its scope from an original focus on teen pregnancy prevention to one that focuses on building various aspects of community capacity through the Padres Unidos (United Parents) and Al-Huda Society initiatives.

Padres Unidos targets newcomer parents who are primarily from Central and South America and other adults who share a central goal of increasing their leadership capacity to organize and lead in making school system decisions affecting their children's education. Stated goals are "1. Share information on the governance of school systems; 2. Develop relationships between administrators and teachers in the school system and Spanish speaking parents in the Latino community; and 3. Develop pathways to increase the participation and leadership of Latino parents in the middle and secondary schools in Chelsea" (organization document). The Al-Huda Society, based in the city of Lynn, is a community partner of ROCA and is a weekend school for Muslim youth.

The Healthy Families Program, in partnership with Massachusetts General Hospital, specifically serves adolescents and young adult mothers during their pregnancy and the first three years of parenthood. This program provides home visiting and outreach to young parents under the age of 20. In addition, a weekly Drop-in Center at ROCA is available on Thursday nights for parents and children to participate in Peacemaking Circles, meet other parents, socialize, and work on projects together. The program also provides ongoing support groups for young parents and offers medical care for sports injuries, high-risk assessments, hepatitis testing, tuberculosis testing, regular checkups, mental health assessment, and referrals to health services when necessary. The Healthy Families Program also provides a much-needed daycare service for these families to facilitate their involvement in educational, job training, and employment programs.

The Lynn Project specifically focuses on street and gang-involved young people and community building within the Cambodian community. Lynn is recognized as having the third-largest concentration of Cambodians in the United States. The Lynn Project is in response to migration of a large number of Cambodians from the greater Boston area to Lynn, which is located 14 miles north. Three primary strategies are utilized within this project: (1) street outreach with youth, (2) restorative justice and community peacemaking, and (3) community organizing and leadership development. ROCA, as a result, has focused on helping Cambodian youth develop trusting relationships with community members and has youth play an increasingly more active and leadership role within their community.

Project Victory is an intensive after-school program for youth aged 12 to 15 years old that utilizes a variety of approaches to meeting their needs. Services include educational support, leadership development, and community service. The underlying goal is focused on youth achieving school success and positive life development. The program spans the entire calendar year. The activities used in the after-school program cover a wide range and includes a combination of education, sports, arts, and cultural programs.

The Youth STAR Program is an AmeriCorps program involving 30 youth and young adults and providing a variety of services such as community health and HIV/AIDS prevention education, as well as organizing and leading observation and environmental services in Chelsea and Revere (neighboring city). Youth participate in a food pantry, take part in an HIV/AIDS peer-to-peer initiative, or work in the adolescent health clinic. Youth STAR members are encouraged to develop important leadership skills and to attain pre-set educational goals focused on obtaining GEDs and a college education. Environmental-focused projects provide youth participants with an opportunity to help conservation and create "green spaces" throughout the community.

Finally, the VIA Project is a multifaceted project with educational and career/employment goals for 16- to 26-year-olds and typifies how the organization has responded to the influx of newcomer youth. The VIA Project was established in 2002 with funding from a variety of sources, with the primary funder being the W. K. Kellogg Foundation. Being true to the mission of ROCA, VIA has an extensive collaborative network: the Massachusetts Department of Youth Services, Employment Resources, Inc., the Metro North Workforce Investment Board Youth Board, the Center for Restorative Justice of Suffolk University (Boston), and Brandeis University—The Center for Youth and Communities. This collaborative network is dynamic and able to incorporate other programs and services depending on the evolving needs of VIA participants. The VIA Project utilizes a two-prong approach toward services—Street School and collaboration with Engaged Institutions. The Street School includes basic education and ESL, developing individual learning plans, employment readiness training, community service opportunities, counseling on demand, substance users' support, harm reduction, gang involvement support, and Peacemaking Circle groups. The Engaged Institutions component, in turn, seeks to create community and systemic change deemed necessary to support young people in their quest to have more options for education and employment.

As evidenced by the type and range of programs described above and its focus on newcomers to the city, ROCA can best be described as a model. True to its mission, these programs strive to provide valuable services but at the same time seek to enhance the community's capacity in the process of doing so. Each of the preceding programs targets a specific aspect of life for residents, yet can be considered complementary and supportive of each other. It would not be surprising to return to this organization 5 or 10 years from the time this study was conducted without finding an array of new programs that take into account ecological changes within Chelsea.

Funding.   Reaching Out to Chelsea Adolescents has managed to attract funding from a wide variety of private and public funding sources. It has an estimated $4 million annual budget and over 80 major funders. The Edna McConnell Clark Foundation provided a five-year grant to help ROCA develop a comprehensive business plan. The W. K. Kellogg Foundation has provided funding for ROCA to organize, coordinate, and lead a national conference on diversity and youth. The active use of volunteers and interns plays a prominent role within any discussion of organizational resources. In many ways, this form of resource is much more valuable than actual dollars from a grant because of its tremendous public relations value and the opportunities it provides outsiders and community residents to be a part of an organization's mission.

Evaluation.   Program evaluation activities have taken on significant influence in youth development-focused programs in the past decade and, not surprisingly, ROCA has embraced a strong commitment toward evaluating its programs and services: "Each program at ROCA . . . has program- and funding-specific evaluations. Programs utilize workplanning systems and have an annual review of learning organization questions focusing on what works, challenges, and lessons learned" (organization document). ROCA's evaluation approach took two years to plan and implement and involved input from community partners, youth, evaluators, youth development professionals, funding partners, and the specific support of the Surdna Foundation. Typically, these evaluation efforts have focused on obtaining input from youth themselves not only in helping to shape research questions but also in carrying out the other facets associated with program evaluation.

The current Director of Evaluation, Mr. Omar Ortez, notes that ROCA has experienced a major "growth moment" and is now focused on "consolidating" this growth. Although the evaluation data clearly help meet funding requirements, Ortez states that the real motivation for serious evaluation is ROCA's own growth and "desire to know." Ideally, the in-depth evaluation process will document if and how the ROCA model works, allowing the organization to then share the model with others and also to seek additional funds. For the past few years, evaluation efforts have focused primarily on the youth participants. Multiple assessment tools were developed that have well captured the youth's "sense of belonging" and "generosity." These instruments, such as the Structured Interview and Street Log, were developed with considerable input from both staff and the youth themselves. However, these tools have not been as successful in capturing the youth's "level of competency" and "sense of independence." Ortez is thus in the process of developing additional indicators to better measure these domains. He is also developing tools to measure ROCA's work with families and the community, which to date has received minimal evaluation attention.

Omar Ortez "pilots" all new forms, as well as offers training to staff on their use. He also does "workout sessions" with staff when his report/analysis is complete, so that collectively they can try to understand what they are seeing, what's happening. He notes that there is an "additional layer" in the evaluation process in a community-based organization like ROCA, since there is a different way of processing things and "street skills are mixed with other kinds of skills." Ortez finds there is more "need for conversation" with staff and with youth participants before the evaluation process can proceed.

While still developing the database, Ortez is already contemplating the "decentralization" of some of the data so that staff can more readily access and better see areas of challenge and accountability issues. He also believes that certain data could provide useful leverage to parents' groups, such as Padres Unidos, in their conversations with the school system. However, he recognizes there are issues of confidentiality involved in any decentralization of the database. In the future, Ortez hopes to add another layer to the evaluation by connecting the quantitative data with "stories" of participants. He dreams of doing multiple individual in-depth interviews and generating qualitative data that will further document and bring to life ROCA's work. Meanwhile, as the only staff member officially charged with program evaluation, Ortez struggles with the challenge of how to make the most of his scarce resources.

Peacemaking Circles

There are many distinctive qualities about ROCA. However, the role and emphasis placed on Peacemaking Circles throughout the organization stand out because of how systematically it has been applied and the nature of the values it stresses. The importance of developing community bonds is well articulated through the use of Peacemaking Circles. In 1999, ROCA brought together a wide range of community members to participate in Peacemaking Circles over a four-day period. The introduction of this method was considered a key milestone for the organization and Peacemaking Circles and its principles have been integrated throughout all of the organization.

Peacemaking Circles have a long and distinguished history within aboriginal and Native American traditions and serve to provide every participant with an opportunity to share their voice with the group:

> In a peacemaking circle, all participants, regardless of age or occupation, are equals in the discussion. Participants feel comfortable speaking freely and often listen to one another for the very first time because the environment is free of pressures and interruptions. Says Baldwin, "Peacemaking circles have been so effective in bringing disparate individuals together that we have integrated these principles into all our programs." (Edna McConnell Clark Foundation, 2003)

Best Practices

How does this case study relate to the issues and best practices identified earlier in this book? The best practices identified and addressed in Chapter 5 and the newcomer issues and needs covered in Chapter 4 can be seen throughout this case study. The importance of youth forming partnerships with adults is evident, as well as the importance of having youth fulfill decision-making roles within an organization. The importance of peers working together toward positive social change rather than engaging in risk-taking behaviors offers much hope for the field.

The role youth development principles play in helping to guide organizational interventions is prominent in ROCA's vision and mission. These principles are also clearly reflected in the following analogy offered by Ms. Sayra Pinto, Director of the VIA Project. Noting the constant availability of a "food table" available to participants at a recent conference, she observed that youth need a "food table"—of acceptance, engagement, and opportunity—constantly available to them. Susan Ulrich, Director of the Youth Star Program, underscored this emphasis on nurturance and empowerment, simply stating, "It's not 'young people have problems,' but young people have talents. These kids, this community are not 'broken,' it's about growth." Youth development principles can be clearly seen in how the six best practices identified in Chapter 5 are carried out on a daily basis.

Enhancement of Adult Caring Relationships with Newcomer Youth.   It is no mistake that ROCA has cast the importance of caring and trusting relationships between youth and adults as a central theme of their vision and mission. The VIA Project's director, Sayra Pinto, comments on the importance of caring adults in the lives of youth: "So many young people in our communities talk about the lack of caring, supportive adults in their lives" (Edna McConnell Clark Foundation, 2003). Thus, the importance of staff goes far beyond competence in particular activities or subject areas and transcends into the arena of adult-youth relationships.

This is such a critical element of ROCA that the authors heard it echoed again and again by staff, who noted that they are frequently the only adult role models the youth have. Staff underscored that their work can only result in success in the context of a real relationship with each youth, and they described multiple ingredients required in building such relationships: the need for outreach to build relationships with youth even before they come to ROCA; the understanding that it takes considerable time for some youth to be "ready" to be in formal programs, yet meanwhile they may still be able to come into the building and just feel "safe"; the importance of a designated "building coverage person" at all times to be available to greet/connect with new youth who drop by; the value of multiple staff knowing the youth and thus the importance of collaborating across programs; and finally, the need to remember that each young person can engage and grow only at his or her own pace.

Enhancement of adult caring relationships with newcomer youth is facilitated when adult staff has a history of participation as youth in ROCA. Investment in staff becomes a prominent part of ROCA's mission, particularly since investment in staff can easily be equated with investment in the Chelsea community. The emphasis on providing employment opportunities to youth participants to make the shift to staff recognizes the talent, values, and commitment youth participants have toward the organization. For example, 16 of the 17 current AmeriCorps volunteers in the Youth Star Program had previously participated in other ROCA programs, and several of the adult staff described themselves as "growing up at ROCA." There is an understanding, however, that making this shift from participant to staff requires patience and investment of time, energy, and resources that often go beyond what is typically experienced in human service programs that do not embrace a youth development or community capacity enhancement paradigm.

Most programs tend to emphasize the importance of educational credentials and internship or employment experience in the field. ROCA recognizes that many of the youth participants who have worked their way into staff positions would normally not be hired by other organizations. These youth participants may not fit a "model profile" that many programs embrace. Consequently, it is expected that making a shift from program participant to staff may require a transition period of anywhere from three to six months. Also, the initial venture into a staff position may not be successful. An unsuccessful transition does not mean that these individuals must leave the organization and never come back. There are instances, however, where this has happened—where former staff members have matured in the time period they were out of ROCA and reapplied and were given a staff position once again.

Caring relationships between adult and youth are only one part of the equation. Staff must also establish and maintain caring relationships among themselves, too. The same commitment and intensity that staff display toward youth is required of staff toward staff. The concept of *burnout* is recognized by staff and there is constant vigilance to make sure that they receive validation and support, and can exercise the right to take time off as an attempt to reenergize themselves. Nevertheless, the satisfaction derived from the work they do with youth and the community is a powerful antidote for burnout.

There is also wide recognition among staff that although there are always many opportunities to seek employment in other youth-serving organizations, there is no other organization like ROCA. Several staff mentioned that ROCA serves the most challenging and needy youth—youth whom "other agencies don't want, don't try or can't serve." Ms. Mehrnoush, educational coordinator of the VIA Project, describes her students as "more desperate for work . . . their other problems more intense," compared to those she's worked with at other agencies. In many ways the uniqueness of ROCA serves to place tremendous expectations and stress on staff but also serves to reinforce the importance of the work that they do and the role of the organization in helping them achieve both personal and community-centered goals for their work.

Successful Brokering between Parental and Peer Influences.   The goal of brokering parental and peer pressure is quite complex because of the interplay of various social factors, such as: (1) youth who do not have family in this country or have family who wish to have nothing to do with them; (2) the family is dysfunctional and playing an active role in encouraging their children to engage in risk-taking behavior; (3) the family may be overly protective, particularly in the case of daughters, and view participation in outside school activities with great suspicion; and (4) the family (particularly those who are recent newcomers) may simply be overwhelmed with trying to survive.

Parents of newcomer youth may fear losing their children as a result of engaging in ROCA activities such as GED classes. On one level, they wish to see their children progress by participating in ROCA. However, participation may well mean that this is a significant step in their children's acculturation in the broader society. Having ROCA staff achieve success with their children can also create feelings of guilt because they were not able to have their children achieve success. ROCA staff must seek to gain the support of parents but not compromise the important work they do with their children. Thus, establishment of adult caring relationships with newcomer youth must, by necessity, carry over to establishment of caring relations with adults, too.

The staff at ROCA must make an assessment of the status of family in the life of youth participants and act accordingly. In cases where family is not present, ROCA in effect becomes a parental substitute in the lives of these newcomer youth. In situations where the family is dysfunctional, ROCA may have to file necessary complaints, to the Department of Social Services for example, and actively seek to have these youth placed in alternative living situations.

In cases where the family is overprotective, much work needs to be undertaken to allay the fears parents may have about their children. This often entails having many home visits to meet with parents and establish a relationship based on mutual trust. Having parents visit ROCA and possibly having them enroll in programs and activities themselves so they can personaly experience the climate of the organization is highly beneficial. Youth participants may even be provided transportation to and from their homes as another way of allaying the concerns of parents. This commitment to help parents work through their concerns and anxieties about their children expanding their contact with the broader community is considered an everyday part of the work of staff.

It is considered to be artificial to separate youth from their parents for the purposes of providing services. Youth benefit from participating and parents can too. As one staff member observed, there is a need to "build parents' capacity so they can understand their child," and within some families, "the need to teach them to love their child differently." Thus, a holistic perspective toward engagement results in youth as well as adults finding a welcoming climate. Parents, if they wish, can visit ROCA to see their children perform in dance or basketball games, for example. Soccer games have been developed that consist of both youth and adults, thus allowing parents and their children to participate in the same activities.

Reinforcement of Language and Culture.   The ROCA organization explicitly affirms and reinforces language and culture throughout its programs. Upon entering the building, one sees banners depicting different cultural heritages and hears multiple languages being spoken and a rich mix of music being played. In addition, on some days there will be the delicious smells of "ethnic dishes" wafting through the hallways. A range of holidays are observed, and information on language and cultural ancestry is carefully collected on all program evaluation forms. Coming into contact with people from diverse backgrounds may be a totally new experience for some newcomer youth, as in the case of Bethlehem Dejene:

> I arrived here two years ago to mingle with the diverse people of Chelsea. In Ethiopia we were not lucky enough to have a place like ROCA, where we can meet other people and share their culture and experiences. (ROCA, 1999, p. 15)

As noted throughout this book, language and culture very often represent the cornerstone of any culturally competent approach toward social work services involving newcomers. An ability to communicate and understand and embrace the value of cultural traditions, beliefs, and values serves as a bridge between a social worker and the newcomer consumer regardless of their age. Thus, youth development programming must effectively integrate these key elements to ensure that practice resonates with the newcomer and his or her community. The story of Thai Taing does a wonderful job of showing the importance of culture in helping newcomer youth meet the challenges of life in this country:

> I grew up in this organization. I was exposed to different things. I got interested in things. The street work caught me. When I was a youth member, I wanted to be a street worker, myself. Myself, I had a goal, a reflection of me, who I could be. We had a lot of racial issues that I went through personally. The history of myself, my family, racially, and ethnically—that is who I am today. I identify myself as Cambodian Chinese. The challenges I faced growing up were addressed to me as a Cambodian citizen. Now as I grow up and make noise, I want them to address me as a Cambodian. Yes, this is the same Cambodian person that you ridiculed, made fun of—so what. I am lost and found. I started as Cambodian. I was raised American. ROCA has built an opportunity to revisit my cultures with my mentors. I didn't grow up in Cambodia. I grew up here. They shared with me what my people went through, the wars, the killing. Now I can share with other young people what it is like. Now they can look up to me. (ROCA, 1999, p. 13)

Bringing together youth from many different cultures in itself serves to help an organization such as ROCA develop its own distinctive organizational culture, as noted by Saroeum Poung:

> ROCA has its own way of culture. It is very rich. It is about everything that people bring with them—wisdom, inspiration, knowledge, dealing with the truth, and what is right. How we can grow and be better, that is our culture. Unified all cultures, no matter what, who you are, you can be at ROCA. (ROCA, 1999, p. 14)

An organization's capacity to carry out goals that reinforce the importance of language and culture can easily be measured by the capacities of its staff to communicate in multiple languages and by getting programming to integrate important cultural values. Thus, the extent of ROCA's staff who have the capacity to speak more than one language represents an initial building block for this best practice. Over 75 percent of ROCA's staff speak at least two languages. The high percentage of ROCA staff speaking another language besides English is a testament to the importance of language in reaching and engaging youth and their parents.

Malika Bey provides a vivid description of the importance of a diverse staff at ROCA:

> Staff are diverse. They each bring different cultures. ROCA respects everyone's culture. We have the freedom to celebrate our own cultures. We allow other people to celebrate their culture. (ROCA, 1999, p. 14)

Bey's description of an interaction of two ROCA participants from different cultural backgrounds highlights the richness of experiences at the organization:

> The Cambodian women went to the Somali women's aerobics. Then one of the Cambodian women spoke French and one of the Somali women spoke French and they started to talk to each other. (ROCA, 1999, p. 14)

The grounding of organizational mission and services within a cultural context, although noble in character, is quite challenging. This grounding in the values, beliefs, and traditions of newcomer youth and their families is also not without its share of conflicts. Peacemaking Circles have been embraced for a variety of very important reasons, not the least of which is the emphasis on respect, values, beliefs, and traditions. The valuing of diversity in participation and staff brings with it a host of challenges to organizations such as ROCA. The constant infusion of new ethnic groups into Chelsea results in a need for the organization to be responsive to these changes and needs. This invariably means hiring staff that reflects the cultural traditions and languages of these new groups, and making a commitment that all staff will learn about the new groups.

Yet another challenge lies in the question of identity in the lives of newcomer youth. Staff certainly recognize that these youth are in the process of further forming their self-identities, both as adolescents/young adults and as "New Americans," and offer support in their ongoing identity development. However, they also realize there may be unique challenges for those who are undocumented. Situations of youth claiming ethnic identities other than their own is often done for the purposes of being able to obtain employment, such as in the case of one individual from Central America claiming to be from Puerto Rico. The consequence of this falsification takes on greater prominence in young participants because it necessitates that they lie to the external world and, in many cases, to their peers. Fears of being "found out" are ever present, with deportation a constant threat. Since staff are aware of these issues, and indeed some staff have themselves experienced them, they are able to supportively discuss them with the youth.

Finally, ROCA recognizes that tensions that are often inherent within the community between different newcomer groups find their way into the organization. There are instances when relations between these groups having tension in the community are cordial within ROCA. Participants, nevertheless, upon leaving the confines of ROCA, may revert back to perceptions of other newcomer groups that are less than favorable. However, discrimination of any kind is not acceptable at ROCA. The search for models or frameworks stressing collaboration and trust between groups to use during in-service training is an ever-constant search. Staff sharing their experiences with participants is considered one way of developing trust and openness between groups with histories of antagonisms.

Reinforcement of language and culture serves not only to instill pride in participants but also to serve as a mechanism for bridging differences between groups, which will hopefully carry over into community interactions. The similarities between groups are far greater than the differences, and they all share a dream of life in this country.

Interventions That Are Culturally Harmonious.   Interventions must be culturally syntonic and respect the values, beliefs, and traditions held by newcomer families and youth. No youth development program stressing the importance of community can afford to limit its scope to the confines of a program with a very limited vision of influence. No program, after all, can be considered an island, although it can certainly be an oasis for youth facing incredible stressors and challenges in their lives. ROCA's drive to change the environment newcomer youth live in, and at the same time broaden the youth's reach by participating in the lives of the general community, typifies this best practice and is embraced and carried out throughout all facets of programming and organizational life.

When staff represent the same ethnic backgrounds of youth participants, they are able to assume a very influential role in the lives of youth by role modeling behavior and attitudes that are culturally syntonic and respectful of cultural traditions. Thus, staff are placed in a position of helping youth struggle with the tensions inherent in cultural clashes common in this society for newcomer youth and their families. Staff are able to share stories and strategies with youth and provide them with knowledge and competencies that help them socially navigate their way through school and other important institutions in their lives.

Respect for cultural values is also reflected in specific program activities. For example, during a visit to a Project VIA class, the authors observed that students were not only asked to help translate for each other but they were also asked to think about how ROCA could help the younger children in ROCA programs. Such an approach clearly reflects a "sense of community" and responsibility for those who are younger—values that are inherent in many of the newcomer groups represented in the class. ROCA's ability to successfully engage parents and community leaders from specific ethnic/religious communities (i.e., Cambodian, Muslim, and Central American) also obviously speaks to its respect for cultural values and beliefs. Indeed, the core components of cultural competence, as outlined in Chapter 7, are well demonstrated throughout ROCA's programs and by its staff.

Interventions That Integrate.   Interventions must not only be driven from the perspective of the newcomer but they must also actively integrate newcomers within the broader community. Many newcomer youth participants in ROCA's programs bring with them a host of experiences that can best be classified as traumatic and, as is often the case, a limited exposure to peoples from other cultures, as in the case of Misald Alhodzic from Bosnia:

> I came to ROCA because I know that they could help me get my friends off of drugs and violence and back into school. I left Bosnia when I was 12, in 1993. I remember seeing people killed right in front of me—not just one person, but many. I was lucky we didn't lose any family, but many friends were killed. When I got here and everything was normal, it took me a while to get used to it. America was a new country for me, I never saw so many people who spoke a different language than me. Never knew that there were so many people that didn't know that Bosnia existed and didn't know people were dying. (ROCA, 1999, p. 14)

The ROCA organization also helps to further integrate newcomer youth into the community at the individual level, as staff respond to issues of trust and accountability. Newcomer youth pose incredible challenges for an organization when trust has not been established prior to engaging youth. What name they go by may change over a period of time to reflect their increased trust. What do the authors mean by this? Simply, newcomer youth may be untrusting of any organization wishing to engage them because of their past experiences with organizations. Thus, they may provide one name upon entry into a program. As their trust level increases, they will be more likely to provide their real names. Staff, as a result, must be prepared to make necessary adjustments to records and be prepared to use the proper names during program activities.

This shifting toward a more reality base to their identities reflects an important phase in an organization being better able to help youth integrate into the broader society. Another positive step in this direction is having newcomer youth be more willing to accept responsibility in events in their lives that have been problematic, as in the case of formal schooling, for example. Stories related to unpleasant experiences in these systems generally take a one-sided perspective and neglect to assign any fault on their part. Ownership of responsibility is critical in better preparing newcomer youth to be willing to engage institutions to their benefit.

The ROCA organization has ongoing activities that focus on collaboration and intersect with broader social systems, such as schools, health, law enforcement, and social services. These partnerships are one means of ROCA seeking to integrate newcomers within the broader community. This process, needless to say, necessitates staff undertaking numerous meetings with these systems as a means of facilitating relationship development and sustaining existing partnerships.

Youth organizations that have been successful in reaching hard-to-reach youth have never had the luxury of just providing a sanctuary for these youth and being oblivious to the events surrounding their lives in the community. For example, there was a one-week period during the authors' visits to ROCA when there were five drug-related overdoses, two of which resulted in deaths. One of the deaths involved a 15-year-old girl who overdosed on heroin. There was also a mass arrest of 22 youth from Central

America under suspicion of planning to engage in gang-related violence. Needless to say, these events occurred in Chelsea since their implications found their way into ROCA. Youth participants were affected. There were serious concerns about their safety and the safety of loved ones. Planned activities experienced an excessive overflow of youth participants during this period, with many of them being new to ROCA. The crisis in the community became a crisis for ROCA staff to handle.

In addition to responding to such community crises, ROCA has proactive activities within their programs that facilitate the integration of newcomers in the broader community. For example, almost half of the Youth Star Program participants are assigned to work in the community, focusing on health education and community service. Another example is Project VIA students' participation in an art exhibit in a museum in Lowell, Massachusetts. Their teacher noted, this "exposes kids, gets them out of Chelsea." She described a strong ripple effect of this art project, reflected in a visibly increased confidence among these young adults.

The Peacemaking Circle trainings have been of tremendous value in strengthening community partnerships, and staff from multiple agencies (schools, police, child protection, juvenile justice, and victim witness) have participated. Several ROCA staff describe how the "conversation has changed" as a result, with a shift from rather negative assumptions about each other to a mutual focus on what the youth need and how staff can support each other and this process.

The mission of ROCA has translated into a service/recreational/educational focus on youth and families that many other systems have either given up on or do not wish to address. Thus, specifically seeking to reach newcomer youth does minimize, although not totally eliminates, adverse reactions from other organizations within the community. Success with youth who have not been successful in other institutions—such as schools, for example—does cause discomfort on the part of these institutions, making ROCA staff having to work even more diligently to achieve their goals of helping youth transform themselves from "losers" to "heroes" and "winners." This statement may well appear to be foreign to many of the readers of this book. However, it is sad to say that turf issues and rivalries are very much an operative reality in the world of youth services. Nonetheless, the participation of a wide range of community service providers in the Peacemaking Circle trainings does appear to be mitigating some of these inherent tensions.

Interventions That Empower.   Interventions need to empower and address issues of racism and nativism through the use of advocacy and reforming existing laws that seek to limit or prohibit newcomer youth from maximizing their potential within this society. An organization's ability to advocate and seek reforms of laws and practices detrimental to newcomer youth—as well as provide a range of educational, recreational, and social services—is challenging at best and possibility undoable in the vast majority of the cases. As a result, ROCA, must walk a thin line between empowering youth participants and seeking to achieve social change in the broader community. The latter approach can result in significant political backlash and poses a constant struggle for this and other organizations seeking to serve individuals and embracing a broad social change agenda. Tensions are inherent in these situations and ROCA is no exception to this scenario.

Programs targeting the needs of newcomer youth and their community cannot ignore the deleterious influence of racism on the lives of these youth by focusing specifically on instrumental or expressive-related services. Thus, it is incumbent on program staff to actively identify the presence of social and economic justice issues that embrace racism and nativism tendencies and that can be manifested at the local level through various institutions with specific mandates for serving youth.

The VIA Project, for example, actively promotes systemic changes by serving as a catalyst in the creation of opportunities in the lives of youth participants. This role can take on various manifestations, such as entering into active partnerships and collaborations with other social organizations. However, it can also take on an advocacy role involving youth as social change agents in pursuit of social and economic justice for themselves and their community. Peacemaking Circles, too, influence this best practice, as noted by Baldwin: It is "a unique and highly effective method of problem solving that successfully builds lines of communication across diverse cultures, groups, ages, gender, builds trust within communities, and instigates collective social change" (Edna McConnell Clark Foundation, 2003).

Controversy surrounding work with gangs typifies many of the challenges an organization must contend with when actively addressing a major social issue. Invariably, there are many community misunderstandings pertaining to what kind of work is necessary to address gangs, and in this case, those consisting of newcomer youth. ROCA's street work as part of the Victory Program is an excellent example. Staff has been accused of sheltering, warning gang members of upcoming raids, covering up gang crimes, and even condoning their activities. Organizations reaching out to controversial groups will encounter similar reactions from the broader community. However, how effective can ROCA be if it essentially turns its back on a young group because of fears about community backlash? In essence, all youth are welcomed and those with controversy could probably benefit the most from participation in ROCA programming.

Within ROCA, staff also are acutely aware of issues of racism and the backlash against immigrants, particularly those who are undocumented. Although one staff person noted that institutionalized racism is so pervasive that the youth are simply "desensitized to it," staff do address lack of power/access and actively support the youth in talking about their experiences. Further, as an organization, ROCA consistently and visibly demonstrates its commitment to serving all youth, regardless of race, ethnicity, religion, and/or legal status.

Role of Social Workers at ROCA

The involvement of social workers within ROCA has historically and currently been very limited. This revelation did not come as any great surprise to the authors of this book, having been involved in numerous innovative youth-focused programs throughout the country. Rarely have social workers found their way into these types of organizations. In ROCA's case, involvement has been limited to one social worker providing clinical supervision/consultation and graduate social work interns.

Why has there been a near-absence of social workers? Well, the answer did not come as any great surprise to the authors either. Professional social workers have become so professional that they cannot function effectively in grass-roots community organizations, although the history of social work origins date back to urban centers and communities. Many social forces have shaped social work's mission over the years and this evolution has effectively created barriers between social workers and the people they seek to serve.

Conclusion

It becomes quite evident that the history of ROCA cannot be disentangled from the history of Chelsea. The city's history as a refuge for newcomer groups to the United States has continued to where it is today. However, the present day has Latinos from many different countries throughout Central and South America shaping Chelsea's future and its youth in particular shaping how key institutions in their lives can be more responsive to their capacities and needs.

Youth service-oriented organizations must be prepared to change and take into account shifting demographic profiles, issues, and challenges, not only to survive but thrive in a social-political climate of great uncertainty. ROCA is an organizational example of how the ecology of urban areas in the United States has changed over the past two decades and will no doubt continue to do so in the future. Its uniqueness and effectiveness, as noted by Baldwin, can be attributed to its vision and values: "It is the vision and values of belonging (that everyone has a place in our community and society) and generosity that are the foundation. . . . ROCA grows and adapts to the changing needs of the communities and with each other. We continually ask, 'What is working, what are the challenges, what are the lessons, and what are the priorities?' It is this vision that drives the organization."

The integration of key youth development principles into practice with new-comer youth is not only possible but can be quite effective in helping them and their community make a successful transition to this country. The absence of social work within the organization and the reasons behind this absence are very distressing for the authors of this book and raise critical questions about what role, if any, social workers will play in organizations such as ROCA across the country. A lack of influence in helping to shape interventions with newcomer youth means that social work will take a backseat to engaging one of this country's fastest growing demographic groups in the early part of this century. This as well as other topics will be addressed in the next and final chapter of this book.

Part V

Themes for Future Directions

Even a cursory review of immigration as a research topic shows that this is not an issue limited to the U.S. or even to the Americas . . . all indicators show that migration is a global phenomenon. . . . The world, however, looks at the U.S. as a country where immigrants have met unprecedented access, consequently special responsibilities accrue to the U.S. democracy.

—Martinez-Brawley & Zorita, 2002, pp. 63–64

10

Epilogue

> *Tolerance, inclusion, equality and effective inter-group relations are not mere philosophical or theoretical abstractions that can be easily ignored. They are the indispensable elements of the societies in which we now live. This holds true whether or not a country's national mythology has caught up with the reality of immigrants and immigration, and whether or not its politicians have acknowledged that advanced industrial societies are in fact multi-ethnic societies.*
>
> —Feldblum & Klusmeyer, 1999, p. 5

Introduction

This chapter draws on a multitude of common themes from the ROCA case illustration presented in Chapter 9 and integrates key concepts from the literature. It provides an opportunity to reflect on the subject matter and to identify key areas that the authors believe will be prominent in practice with refugee and immigrant youth in the early part of the twenty-first century.

Critical Themes

The writing of a book is very much like a journey or adventure. This chapter will hopefully capture for the reader the joy and pain experienced in writing this book by identifying nine critical and cross-cutting themes that emerged for the authors based on our experience in researching and writing this book. The reader, of course, may not agree with this list. However, it is undeniable that these themes strike at the heart of what will eventually emerge as best practices with newcomer youth in the coming years.

Terminology

It is remarkable how terms and labels seem to develop a life of their own in professional circles. The field of newcomers is no exception. Terms such as *immigrant, asylee, illegal alien, undocumented, refugee, newcomer,* and *native* do not do justice to the human experience newcomers bring with them to their new homeland. These terms unfortunately provide a much too narrow perspective on this phenomenon.

The authors' attempt to develop a new term that best captures the commonalties of the experiences of different groups proved unsuccessful. Thus, we, too, were relegated to using terms that we did not think accurately portrayed the experiences of newcomer youth, their families, or communities. Perhaps these terms and labels had much greater meaning at the turn of the twentieth century, but some may well argue that they did not capture well the experiences of early migration groups either.

Talent and Success

One cannot help but be in awe of newcomer youth and their incredible abilities to bounce back, thrive, and even succeed beyond their parents' wildest wishes. These youth have developed a very focused purpose in life that, in many ways, is a source of strength for them and an inspiration for others. In addition, these youth have managed to keep a firm grasp of their cultural heritage yet are able to embrace their new status and perspective of life in this country. This is not to say, however, that these youth did not experience incredible challenges or did not have critical needs that were going unmet. The literature is well grounded in the needs, issues, and challenges of these youth. Equal attention, however, must now be given to their competencies and abilities to navigate socially without penalty of social death occurring.

Best Practices

Social work and best practices with newcomer youth—are we there yet? Social workers face incredible challenges in practice with newcomer youth. On one hand, workers need to help them obtain the social tools to successfully navigate their way through life in the United States. Unfortunately, this occurs during a time when there are renewed hostilities toward newcomers. On the other hand, workers need to protect newcomer youth because once they enter this country, they are entering an environment that can be classified as toxic to their health—a danger zone, if you wish. Consequently, best practices with newcomer youth mean establishment of a buffer around them to protect them at all times. Of course, this is not possible. Nevertheless, some practitioners may argue that it is still a goal that should be sought in any form of best practices. The reality is that the more acculturated newcomer youth become, the higher the likelihood of them participating in social and health risk behaviors.

Newcomers' Contributions

Can this nation really exist without the contributions of newcomers? There is absolutely no denying that newcomers, be they undocumented or otherwise, are as much a part of the nation's social fabric as their predecessors were during the nineteenth and much of the twentieth centuries. The controversy surrounding this nation's policies toward newcomers reflects a tremendous amount of ambivalence. This country, like it or not, has become very dependent on the presence of newcomers. The United States needs newcomers to carry out many of the functions that "ordinary Americans" are no longer willing to carry out either because of low wages, low status, or danger. However, as a whole, the nation does not want to acknowledge this dependence or accept these new members of society as fellow "citizens." The country invariably seeks to deprive them of legal rights for obtaining services to have their social, health, and educational needs met, particularly if it involves use of tax dollars. Ironically, these individuals, with few exceptions, are law abiding and taxpayers and, in the case of the undocumented, cannot possibly receive social security payments if they reach retirement age.

Much talk has surfaced since September 11th about closing the nation's borders to prevent undocumented persons from entering the country. The authors simply do not believe it is possible to close our borders, however. The nation certainly has not been able to do so to prevent the influx of drugs, a much less challenging task. The number of undocumented people entering this country has largely gone unabated since the terrorist attacks of September 11th.

Also, the significant drop in refugee admissions (lowest in the past 28 years) since September 11th is another indicator of the negative sentiment toward immigrants. Keep in mind that refugees are legal immigrants and none of the individuals who carried out the attack against the United States entered the country as a refugee. Terrorized and tortured refugees are seeking a safe haven in the United States, and it would be a mistake to assume that these individuals are trying to harm this country.

Currently, there is no youth component in the United States refugee admission program. Adding a youth component to the standard resettlement services for refugees would be one way to ensure that immigrant youth will not be left on their own. This could be done either by adding youth services to agencies that resettle refugees or having proper referral services to programs where youth can receive appropriate services.

Racial Dynamics

Many people would argue that this nation's view of the world was greatly shaped and influenced by the centrality of slavery in the nation's social fabric. As a result, race relations have historically been viewed from a Black-White perspective. However, the shift in demographic composition has largely been fueled by immigration. The number of newcomers from Latino countries in the Western Hemisphere, as noted in Chapter 2, has been so pronounced that this trend, combined with high fertility and low-death rates, have converged to make Latinos the largest "minority" in the United States.

All demographic data indicate that the numerical gap between African Americans and Latinos will only continue to widen in the next 50 years, raising important social and political questions about how this nation will address issues of diversity, access, and social-economic justice. When placing the subject of *urban* into the discussion, since the vast majority of newcomers are settling in urban areas that have historically been home to the nation's communities of color, then any discussion of race relations will require that the ethnic and racial backgrounds of newcomers be considered. Social navigation, as a result, needs to be contextualized within an urban environment with a multitude of ethnic and racial groups being a part of this experience.

Where Is Social Work?

It is ironic that a book devoted to social work practice with newcomer youth would use a case study to illustrate best practices in which social workers are virtually absent. It was noted in the case study in Chapter 9 that social workers were really not present in any significant degree within ROCA; this both surprised and did not surprise the authors.

Previous case studies in organizations providing innovative services to marginalized youth did not have social workers playing significant roles other than possible referral agents. The history of the profession had workers playing important roles in helping newcomers to this country through the birth of the settlement house movement. Although these efforts were far from perfect, they still represented a substantial commitment and vision on the part of the profession to reach out and engage newcomer groups in urban communities. Urban communities, particularly those on the coasts, were the primary ports of entry into this country.

Has the profession become so professionalized that work in community-based organizations that embrace principles of empowerment and decision-making participation are not considered attractive enough to warrant involvement? The authors' sincere hope is that this is not the case over the long run and that all social workers rediscover their origins and be prepared to commit to the valuable work that is inherent in working with newcomers to this country's shores.

Another area in which social workers could play an important role is advocacy and policy change on behalf of immigrants. The average American would likely have a difficult time navigating "the system"—it becomes much more difficult for a newcomer who is trying to learn the basics about living in a new country and culture. Thus, immigrants become an easy target for policymakers who seek to fix the financial problems and budget deficit by cutting services to them, because the possibility of immigrants getting heard or uprising is much lower than any other group.

Advocacy on behalf of asylum seekers, a group who is not entitled to any basic services, is an area in need of much attention and work. For fear of being detained and deported, asylum seekers never object to their extremely difficult living conditions during the asylum process. In many European countries, asylum seekers are entitled to housing and work authorization or financial assistance from the government. The hope of the authors is that a similar system will be put in place in the United States.

Mutual Learning

The prevailing discourses regarding newcomers generally seem to focus on how to keep them out or how to assimilate them once they're here. Far too seldom do we consider what we can learn from them and their cultures. In an era of scarce resources, concerns about national security, and an increased focus on "family" and "home," this question seems particularly pertinent.

Certainly, many newcomer youth, parents, and communities know a great deal about managing with scarce resources, both in their homelands and in the United States. Some have strong traditions of collective support, informal "lending" associations, and creative use of indigenous materials. The majority of newcomers, unfortunately, have also had experience with war or security issues in their homelands, yet somehow they have found ways—tapping individual, cultural, community, and/or spiritual resources—to go on living their lives despite the uncertainties.

Finally, most newcomers have strong traditions related to family. Even if they are separated by miles and migration, they find ways to remain connected and to support each other. Ideally, whether practitioners work with newcomers in youth development programs, schools, medical/mental health settings, or community-based organizations, social workers will take the time to consider not only how they may best serve newcomers, but how and what can be learned from them. This kind of "mutual learning" requires active curiosity and genuine respect for other cultures, as well as "cultural humility" related to one's own beliefs and systems. If pursued, it can enrich social workers both as individuals and as practitioners, as well as agencies and communities as a whole.

Bicultural/Bilingual Social Workers

The latest census documents the ever-increasing diversity in the United States. This diversity clearly brings great richness to U.S. society, but it also brings unique challenges for human services consumers and providers alike. At hospitals, schools, child welfare agencies, mental health clinics, and youth programs around the country, far too many current and potential clients or consumers face significant cultural and linguistic barriers. Clearly, all social workers need to become more culturally competent so they can better serve diverse populations; however, the profession also desperately needs to have more bicultural/bilingual social workers, particularly those who represent the newest population groups.

Multiple measures can be taken to ensure this:

1. Schools of social work can look to their recruitment strategies, scholarship opportunities, curriculum content, faculty composition, and student support services.
2. Specialized educational programs can be developed that reach out to newcomer populations in order to understand their beliefs regarding health and illness, to demystify formal Western-style social work practice, to introduce social work as a profession/career to be considered, and to establish credibility within these communities.
3. Government-sponsored social work scholarship and training programs, such as those targeting African Americans and Latinos in the past, would ideally now be made available for the wide spectrum of newcomer populations.
4. More agencies can make the hiring of bicultural/bilingual staff a priority, commit to creating an agency environment that values and supports them, and recognize that their work with newcomer communities may well require additional agency flexibility and creativity.

Lives of Hope

Writing this book has, of course, had its moments of frustrations as well as the inevitably missed deadlines. Mostly, however, it has been a journey of joy. There is a growing wealth of literature on newcomers and expansive materials on youth development; the challenge for the authors has been to better link the two. Working with colleagues who each brought special expertise and diverse perspectives has made for a lively and fruitful cross-fertilization process, and there was a true "luxury of learning" in the many hours of reading and interviewing.

There was also exposure to great passion—in researchers' rich data analysis, in the lives and stories of newcomer youth themselves, and in the energy and dedication of the ROCA staff. Such passion is surely contagious and serves to strengthen the authors' own commitment to these issues. Finally, throughout this process, the authors have been privileged to come to know so many "lives of hope"—newcomer youth, their parents, and the communities who are successfully rebuilding their lives in this country and enriching us all.

Conclusion

It is fitting to end this book with a quote. Breitbart (1998) has issued a challenge for all those who embrace a mission of service involving youth that has relevance to the perspective and work proposed in this book:

> In the process of imposing adult derived theories of social change, . . . we must be careful not to obscure the important role that young people's creative environmental interventions can play as a mode of survival—a survival that depends as much on youth opportunities to "play" and nurture hope as it does on generating new collective redefinitions of neighbourhood and lessons for adults about the necessary components of urban revitalisation. (p. 325)

References

Aarim-Heriot, N. (2003). *Chinese immigrants, African-Americans, and racial anxiety in the United States, 1848–82*. Urbana: University of Illinois Press.

Abbady, T. (2002, March 3). Venezuelans are flocking to South Florida. *The Miami Herald*, p.1.

Abraham, Y. (2003, April 19). Minus ending, immigrant family's story's is familiar. *Boston Globe*, p. B6.

Agbayani-Siewart, P. (1994). Filipino American culture and family: Guidelines for practitioners. *Families in Society*, 75, pp. 429–238.

Aguilar, L. (2001, August 6). Colorado a haven for immigrants; Hispanic, Asian influx reaches beyond cities. *Denver Post*, p. A7.

Aitken, S.C. (2001). *Geographies of young people: The morally contested spaces of identity*. New York: Routledge.

Alaggia, R., Chau, S., & Tsang, K.T. (2001). Astronaut Asian families: Impact of migration on family structure from the perspective of the youth. *Journal of Social Work Research*, 2, pp. 295–306.

Albro, W. (Ed.) (1998, August 1). Minorities, immigrants become home-market force, p. TR8 (http://www.realtor.org/rmomag.nsf/pages/Minorities199Archive1998Aug).

Alvarez, M. (1999). The experience of migration: A relational approach in therapy. *Journal of Feminist Therapy*, 11, pp. 1–29.

American Civil Liberties Union (ACLU). (2002). *Immigrants rights*. New York: Author.

American Civil Liberties Union of Northern California. (2002, November 13). New ACLU report profiles individuals caught in post-Sept. 11 backlash in northern California.

Amodeo, M., & Jones, K. (1997). Viewing alcohol and other drug use cross-culturally: A cultural framework for clinical practice. *Families in Society*, 78, pp. 240–254.

Amodeo, M., Peou, S., Grigg-Saito, D., Berke, H., Pin-Riebe, S., & Jones, K. (1999). Designing culturally specific programs: Early lessons from a Cambodian substance abuse intervention project. Unpublished manuscript.

Amodeo, M., Robb, N., Peou, S., & Tran, H. (1996). Adapting mainstream substance-abuse interventions for Southeast Asian clients. *Families in Society*, 7, pp. 403–412.

Anderson, E. (1999). *Code of the streets: Decency, violence, and the moral of the inner city*. New York: Norton.

Anderson, G.M. (2000). Immigrants in detention: I.N.S. officials claimed that Bible study offered "unreasonable hope" to detainees. *America*, 182, pp. 13–14.

Andino, A.T. (2002, September 2). Refugees work to keep area thriving: Businesses set pace with fruitful jobs. *Florida Times-Union* (Jacksonville), p. B1.

Anguiano, R.P.V. (2001). Planting Seeds Family Enrichment Program: Serving rural immigrant Hispanic families and their youth in eastern North Carolina. *Journal of Extension*, 39, pp. 1–4.

Anonymous. (2002). Positive youth development through community-based programs. *Leadership for Student Activities*, 30, pp. 46–47.

Antony, E.J. (1987). Risk, vulnerability and resilience. An overview. In E.J. Anthony & B. Cohler (Eds.), *The invulnerable child* (pp. 3–48). New York: Guilford.

Apfel, R.J., & Simon, B. (1996). Psychosocial interventions for children of war: The value of a model of resiliency. *Medicine & Global Survival*, 3, pp. 70–99.

Arizona Republic. (2001, August 26). Dying to work, p. 1.

Armas, G.C. (2003, January 21). Hispanics now outnumber Blacks in U.S. *Associated Press Release*, p. 1.

Armas, G.C. (2002, December 6). Immigrants fuel rise in labor force, report says. *Boston Globe*, p. A4.

Asian American Legal Defense and Education Fund (AALDEF). (2003). *Voting rights* (http://www.aaldef.org/voting.html).

Associated Press. (2001, December 11). DA drops investigation of immigrant health Care. State and Regional Section, p. 1.

Associated Press State & Local Wire. (2003a, March 2). Undocumented immigrants get fewer organs than they donate, p. 1.

Associated Press State & Local Wire. (2003b, January 22). Hispanics majority in Phoenix by 2007, p. 1.

Associated Press State & Local Wire. (2001, January 5). New INS standards could force changes at privately owned prisons, jails, p. 1.

Audi, T. (2003, April 9). Special federal teams expelling large numbers of immigrants. *Detroit Free Press*, p. 1.

Azima, F.J.C., & Grizenko, N. (Eds.). (2002). *Immigrant and refugee children and their families: Clinical, research, and training issues.* Madison, CT: International Universities Press.

Bailer, J. (1998). Locked away: Immigration detainees in jails in the U.S. *Human Rights Watch*, 10, pp. 1–86.

Baines, T.R., & Selta, J.R. (1999). Raising the rest of the neighborhood. *Reclaiming Children and Youth*, 8, pp. 25–30.

Bakewell, O. (2000). Can we ever rely on refugee statistics? *Radical Statistics: The Journal* (http://www.radstats.org.uk/no072article1.htm).

Balcazar, H., & Qian, Z. (2000). Immigrant families and sources of stress. In P. McKenry & S. Price (Eds.), *Families and change: Coping with stressful events and transitions* (2nd ed., pp. 359–377). Thousand Oaks, CA: Sage.

Baldassare, M. (2000). *California in the new millennium: The changing social and political landscape.* Berkeley, CA: University of California Press.

Balgopal, P.R. (Ed.). (2000). *Social work practice with immigrants and refugees.* New York: Columbia University Press.

Ball, A., & Heath, S.B. (1993). Dances of identity: Finding an ethnic self in the arts. In S.B. Heath & M.W. McLaughlin (Eds.), *Identity and inner-city youth: Beyond ethnicity and gender* (pp. 69–93). New York: Teachers College Press.

Bandura, A. (1995). Exercise of personal and collective efficacy in changing societies. In Bandura (Ed.), *Self-efficacy in changing societies* (pp. 1–45). New York: Cambridge University Press.

Bandura, A. (1989). Human agency in social cognition theory. *American Psychologist*, 44, pp. 1175–1184.

Banks, E. (1997). The social capital of self-help mutual groups. *Social Policy*, 28, pp. 30–38.

Bankston, C.L., & Zhou, M. (1996). The ethnic church, ethnic identification, and the social adjustment of Vietnamese adolescents. *Review of Religious Research*, 38, pp. 18–37.

Barabak, M.Z. (2001, May 20). Blacks see a shrinking political role in California; Population: Their numbers stagnate as Latino and Asian communities surge. *Los Angeles Times*, p. A1.

Barker, G., Knaul, F., Cassaniga, N., & Schrader, A. (2000). *Urban girls: Empowerment in especially difficult circumstances.* New York: Intermediate Technology Publications.

Barron-McKeagney, T., Woody, J.D., & D'souza, H.J. (2000). Mentoring at-risk Chicano children and their parents: The role of community: Theory and practice. *Journal of Community Practice*, 8, pp. 37–56.

Barry, D. (2003, July 30). Mexican, but the dream is American. *New York Times*, p. A16.

Barwick, C.L., Beiser, M., & Edwards, G. (2002). Refugee children and their families: Exploring mental health risks and protective factors. In F.J.C. Azima & N. Grizenko (Eds.), *Immigrant and refugee children and their families: Clinical, research, and training issues* (pp. 37–63). Madison, CT: International Universities Press.

Bayor, R.H. (1978). *Neighbors in conflict: The Irish, Germans, Jews, and Italians of New York City, 1929–1941.* Baltimore, MD: Johns Hopkins University Press.

Beauvais, F., & Oetting, E.R. (1999). Drug use, resilience, and the myth of the golden child. In M.D. Glantz & J.L. Johnson (Eds.), *Resilience and development: positive life adaptations* (pp. 101–107). New York: Kluwer Academic/Plenum Publishers.

Beedy, J.P., & Zierk, T. (2000). Lessons from the field: Taking a proactive approach to developing character through sports. *CYD Journal Community Youth Development*, 1, pp. 6–13.

Bemak, F., Chung R.C., & Bornemann, T.H. (1996). Counseling and psychotherapy with refugees. In P.B. Pederson, W.L. Draguns, W.L. Lonner, & J.E. Trimble (Eds.), *Counseling across cultures* (4th ed., pp. 243–265). Thousand Oaks, CA: Sage.

Benard, B. (1999). Applications of resilience: Possibilities and promise. In M.D. Glantz & J.L. Johnson (Eds.), *Resilience and development: Positive life adaptations* (pp. 269–277). New York: Kluwer Academic/Plenum Publishers.

Benard, B. (1997). Drawing forth resilience in all our youth. *Reclaiming Children and Youth: Journal of Emotional and Behavioral Problems*, 6, pp. 29–32.

Benard, B. (1991). *Fostering resiliency in kids: Protective factors in the family, school, and community.* Portland, OR: Northwest Regional Educational Laboratory. (ERIC Document Reproduction Service No. ED 335 781).

Benard, B., & Constantine, N. (2000). *Supporting positive youth development in our schools: A research-based guide to approaches that work.* Washington, DC: American Association of School Administrators.

Bendtro, L.K., Brokenleg, M., & Van Bockern, S. (2002). *Reclaiming youth at risk: Our hope for the future* (rev. ed.). Lanham, MD: American Correctional Association.

Benedick, R., & Peltz, J. (2001, July 25). Census 2000: Economics, politics and culture keep door to Latin America open both ways. *South Florida Sun Sentinel*, p. 1.

Benson, P. (2002). Ethnicity, spirituality, and religion as a source of meaning. *Positive Youth Development Working Group* (p. 3). Society for Research on Adolescence. Ninth Biennial Meeting, New Orleans.

Berger, J. (2003, March 25). Korean? Spoken here? Two affluent areas of Queens are adjusting to a new ethnic mix. *New York Times*, p. A14.

Besharov, D.I. (Ed.). (1999). *America's disconnected youth: Toward a preventive strategy*. Washington, DC: Child Welfare League of America.

Biehl, J. (2001). Social death. *Anthropological Quarterly*, 74, pp. 147–148.

Birman, D. (1998). Biculturalism and perceived competence of Latino immigrant adolescents. *American Journal of Community Psychology*, 26, pp. 335–353.

Blake, S.M., Ledsky, R., Goodenow, C., & O'Donnell, L. (2001). Recency of immigration, substance use, and sexual behavior among Massachusetts adolescents. *American Journal of Public Health*, 91, pp. 794–798.

Blake, D. (2002). Saving Buffalo from extinction. In F. Siegel & J. Rosenberg (Eds.), *Urban society* (11th ed., pp. 99–102). Guilford, CT: McGraw-Hill/Duskin.

Bloch, A. (2002). *The migration and settlement of refugees in Britain*. New York: St. Martin's Press.

Bloom, D. & Padilla, A.M. (1979). A peer interviewer model for conducting surveys among Mexican-American youth. *Journal of Community Psychology*, 7, pp. 129–136.

Board on Children and Families. (1995). Immigrant children and their families: Issues for research and policy. *The Future of Children*, 5, pp. 72–89.

Board of Children and Families, Commission on Behavior and Research Council, Institute of Medicine. (1995). Immigrant children and their families: Issues of children and their families. *The Future of Children*, 5, pp. 72–89.

Bobo, L., Zubrinsky, C.L., Johnson, J.H., & Oliver, M.L. (1994). Public opinion before and after a spring of discontent. In M. Baldassare (Ed.), *The Los Angeles riots: Lessons for the urban future* (pp. 103–133). Boulder, CO: Westview.

Boston Globe. (2002, October 2). Kennedy calls for rise in refugee admissions, p. A2.

Botvin, G.J., Baker, E., Renick, N., & Filazzola, A. (1984). A cognitive-behavioral approach to substance abuse prevention. *Addictive Behaviors*, 9, pp. 137–147.

Boyle, D.P., Nackerud, L., & Kilpatrick, A. (1999). The road less traveled: Cross-cultural, international experiential learning. *International Social Work*, 42, pp. 201–214.

Boyle, D.P., & Springer, A. (2001). Toward a cultural competence measure for social work with specific populations. *Journal of Ethnic and Cultural Diversity in Social Work*, 9, pp. 53–71.

Bozorgmehr, M., Der-Martirosian, C., & Sabagh, G. (1996). Middle Easterners: A new kind of immigrant. In R. Waldinger & M. Bozorgmehr (Eds.), *Ethnic Los Angeles* (pp. 345–378). New York: Russell Sage Foundation.

Bracken, P. (2002). *Demoralised asylum seekers develop mental health problems*. London: Royal College of Psychiatrists.

Brave Heart, M.Y.H. (2001). In R. Fong & S. Furuto (Eds.), *Culturally competent practice: Skills, interventions and evaluation* (pp. 163–177). Boston: Allyn and Bacon.

Brazil, E. (2001, June 24). Sending dollars to Latin America: Wiring money home—cheaply, credit unions cut costs for immigrants. *San Francisco Chronicle*, p. 1.

Breitbart, M.M. (1998). "Dana's mystical tunnel": Young people's designs for survival and change in the city. In T. Skelton & G. Valentine (Eds.), *Cool places: Geographies of youth cultures* (pp. 305–327). New York: Routledge.

Broder, T., & Wiley, M. (2002). *Immigrants' eligibility for federal benefits*. Washington, DC: National Center on Poverty Law.

Bronfenbrenner, U. (1979). *The ecology of human development: Experiments by nature and design*. Cambridge, MA: Harvard University Press.

Bruni, F. (2002, September 23). Off Sicily, tide of bodies roils the debate over immigrants. *New York Times*, pp. A1, A8.

Bruno, A., & Bush K. (2002, January 22). *Refugee admissions and resettlement policy*. CRS Report for Congress.

Buchbinder, J. (Ed.) (2002). A portrait of new Americans. *The Magazine of the Harvard Graduate School of Education*, XLVI, pp. 18–23.

Buetler, M.E., Briggs, M., Hornibrook-Hehr, D., & Warren-Sams, B. (1998). *Improving education for immigrant students: A resource guide for K-12 educators in the Northwest and Alaska*. Portland, OR: Northwest Regional Educational Laboratory.

Buffalo News. (1999, November 14). There's no excuse for not investing in children, p. 3H.

Burt, M.R., Resnick, G., & Novick, E.R. (1998). *Building supportive communities for at-risk adolescents: It takes more than services.* Washington, DC: American Psychological Association.

Burton, L.M. (2001). One step forward and two steps back: Neighborhoods, adolescent development, and unmeasurable variables. In A. Booth & A.C. Crouter (Eds.), *Does it take a village?: Community effects on children, adolescents, and families* (pp. 149–159). Mahwah, NJ: Lawrence Erlbaum.

Calvan, B.C. (2003, May 24). Calif. debates immigrants' privileges: Measures would aid the undocumented. *The Boston Globe,* p. A3.

Camarillo, A.M., & Bonilla, F. (2001). Hispanics in a multicultural society: A new American dilemma? In N.J. Smelser, W.J. Wilson, & F. Mitchell (Eds.), *America becoming: Racial trends and their consequences,* (vol. 1. pp. 103–134). Washington, DC: National Academy Press.

Camino, L.A. (1994). Refugee adolescents and their changing identities. In L.A. Camino & R.M. Krulfeld (Eds.), *Reconstructing lives, recapturing meaning: Refugee identity, gender, and culture change* (pp. 29–56). Washington, DC: Gordon and Breach.

Campinha-Bacote, J. (1991). *The process of cultural competence: A culturally competent model of care.* Cincinnati, OH: Transcultural C.A.R.E. Associates.

Canda, E.R., & Furman, L.D. (1999). *Spiritual diversity in social work practice.* New York: The Free Press.

Canda, E.R., & Phaobtong, T. (1992). Buddhism as a support system for Southeast Asian refugees. *Social Work,* 37, pp. 61–67.

Canedy, D. (2002, August, 25). Hospitals feeling strain from illegal immigrants. *The New York Times,* National Report, p. 12.

Canino, I.A., & Spurlock, J. (2000). *Culturally diverse children and adolescents: Assessment, diagnosis, and treatment.* New York: Guilford.

Capps, R. (2001). *Hardships among children of immigrants: Findings from the 1999 national survey of America's families.* Washington, DC: Urban Institute.

Caring for Immigrants. (2001). *Health care safety nets in Los Angeles, New York, Miami, and Houston: Executive summary.* Washington, DC: Author.

Carney, M., & Gedajlovic, E. (2002). The co-evolution of institutional environments and organizational strategies: The rise of family business groups in the ASEAN region. *Organizational Studies,* 23, pp. 1–13.

Carr, J. (2001, January 19). Movie review: The House of Mirth. *The Boston Globe,* p. D1.

Carroll, S.D. (1996). *Resiliency and the Hmong child growing up in Fresno: An ethnographgic narrative with drawings.* Fresno: California School of Professional Psychology.

Cartledge, G. (1996). *Cultural diversity and social skills instruction: Understanding ethnic and gender differences.* Champaign, IL: Research Press.

Casanova, C. (1996). *Stressors in the lives of immigrant children* (http://www.guidancechannel.org/detail.asp?index=1032@cat=1)

Castex, G.M. (1997). Immigrant children in the United States. In N.K. Phillips & S.L.A. Straussner (Eds.), *Children in the urban environment: Linking social policy and clinical practice* (pp. 43–60). Springfield, IL: Charles C. Thomas.

Catherall, D.R. (1995). Preventing institutional secondary traumatic stress disorder. In C.R. Figley (Ed.), *Compassion fatigue: Coping with secondary traumatic stress disorder in those who treat the traumatized* (pp. 232–247). New York: Brunner/Mazel.

Center for Applied Linguistics. (1998). *Welcome to the United States: A guidebook for refugees* (http://www.cal.org.rsc.).

Center for Youth Development and Policy Research. (1995). *Definitions, language, and concepts for strengthening the field of youth development work.* Washington, DC: Academy for Educational Development.

Cervantes, J.M., & Ramirez, O. (1992). Spirituality and family dynamics in psychotherapy with Latino children. In J.D. Koss-Chioino & L.A. Vargas (Eds.), *Working with culture: Culture, development, and context* (pp. 103–128). San Francisco: Jossey-Bass.

Champassak, N.N. (2001). Helping traumatized children: A Canadian program successfully helps disturbed refugee children. *Refugees,* 1, p. 20.

Chapa, J. (2002). Affirmative Action, x percent plans, and Latino access to higher education in the twenty-first century. In M.M. Suarez-Orozco & M.M. Paez (Eds.), *Latinos remaking America* (pp. 375–388). Berkeley: University of California Press.

Chau, K.L. (1991). Social work with ethnic minorities: Practice issues and potentials. *Journal of Multicultural Social Work,* 1, pp. 23–39.

Chau, K.L. (1989). Sociocultural dissonance among ethnic minority populations. *Social Casework,* 70, pp. 224–230.

Chaukin, N.F., & Gonzalez, J. (2000, October). Mexican immigrant youth and resiliency: Research and promising programs. *ERIC Digest,* pp. 1–5.

Chavez, E. (1998). Facial faultlines: The historical origins of white supremacy in California. *Mexican Studies—Estudios Mexicannos*, 14, pp. 213–235.

Chazin, R. (1997). Working with Soviet Jewish immigrants. In E.P. Congress (Ed.), *Multicultural perspectives in working with families* (pp. 142–166). New York: Springer.

Checkoway, B., & Richards-Schuster, K. (2002). *Youth participation in community research*. Ann Arbor: Center for Community Change, School of Social Work, University of Michigan.

Chen, D.W. (2002, June 27). Struggling to sort out 9/11 aid to foreigners. *New York Times*, p.A1.

Cheng, M.M. (2002a, February 7). U.S. foreign-born population peaks. *Newsday*, p. A19.

Cheng, M.M. (2002b June 5). Data tell of rise in immigrants. *Newsday*, p. 1.

Chow, J. (1999). Multiservice centers in Chinese American immigrant communities: Practice principles and challenges. *Social Work*, 44, pp. 70–81.

Chrispin, M.C. (1999, May). *Resilient adaptation of church-affiliated young Haitian immigrants: A search for protective resources*. Dissertation Abstracts International, A (Humanities and social sciences), Vol. 59 (10A).

Christian Science Monitor. (2002, February 7). Now, a nation of more immigrants than ever, p. 1.

Clemetson, L. (2003, January 22). Hispanics now largest minority, census shows. *New York Times*, p. A1.

Clemetson, L. (2002, October 7). A neighborhood clinic helps fill the gap for Latinos without health care. *New York Times*, p. A12.

Coleman, D. (1992, April 21). Black scientists study the "pose" of the inner city. *New York Times*, p. C1.

Collingwood, T.R. (1997). *Helping at-risk youth through physical fitness programming*. Champaign, IL: Human Kinetics.

Colson, E. (1999). Gendering those uprooted by "development." In D. Indra (Ed.), *Engendering forced migration: Theory and practice* (pp. 23–39). New York: Berghahn Books.

Comas-Diaz, L. (1999). Foreword II. In J.D. Koss-Chioino & L.A. Vargas (Eds.), *Working with Latino youth: Culture, development, and context* (pp. ix–xi). San Francisco: Jossey-Bass.

Commerce Business Daily. (2000, February 3). Constructing communities to promote youth development. PSA-2526.

Community Association of Progressive Dominicans. (1999). *Sex education and HIV prevention*. New York: Author.

Congress, E.P. (1999). *Social work values and ethics*. Chicago: Nelson-Hall.

Connell, J.P., Aber, J.L., & Walker, G. (1999). How do urban communities affect youth? Using social science research to inform the design and enhancement of comprehensive community initiatives. In J.P. Connell, A.C. Kubish, L. Shorr, & Weiss, C.H. (Eds.), *New approaches to enhancing community initiatives* (pp. 11–21). Washington, DC: Aspen Institute.

Connolly, P. (2000). Racism and young girls' peer-group relations: The experiences of South Asian girls. *Sociology*, 34, pp. 499–511.

Cooper, C.R., Denner, J., & Lopez, E.M. (1999). Cultural brokers: Helping Latino children on pathways towards success. *The Future of Children*, 9, pp. 51–57.

Corey, G., Corey, M.S., & Callanan, P. (2003). *Issues and ethics in the helping profession* (6th ed.). Pacific Grove, CA: Brooks/Cole.

Cornelius, W.A. (2002). Ambivalent reception: Mass public responses to the "new" Latino immigration to the United States. In M.M. Suarez-Orozco & M.M. Paez (Eds.), *Latinos remaking America* (pp. 165–189). Berkeley: University of California Press.

Coutin, S.B. (2000). *Legalizing moves: Salvadoran immigrant's struggle for U.S. residency*. Ann Arbor: University of Michigan Press.

Covey, S. (1989). *The seven habits of highly effective people: Powerful lessons in personal change*. New York: Simon and Schuster.

Cox, L. (2002). Fragile families: When undocumented immigrants lose children to the child welfare system. *Covering the Youth Beat: The lives of children in New York City, 2002*. New York: Columbia University, School of Journalism, pp. 1–12.

Credit Union Journal. (2003, January 6). Immigrants: One word for many groups, possibilities, p. 16.

Cross, M., & Moore, R. (Eds.). (2002). *Globalization and the new city*. New York: St. Martin's Press.

Cross, T.L., Bazron, B.J., Dennis, K.W., & Issacs M.R. (1989). *Toward a culturally competent system of care*. Washington, DC: Georgetown University Child Development Center.

CDY Journal. (2002). Youth engagement in community evluation research. Volume 4, p. 1.

Daily Telegraph (Sydney). (2001, August 10). Youth empowered by mobile phones, p. 10.

Damico, J.S., & Damico, S.K. (1993). Language and social skills from a diversity perspective: Considerations for the speech-language pathologists. *Language, Speech, and Hearing Services in Schools*, 24, pp. 236–243.

Danieli, Y. (1996). Who takes care of the caretakers? In R.J. Apfel & B. Simon (Eds.), Minefields in their hearts: *The mental health of children in war and communal violence* (pp. 189–205). New Haven, CT: Yale University Press.

Dao, J. (1998, March 18). New York City grows, even as many leave: Newcomers and newborns offset loss if more than a million people. *New York Times*, p. A23.

Davis, M. (1995, November 12). The social origins of the referendum (Proposition 187) (The immigration backlash). *NACLA Report on the Americas*, 29, pp. 24–30.

Davis, R. (2001, September 6). Health care, without question. *USA Today*, p. 9D.

Dean, R.G. (2001). The myth of cross-cultural competence. *Families in Society*, 82, pp. 623–630.

De Anda, D. (1984). Bicultural socialization: Factors affecting the minority experience. *Social Work*, 29, pp. 172–181.

De la Rosa, M. (in press). Onset of drug use among Latino gang members: A preliminary analysis. *Alcoholism Treatment Quarterly*.

De la Rosa, M., Segal, B., & Lopez, R. (Eds.). (1999). *Conducting drug abuse research with minority populations: Advances and issues.* New York: Haworth.

De la Rosa, M., Vega, R., & Radisch, M.A. (2000). The role of acculturation in the substance abuse behavior of African-American and Latino adolescents: Advances, issues, and recommendations. *Journal of Psychoactive Drugs*, 32, pp. 33–50.

Delgado, M. (in press). *Social youth entrepreneurship and youth development: The potential for youth and community transformation.* Westport, CT: Praeger.

Delgado, M. (2003). *Death at an early age and the urban scene: The case for memorial murals and community healing.* Westport, CT: Praeger.

Delgado, M. (2002a). *New frontiers for youth development in the twenty-first century: Revitalizing and broadening youth development.* New York: Columbia University Press.

Delgado, M. (2002b). *Where are all of the young men and women of color? Capacity enhancement practice and the criminal justice system.* New York: Columbia University Press.

Delgado, M. (2000a). *New arenas for community social work practice with urban youth: Use of the arts, humanities, and sports.* New York: Columbia University Press.

Delgado, M. (2000b). *Community social work practice in an urban context: The potential of a capacity-enhancement perspective.* New York: Oxford University Press.

Delgado, M. (1998). Community asset assessment and substance abuse prevention: A case study involving the Puerto Rican community. In M. Delgado (Ed.), *Social services in Latino communities: Research and strategies* (pp. 5–23). New York: Haworth.

Delgado, M. (1981). Using Hispanic adolescents to assess community needs. *Social Casework: The Journal of Contemporary Social Work*, 62, pp. 607–613.

Delgado, M. (1979). A grass-roots model for needs assessment in Hispanic communities. *Child Welfare*, 58, pp. 571–576.

Delgado, M. (1999). *Social work practice in nontraditional urban settings.* New York: Oxford University Press.

Delgado, M., & Barton, K. (1998). Murals in Latino communities: Social indicators of community strengths. *Social Work*, 43, pp. 346–356.

Delgado, R. (2002, December 20). S.F. students honored for helping others. *San Francisco Chronicle*, p. 2.

DeMonchy, M.L. (1991). Recovery and rebuilding: The challenge for refugee children and service providers. In F.L. Ahearn, Jr. & J.L. Athey (Eds.), *Refugee children: Theory, research, and services* (pp. 163–180). Baltimore, MD: John Hopkins University Press.

Denner, J., & Griffin, A. (2003). The role of gender in enhancing programs strategies for healthy youth development. In F.A. Villarruel, D.F. Perkins, L.M. Borden, & J.G. Keith (Eds.), *Community youth development programs, policies, and Practices* (pp. 118–145). Thousand Oaks, CA: Sage.

de Rios, M.D. (2001). *Brief psychotherapy with the Latino immigrant client.* New York: Haworth.

DeVoe, P.A. (1994). Refugees in an educational setting: A cross-cultural model of success. In L.A. Camino & R.M. Krulfeld (Eds.), *Reconstructing lives, recapturing meaning: Refugee identity, gender, and culture change* (pp. 235–249). Washington DC: Gordon and Breach Publishers.

Devore, W., & Schlesinger, E.G. (1999). *Ethnic-sensitive social work practice* (5th ed.). Boston: Allyn and Bacon.

Devore, W., & Schlesinger, E.G. (1995). *Ethnic-sensitive social work practice* (4th ed.). Boston: Allyn and Bacon.

Devore, W., & Schlesinger, E. (1981). *Ethnic-sensitive social work practice.* St. Louis: C.V. Mosby.

Dianne, S.A. (2001). *Current population reports, Series P23–206, Profile of the foreign-born population in the United States, 2000.* Washington, DC: U.S. Government Printing Office.

Didion, J. (1987). *Miami.* New York: Pocket Books.

Dinh, K.T., Roosa, M.W., Tein, J.Y., & Lopez, V.A. (2002). The relationship between acculturation and problem behavior proneness in a Hispanic youth sample: A longitudinal mediation model. *Journal of Abnormal Child Psychology*, 30, pp. 295–317.

Do, P.V. (2002). Between two cultures: Struggle of Vietnamese American adolescents. *The Review of Vietnamese Studies*, 2, pp. 1–18.

Doucette, J.H. (2001, February 28). Keeping TB in check: Clinic reaches out to reassure immigrants about tests. *Newsday*, p. A27.

Dow, W.N. (1997). An urbanizing world. In U. Kindar (Ed.), *Cities fit for people* (pp. 29–49). New York: United Nations Publications.

Doyle, R. (2002, February 23). Assembling the future: How international migrants are shaping the 21st century. *Scientific America*, p. 2.

Drachman, D. (1995). Immigration statuses and their influence on service provision, access and use. *Social Work*, 40, pp. 188–197.

Druley, L. (2002, September 23). Immigrant youth walk middle ground. *Minnesota Public Radio* (Transcript), pp. 1–3.

Dugger, C.W. (1998, March 22). Immigrants' young blend in. *Los Angeles Daily News*, p. 1.

Dugger, C.W. (1997a, March 27). With new restrictions at hand, U.S. tries to allay fear among immigrants. *New York Times*, p. A32.

Dugger, C.W. (1997b, November 10). Study shows Dominicans sink deeper into poverty. *New York Times*, p. A31.

Duggar, C.W. (1996, March 10). Immigrant voters reshape politics. *New York Times*, pp. 1, 28.

Dulwich Centre. (1990). Introduction: The New Zealand and agency context. *Dulwich Centre Newsletter*, 1, p. 1.

Dunn, D. (1994). *Resilient reintegration of married women with dependent children: Employed and unemployed.* Doctoral Dissertation, Department of Health Education, University of Utah, Salt Lake City.

Earls, F. (1993). Health promotion for minority adolescents: Cultural considerations. In S.G. Millstein, A.C. Petersen, & E.O. Nightingale (Eds.), *Promoting the health of adolescents: New directions for the twenty-first century* (pp. 58–72). New York: Oxford University Press.

Eccles, J., & Gootman, J.A. (2002). *Community programs to promote youth development.* Washington, DC: National Academy Press.

Economist. (2002, August 24). Half a billion Americans? Demography and the west, pp. 1–2.

Edna McConnell Clark Foundation. (2003). ROCA, Inc.: Young people and families striving for change (http://www.emcf.org/programs/youth/roca.htm).

Ehrlich, P.R., Biderback, L., & Ehrlich, A.H. (1981). *The golden door: International migration, Mexico, and the United States.* New York: Wideview Books.

Eisenbrunch, M. (1991). From post-traumatic stress disorder to cultural bereavement: Diagnosis of Southeast Asians refugees. *Social Science Medicine*, 33, pp. 673–680.

Elickson, P.L. (1984). *Project ALERT: A smoking and drug prevention experiment.* Santa Monica, CA: Rand Corporation.

Elliott, G.R., & Feldman, S. (1990). (Eds.) *At the threshold: The developing adolescent.* Cambridge, MA: Harvard University Press.

Endelman, G. (2000, August 4). Guest commentary: Immigration and the American city: A source of renewal, not a cause for concern. *Siskind's Immigration Bulletin*, pp. 1–4.

Erwin, P.G. (1994). Effectiveness of social skills training with children: A meta-analytic study. *Counseling Psychology Quarterly*, 7, pp. 305–310.

Evans, D.W. (1998). Tobacco use and adolescents. In A. Henderson, S. Champlin, & W. Evashwick (Eds.), *Promoting teen health: Linking schools, health organizations, and community* (pp. 46–57). Thousand Oaks, CA: Sage.

Evans, I.M., & Ave, K.T. (2000). Mentoring children and youth: Principles, issues, and policy implications for community programmes in New Zealand. *New Zealand Journal of Psychology*, 29, pp. 41–56.

Ewing, M. (1997). *Promoting social and moral development through sports* (http://ed-web3.educ.msu/ysi/Spotlight`997/social.html).

Fabricant, M.B., & Fisher, R. (2002). *Settlement houses under siege: The struggle to sustain community organizations in New York City.* New York: Columbia University Press.

Fadiman, A. (1997). *The spirit catches you and you fall down: A Hmong child, her American doctors, and the collision of two cultures.* New York: Farrar, Straus & Giroux.

Falicov, C.J. (2003). Immigrant family process. In F. Walsh (Ed.), *Normal family processes: Growing diversity and complexity* (3rd ed., pp. 280–300). New York: Guilford.

Falicov, C.J. (2002). Ambiguous loss: Risk and resilience in Latino immigrant families. In M.M. Surarez-Orozco & M.M. Paez (Eds.), *Latinos remaking America* (pp. 274–288). Berkeley: University of California Press.

Falicov, C. (1995). Training to think culturally: A multidimensional framework. *Family Process*, 34, pp. 373–388.

Family Life Matters. (1998). Latino/Latina youth—Special challenges, special opportunities, 33, pp. 1–6.

Fang, S.S., & Wark, L. (1998). Developing cross-cultural competence with traditional Chinese Americans in family therapy: Background information and the initial therapeutic contact. *Contemporary Family Therapy*, 20, pp. 59–77.

Farrington, B. (2001a, September 30). Little Havana is no longer just Cuban. *South Florida Sun-Sentinel*, p. 1.

Farrington, B. (2001b, September 7). *Latin American immigrants flood Miami.* AP Online (wysiwyg://12http://library.norther...).

Fears, D. (2002, February 24). A diverse—and divided—Black community: As foreign-born population grows, nationality trumps skin color. *Washington Post*, p. A1.

Feder, B.J. (1995, July 4). Dead end jobs? *New York Times*, p. 27.

Feldblum, M., & Klusmeyer, D. (1999). Immigrants and citizenship today: A comparative perspective. *Research Perspectives on Migration*, 2, pp. 1–5.

Fetterman, D.M. (2001). *Foundations of empowerment research.* Thousand Oaks, CA: Sage.

Feuer, A. (2003, September 6). Ethnic chasm in El Barrio: Changes pit Mexicans against Puerto Ricans. *New York Times*, p. A10.

Fidler, S. (2001, May 16). Migrants spur growth in remittances. *The Financial Times*, p. 1.

Fields, R. (2001, August 6). 90s saw a tide of new people. *Los Angeles Times*, p. A1.

Firestone, D. (1995, March 29). Major ethnic changes under way. *New York Times*, pp. B1–B2.

Fix, M., & Passel, J.S. (1994). *Immigration and immigrants: Setting the record straight.* Washington, DC: Urban Institute.

Flanagan, C., & Horn, B.V. (2003). Youth civic development: A logical next step in community youth development. In F.A. Villarruel, D.F. Perkins, L.M. Borden & J.G. Keith (Eds.), *Community youth development programs, policies, and practices* (pp. 273–296). Thousand Oaks, CA: Sage.

Flores, J. (2002). Islands and enclaves: Caribbean Latinos in historical perspectives. In M.M. Suarez-Orozco & M.M. Paez (Eds.), *Latinos: Remaking America* (pp. 39–74). Berkeley: University of California Press.

Fogey, M.A. (2000). Capitalizing on strengths: A resilience enhancement model for at-risk youth. In E. Norman (Ed.), *Resiliency enhancement* (pp. 211–226). New York: Columbia University Press.

Foner, N. (Ed.). (2001b). Introduction: New immigrants in a new New York. In N. Foner (Ed.), *New immigrants in New York* (pp. 1–31). New York: Columbia University Press.

Foner, N. (2000). *From Ellis Island to JFK: New York's two great waves of immigration.* New Haven, CT: Yale University Press.

Foner, N., Rumbaut, R.G., & Gold, S.J. (2000). Immigration and immigration research in the United States. In N. Foner, R.G. Rumbaut, & S.J. Gold (Eds.), *Immigration research for a new century: Multidisciplinary perspectives* (pp. 1–19). New York: Russell Sage Foundation.

Fong, R. (2001). Culturally competent social work practice: Past and present. In R. Fong & S. Furuto (Eds.), *Culturally competent practice: Skills, interventions, and evaluation* (pp. 1–9). Boston: Allyn and Bacon.

Fong, R., & Furuto, S. (Eds.). (2001). *Culturally competent practice: Skills, interventions, and evaluation.* Boston: Allyn and Bacon.

Forest, A.D. (2002, December 30). Latin teenagers face suicide risk: Health professionals still learning what creates crisis for immigrant children. *The Herald-Sun* (Durham, NC), p. C1.

Forum for Youth Investment. (2002a). Youth contributing to communities, communities supporting youth. *FYI Newsletter*, 2, pp. 1–5.

Forum for Youth Investment. (2002b). What is the impact of meaningful youth action? On youth? On communities? *FYI Newsletter*, 2, pp. 7–8.

Fountain, J.W., & Yardley, J. (2002, October 16). Skeletons tell tale of gamble by immigrants. *New York Times*, pp. A1, A17.

Frank, G. (1998). Nutrition for teens. In A. Henderson, S. Champlin, & W. Evashwick (Eds.), *Promoting teen health: Linking schools, health organizations, and community* (pp. 28–45). Thousand Oaks, CA: Sage.

Franklin, C. (2001). Onward to evidence-based practices for schools. *Children & Schools*, 23, pp. 131–134.

Franklin, C., & Corcoran, J. (2000). Preventing adolescent pregnancy: A review of programs and practices. *Social Work*, 45, pp. 40–52.

Fraser, M.W. (Ed.). (1997). *Risk and resilience in childhood.* Washington, DC: NASW Press.

Freedman, M. (1993). *The kindness of strangers: Adult mentors, urban youth, and the new voluntarism.* San Francisco: Jossey-Bass.

Freidman, A.R. (1992). Rape and domestic violence: The experience of refugee women. *Women and Therapy*, 13, pp. 65–78.

Frelick, B. (2002a). The year in review. In *World refugee*

survey, 2002 (pp. 14–23). Washington, DC: U.S. Committee for Refugees.

Frelick, B. (2002b). Rethinking U.S. refugee admissions: Quantity and quality. In *World Refugee Survey, 2002* (pp. 28–37). Washington, DC: U.S. Committee for Refugees.

Frosina Information Network. (Undated). *Report shows immigrants boost economy* (http://www.frosina.org/ advisories/immsboostecon.shtml).

Fuentes, A. (2001, March 13). Clinic casts lifeline to isolated migrant workers. *New York Times*, Section F, p. 5.

Fukuyama, M.A., & Sevig, T.D. (1999). *Integrating spirituality into multicultural counseling*. Thousand Oaks, CA: Sage.

Fulton, W. (2001). *The reluctant metropolis: The politics of urban growth in Los Angeles*. Baltimore: Johns Hopkins University Press.

Furstenberg, F. F. (1998). When will teenage childbearing become a problem? The implications of western experience for developing countries. *Studies in Family Planning*, 29, pp. 246–254.

Furstenberg, Jr., F.F., Cook, T.D., Eccles, J., Elder, Jr., G.H., & Sameroff, A. (1999). *Managing to make it: Urban families and adolescent success*. Chicago: University of Chicago Press.

Galambos, N.L., & Ehrenberg, M.F. (1997). The family as health risk and opportunity: A focus on diverse and working families. In J. Schulenberg, J.L. Maggs, & K. Hurrleman (Eds.), *Health risks and developmental transitions* (pp. 139–160). New York: Cambridge University Press.

Gallegos, J.S., Bondavalli, D., & Chandler, S. (2000, August 1). *Using international social work to educate students for culturally competent practice in the 21st century*. Presentation at the Joint Conference of the International Federation of Social Workers and the International Association of Schools of Social Work, Montreal, Quebec, Canada.

Galloro, V. (2001, November 5). Disproportionate burden: Providers near U.S.-Mexico border face a flood of problems in caring for immigrants. *Modern Healthcare*, p. 24.

Gandara, P. (2002). Learning English in California: Guideposts for the nation. In M.M. Suarez-Orozco & M.M. Paez (Eds.), *Latinos remaking America* (pp. 339–358). Berkeley: University of California Press.

Garbarino, J. (1985). Human ecology and competence in adolescence. In J. Garbarino (Ed.), *Adolescent development: An ecological perspective* (pp. 40–86). Columbus, OH: Merrill.

Garmezy, N., & Masten, A.S. (1986). Stress, competence, and resilience: Common frontiers for therapists and psychopathologists. *Behavior Therapy*, 57, pp. 159–174.

Gavagan, T., & Brodyaga, L. (1998). Medical care for immigrants and refugees. *American Family Physician*, 57, pp. 106–116.

Gee, J.P. (1989). Literacy, discourse, and linguistics: An introduction. *Journal of Education*, 171, pp. 5–17.

Genero, N.P. (1995). Culture, resiliency, and mutual psychological development. In H.I. McCubbin, E.A. Thompson, A.I. Thompson, & J.A. Futrell (Eds.), *Resiliency in ethnic minority families* (pp. 31–48). Madison: The University of Wisconsin System.

Gerzon-Kessler, A. (2000). Sports: A forum for collaboration, connection and community. *CYD Journal Community Youth Development*, 1, pp. 20–23.

Gibbs, J.T., & Bankhead, T. (2001). *Preserving privilege: California politics, propositions and people of color*. Westport, CT: Praeger.

Gilliam, B., & Scott, D. (1998). The course to expect greatness from our children. Reclaiming Children and Youth: *Journal of Emotional and Behavioral Problems*, 7, pp. 176–178.

Gilligan, R. (1999). Enhancing the resilience of children and young people in public care by mentoring their talents and interests. *Child and Family Social Work*, 4, pp. 187–196.

Gillilan, L. (2000, October 12). Space: Inner space: Twenty quid genius. *The Guardian* (London), p. 10.

Gillock, K.L., & Reyes, O. (1999). Stress, support, and academic performance of urban, low-income, Mexican-American adolescents. *Journal of Youth and Adolescence*, 28, pp. 259–271.

Giuliani, R. (1997, June). *New York City conference on immigration, Ellis Island*. New York.

Glantz, M.D., & Johnson, J.L. (Eds.). (1999). *Resilience and development: Positive life adaptations*. New York: Kluwer Academic/Plenum Publishers.

Glantz, M.D., & Sloboda, Z. (1999). Analysis and reconceptualization of resilience. In M.D. Glantz & J.L. Johnson (Eds.), *Resilience and development: Positive life adaptations* (pp. 109–126). New York: Kluwer Academic/ Plenum Publishers.

Gold, S. (1993). Migration and family adjustment. In H. McAdoo (Ed.), *Family ethnicity: Strength in diversity* (pp. 300–314). Newbury Park, CA: Sage.

Goldberg, M. (2000). Conflicting principles in multicultural social work. *Families in Society*, 81, pp. 12–21.

Goldsmith, S. (2002, June 20). Border buster: Critics say L.A. lawyer Peter Schey is ruining America by helping hordes of illegal immigrants stay here. *New Times Los Angeles*, p. 1.

Golledge, R.G. (1999). *Wayfinding behavior: Cognitive mapping and other spatial processes*. Baltimore, MD: Johns Hopkins University Press.

Gonzalez, A. (2002, August 15). *Is the education of child immigrants affected by their age at arrival? Findings and policy implications* (http://www.realtor.org/rmomag.nsf/pages/Minorities199Archive1998Aug).

Gonzalez, M. (2002). Mental health intervention with Hispanic immigrants: Understanding the influence of the client's worldview, language and religion. *Journal of Immigrant and Refugee Services*, 1, pp. 81–92.

Gonzalez, R., & Padilla, A.M. (1997). The academic resilience of Mexican American high school students. *Hispanic Journal of Behavioral Sciences*, 19, pp. 301–317.

Gonzalez-Ramos, G., & Sanchez-Newster, M. (2001). Responding to immigrant children's mental health needs in the schools: Project M. Tierra/My country. *Children & Schools*, 23, pp. 49–62.

Gopaul-McNicol, S.A. (1993). Working with West Indian families. In S.A. Gopaul-McNicol (Ed.), *Working with West Indian families* (pp. 102–120). New York: Guilford.

Gopaul-McNicol, S., & Thomas-Presswood, T. (1998). *Working with linguistically and culturally different children: Innovative clinical and educational approaches*. Boston: Allyn and Bacon.

Gordon, E.W., & Song, L.D. (1994). Variations in the experience of resilience. In M.C. Way & E.W. Gordon (Eds.), *Educational resilience in inner-city America* (pp. 27–43). Hillsdale, NJ: Lawrence Erlbaum.

Gore, A. (2003) Foreword: Family-centered community building and developmental assets for youth. In R.M. Lerner & P.L. Benson (Eds.), *Developmental assets and asset-building communities* (pp. vii–ix). New York: Kluwer Academic/Plenum Publishers.

Gori, G., (2002, July 6). A card allows U.S. banks to aid Mexican immigrants. *New York Times*, p. C3.

Gould, S.J. (1994). In the mind of the beholder. *Natural History*, 103, pp. 16–23.

Graham, H.D. (2002). *Collision course: The strange convergence of affirmative action and immigration policy in America*. New York: Oxford University Press.

Gray, T.W. (1998). Meeting the needs of immigrants: Must acculturation be a condition of agency service? In J.C. Rothman (Ed.), *From the frontlines: Student cases in social work ethics* (pp. 139–147). Boston: Allyn and Bacon.

Green, J.W. (1982). *Cultural awareness in the human services*. Englewood Cliffs, NJ: Prentice-Hall.

Greene, R.R., & Watkins, M. (Eds.). (1998). *Serving diverse constituencies: Applying the ecological perspective*. New York: Aldine de Gruyter.

Grieger, I., & Ponterotto, J.G. (1995). A framework for assessment in multicultural counseling. In J.G. Ponterotto, J.M. Casas, C.A. Suzuki, & C. Alexander (Eds.), *Handbook of multicultural counseling* (pp. 357–374). Thousand Oaks, CA: Sage.

Grimmett, D. (1998). Physical activity and fitness. In A. Henderson, S. Champlin, & W. Evashwick (Eds.), *Promoting teen health: Linking schools, health organizations, and community* (pp. 22–27). Thousand Oaks, CA: Sage.

Grinberg, L., & Grinberg, R. (1989). *Psychoanalytic perspectives on migration and exile*. New Haven, CT: Yale University Press.

Grindle, M.S. (2002). Commentary. In M.M. Suarez-Orozco & M.M. Paez (Eds.), *Latinos remaking America* (pp. 146–149). Berkeley: University of California Press.

Gross, G.D. (2000). Gatekeeping for cultural competence: Ready or not? Some post and modernist doubts. *The Journal of Baccalaureate Social Work*, 5, pp. 47–66.

Guardian. (1999, October 1). Triumphs, trick, and marking time, p. 13.

Guest, H.E. (1995). A national youth agenda: Returning the community interest to the community. In American Youth Policy Forum, *Contract with America's youth* (pp. 26–27). Washington, DC: AYPF.

Guo, J., Hill, K.G., Hawkins, J.D., Catalano, R.F., & Abbott, R.D. (2002). A developmental analysis of sociodemographic, family, and peer effects on adolescent illicit drug initiation. *Journal of the American Academy of Child and Adolescent Psychiatry*, 41, pp. 838–845.

Gutfeld, R. (2003, Fall). Citizens and persons. *Ford Foundation Report*, pp. 10–14.

Gutierrez, L.M., & Lewis, E.A. (1999). *Empowering women of color*. New York: Columbia University Press.

Hagan, J., & Rodriguez, N. (2002). Resurrecting exclusion: The effects of 1996 U.S. immigration reform on communities and families in Texas, El Salvador and Mexico. In M.M. Suarez-Orozco & M.M. Paez (Eds.), *Latinos remaking America* (pp. 190–201). Berkeley: University of California Press.

Hahn, A., & Raley, G. (1999). *Youth development: On the path towards professionalization.* Washington, DC: National Assembly.

Halper, S.J., Cusack, G., Raley, R., O'Brien, R., & Wills, J. (1995). *Contract with America's youth: Toward a national youth development agenda.* Washington, DC: American Youth Policy Forum.

Hamm, M. (1995). *The abandoned ones: The imprisonment and uprising of the Mariel Boat People.* Boston: Northeastern University Press.

Harden, M. (2001, October 2). Thirst with Michael Harden. *Herald Sun* (Durham, NC), p. 44.

Harker, K. (2001). Immigrant generation, assimilation, and adolescent psychological well-being. *Social Forces, 79,* pp. 969–1004.

Harrell, W.A., Bowlby, J.W., & Hall-Hoffarth, D. (2000). Directing wayfinders with maps: The effects of gender, age, route complexity, and familiarity with the environment. *Journal of Social Psychology, 140,* pp. 169–178.

Harris, J. (1998). *The nurture assumption: Why children turn out the way they do.* New York: The Free Press.

Hart, D., Atkins, R., & Ford, D. (1998). Urban America as a context for the development of moral identity in adolescence. *Journal of Social Issues, 54,* pp. 513–530.

Haslip-Viera, G., & Baver, S.L. (1996). *Latinos in New York: Communities in transition.* Notre Dame, IN: University of Notre Dame Press.

Haughney, C. (2002, July 22). The Northeast's shifting labor supply; in '90s, foreign-born population surged while young, educated workers left, study finds. *Washington Post,* p. A3.

Hawthnorne, S. (2001, Autumn). Hamptom leads in youth engagement. *Assets Magazine,* pp. 1–6.

Hayes-Bautista, D., & Rodriguez, G. (1995, February 13). In South Central se habla espanol: Latinization of L.A. *The Nation* (Los Angeles), pp. 202–206.

Hayes-Bautista, D., Schink, W.O., & Chapa, J. (1988). *The burden of support: Young Latinos in an aging society.* Palo Alto, CA: Stanford University Press.

Health Law. (undated). *Use of family members or friends including minors as interpreters.* http://www.healthlaw.crg/docs/ocrappendix.pdf.

Hecht, T. (1998). *At home in the street: Street children of Northeast Brazil.* New York: Cambridge University Press.

Hee-og, S. (2000). Relationship of daily hassles and social support to depression and antisocial behavior among early adolescents. *Journal of Youth and Adolescence, 29,* pp. 647–658.

Hegstrom, E. (2002, August 10). A risky border business; INS reports a growing number of illegal workers paying smugglers to bring their families to U.S. *Houston Chronicle,* p. A1.

Hellison, D., Cutforth, N., Kallusky, J., Martinek, T., Parker, M., & Stiehl, J. (2000). *Youth development and physical activity: Linking universities and communities.* Campaign, IL: Human Kinetics.

Helm, K. (1991, December 17). Coining: Home remedy. *Long Beach Press-Telegram* (CA), p. 1.

Henderson, T., Epstein Nieves, G., & Bolstad, E. (2002, April 29). Migration still fuels area's growth. *Miami Herald,* p. 1.

Hendricks, T. (2003, January 22). America's ethnic shift; Latinos surpass blacks unless you count black Latinos. *San Francisco Chronicle,* p. A3.

Hendricks, T. (2002a, June 5). Foreign-born residents on rise, census reports; the proportion of "new Americans" increased from 4.7% to 11.1% in 30 years. *San Francisco Chronicle,* p. A17.

Hendricks, T. (2002b, August 27). All roads lead to the Bay Area; number of foreign-born residents climbs to 27.5%. *San Francisco Chronicle,* p. A1.

Heredia, C., & Haddock, V. (2001, April 3). State's kids even more diverse than its adults. *San Francisco Chronicle,* p. 1.

Hernandez, D. (2003a, April 15). Tax day puts illegal immigrants in a special bind. *New York Times,* p. A19.

Hernandez, D. (2003b, July 14). Sending more home despite tough times: Money still flows to Latin America. *New York Times,* p. A16.

Hernandez, D.J. (Ed.). (1999). *Children of immigrants: Health, adjustment, and public assistance.* Washington, DC: National Academy Press.

Hernandez, D.J., & Charney, E. (Eds.). (1998). *From generation to generation: The health and well-being of children in immigrant families.* Washington, DC: National Academy Press.

Hernandez, R., Siles, M., & Rochin, R.I. (2000). Latino youth: Converting challenges to opportunities. In M. Montero-Sieburth & F.A. Villarruel (Eds.), *Making invisible Latino adolescents visible: A critical approach to Latino diversity* (pp. 1–28). New York: Falmer.

Hernandez, R., & Torres-Saillant, S. (1996). Dominicans in New York: Men, women and prospects. In G. Haslip-Viera & L. Baver (Eds.), *Latinos in New York: Communities in transition* (pp. 30–56). Notre Dame IN: University of Notre Dame Press.

Higgerson, M.L. (1998). In my view: Restoring hope and building leaders. *Kappa Delta Pi: Record, 35,* pp. 6–7.

Hodge, D.R. (2002). Working with Muslim youths: Understanding the values and beliefs of Islamic discourse. *Children & Schools*, 24, pp. 6–15.

Hoffman, J. (2003, July 30). Treating torture victims, body and soul. *New York Times*, p. A17.

Hondagneu-Sotelo, P. (2002). Families on the frontier: From Braceros in the fields to Braceras in the home. In M.M. Surez-Orozco & M.M. Paez (Eds.), *Latinos: Remaking America* (pp. 259–273). Berkeley: University of California Press.

Hong, P.Y., & McDonnell, P.J. (2002, February 7). Proportion of immigrants in U.S. population has doubled since '70. *Los Angeles Times*, p. 24.

Hong, P.Y. & Yi, D. (2001, March 30). Census 2000 focus: Asians; fastest growth of any ethnic group in state; biggest increase was in the suburbs. Southern California's expansion was geographic and economic. *Los Angeles Times*, p. U5.

Horsch, K., Little, P.M.D., Smith, J.C., Goodyear, L., & Harris, E. (2002). Issues and opportunities in out-of-school time evaluation briefs. *Youth Involvement in Evaluation and Research*, 1, pp. 1–15.

Hovey, J.D. (2000). Psychosocial predictors of acculturative stress in Mexican immigrants. *Journal of Psychology*, 134, pp. 490–500.

Howard, C. A., Andrade, S.J., & Byrd, T. (2001). The ethical dimensions of cultural competence in border health care settings. *Family Community Health*, 23, pp. 36–49.

Howard, M.O., & Jenson, J.M. (1999a). Clinical practice guidelines: Should social work develop them? *Research on Social Work Practice*, 9, pp. 283–301.

Howard, M.O., & Jenson, J.M. (1999b). Barriers to development, utilization and evaluation of social work practice guidelines: Toward an action plan for social work. *Research on Social Work Practice*, 9, pp. 347–364.

Huang, Z.J. (2002, November 12). *Health status and health services by children from immigrant families: An analysis of 1999 national survey of American families.* Paper presented at the 130th Annual Meeting of the American Public Health Association, Atlanta, GA.

Huber, M.S.Q., Frommeyer, J., Weissenbach, A., & Sazama, J. (2003). Giving youth a voice in their own community and personal development. In F.A. Villarruel, D.F. Perkins, L.M. Borden, & J.G. Keith (Eds.), *Community youth development programs, policies, and practices* (pp. 297–323). Thousand Oaks, CA: Sage.

Huebner, A.J. (2003). Positive youth development: The role of competence. In F.A. Villarruel, D.F. Perkins, L.M. Borden, & J.G. Keith (Eds.), *Community youth development programs, policies, and practices* (pp. 341–357). Thousand Oaks, CA: Sage.

Huff, C.R. (Ed.). (1990). *Gangs in America*. Newbury Park, CA: Sage.

Hughes, D.M. (2000). Hope: The life source. *CYD Journal: Community Youth Development*, 1, pp. 12–17.

Hughes, D.M., & Nichols, N. (1995). Changing the paradigm to community youth development. In American Youth Policy Forum, *Contract with America's youth* (pp. 30–32). Washington, DC: AYPF.

Hughes, D.M. (2002). Young people as catalysts for change in their families and communities. *CYD Journal: Community Youth Development*, 3, pp. 54–55.

Huitt, W. (2000). *Moral and character development* (http://chiron.valdosta.edu/whuitt/col/morchr/morchr.html).

Human Rights Watch. (2003, March 26). *U.S. "Operation Liberty Shield" undermines asylum seekers' rights* (http://www.hrw.org/press/2003/03/us032603.htm).

Hutchinson, E.O. (2002, April 24). Commentary; 10 years after the riots, we stick with our own; put money behind efforts to bridge the racial divide. *Los Angeles Times*, p. B13.

Hwang, C. (1998, September 21). The good daughter. *Newsweek*, p. 16.

Hyman, I., Vu, N., & Beiser, M. (2000). Post-immigration stresses among Southeast Asian refugee youth in Canada: A research note. *Journal of Comparative Family Studies*, 31, pp. 281–294.

IAC Fifth Regional Conference. (2001). Female genital mutilation. *WIN News*, 27, p. 60.

Ifill, M.B. (1996). *Slavery: Social death or communal victory*. Port of Spain, Trinidad: Economics and Business Research.

Imber-Black, E. (1997). Developing cultural competence: Contributions from recent family therapy literature. *American Journal of Psychotherapy*, 51, pp. 607–610.

Immigration Forum. (undated). *A fiscal portrait of the newest Americans: Executive summary* (http://www.immigrationforum.org/currentissues/legal/%20immigration/tax.html).

Immigration Policy Reports. (2001a). *U.S. benefits from foreign-born: Population survey supports the contributions of immigrants.* Washington, DC: American Immigration Law Foundation.

Immigration Policy Reports. (2001b). *Realities of immigration emerge in 2000 census.* Washington, DC: American Immigration Law Foundation.

Immigration and Refugee Services of America. (2003, June). *Refugee Reports: FY 2003: Refugee resettlement still stalled,* 24, p. 4.

Indra, D. (Ed.). (1999). *Engendering forced migration: Theory and practice.* New York: Berghahn Books.

Institute for Cultural Partnerships. (1999). *Multi-ethnic community resources project.* Harrisburg, PA: Author.

IOM's Mission, Objectives and Functions (undated) (http://www.oim.pt/body_mission.html).

Jablon, R. (2003, February 6). Hispanic babies majority of newborns in California. *Associated Press State & Local Wire,* p. 1.

Jackson, B.W., & Holvino, E. (1988). *Multicultural organizational development.* Working Paper #11. Program on Conflict Management Alternatives. Ann Arbor: University of Michigan Press.

Jacoby, T. (2002, April 1). Too many immigrants. *Commentary,* 113, pp. 37–47.

Jakarta Post. (1998, December 29). Habibie urged to release all political prisoners unconditionally, p. 1.

Jaret, C. (1999). Troubled by newcomers: Anti-immigrant attitudes and action during two eras of mass immigration to the United States. *Journal of American Ethnic History,* 18, pp. 9–39.

Jayaratne, S., Croxton, T., & Mattison, D. (1997). Social work professional standards: An exploratory study. *Social Work,* 42, pp. 187–198.

Jennings, Z.H. (2002, December 22). Moving down to move up. *Boston Globe,* pp. C1, C9.

Jensen, L. (2002). Coming of age in a multicultural world: Adolescent cultural identity formation. *Positive Youth Development Work Group* (p. 4). Society for Research on Adolescence Ninth Biennial Meeting, New Orleans.

Johns, S.E. (2001). Using the Comer model to educate immigrant children. *Chidhood Education,* 77, pp. 268–274.

Johnson, A.C. (1995). Resiliency mechanisms in culturally diverse families. *The Family Journal: Counseling and Therapy for Couples and Families,* 3, pp. 316–324.

Johnson, J.L. (1999). Commentary: Resilience as transactional equilibrium. In M.D. Glantz & J.L. Johnson (Eds.). *Resilience and development: Positive life adaptations* (pp. 225–228). Kluwer Academic/Plenum Publishers.

Johnson, S. (2000, August 11). Music: Crowd control. *The Guardian* (London), p.14.

Jones, K., & Lane, T. (2000, August 1). *The global challenge of refugees and immigrants: One school of social work's local response.* Presentation at the Joint Conference of the International Federation of Social Workers and the International Association of Schools of Social Work, Montreal, Quebec, Canada.

Jones-Correa, M. (1998). *Between two nations: The political predicament of Latinos in New York City.* Ithaca, NY: Cornell University Press.

Kahn, R.S. (1996). *Other people's blood: U.S. immigration prisons in the Reagan decade.* Boulder, CO: Westview.

Kamya, H. (1997). African immigrants in the U.S.: The challenge for research and practice. *Social Work,* 42, pp. 154–165.

Kanner, A.D., Coyne, J.C., Schaefer, C., & Lazarus, R.S. (1981). Comparison of two modes of stress measurement: Daily hassles, uplifts and major life events to health status. *Journal of Behavioral Medicine,* 4, pp. 1–39.

Kaplan, F. (1997, April 12). In NYC, Dominicans feeling political clout. *Boston Globe,* pp. A1, A8.

Kaplan, H.B. (1999). Toward an understanding of resilience: A critical review of definitions and models. In M.D. Glantz & J.L. Johnson (Eds.), *Resilience and development: Positive life adaptations* (pp. 17–83). New York: Kluwer Academic/Plenum Publishers.

Kaur, M. (2003, February 21–27). How did the Washington school system let one Sikh American boy be bullied for seven years? *AsianWeek.Com,* pp. 1–6(http://www.asianweek.com/2003_02_21/feature.html).

Kazin, A. (2002). Fear of the city, 1783–1983. In F. Siegel & J. Rosenberg (Eds.). *Urban society* (11th ed., pp. 2–7). Guilford, CT: McGraw-Hill/Dushkin.

Keating, R. (2001, September), *A nation of immigrants, an economy of immigrants, analysis 4.* Washington, DC: Small Business Survival Committee.

Kehret, P. (2001, December). Encouraging empathy. *School Library Journal,* pp. 1–2.

Kelen, J.A., & Kelen, L.G. (2002). *Faces and voices of refugee youth.* Logan: Utah State University Press.

Kelley, S., & Enslein, J.C. (2001). Cultural barriers to care: Inverting the problems. *Diabetes Spectrum,* 14, pp. 13–22.

Kelly, M.P.F., & Schauffler, R.(1996). Divided fates: Immigrant children and the new assimilation. In A. Portes (Ed.), *The new second generation* (pp. 30–53). New York: Russell Sage Foundation.

Kempler, B. (2002). The resilience of the human spirit. *Connections,* 3, pp. 2–7.

Kennedy, P. (1998, October 13). Don't say pleased to meet you. *The Times* (London), p. 1.

Kershaw, S. (2003, January 18). Freud meets Buddha: Therapy for immigrants. *New York Times,* p. A15.

Kerwin, D. (2001). Looking for asylum, suffering in detention. *Human Rights*, 28, pp. 3–5.

Kielsmeir, J., & Klopp, C. (2002). Service-learning: Positive youth development in the classroom and community. *CYD Journal: Community Youth Development*, 3, pp. 33–39.

Kim, D.H. (1990). *A cultural program as an effective means of ministry with the second generation youth in the USA*. Philadelphia, PA: Drew University.

Kim, U. (1994). Individualism and collectivism: Conceptual clarification and elaboration. In U. Kim, H. C. Triandis, C. Kagitcibasi, S.-C. Choi, & G. Yoon (Eds.), *Individualism and collectivism: Theory, methods, and applications* (pp. 19–40). Thousand Oaks, CA: Sage.

Kinzie, J.D. (1994). Countertransference in the treatment of Southeast Asian refugees. In J.P. Wilson & J.D. Lindy (Eds.), *Countertransference in the treatment of PTSD* (pp. 249–262). New York: Guilford.

Kinzie, J.D. (2001). Psychotherapy for massively traumatized refugees: The therapist variable. *American Journal of Psychotherapy*, 55, pp. 475–490.

Kirova, A. (2001). Loneliness in immigrant children: Implications for classroom practice. *Childhood Education*, 77, pp. 260–267.

Kiselica, M.S., & Robinson, M. (2001). Bringing advocacy counseling to life: The history, issues, and human dramas of social justice work in counseling. *Journal of Counseling and Development: JCD*, 79, pp. 387–397.

Kleinman, A., Eisenberg, L., & Good, B. (1978). Culture, illness and care: Clinical lessons from anthropologic and cross-cultural research. *Annals of Internal Medicine*, 88, pp. 251–258.

Klerman, L.V. (1993). The influence of economic factors on health-related behaviors in adolescents. In S.G. Millstein, A.C. Petersen, & E.O. Nightingale (Eds.), *Promoting the health of adolescents: New directions for the twenty-first century* (pp. 38–57). New York: Oxford University Press.

Kodluboy, D.W., & Evinrude, L. (1993). School-based interventions: Best practice and critical issues. In A.P. Goldstein & C.R. Huff (Eds.), *The gang intervention handbook* (pp. 257–300). Champaign, IL: Research Press.

Korbin, J. (1991). Child maltreatment and the study of child refugees. In F. Ahern & J. Athey (Eds.), *Refugee children: Theory, research and services* (pp. 39–49). Baltimore, MD: Johns Hopkins University Press.

Koss-Chioino, J.D., & Vargas, L.A. (1999). *Working with Latino youth: Culture, development, and context*. San Francisco: Jossey-Bass.

Kotkin, J. (2002). Movers and shakers: How immigrants are reviving neighborhoods given up for dead. In F. Siegel & J. Rosenberg (Eds.), *Urban society* (11th ed., pp. 106–111). Guilford, CT: McGraw-Hill/Dushkin.

KQED. (2002). *Youth media corps: Immigrant voices: Stories and writing*. San Francisco: Author.

Kraly, E.P., & Miyares, I. (2001). Immigration to New York: Policy, population and patterns. In N. Foner (Ed.), *New immigrants in New York City* (pp. 33–79). New York: Columbia University Press.

Krauss, C. (2002, October 2). Immigrant families are courted to revive Canada's hinterland. *New York Times*, pp. A1, A8.

Krikorian, G., Mena, J., & Miller, T.C. (2002, August 14). Desperate parents keep child smuggling alive. *Los Angeles Times*, p. 1.

Kritz, M.M. (2001). Population growth and international migration: Is there a link. In A.R. Zolberg & P.M. Benda (Eds.), *Global migrants, global refugees: Problems and solutions* (pp. 19–41). New York: Berghahn Books.

Krulfeld, R.M. (1994). Buddhism, maintenance, and change: Reinterpreting gender in a Lao refugee community. In L.A. Camino & R.M. Krulfeld (Eds.), *Reconstructing lives, recapturing meaning: Refugee identity, gender, and culture change* (pp. 97–128). Washington, DC: Gordon and Breach.

Kugel, S. (2002, September 1). Some Dominicans balk at a diplomatic import. *New York Times*, p. 4.

Kulynych, J. (2001). No playing in the public sphere: Democratic theory and the exclusion of children. *Social Theory & Practice*, 27, pp. 231–264.

Kumpfer, K.L. (1999). Factors and processes contributing to resilience: The resilience framework. In M.D. Glantz & J.L. Johnson (Eds.), *Resilience and development: Positive life adaptations* (pp. 179–224). New York: Kluwer Academic/Plenum Publishers.

Kuoch, T., Miller, R.A., & Scully, M.F. (1992). Healing the wounds of the Mahantdori. *Women and Therapy*, 13, 1/2, pp. 191–207.

Kurth-Sehai, R. (1998). The role of youth in society: A reconceptualization. *Educational Forum*, 53, pp. 113–132.

Kuthiala, S.K. (2001). Who benefits from immigration and immigrants. *Migration World Magazine*, 29, pp. 6–13.

Ladd, G.W. (1990). Having friends, keeping friends, making friends, and being liked by peers in the classroom: Predictors of children's early school adjustment? *Child Development*, 61, pp. 312–331.

Ladd, G.W., & Price, J.M. (1987). Predicting children's social and school adjustment following the transition from preschool to kindergarten. *Child Development*, 57, pp. 1168–1189.

Ladd, G.W., Price, J.M., & Hart, C.H. (1988). Predicting preschoolers' peer status from their playground behaviors. *Developmental Psychology*, 59, pp. 986–992.

Laird, J. (1998). Theorizing culture: Narrative ideas and practice principles. In M. McGoldrick (Ed.), *Revisioning family therapy: Race, culture, and gender in clinical practice* (pp. 20–36). New York: Guilford.

Lakes, R.D. (1995). *Youth development and critical education: The promise of democratic action.* New York: State University of Buffalo Press.

Landau-Stanton, J. (1990). Issues and methods of treatment for families in cultural transition. In M.P. Mirkin (Ed.), *The social and political contexts of family therapy* (pp. 251–275). Boston: Allyn and Bacon.

Lao-Montes, A. (2001). Introduction. In A. Lao-Montes & A. Davila (Eds.), *Mambo montage: The Latinization of New York* (pp. 1–53). New York: Columbia University Press.

Lao-Montes, A., & Davila, A. (2001). *Mambo montage: The Latinization of New York.* New York: Columbia University Press.

Lappin, J. (1983). On becoming a culturally conscious family therapist. In J. Hansen & Falicov (Eds.), *Cultural perspectives in family therapy* (pp. 122–136). Rockville, MD: Aspen.

Larkin, M.A. (1999). Nationality in Mexico. *Research Perspectives on Migration*, 2, pp. 15–16.

Laslett, J.H.M. (1996). Historical perspectives: Immigration and the rise of a distinctive urban region, 1900–1970. In R. Waldinger & M. Bozorgmehr (Eds.), *Ethnic Los Angeles* (pp. 79–107). New York: Russell Sage Foundation.

Laursen, B.K. (2002). Seven habits of reclaiming relationships. *Reclaiming Children and Youth*, 11, pp. 10–15.

Lawrence, D.H. (1998). Positive youth development promotes pathways of growth. *Common Ground*, 15, p. 9.

Lecca, P.J., Quervalu, I., Nunes, J.V., & Gonzales, H.F. (1998). *Cultural competency in health, social and human services.* New York: Garland.

Le-Doux, C., & Stephens, K.S. (1992). Refugee and immigrant social service delivery: Critical management issues. In A.S. Ryan (Ed.), *Social work with immigrants and refugees* (pp. 31–45). New York: Haworth.

Lee, E. (1990). Family therapy with Southeast Asian families. In M.P. Mirkin (Ed.), *The social and political contexts of family therapy* (pp. 331–354). Boston: Allyn and Bacon.

Lee, F.R. (2003, February 1). New topic in Black studies debate: Latinos. *New York Times*, pp. A1, A21.

Lee, J. (1994). *The empowerment approach to social work practice.* New York: Columbia University Press.

Lee, R.M., & Ramirez, III, M. (2000). The history, current status, and future of multicultural psychotherapy. In I. Cuellar & F.A. Paniagua (Eds.), *Handbook of multicultural mental health: Assessment and treatment of diverse populations* (pp. 279–309). Boston: Academic Press.

Lerner, R.M. (1995). *America's youth in crisis: Challenges and options for programs and policies.* Thousand Oaks, CA: Sage.

Lerner, R.M., Brentano, C., Dowling, E.M., & Anderson, P.M. (2002). Positive youth development: Thriving as the basis of personhood and civil society. In R.M. Lerner, C.S. Taylor, & A.V. Eye (Eds.), *New directions for youth development: Pathways to positive development among diverse youth* (pp. 11–33). San Francisco: Jossey-Bass.

Lerner, R.M., Taylor, C.S., & Eye, A.V. (2002). *New directions for youth development: Pathways to positive development among diverse youth.* San Francisco: Jossey-Bass.

Leung, P., & Cheung, M. (2001). Competencies in practice evaluation with Asian American individuals and families. In R. Fong & S. Furuto (Eds.), *Culturally competent practice: Skills, interventions, and evaluation* (pp. 428–436). Boston: Allyn and Bccon.

Levine, J. (2001). Working with victims of persecution: Lessons from Holocaust survivors. *Social Work*, 46, pp. 350–360.

Levitt, P. (2002). Two nations under God? Latino religious life in the United States. In M.M. Suarez-Orozco & M.M. Paez (Eds.), *Latinos remaking America* (pp. 150–164). Berkeley: University of California Press.

Levitt, P. (2001). *The transnational villagers.* Berkeley: University of California Press.

Lichtblau, E. (2003, June 3). U.S. report faults the roundup of illegal immigrants after 9/11. *New York Times*, pp. A1, A14.

Linden, J.A. van, & Fertman, C.I. (1998). *Youth leadership: A guide to understanding leadership development in adolescents.* San Francisco: Jossey-Bass.

Liptar, A. (2003, June 3). For jailed immigrants, a presumption of guilt. *New York Times*, p. A14.

Little, J.S., & Triest, R.K. (2001). *Seismic shifts: The economic impact of demographic change.* An overview. Federal Reserve Bank of Boston, Conference Series, pp. 1–29.

Locke, D.C. (1992). *Increasing multicultural understanding: A comprehensive model.* Newbury Park, CA: Sage.

London, J. (2002, June 7–9). *Youth involvement in community research and evaluation: Mapping the field—Draft discussion paper.* Presented at the Wingspread Symposium on youth involvement in community research and evaluation. Racine, WI.

Long, P.D. (1995). *The dream shattered: Vietnamese gangs in America.* Boston: Northeastern University Press.

Lopez, B., Nerenberg, L., & Valdez, M. (2000). Migrant adolescents: Barriers and opportunities for creating a promising future. In M. Montero-Sieburth & F.A. Villarruel (Eds.), *Making invisible Latino adolescents visible: A critical approach to Latino diversity* (pp. 289–307). New York: Falmer.

Lopez, D.E., Popkin, E., & Telles, E. (1996). Central Americans: At the bottom, struggling to get ahead. In R. Waldinger & M. Bozorgmehr (Eds.), *Ethnic Los Angeles* (pp. 279–304). New York: Russell Sage Foundation.

Los Angeles City Planning Department. (2001). *City of Los Angeles—Census 2000 race/ethnicity composition 1970–2000.* Los Angeles: Author.

Loue, S. (Ed.). (1998). *Handbook of immigrant health.* New York: Plenum.

Lowry, D.S. (2002, November 12). *Raised in different places: Immigrant and refugee relationships across generations.* Paper presented at the Annual Meeting of the American Public Health Association, Atlanta, GA.

Lum, D. (Ed.). (2003). *Culturally competent practice: A framework for understanding diverse groups and justice issues* (2nd ed.). Pacific Grove, CA: Brooks/Cole.

Lynch, W.W. (1991). From culture shock to cultural learning. In E.W. Lynch & M.J. Hanson (Eds.), *Developing cross-cultural competence: A guide for working with young children* (pp. 19–34). Baltimore, MD: Paul H. Brooks.

Ly-Phin, P. (1998). Ren and the process of coping. *The World & I*, 13, pp. 229–233.

Macias, R.F. et al. (2000). *Summary report of the survey of the states' limited English proficient students and available educational programs and services, 1997–1998.* Washington, DC: National Clearinghouse for Bilingual Education.

Mahler, S.J. (1995). *Salvadorans in suburbia: Symbiosis and conflict.* Boston: Allyn and Bacon.

Maier, T.W. (2001, October 29). Surge in immigrant worker deaths. *Newsday*, p. A14.

Maier, T.W., & Paige, S. (1999, August 23). The people smugglers. *Insight on the News*, pp. 14–17.

Malik, S., & Velazquez, J. (2002, July/August). Cultural competence and the "New Americans." *Children's Voice*, pp. 1–7.

Malone, J. (2003, January 31). Illegal population grew by more than a million in last four years. *Cox News Service*, p. 1

Manning, S.S. (2003). *Ethical leadership in human services: A multi-dimensional approach.* Boston: Allyn and Bacon.

Mar, P. (1998). Just the place is different: Comparisons of place and settlement practices of some Hong Kong migrants in Sydney. *The Australian Journal of Anthropology*, 9, pp. 58–73.

Margolis, M.L. (1998). *An invisible minority: Brazilians in New York City.* Boston: Allyn and Bacon.

Market Europe. (1998). Trendwatch: The macro view: The future belongs to youth. Author, 9, pp. 1–8.

Markowitz, L.M. (1994, July-August). The cross-currents of multiculturalism. *Networker*, pp. 18–27, 69.

Marotta, S.A. (2000). Best practices for counselors who treat posttraumatic stress disorder. *Journal of Counseling & Development*, 78, pp. 492–495.

Marquez, S. (2002, September 2). California immigrants thrive where little English is spoken. *Associated Press State and Local Wire*, p. 1.

Marquis, C. (2002a, October 13). Slowdown on U.S. visas stalls business, science, and personal travel plans. *New York Times*, p. 12.

Marquis, C. (2002b, April 9). A nation challenged: Immigration; I.N.S. proposes new limits on the length of visas. *New York Times*, p. A17.

Marsiglia, F.F., & Holleran, L. (1999). I've learned so much from my mother: Narratives from a group of Chicana high school students. *Social Work in Education*, 4, pp. 220–228.

Martin, P. & Teitelbaum, M. (1998, April 27). *Migration dialogue: Report of the seminar on integration issues and immigration policy: Focus on Southern Florida.* Conference in Miami.

Martin, P., & Widgren, J. (2002). International migration: Facing the challenge. *Population Bulletin*, 57, pp. 1–40.

Martin, T. (2002). Advancing social justice: Connecting youth service to environmental justice. *CYD Journal: Community Youth Development*, 3, pp. 48–49.

Martinez-Brawley, E.E., & Zorita, P.M.-B. (2002). Immigrants, refugees and asylum seekers: The challenge of services in the Southwest. *Journal of Ethnic & Cultural Diversity in Social Work*, 10, pp. 49–67.

Masaki, B., & Wong, L. (1997). Domestic violence in the Asian community. In E. Lee (Ed.). *Working with Asian-Americans* (pp. 439–451). New York: Guilford.

Mask, T. (2002, September 5). Report highlights effect of Sept. 11 on immigrants. *Chicago Daily Herald*, pp. F1, F2.

Massachusetts Immigrant and Refugee Advocacy Coalition. (2002). *Changes in Massachusetts benefits programs: Food stamps and cash assistance*. Boston: Author.

Masten, A.S. (1999). Commentary: The promise and perils of resilience research as a guide to prevention interventions. In M.D. Glantz & J.L. Johnson (Eds.), *Resilience and development: Positive life adaptations* (pp. 251–257). New York: Kluwer Academic/Plenum Publishers.

Masten, A.S. (1994). Resilience in individual development: Successful adaptation despite risk and resiliency. In M.C. Way & E.W. Gordon (Eds.), *Educational resilience in inner-city America* (pp. 3–25). Hillsdale, NJ: Lawrence Erlbaum.

Mathews, H. (1995). Culture, environment experience and environmental awareness: Making sense of young Kenyan children's views of place. *The Geographical Journal*, 161, pp. 285–297.

Matthews, K. (2002, January 14). WTC day laborers to get toxin tests. *AP Online*, Domestic News section.

Mayadas, N.S., & Segal, U.A. (2000). Refugees in the 1990s: A U.S. perspective. In P.R. Balgopal (Ed.), *Social work practice with immigrants and refugees* (pp. 198–227). New York: Columbia University Press.

McAdoo, H.P. (Ed.). (1999). *Family ethnicity* (2nd ed.). Thousand Oaks, CA: Sage.

McCabe, M. (2002). Pathways to change: Linking service to sustainable change. *CYD Journal: Community Youth Development*, 3, pp. 40–47.

McCarthy, K.F., & Vernez, G. (1997). *Immigration in a changing economy: California's experience*. Santa Monica, CA: Rand Corporation.

McClain, C. (1998). *In search of equality: The Chinese struggle against discrimination in 19th century America*. Berkeley: University of California Press.

McCubbin, H., Thompson, E.A., Thompson, A.I., & Fromer, J.E. (Eds.), (1998). *Resiliency in Native American and immigrant families*. Thousand Oaks, CA: Sage.

McDonnell, L.M., & Hill, P.T. (1993). *Newcomers in American schools: Meeting the educational needs of immigrant youth*. Santa Monica, CA: Rand Corporation.

McDonnell, P.J. (2002, May 9). A Latino census recount; population: Tally failed to identify 200,000 Central Americans in an area, an analysis finds. *Los Angeles Times*, p. B1.

McGoldrick, M. (2003). Culture: A challenge to concepts of normality. In F. Walsh (Ed.), *Normal family processes* (3rd ed., pp. 235–259). New York: Guilford.

McGoldrick, M., & Giordano, J. (1996). Overview: Ethnicity and family therapy. In M. McGoldrick, J. Giordano, & J.K. Pearce (Eds.), *Ethnicity and family therapy* (2nd ed., pp. 1–27). New York: Guilford.

McGoldrick, M., Giordano, J., & Pearce, J.K. (Eds.). (1982). *Ethnicity and family therapy*. New York: Guilford Press.

McGoldrick, M., Pearce, J., & Giordano, J., & Pearce, J.K. (Eds.). (1996). *Ethnicity and family therapy* (2nd ed.). New York: Guilford.

McGreevy, P. (2001, December 21). The Valley; panel is urged to offset census under-count; City Council: activists ask committee redrawing districts to balance minority representation. *Los Angeles Times*, p. B3.

McIntosh, P. (1989, July/August). White privilege: Unpacking the invisible knapsack. *Peace and Freedom*, pp. 10–12.

McLaughlin, M.W., & Heath, S.B. (1993). Casting the self: Frames for identity and dilemmas for policy. In S.B. Heath & M.M. McLaughlin (Eds.), *Identity and inner-city youth* (pp. 210–239). New York: Teachers College Press.

McLaughlin, M.W., Irby, A., & Langman, J. (1994). *Urban sanctuaries: Neighborhood organizations in the lives and futures of inner-city youth*. San Francisco: Jossey-Bass.

McMillen, J.C. (1999). Better for it: How people benefit from adversity. *Social Work*, 44, pp. 455–467.

McMorris, B.J., Tyler, K.A., Whitbeck, L.B., & Hoyt, D.R. (2002). Familial and on-the-street risk factors associated with alcohol use among homeless and runaway adolescents. *Journal of Studies on Alcohol*, 63, pp. 34–51.

Mejia, M., & Prado, M.A. (2000). *Portland Latino and Asia Pacific youth produce TV and organize conferences* (http://www.afsc.org/pnro/su2K05.htm).

Melchior, A. (2002). Connecting service-learning and CYD. *CYD Journal*, 3, pp. 5.

Mendell, D. (2002). Changing faces and places: What the 2000 census means for Chicago: During the 1990s, the six-county region became more diverse ethnically and racially than even the boldest demographer would have predicted. *Planning*, 68, pp. 4–12.

Mendler, A.N. (2000). *Motivating students who don't care: Successful techniques for educators*. Lanham, MD: American Correctional Association.

Menjivar, C. (1997). Immigrant kinship networks: Vietnamese, Salvadoreans and Mexicans in comparative perspective. *Journal of Comparative Family Studies,* 28, pp. 1–21.

Merighi, J.R., & Grimes, M.D. (2000). Coming out to families in a multicultural context. *Families in Society,* 81, pp. 32–41.

Metro: Boston Edition. (2003, January 15). Bush pushes welfare refom, p. 3.

Meyers, D.W. (1998, May). *Migrant remittances to Latin America: Reviewing the literature.* The Tomas Rivera Policy Institute, pp. 1–30.

Midobuche, E. (2001). More than empty footprints in the sand: Educating immigrant children. *Harvard Educational Review,* 71, pp. 529–535.

Miley, K.K., O'Melia, M., & DuBois, B.I. (1998). *Generalist social work practice: An empowering approach.* Boston: Allyn and Bacon.

Miller, S.C. (1969). *The unwelcome immigrant: The American image of the Chinese, 1785–1882.* Berkeley: University of California Press.

Millman, J. (1997). *The other America: How immigrants renew our country, our economy, and our values.* New York: Viking.

Millstein, S.G. (1993). A view of health from the adolescent's perspective. In S.G. Millstein, A.C. Petersen, & E.O. Nightingale (Eds.), *Promoting the health of adolescents: New directions for the twenty-first century* (pp. 97–118). New York: Oxford University Press.

Min, P.G. (2001). Koreans: An "institutionally complete community" in New York. In N. Foner (Ed.), *New immigrants in New York* (pp. 173–199). New York: Columbia University Press.

Mirkin, M.P. (1998). The impact of multiple contexts on recent immigrant families. In M. McGoldrick (Ed.), *Revisioning family therapy* (pp. 370–383). New York: Guilford.

Mirsky, J., & Prawer, L. (1992). *To immigrate as an adolescent: Immigrant youth from FSU to Israel.* Jerusalem, Israel: The Van Leer Institute and the Association for the Development and Advancement of Manpower in Social Services in Israel.

Mishra, R.C. (1994). Individualistic and collectivist orientations. In U. Kim, H.C. Triandis, C. Kagiticibasi, S.C. Choi, & G. Yoon (Eds.), *Individualism and collectivism: Theory, methods, and applications* (pp. 225–238). Thousand Oaks, CA: Sage.

Mize, J., & Abell, E. (1996). Encouraging social skills in young children: Tips teachers can share with parents. *Dimensions of Early Childhood,* 24, pp. 23–30.

Mohan, B. (1992). Trans-ethnic adolescence, confluence and conflict: An Asian Indian paradox. In S.M. Furuto, R. Biswas, K. Murase, & F. Ross-Sheriff (Eds.), *Social work practice with Asian Americans* (pp. 213–226). Newbury Park, CA: Sage.

Moje, E.B. (2002). But where are the youth? On the value of integrating youth culture into literacy theory. *Educational Theory,* 52, pp. 97–121.

Moon, D.G. (1996). Concepts of "culture": Implications for intercultural communication research. *Communication Quarterly,* pp. 70–81.

Moorthy, S. (2000). Merging social work and social advocacy in response to the plight of unaccompanied child refugees in the United States. *Advocates' Forum,* 6, pp. 35–40.

Morrison, P.A., & Lowry, I.S. (1994). A riot of color: The demographic setting. In M. Baldassare (Ed.), *The Los Angeles riots: Lessons for the urban future* (pp. 19–46). Boulder, CO: Westview.

Morse, A. (2002, July 7). *Tuition and immigrant students.* Washington, DC: National Council of State Legislatures.

Munroe, J.F., Shay, J., Fisher, L., Makary, C., Rapperport, K., & Zimering, R. (1995). Preventing compassion fatigue: A team treatment model. In C.R. Figley (Ed.), *Compassion fatigue: Coping with secondary traumatic stress disorder in those who treat the traumatized* (pp. 209–231). New York: Brunner/Mazel.

Murdock, S.H. (1998). *American challenge.* Washington, DC: Heritage Foundation.

Murdock, S.H. (1995). *An America challenged: Population change and the future of the United States.* Boulder, CO: Westview.

Murphy, D.E. (2003, February 17). New Californian identity predicted by researchers: Most newborns in state are now Hispanic. *New York Times,* p. A13.

Mydans, S. (2002, August 9). Dead end for Cambodians who grew so American. *New York Times,* p. A3.

Nanji, A. (1993). The Muslim family in North America: Continuity and change. In H. P. McAdoo (Ed.), *Family ethnicity: Strength in diversity* (pp. 229–242). Newbury Park, CA: Sage.

Nassar, R. (2002). Social justice advocacy by and for Tibetan immigrants: A case example of international and domestic empowerment. *Journal of Immigrant and Refugee Services,* 1, pp. 21–32.

National Academy Press. (1999). *Risks and opportunities: Synthesis of studies on adolescence.* Washington, DC: National Research Council.

National Academy Press. (1993). *Losing generations: Adolescents in high-risk settings.* Washington, DC: National Research Council.

National Assembly and the National Collaboration for Youth. (2000). Talking about "youth development" (http://www.touchlife.net/mall/fpseya//talking.htm).

National Immigration Forum. (2003, September 16). *Publications and resources: Immigrants and public benefits.* Washington, DC: Author.

National Immigration Forum. (2001). *Cycles of nativism in U.S. history.* Washington, DC: Author.

National Immigration Forum. (2000). *Immigrants and the American economy.* Washington, DC: Author.

National Immigration Forum. (1999). *Facts on refugees and asylees* (http://www.immigrationforum.org/refugees&asylees.htm).

National Immigration Law Center. (2002). *Guide to immigrant eligibility for federal programs.* Los Angeles: Author.

National Immigration Law Center. (2001, August 31). Immigrants and public benefits: Miscellaneous issues. *Immigrants' Rights Update,* 5, p. 5.

National Immigration Law Center. (undated). *Immigration, employment and public benefits* (http://www.nilc.org/immspbs/research/factsaboutimms.htm).

National Research Council. (1993). *Losing generations: Adolescents in high-risk settings.* Washington, DC: Author.

National Technical Information Service. (1971). *Youth development program models.* Washington, DC: Department of Commerce.

Navarro, M. (2003a, January 28). Mariachis made in Manhattan: Teaching the children the music of Old Mexico. *New York Times,* p. A21.

Navarro, M. (2003b, April 28). Among New York's Black Latinos, a growing racial consciousness. *New York Times,* p. A23.

Navarro, M. (2003c, November 9). Going beyond black and white, Hispanics in census pick "other." *New York Times,* pp. 1, 21.

Navarro, M. (1999, September 19). Latinos gain visibility in cultural life of U.S.: Numbers and influence are on the rise. *New York Times,* p. 18.

Neiger, B.L. (1991). *Resilient reintegration: Use of structural equations modeling.* Doctoral Dissertation, University of Utah, Salt Lake City.

Nettles, S.M., Mucherah, W., & Jones, D.S. (2000). Understanding resilience: The role of social resources. *Journal of Education for Students Placed at Risk,* 5, pp. 47–60.

Nevins, J. (2002). *Operation gatekeeper: The rise of the "illegal alien" and the remaking of the U.S.-Mexico boundary.* New York: Routledge.

New York City Department of Planning. (2002). *Demographic profile—New York City 1990–2000.* New York: Author.

New York Times. (2002a, March 28). U.S. weighs the fate of child immigrants. p. A24.

New York Times. (2002b, June 5). Judges are told to aid children who immigrate to U.S. alone, p. A27.

New York Times. (2002c, April 11). Guinean immigrant in custody is a minor, agency concedes, p. A20.

New York Times. (2002d, November 27). Shift of care for immigrant children alone, p. A12.

Newsday. (2000, June 10). Forum exposes plight of widows, p. A12.

Nieves, E. (2002, August 6). Illegal immigrant death rate rises sharply in barren areas. *New York Times,* pp. A1, A12.

Norman, E. (Ed.). (2000a). *Resiliency enhancement.* New York: Columbia University Press.

Norman, E. (2000b). Introduction: The strengths perspective and resiliency enhancement—A natural partnership. In E. Norman (Ed.), *Resiliency enhancement* (pp. 1–16). New York: Columbia University Press.

Northwest Regional Educationl Laboratory. (2001). *The immigrant experience* (http://www.nwrel.org/cnorse/booklets/immigration/4.html).

Northwest Regional Educational Laboratory. (1999). *Lessons from the cities, part two: The strengths of city kids* (http://www.nwrel.org/nwedu/winter99/lessons2.html).

Norton, D. G. (1978). *The dual perspective: Inclusion of ethnic minority content in the social work curriculum.* New York: Council on Social Work Education.

Nucci, L. (2002). *Moral development and moral education: An overview* (http://tigger.uic.edu/lnucci/MoralEd/overview.html).

Nucci, L. (Ed.). (1989). *Moral development and character education: A dialogue.* Berkeley CA: McCutchan.

Oberg, K. (1960). Culture shock: Adjustment to new cultural environments. *Practical Anthropology,* 7, pp. 177–182.

O'Brien, K. (1998, October 18). Hanging on by a string; most toys need an ad campaign to make them a success. *The Independent* (London), p. 2.

Ochs, R. (2001, September 11). In the vanguard of pediatric medicine: Mobile unit puts "continuity of care" on wheels. *Newsday,* p. C06.

O'Connor, A.M. (2002, August 25). Gathering fights those who deal in human lives; Border: Social workers, law enforcement and human rights activists meet to devise strategies to combat criminals who prostitute thousands of women and children. *Los Angeles Times,* p. 10.

O'Connor, B.B. (1998). Healing practices. In S. Loue (Ed.), *Handbook of immigrant health* (pp. 145–161). New York: Plenum Press.

O'Donnell, J., Hawkins, J.D., Catalano, R.F., Abbott, R.D., & Day, L.E. (1995). Preventing school failure, drug use, and delinquency among low-income children: Long-term intervention in elementary schools. *American Journal of Orthopsychiatry*, 65, pp. 87–100.

Ogbu, J. (1994). From cultural differences to differences in cultural frame of reference. In P.M. Greenfield & R.R. Cocking (Eds.), *Cross-cultural roots of minority child development* (pp. 365–390). Hillsdale, NJ: Lawrence Erlbaum.

Ojito, M. (1998, December 15). U.S. deporting record numbers of immigrants. *The Patriot Ledger* (Quincy MA), pp1–2.

Ojito, M. (1997, December 16). Dominicans, scrabbling for hope. *New York Times*, p. A31.

Okazaki, S. (2002). Influences of culture on Asian American sexuality. *Journal of Sex Research*, 39, pp. 34–41.

Oldfield, G. (2002). Commentary. In M.M. Suarez-Orozco & M.M. Paez (Eds.), *Latinos remaking America* (pp. 389–397). Berkeley: University of California Press.

O'Leary, V.E. (1998). Strength in the face of adversity: Individual and social thriving. (Thriving: Broadening the paradigm beyond illness and health*). Journal of Social Issues*, 54, pp. 425–446.

Olive, E. (2003). The African American child and positive youth development: A journey from support to sufficiency. In F.A. Villarruel, D.F. Perkins, L.M. Borden, & J.G. Keith (Eds.), *Community youth development programs, policies, and practices* (pp. 27–46). Thousand Oaks, CA: Sage.

Olsen, J.R., & Pace, K. (2002). *Character education*. East Lansing: Michigan 4–H Youth Development, Michigan State University.

Onaga, E., Carolan, M., Maddalena, C., & Villarruel, F.A. (2003). Positive development for youth with disabilities: Lessons learned from two stories of success. In F.A. Villarruel, D.F. Perkins, L.M. Borden, & J.G. Keith (Eds.), *Community youth development programs, policies, and practices* (pp. 162–178). Thousand Oaks, CA: Sage.

Orellana, M.F. (2001). The work kids do: Mexican and Chicano American immigrant children's contribution to households and schools in California. *Harvard Educational Review*, 3, pp. 366–389.

Orleck, A. (2001). Soviet Jews: The city's newest immigrants transform New York Jewish life. In N. Foner (Ed.), *New immigrants in New York* (pp. 111–140). New York: Columbia University Press.

Pace, K.L. (2003). The character of moral communities: A community youth development approach to enhancing character development. In F.A. Villarruel, D.F. Perkins, L.M. Borden, & J.G. Keith (Eds.), *Community youth development programs, policies, and practices* (pp. 248–272). Thousand Oaks, CA: Sage.

Padilla, Y.C. (1997). Immigrant policy: Issues for social work practice. *Social Work*, 42, pp. 595–606.

Pan, P.L.P. (1998, December 1). Ren and the process of coping. *The World & I*, 13, pp. 229–233.

Parks, S.D. (2000). *Big questions, worthy dreams: Mentoring young adults in their search for meaning, purpose, and faith*. San Francisco: Jossey-Bass.

Parrillo, V.N. (1991). The immigrant family: Securing the American dream. *Journal of Comparative Family Studies*, 22, pp. 131–145.

Parsons, R.D. (2001). *The ethics of professional practice*. Boston: Allyn and Bacon.

Patistea, E., & Siamanta, H. (2000). Family life, two cultures and a serious childhood illness. *Community Practitioner*, 73, pp. 566–576.

Patterson, O. (1982). *Slavery and social death: A comparative study*. Cambridge, MA: Harvard University Press.

Paulino, A., & Burgos-Servido, J. (1997). Working with immigrant families in transition. In E.P. Congress (Ed.), *Multicultural perspectives in working with families* (pp. 125–141). New York: Springer.

Pear, R. (1992, December 4). New look at the U.S. in 2050: Bigger, older and less white. *New York Times*, pp. 1, D18.

Pedersen, P.B. (1995). Culture-entered ethical guidelines for counselors. In J.G. Ponterotto, J.M. Casas, L.A. Suzuki, & C.M. Alexander (Eds.), *Handbook for multicultural counseling* (pp. 34–49). Thousand Oaks, CA: Sage.

Pedersen, P.B. (1994). *A handbook for developing multicultural awareness*. Alexandria, VA: American Counseling Association.

Pedersen, P.B., Draguns, J.G., Lonner, W.J., & Trimble, J.E. (Eds.). (1989). *Counseling across cultures* (3rd ed.). Honolulu: University of Hawaii.

Pentz, M.A., Dwyer, J., Mackinnon, D., Flay, B.R., et al. (1989). A multicommunity trial for primary prevention of adolescent drug abuse. *Journal of the American Medical Association*, 261, pp. 3250–3266.

Penuel, W.R. (1995). *Adult guidance in youth development revisited: Identity construction in youth organizations*. Worcester, MA: Clark University.

Perez-Foster, R.M. (2001). When immigration is trauma: Guidelines for the individual and family clinician. *American Journal of Orthopsychiatry*, 71, pp. 153–170.

Perkins, D.F., & Borden, L.M. (2003). Key elements of community youth development programs. In F.A.

Villarruel, D.F. Perkins, L.M. Borden, & J.G. Keith (Eds.), *Community youth development programs, policies, and practices* (pp. 327–340). Thousand Oaks, CA: Sage.

Perry, C.L., Kelder, S.H., & Komro, K.A. (1993). The social world of adolescents: Family peers, schools, and the community. In S.G. Millstein, A.C. Petersen, & E.O. Nightingale (Eds.), *Promoting the health of adolescents: New directions for the twenty-first century* (pp. 73–96). New York: Oxford University Press.

Pessar, P.R. (1995). *A visa for a dream: Dominicans in the United States.* Boston: Allyn and Bacon.

Pessar, P.R. (1987). The Dominicans: Women in the household and the garment industry. In N. Foner (Ed.), *New immigrants in New York* (pp. 103–129). New York: Columbia University Press.

Pessar, P.R., & Graham, P.M. (2001). Dominicans: Transnational identities and local politics. In N. Foner (Ed.), *New immigrants in New York* (pp. 251–273). New York: Columbia University Press.

Petersilia, J., & Abrahamse, A. (1994). A profile of those arrested. In M. Baldassare (Ed.), *The Los Angeles riots: Lessons for the urban future* (pp. 135–147). Boulder, CO: Westview.

Pettys, G.L., & Balgopal, P.R. (1998). Multigenerational conflicts and new immigrants: An Indo-American experience. *Families in Society, 79*, pp. 410–423.

Phillips, N.K., & Straussner, S.L.A. (2002). *Urban social work: An introduction to policy and practice in the cities.* Boston: Allyn and Bacon.

Phinney, J.S., Romero, I., Nava, M., & Huang, D. (2001). The role of language, parents, and peers in ethnic identity among adolescents in immigrant families. *Journal of Youth and Adolescence, 30*, pp. 135–143.

Physicians for Human Rights. (2003). *From persecution to prison: The health consequences of detention for asylum seekers.* Boston: Author.

Pianta, R.C., Stubbman, M.W., & Hamre, B.K. (2002). How schools can do better: Fostering stronger connections between teachers and students. In J.E. Rhodes (Ed.), *New directions for youth development: A critical view of youth mentoring* (pp. 91–107). San Francisco: Jossey-Bass.

Pierce, W.J., & Elisme, E. (1997). Understanding and working with Haitian immigrant families. In P.M. Brown & J. S. Shalett (Eds.), *Cross-cultural practice with couples and families* (pp. 49–65). New York: Haworth (pp. 125–141). New York: Springer.

Pikes, T., Burrell, B., & Holliday, C. (1998). Using academic strategies to build resilience. *Reaching Today's Youth: The Community Circle of Caring Journal, 2*, pp. 44–47.

Pinderhughes, E. (1990). Legacy of slavery: The experience of Black families in America. In M.P. Mirkin (Ed.), *The social and political contexts of family therapy* (pp. 289–305). Boston: Allyn and Bacon.

Pinderhughes, E. (1989). *Understanding race, ethnicity, and power.* New York: The Free Press.

Pipher, M. (2002). *The middle of everywhere: The world's refugees come to our town.* New York: Harcourt.

Pittman, K.J. (1996). Community, youth, development: Three goals in search of connection. *New Designs for Youth Development, 12*, pp. 4–8.

Pittman, K.J., & Zeldin, S. (1995). *Premises, principles and practices: Defining the why, what, and how of promoting youth development through organizational practice.* Washington, DC: Academy for Educational Development.

Poe, J. (2002, February 7). 10 percent in U.S. are foreign-born. *Atlanta Constitution*, p. 1.

Population Reference Bureau. (2002). *1 million Arab Americans in the United States.* Washington, DC: Author.

Population Resource Center. (2002). *Executive summary: A demographic profile of Hispanics in the U.S.* Washington, DC: Author.

Population Resource Center. (1997). *Immigration to California.* Washington, DC: Author.

Porter. (2001, August 29). UCLA study says legalization of undocumented would have positive economic impact. *Wall Street Journal*, Washington News, p. 1.

Portes, A., & Rumbaut, R.G. (2001a). *Legacies: The story of the immigrant second generation.* Berkeley: University of California Press.

Portes, A., & Rumbaut, R.G. (Eds.). (2001b). *Ethnicities: Children of immigrants in America.* Berkeley: University of California Press.

Portes, A., & Rumbaut, R.G. (1997). *Immigrant America: A portrait.* Berkeley: University of California Press.

Portes, A., & Zhou, M. (1993, November). The new second generation: Segmented assimilation and its variants. *Annals of the American Academy of Political and Social Sciences, 503* (November), pp. 74–96.

Positive Youth Development Working Group. (2002). *The adolescent search for purpose: The roles of moral, civic and spiritual development.* Society for Research on Adolescence Ninth Biennial Meeting, New Orleans.

Potocky, M. (1996). Refugee children: How are they faring economically as adults? *Social Work, 41*, pp. 364–373.

Potocky-Tripodi, M. (2002). *Best practices for social work with refugees and immigrants.* New York: Columbia University Press.

Power, A. (1996). Area-based poverty and resident empowerment. *Urban Studies*, 33, pp. 1535–1565.

Proctor, E.K. (2001). Building and consolidating knowledge for practice. *Social Work Research*, 25, pp. 195–197.

Pryor, C.B. (2001). New immigrants and refugees in American schools: Multiple voices. *Childhood Education*, 77, pp. 275–283.

Purdum, T.S. (2001, March 30). California census confirms whites are in minority. *New York Times*, pp. A1, A16.

Pynoos, R.S., Steinberg, A.M., & Goenjian, A. (1996). Traumatic stress in childhood and adolescence: Recent developments and current controversies. In B. Van der Kolk, A.C. McFarlane, & L. Weisrath (Eds.), *Traumatic stress* (pp. 331–358). New York: Guilford.

Quinn, J. (1999). Where need meets opportunity: Youth development programs for early teens. *The Future of Children: When School Is Out*, 9, pp. 96–116.

Quinton, D., Pickles, A., Maughan, B., & Rutter, M. (1993). Partners, peers, and pathways: Assortive pairing and continuities in conduct disorder. *Development and Psychopathology*, 5, pp. 763–783.

Rahman, M.A. (1999, November 19). Challenges facing youth development: National and global perspectives. *The Independent*, pp. 3–6.

Ramirez, E. (2003, June 23). Turning to the temple. *The Boston Globe*, p. B5.

Ramsey, M. (1994). Use of a Personal Cultural Perspective Profile (PCPP) in developing counselor multicultural competence. *International Journal for the Advancement of Counseling*, 17, pp. 283–290.

Rapport, A.L. (2002). Building social and civic capital through service-learning: In practice and in systematic study. *CYD Journal: Community Youth Development*, 3, pp. 26–32.

Rauner, D.M. (2000). *The role of caring in youth development and community life*. New York: Columbia University Press.

Ray, D. (2000, March 20). Miami's thriving Little Havana. *The Washington Times*, pp. 1–2.

Reamer, F.G. (1999). *Social work values and ethics* (2nd ed.). New York: Columbia University Press.

Reardon-Anderson, J., Capps, R., & Fix, M.E. (2002). *The health and well-being of children in immigrant families*. Washington, DC: Urban Institute.

Rees, S. (1998). Empowerment of youth. In L.H. Gutierrez, L.M. Parsens, & E.O. Cox (Eds.). *Empowerment in social work: A sourcebook* (pp. 130–145). Pacific Grove, CA: Brooks/Cole.

Refugee and Immigrant Coordination Program. (2002). *Asian American youth leadership conference*. Portland, OR: Author.

Renwick, L. (1993, January 3). The myth of South-Central; more of a stereotype than a place, it is defined by ethnicity and negative media images rather than street boundaries. *Los Angeles Times*, p. 17.

Reuters. (2003, January 15). Bush pushes welfare reform. *Boston Metro*, p. 3.

Reyes, A. (1999). From urban area to refugee camp: How one thing leads to another. *Ethnomusicology*, 43, pp. 201–216.

Rhodes, J.E. (2002a). *Stand by me: The risks and rewards of mentoring today's youth*. Cambridge, MA: Harvard University Press.

Rhodes, J.E. (Ed.). (2002b). *New directions for youth development: A critical view of youth mentoring*. San Francisco: Jossey-Bass.

Rich, J.M., & DeVitis, J.L. (1994). *Theories of moral development*. Springfield, IL: Charles C. Thomas.

Richardson, L., & Fields, R. (2003, February 6). The nation; Latino majority arrives—Among state's babies. *Los Angeles Times*, p. 1.

Riddle, A. (2001, March 28). Census: Hispanics top blacks as largest minority group in Florida. *Naples Daily News*, p. 1.

Ridley C.R., Baker, D.M., & Hill, C.L. (2001). Critical issues concerning cultural competence. *The Counseling Psychologist*, 29, 6, pp. 822–832.

Rieff, D. (1999). *Going to Miami: Exiles, tourists and refugees in the new America*. Gainsville: University Press of Florida.

Rieff, D. (1991). *Los Angeles: Capital of the third world*. New York: Simon and Schuster.

Rivera, B.D., & Rogers-Atkinson, D. (1997). Culturally sensitive interventions: Social skills training with children and parents from culturally and linguistically diverse backgrounds. *Intervention in School and Clinic*, 33, pp. 75–80.

Roberts, D. (2002). *Shattered bonds: The color of child welfare*. New York: Basic Civitas Books.

ROCA. (2003). *Year I Report to W.K. Kellogg Foundation*. Chelsea, MA: Author.

ROCA. (1999). ROCA: A multicultural way of life. *New Designs for Youth Development*, 15, pp. 13–18.

Rockwell, S. (1998). Overcoming four myths that prevent fostering resilience. *Reaching Today's Youth: The Community Circle of Caring Journal*, 2, pp. 14–17.

Rodriguez, C. (2003, February 2). Pursuing a dream: Identity-card program offers an opportunity for Mexican workers. *Boston Globe*, pp. B1, B8.

Rodriguez, C. (2002, July 22). Top Salvador official makes pitch: Courts business in Boston area. *Boston Globe*, p. B2.

Rodriguez, L.J. (1997). Hearts and hands: A new paradigm for work with youth and violence (Losing a generation: Probing the myths and reality of youth and violence). *Social Justice*, 24, pp. 7–20.

Rodriguez, M.C., Morrobel, D., & Villarruel, F.A. (2003). Realities and vision of success for Latino youth development. In F.A. Villarruel, D.F. Perkins, L.M. Borden, & J.G. Keith (Eds.), *Community youth development programs, policies, and practices* (pp. 47–78). Thousand Oaks, CA: Sage.

Roehlkepartain, E.C. (2001, Summer). Connecting with boys: Closing the asset gap. *Assets Magazine*, pp. 20–24.

Roffman, J.G., Suarez-Orozco, C., & Rhodes, J.E. (2003). Facilitating positive development in immigrant youth: The role of mentors and community organizations. In F.A. Villarruel, D.F. Perkins, L.N. Borden, & J.G. Keith (Eds.), *Community youth development programs, policies, and practices* (pp. 90–117). Thousand Oaks, CA: Sage.

Rogler, L.H., Malgady, R.G., & Rodriguez, O. (1989). *Hispanics and mental health: A framework for research*. Malabor, FL: Krieger.

Rosenberg, T. (1997, December 28). To hell and back. *The New York Sunday Times Magazine*, pp. 32–36.

Roth, J., Brooks-Gunn, J., Murray, L., & Foster, W.H. (1998). Promoting healthy adolescents: Synthesis of youth development program evaluations. *Journal of Research on Adolescence*, 8, pp. 423–459.

Roth, J., Murray, L.F., Brooks-Gunn, J., & Foster, W.H. (1999). Youth development programs. In D.B. Besharov (Ed.), *America's disconnected youth: Toward a preventive strategy* (pp. 267–294). Washington, DC: Child Welfare League of America Press.

Rothstein, R. (2002, August 7). Schools can use help teaching parents to get involved. *New York Times*, p. A16.

Rousseau, C. (1995). *The mental health of refugee children: A longitudinal study*. Canada: McGill Division of Social and Transcultural Psychiatry (http://ww2.mcgill.ca/psychiatry/transcultural/immig.html).

Rousseau, C., Gagne, M., & Bibeau, G. (1998). Resilience in unaccompanied minors from north of Somalia. *Psychoanalytic Review*, 85, pp. 615–629.

Roy, J.M. (2002). *Love to hate: America's obsession with hatred and violence*. New York: Columbia University Press.

Roylance, F.D. (2001, August 6). State's population of foreign-born soars; 60% rise since 1990; most settle near D.C. *Baltimore Sun*, p. 4A.

Ruiz-de-velasco, J., Fix, M., & Clewell, B.C. (2000). *Overlooked and underserved: Immigrant students in U.S. secondary schools*. Washington, DC: The Urban Institute.

Rumbaut, R. (1998). Coming of age in immigrant America. *Research Perspectives on Migration*, 1, pp. 1–14.

Rumbaut, R. (1996). The crucible within: Ethnic identity, self-esteem, and segmented assimilation among children of immigrants. In A. Portes (Ed.), *The new second generation* (pp. 119–170). New York: Russell Sage Foundation.

Rumbaut, R. (1991). The agony of exile: A study of the immigration and adaptation of Indochinese refugee adults and children. In F.L. Ahearn & J.L. Athey (Eds.), *Refugee children: Theory, research and services* (pp. 53–91). Baltimore, MD: Johns Hopkins University Press.

Rutledge, J.P. (1992). *The Vietnamese experience in America*. Bloomington: Indiana University Press.

Rutter, M., & Quinton, D. (1984). Long-term followup of women institutionalized in childhood: Factors promoting good functioning in adult life. *British Journal of Developmental Psychology*, 18, pp. 225–234.

Ryan, A.S. (1992). *Social work with immigrants and refugees*. New York: Haworth.

Ryu, C. (1992). 1.5 generation. In J.F.J. Lee (Ed.), *Asian Americans* (pp. 50–54). New York: The New Press.

Sabagh, G., & Bozorgmehr, M. (1996). Population change: Immigration and ethnic transformation. In R. Waldinger & M. Bozorgmehr (Eds.). *Ethnic Los Angeles* (pp. 79–107). New York: Russell Sage Foundation.

Sachs, S. (2003, July 28). In Harlem's fabric, bright treads of Senegal. *New York Times*, pp. A1, A17.

Sachs, S. (2002a, March 15). A nation challenged: Illegal immigrants; Long resistant, police start embracing immigration duties. *New York Times*, p. A11.

Sachs, S. (2002b, July 11). Traces of terror: The detainees: U.S. deports most of those arrested during sweeps after 9/11. *New York Times*, p. A20.

Sachs, S. (2002c, August 11). Immigrants see path to riches in phone cards. *New York Times*, pp. 1, 24.

Sachs, S. (2001, March 16). New York City tops 8 million for the first time. *New York Times*, pp. A1, A18.

Sack, W.H., Him, C., & Dickason, D. (1999). Twelve-year follow-up study of Khmer youths who suffered massive war trauma as children. *Journal of the American Academy of Child and Adolescent Psychiatry*, 38, pp. 1173–1202.

Sadowski-Smith, C. (2002a). *Globalization on the line: Culture, capital, and citizenship at U.S. borders*. New York: St. Martin's Press.

Sadowski-Smith, C. (2002b). Reading across Diaspora: Chinese and Mexican undocumented immigration across U.S. land borders. In C. Sadowski-Smith (Ed.), *Gloalization on the line: Culture, capital, and citizenship at U.S. borders* (pp. 69–97). New York: St. Martin's Press.

Saito, R.N., & Roehlkepartain, E.C. (1992). *Variety of programs meet needs of mentors and mentees.* Minneapolis: Search Institute.

Saleebey, D.S. (1996). The strengths perspective in social work practice: Extensions and cautions. *Social Work, 41*, pp. 296–305.

Saleebey, D.S. (Ed.). (1992). *The strengths perspective in social work practice.* New York: Longman.

Sam, D.L. (2000). Psychological adaptation of adolescents with immigrant backgrounds. *The Journal of Social Psychology, 140*, pp. 5–15.

Samaniego, R.Y., & Gonzales, N.A. (1999). Multiple mediators of the effects of acculturation status on delinquency for Mexican American adolescents. *American Journal of Community Psychology, 27*, pp. 189–199.

Sanchez, L. (2003, February 6). Latinos make up majority of babies born in California. *San Diego Union-Tribune*, p. 1

Sandefur, G.D., Martin, M., Eggerling-Boeck, S.E., Mannon, S.E., & Meier, A.M. (2001). An overview of racial and ethnic demographic trends. In N.J. Smelser, W.J. Wilson, & F. Mitchell (Eds.), *America becoming: Racial trends and their consequences*, (vol. 1. pp. 40–102). Washington, DC: National Academy Press.

Saposnick, K. (2003). Living together well in diverse urban communities: An interview with Molly Baldwin. *Leverage Points, 38*, pp. 1–4.

Sawhney, D.N. (Ed.). (2002). *Unmasking L.A.: Third worlds and the city.* New York: St. Martin's Press.

Scales, P.C., & Leffert, N. (1999). *Developmental assets: A synthesis of the scientific research on adolescent development.* Minneapolis: Search Institute.

Scheer, S.D. (1999). Strategies for teaching youth development in the undergraduate program. *College Student Journal, 33*, pp. 154–160.

Scheinfeld, D., Wallach, L.B., & Langendorf, T. (1997). *Strengthening refugee families: Designing programs for refugee and other families in need.* Chicago: Lyceum Books.

Schiller, D. (2002, June 2). These youths have an identity crisis: Jobs, college, drivers' licenses are elusive for the undocumented. *San Antonio Express-News*, p. 1A.

Schmeidl, S. (2001). Conflict and forced migration: A quantitative review, 1964–1995. In A.R. Zolberg & P.M. Benda (Eds.), *Global migrants, global refugees: Problems and solutions* (pp. 62–94). New York: Berghahn Books.

Schmitt, E. (2001a, April 1). U.S. now more diverse, ethnically and racially. *New York Times*, p. 18.

Schmitt, E. (2001b, March 13). For 7 million people in census, one race category isn't enough. *New York Times*, pp. A1, A14.

Schneider, A.C. (2002, December 23). A changing America has changing tastes. *Kiplinger Business Forecasts*, p. 1.

Schulenberg, J., Maggs, J.L., & Hurrelmann, K. (Eds.). (1999). *Health-risks and developmental transitions during adolescence.* New York: Cambridge University Press.

Schwartz, W. (1996, November). *Immigrants and their educational attainment: Some facts and findings.* New York: ERIC Clearinghouse on Urban Education.

Scott, J. (2002, December 5). In simple pronouns, clues to New York Latino culture. *New York Times*, p. A37.

Scott, J. (2002, August 6). Census finds immigrants lower city's income data. *New York Times*, p. A16.

Search Institute. (1995, Winter). Different faiths share common goals. *Youth Update*, pp. 1, 7.

Segal, U.A. (2002). *A framework for immigration: Asians in the United States.* New York: Columbia University Press.

Seidman, E., et al. (1995). Development and validation of adolescent-perceived micro-system scales: Social support, daily hassles, and involvement. *American Journal of Community Psychology, 23*, pp. 355–375.

Seligman, M.E.P. (1991). *Helplessness: On depression, development and death* (2nd ed.). New York: Oxford University Press.

Shaklee, H. (2000). Inventing adolescence: 20th century concepts of youth development. *Journal of Family & Consumer Sciences, 92*, pp. 11–16.

Shapiro, J., Douglas, K., Rocha, O. de la, Radecki, S., Vu, C., & Dinh, T. (1999). Generational differences in psychosocial adaptation and predictors of psychological distress in a population of recent Vietnamese immigrants. *Journal of Community Health, 24*, pp. 95–103.

Sharp, D. (2002, May 14). Little Havana is unimpressed. *USA Today*, p. 3A.

Sharry, F. (2002, September 10). Don't just target immigrants. *USA Today*, p. 10A.

Shear, L. (2000). Learning large: Reclaiming the sacred in youth work. *CYD Journal: Community Youth Development, 1*, pp. 22–29.

Shelton, C.M. (1991). *Morality and the adolescent: A pastoral psychological approach.* New York: Crossroad.

Shenon, P. (2002, December 8). For immigrants, the watchword suddenly is enforcement. *New York Times* (Week in Review), p. 4.

Sherraden, M.S., & Martin, J.J. (1994). Social work with immigrants: International issues in service delivery. *International Social Work*, 37, pp. 369–384.

Shine, J., Shoup, B., & Harrington, D. (1981). *New roles for early adolescence*. New York: The National Commission on Resources for Youth.

Simon, B.L. (1994). *The empowerment tradition in American social work: A history*. New York: Columbia University Press.

Simon, S. (2002, October 24). Latinos take root in Midwest. *Los Angeles Times*, p. 1.

Sims, E.M., Pernell-Arnold, A., Graham, R., & Hughes, R. (1998). Principles of multi-cultural psychiatric rehabilitation services. *Psychiatric Rehabilitation Journal*, 21, pp. 219–226.

Singer, B. (1997). Two California cultures (Whites and Third World immigrants). *Contemporary Review*, 271, pp. 195–201.

Sisneros, J.A. (2002). Social work practice with Mexican immigrants: Steps to understanding. *Social Work Today*, 2, pp. 13–15.

Skaff, M.M., Chesla, C.A., Mycue, V.D.L.S. & Fisher, L. (2002). Lessons in cultural competence: Adapting research methodology for Latino participants. *Journal of Community Psychology*, 30, pp. 305–323.

Smith, J. (2001, August 8). Census undercounts may cost NYC. *Newsday*, p. A34.

Smith, R.C. (2001a). Mexicans: Social, educational, economic, and political problems and prospects in New York. In N. Foner (Ed.), *New immigrants in New York* (pp. 275–300). New York: Columbia University Press.

Smith, R.C. (2001b). "Mexicanness" in New York: Migrants seek place in old racial order. *NACLA Report on the Americas*, 35, pp. 14–18.

Smith, R.C. (1996). Mexicans in New York: Memberships and incorporation in a new immigrant community. In G. Haslip-Viera & S.L. Baver (Eds.), *Latinos in New York: Communities in transition* (pp. 57–103). Notre Dame, IN: University of Notre Dame Press.

Smith, T.J., & Jucovy, K. (1996). *AmeriCorps in the field: Implementation of the National and Community Trust Act in nine states*. Washington, DC: American Youth Policy Program.

Solomon, A. (2002, August 20). Detainees equal dollars. *The Village Voice*, p. 46.

Solomon, B. (1970). *Black empowerment*. New York: Columbia University Press.

Sommer, D. (2002). Afterword: American projections. In M.M. Suarez-Orozco & M.M. Paez (Eds.), *Latinos remaking America* (pp. 457–461). Berkeley: University of California.

Sontag, D., & Dugger, C.W. (1998, July 19). The new immigrant tide: A shuttle between worlds. *New York Times*, pp. 1, 26.

Specht, H., & Courtney, M.E. (1994). *Unfaithful angels: How social work has abandoned its mission*. New York: The Free Press.

Spence, S. (1996, November 21). Record number of deportations. *Workers World*, p. 1.

Spencer, M., Lewis, E., & Gutierrez, L. (2000). Multicultural perspectives on direct practice in social work. In A. Allern-Meares & C. Garvin (Eds.), *The handbook of social work direct practice* (pp. 131–149). Thousand Oaks, CA: Sage.

Stake, R.E. (1995). *The art of case study research*. Thousand Oaks, CA: Sage.

Stanton-Salazar, R.D. (1997). A social capital framework for understanding the socialization of racial minority children and youths. *Harvard Educational Review*, 67, pp. 1–32.

Steinberg, S. (1981). *The ethnic myth: Race, ethnicity, and class in America*. New York: Atheneum.

Stepick, A. (1998). *Pride against prejudice: Haitians in the United States*. Boston: Allyn and Bacon.

Stepick, A., & Stepick, C.D. (2002). Power and identity: Miami Cubans. In M.M. Suarez-Orozco & M.M. Paez (Eds.), *Latinos remaking America* (pp. 75–92). Berkeley: University of California Press.

Stevens, J.W. (2002). *Smart and sassy: The strengths of inner-city Black girls*. New York: Oxford University Press.

Stodolska, M. (1998). Assimilation and leisure constraints: Dynamics of constraints on leisure in immigrant populations. *Journal of Leisure Research*, 30, pp. 521–524.

Stoller, P. (2001). West Africans: Trading places in New York. In N. Foner (Ed.), *New immigrants in New York* (pp. 229–249). New York: Columbia University Press.

Strier, D.R. (1996). Coping strategies of immigrant parents: Directions for family therapy. *Family Process*, 35, pp. 363–376.

Strodl, P. (1993). *The development of social communications curricula: A proposal and a resource compendium*. ERIC Document Reproduction Service (EDRS) ED 355 295. Paper presented at the Annual Meeting of the Eastern Educational Research Association, February 17–21, Clearwater Beach, FL.

Strug, D.L., & Mason, S.E. (2002). Social service needs of Hispanic immigrants: An exploratory study of the Washington Heights community. *Journal of Ethnic & Cultural Diversity in Social Work*, 10, pp. 69–88.

Suarez-Orozco, C. (2001). Afterword: Understanding and serving the children of immigrants. *Harvard Educational Review*, 71, pp. 579–589.

Suarez-Orozco, C., & Suraez-Orozco, M.M. (2001). *Children of immigration*. Cambridge, MA: Harvard University Press.

Suarez-Orozco, C., & Suaraez-Orozco, M.M. (1995). *Transformations: Immigrations, family life, and achievement motivation among Latino adolescents*. Palo Alto, CA: Stanford University Press.

Suarez-Orozco, M. (2001). Globalization, immigration, and education: The research agenda. *Harvard Educational Review*, 71, pp. 364–365.

Suarez-Orozco, M.M., & Paez, M.M. (Eds.). (2002a). *Latinos: Remaking America*. Berkeley: University of California Press.

Suarez-Orozco, M.M., & Paez, M.M. (2002b). Introduction. *Latinos: Remaking America* (pp. 1–37). Berkeley: University of California Press.

Sue, D.W. (2001). Multidimensional facets of cultural competence. *The Counseling Psychologist*, 29, pp. 790–821.

Sue, D.W., Arredondo, P., & McDavis, R. (1992). Multicultural counseling, competencies and standards: A call for the profession. *Journal of Counseling and Development*, 70, pp. 477–486.

Sue, D.W., & Sue, S. (2003). *Counseling the culturally diverse: Theory and practice* (4th ed.). New York: Wiley & Sons.

Sue, D., & Sue, S. (1999). *Counseling the culturally different: Theory and practice* (3rd ed.). New York: Wiley & Sons.

Sue, S. (1998). In search of cultural competence in psychotherapy and counseling. *American Psychologist*, 53, pp. 440–448.

Sullivan, T. (2002, September 11). Immigrants are finding permission to enter U.S. harder to get; legal visits now shorter; red tape snares refugees. *Salt Lake Tribune*, p. AA14.

Sum, A., Fogg, N., & Mangum, G. (2001). Confronting the youth population boom: Labor market prospects of out-of-school young adults. *Challenge*, 44, pp. 30–42.

Summerfield, D. (2000). War and mental health: A brief overview. *British Medical Journal*, 321, pp. 232–239.

Sutner, S. (2002, September 1). State slashes immigrant aid. *Worcester Telegram & Gazette* (Massachusetts), p. A12.

Suzuki, L.A., McRae, M.B., & Short, E.L. (2001). The facets of cultural competence: Searching outside the box. *The Counseling Psychologist*, 29, pp. 842–849.

Swarns, R.L. (2003a, June 17). Asylum seekers suffer psychological setbacks, study finds. *New York Times*, p. A23.

Swarns, R.L. (2003b, June 25). Immigrants feel the pinch of post-9/11 laws. *New York Times*, p. A14.

Swarns, R.L. (2003c, July 20). U.S. a place of miracles for Somali refugees. *New York Times*, p. 1, 23.

Switzer, G.E., Scholle, S.H., Johnson, B.A., & Kelleher, K.J. (1998). The Client Cultural Competence Inventory: An instrument for assessing cultural competence in behavioral managed care organizations. *Journal of Child and Family Studies*, 7, 483–491.

Szanisko, M. (2002, June 6). Immigrant population booming in Bay State. *Boston Herald*, p. 1.

Szapocznik, J., & Kurtines, W.M. (1993). Family psychology and cultural diversity: Opportunities for theory, research, and application. *American Psychologist*, 48, pp. 400–407.

Tambiah, S.J. (2000). Transnational movements, diaspora, and multiple modernities. *Daedalus*, 129, pp. 163–183.

Tani, C.R., Chavez, E.L., & Deffenbacher, J.L. (2001). Peer isolation and drug use among White non-Hispanic and Mexican American adolescents. *Adolescence*, 36, pp. 127–142.

Tarter, R.E., & Vanyukov, M. (1999). Re-visiting the validity of the construct of resilience. In M.D. Glantz & J.L. Johnson (Eds.), *Resilience and development: Positive life adaptations* (pp. 85–100). New York: Kluwer Academic/Plenum Publishers.

Taylor, A.S., & Bressler, J. (2000). *Mentoring across generations: Partnerships for positive youth development*. New York: Kluwer Academic/Plenum Publishers.

Tebo, M.G. (2000). Locked up tight. *American Bar Association Journal*, 86, pp. 44–51.

Terr, L. (1991). Childhood traumas: An outline and overview. American Journal of Psychiatry, 148, pp. 10–20.

Thompson, E. (2002, September 1). They will take advantage of you; children of illegals face challenges. *Sunday Telegram* (Worcester, MA), p. A13.

Thompson, G. (2003, November 3). Littlest immigrants, left in hands of smugglers. *New York Times*, pp. A1, A12.

Thompson, G. (2002, April 8). Guatemala intercepts 49 children illegally bound for U.S. *New York Times*, p. A2.

Tienda, M., & Wilson, W.J. (2002). Comparative perspectives of urban youth: Challenges for normative development. In M. Tienda & W.J. Wilson (Eds.), *Youth in cities: A cross-national perspective* (pp. 3–18). New York: Cambridge University Press.

Torres-Saillant, S., & Hernandez, R. (1998). *The Dominican Americans.* Westport, CT: Greenwood.

Trueblood, L.A. (2000). Female genital mutilation: A discussion of international human rights instruments, cultural sovereignty and dominance theory. *Denver Journal of International Law and Policy*, 28, pp. 437–468.

Tsang, A.K.T., & George, U. (1998). Towards an integrated framework for cross-cultural social work practice. *Canadian Social Work Review*, 15, pp. 73–93.

United Nations High Commissioner for Refugees. (2001). *Women, children and older refugees.* Geneva, Switzerland: Author.

U.S. Census Bureau. (2002a). *Profile of the foreign-born population in the United States: 2000.* Washington, DC: Author.

U.S. Census Bureau. (2002b). *Census 2000: California demographic profile sample data-statements.* Washington, DC: Author.

U.S. Census Bureau. (2002c). *A profile of the nation's foreign-born population from Asia (2000 update).* Washington, DC: Author.

U.S. Census Bureau. (2002d). *Coming to America: A profile of the nation's foreign born (2000 update).* Washington, DC: Author.

U.S. Census Bureau. (2001). *Population by race and Hispanic or Latino origin for the United States: 1990 and 2000.* Washington, DC: Author.

U.S. Census Bureau. (2001). *The Hispanic population in the United States: Population characteristics.* Washington, DC: U.S. Department of Commerce.

U.S. Census Bureau. (2000, June 22). *State population estimates and demographic components of population change: Annual time-series, April 1, 1990 to July 1, 1999.* Washington, DC: Author.

U.S. Committee for Refugees. (2002). *World refugee survey, 2002.* Washington, DC: Author.

U.S. Committee for Refugees. (2002, May). *Refugee Reports*, 23, p. 4. Washington, DC: Author.

U.S. Conference of Catholic Bishops. (2001). *Hispanic affairs.* Washington, DC: Author.

U.S. Department of Justice. (2002, November 25). *Hate crime statistics.* Washington, DC: Federal Bureau of Investigation.

U.S. Department of Justice. Immigration and Naturalization Service. (1999). *Asylees, Fiscal Year 1997.* Washington, DC: Author.

U.S. Department of State. (2001, March 1). *U.S. refugee admissions program: Eligibility for refugee processing priorities FY 2001.* Washington: D.C.: Bureau of Population, Refugees, and Migration.

U.S. Immigration and Naturalization Service. (2002). *2000 statistical yearbook* Washington, DC: Author.

U.S. Immigration and Naturalization Service. (1997). *Statistical yearbook of the Immigration and Naturalization Service, 1995.* Washington, DC: U.S. Government Printing Office.

U.S. Newswire. (2002, October 17). Refugee Council USA dismayed by President's Decision to limit refugee admissions.

University of Minnesota Extension Service. (2001). *Helping youth succeed.* Minneapolis-St. Paul, MN: Author.

Unz, R. (1999). California and the end of white America. *Commentary*, 108, pp. 1–17.

Van Soest, D. (2003) Advancing social and economic justice. In D. Lum (Ed.), *Culturally competent practice: A framework for understanding diverse groups and justice issues* (2nd ed., pp. 345–376). Pacific Grove, CA: Brooks/Cole.

Vang, V., Jiminez, E., & Ruukel, E., (1996). Hardships and dreams (Three young immigrant narratives). *Scholastic Update*, 129, pp. 10–15.

Vernez, G., & Abrahamse, A. (1996). *How immigrants fare in U.S. education.* Santa Monica, CA: Rand Corporation.

Vickerman, M. (2001). Jamaicans: Balancing race and ethnicity. In N. Foner (Ed.), *New immigrants in New York* (pp. 201–228). New York: Columbia University Press.

Vigil, D. (2002). Community dynamics and the rise of street gangs. In M.M. Suarez-Orozco & M.M. Paez (Eds.), *Latinos remaking America* (pp. 97–109). Berkeley: University of California Press.

Vigil, J.D. (1990). Cholos and gangs: Culture change and street youth in Los Angeles. In C.R. Huff (Ed.), *Gangs in America* (pp. 116–128). Newbury Park, CA: Sage.

Vigil, J.D., & Yun, S.C. (1990). Vietnamese youth gangs in Southern California. In C.R. Huff (Ed.), *Gangs in America* (pp. 146–162). Newbury Park, CA: Sage.

Villarruel, F.A., & Lerner, R.M. (1994). Development and context and the contexts of learning. In. F.A. Villarruel & R.M. Lerner (Eds.), *Promoting community-based programs for socialization and learning* (pp. 3–10). San Francisco: Jossey-Bass.

Villarruel, F.A., Perkins, D.F., Borden, L.M., & Keith, J.G. (Eds.). (2003a). *Community youth development programs, policies, and practices.* Thousand Oaks, CA: Sage.

Villarruel, F.A., Perkins, D.F., Borden, L.M., & Keith, J.G. (2003b). Community youth development: Youth voice and activism. In F.A Villarruel, D.F. Perkins, L.M. Borden, & J.G. Keith (Eds.), *Community youth development programs, policies, and practices* (pp. 394–403). Thousand Oaks, CA: Sage.

Vinokurov, A., Trickett, E.J., & Birman, D. (2002). Acculturative hassles and immigrant adolescents: A life-domain assessment for Soviet Jewish refugees. *Journal of Social Psychology*, 142, pp. 425–445.

Vygotsky, L.S. (1978). *Mind in society*. Cambridge, MA: Harvard University Press.

Waldinger, R. (Ed.). (2001a). *Strangers at the gates: New immigrants in urban America*. Berkeley: University of California Press.

Waldinger, R. (2001b). Conclusion: Immigration and the remaking of urban America. In R. Waldinger (Ed.), *Strangers at the gates: New immigrants in urban America* (pp. 308–330). Berkeley: University of California Press.

Waldinger, R. (1996a). Ethnicity and opportunity in the plural city. In R. Waldinger & M. Bozorgmehr (Eds.), *Ethnic Los Angeles* (pp. 445–470). New York: Russell Sage Foundation.

Waldinger, R. (1996b). *African-Americans and new immigrants in postindustrial New York*. Cambridge, MA: Harvard University Press.

Waldinger, R., & Bozorgmehr, M. (Eds.). (1996). *Ethnic Los Angeles*. New York: Russell Sage Foundation.

Waldinger, R., & Lee, J. (2001). New immigrants in urban America. In R. Waldinger (Ed.), *Strangers at the gates: New immigrants in urban America* (pp. 30–79). Berkeley: University of California Press.

Walker, J.A. (2003). The essential youth worker: Supports and opportunities for professional success. In F.A. Villarruel, D.F. Perkins, L.M. Borden, & J.G. Keith (Eds.), *Community youth development programs, policies, and practices* (pp. 373–393). Thousand Oaks, CA: Sage.

Walker, K.J. (1995). *Resiliency in adult children of alcoholic parents: Use of structural equation modeling*. Dissertation, University of Utah, Salt Lake City.

Waters, M.C. (1996a). The intersection of gender, race, and ethnicity in identity development of Caribbean American teens. In B.J. Leadbeater & N. Way (Eds.), *Urban girls: Resisting stereotypes, creating identities* (pp. 54–81). New York: New York University Press.

Waters, M.C. (1996b). Ethnic and racial identities of second-generation black immigrants in New York City. In A. Portes (Ed.), *The new second generation* (pp. 171–196). New York: Russell Sage Foundation.

Waters, T. (1999). *Crime and immigrant youth*. Thousand Oaks, CA: Sage.

Watkins, M., & Iverson, E. (1998). Youth development principles and field practicum opportunities. In R.R. Greene & M. Watkins (Eds.), *Serving diverse constituencies: Applying the ecological perspective* (pp. 167–197). New York: Aldine de Gruyter.

Weaver, H.N. (2003). Cultural competence with First Nations peoples. In D. Lum (Ed.), *Culturally competent practice: A framework for understanding diverse groups and justice issues* (2nd ed., pp. 197–216). Pacific Grove, CA: Brooks/Cole.

Weber, G.H. (1982). Self-help and beliefs. In G.H. Weber & L.M. Cohen (Eds.), *Beliefs and self-help: Cross-cultural perspectives and approaches* (pp. 9–30). New York: Human Sciences Press.

Weisberg, L., & Sanchez, L. (2002, May 15). County's foreign-born population surges 41%. *San Diego Union-Tribune*, p. A1.

Welch, M. (2000). The role of the Immigration and Naturalization Service in the prison-industrial complex. *Social Justice*, 27, pp. 73–89.

Welsh, J.A. (1998). Social competence. In J. Kagan (Ed.), *Gale Encyclopedia of Childhood and Adolescence* (pp. 290–314). Detroit: Gale Publishers.

Werner, E.E. (1990). Protective factors and individual resilience. In S.J. Meisels & J.P. Shonkoff (Eds.), *Handbook of early childhood intervention* (pp. 97–116). New York: Cambridge University Press.

Werner, E.E. (1989). High-risk children in young adulthood. A longitudinal study from birth to 32 years. *American Journal of Orthopsychiatry*, 59, pp. 72–81.

Werner, E.E., & Johnson, J.L. (1999). Can we apply resilience? In M.D. Glantz & J.L. Johnson (Eds.), *Resilience and development: Positive life adaptations* (pp. 259–268). New York: Kluwer Academic/ Plenum Publishers.

Werner, E.E., & Smith, R.S. (1992). *Overcoming the odds: High risk children from birth to adulthood*. Ithaca, NY: Cornell University Press.

Werner, E.E., & Smith, R.S. (1982). *Vulnerable but invincible*. New York: McGraw-Hill.

Werner, E.E., & Smith, R.S. (1977). *Kauai's children come of age*. Honolulu: University of Hawaii Press.

Westby, C. (1997). There's more to passing than knowing the answers. *Language, Speech, and Hearing Services in School*, 28, pp. 274–287.

Westermeyer, J. (1991). Psychiatric services for refugee children: An overview. In F.L. Ahearn & J.L. Athey (Eds.), *Refugee children: Theory, research, and services* (pp. 1–27). Baltimore: Johns Hopkins University Press.

Westermeyer, J., & Wahmanhom, K. (1996). Refugee children. In R. Apfel & B. Simon (Eds.), *Minefields in their hearts: The mental health of children in war and communal violence* (pp. 75–103). New Haven, CT: Yale University Press.

Wholey, D. (1992). *When the worst that can happen already has: Conquering life's most difficult times.* New York: Hyperion.

Williams, B. (2001). Accomplishing cross cultural competence in youth development programs. *Journal of Extension, 39,* pp. 80–83.

Williams, C.C., & Windebank, J. (2000). Self-help and mutual aid in deprived urban neighborhoods: Some lessons from Southampton. *Urban Studies, 37,* pp. 127–138.

Wilson, Y.L. (1993, April 16). South Central, Simi Valley both tarred by stereotypes. *San Francisco Chronicle,* p. A4.

Wingspan Symposium. (2002), Involving young people in community research. *FYI Newsletter, 2,* p. 6.

Witt, P.A. (2002). Youth development: Going to the next level; services for youth need to help reduce problem behaviors, and increase pro-social attitudes and skills. *Parks & Recreation, 37,* pp. 52–58.

Witt, P.A., & Crompton, J.L. (Eds.). (1996). *Recreation programs work for at-risk youth: The challenge of shaping the future.* State College, PA: Venture Publishing.

Wolf, D.L. (1997). Family secrets: Transnational struggles among children of Filipino immigrants. *Sociological Perspectives, 40,* pp. 457–482.

Wolin, S., & Wolin, S.J. (1999). *Project resilience: Challenge Model* (http://projectresilience.com/challenge.htm).

Wolin, S., & Wolin, S.J. (1998). Shaping a brighter future by uncovering survivor's pride. *Reaching Today's Youth: The Community Circle of Caring Journal, 2,* pp. 61–64.

Wong, B. (1998). *Ethnicity and entrepreneurship: The new Chinese immigrants in the San Francisco Bay Area.* Boston: Allyn and Bacon.

Wrenn, C.G. (1985). Afterword: The culturally encapsulated counselor revisited. In P. Pedersen (Ed.), *Handbook of cross-cultural counseling and therapy* (pp. 323–329). Westport, CT: Greenwood.

Wright, R., & Ellis, M. (2001). Immigrants, the native-born and the changing division of labor in New York City. In N. Foner (Ed.), *New immigrants in New York* (pp. 81–110). New York: Columbia University Press.

Wucker, M. (2003, July 1). Civic lessons from immigrants. *Prospect, 14,* p. 7.

Wunder, A. (1995). Foreign inmates in U.S. prisons: An unknown population. *Corrections Compendium, 20,* pp. 4–18.

Yassen, J. (1995). Preventing secondary traumatic stress disorder. In C.R. Figley (Ed.), *Compassion fatigue: Coping with secondary traumatic stress disorder in those who treat the traumatized* (pp. 178–208). New York: Brunner/Mazel.

Yeh, C., & Inose, M. (2002). Difficulties and coping strategies of Chinese, Japanese, and Korean immigrant students. *Adolescence, 37,* pp. 69–76.

Yemma, J. (1997, September 17). America's changing face: South Central Los Angeles exemplifies the melting pot of the 1990s. *Boston Globe,* pp. A1, A18–A19.

Yeoman, B. (2000). Hispanic Diaspora—Down by jobs, Latino immigrants are moving to small towns like Siler City, North Carolina, bringing with them new diversity and new tensions. *Mother Jones, 25,* pp. 34–42.

Yohalem, N. (2003). Adults who make a difference: Identifying the skills and characteristics of successful youth workers. In F.A. Villarruel, D.F. Perkins, L.M. Borden, & J.G. Keith (Eds.), *Community youth development programs, policies, and practices* (pp. 358–372). Thousand Oaks, CA: Sage.

Youness, J., McLellan, J.A., & Yates, M. (1997). What we know about engendering civic identity. *American Behavioral Scientists, 40,* pp. 620–631.

Youth Venture. (2002). Youth ventures (http://www.youthventure.org/ventures,asp).

Yurus, M. (2002, May 15). Ads blame immigrants for economy. *The Review, 127* p. 53.

Zeldin, S., Kimball, M., & Price, L. (1995). *What are the day-to-day experiences that promote youth development? An annotated bibliography of research on adolescents and their families.* Washington, DC: Academy for Educational Development.

Zephir, F. (2001). *Trends in ethnic identification among second-generation Haitian Immigrants in New York City.* Westport, CT: Bergin & Garvey.

Zernike, K., & Thompson, G. (2003, June 29). Deaths of immigrants uncover makeshift world of smuggling. New York Times, pp. 1, 23.

Zhou, Y. (2002, August 5). Wave of pupils lacking English strains schools: Rural immigrants face shortage of teachers. *New York Times,* pp. A1, A11.

Zhou, M. (2001a). Contemporary immigration and the dynamics of race and ethnicity. In N.J. Smelser, W.J. Wilson, & F. Mitchell (Eds.), *America becoming: Racial trends and their consequences* (Vol. 1, pp. 200–242). Washington, DC: National Academy Press.

Zhou, M. (2001b). Chinese: Divergent destinies in immigrant New York. In N. Foner (Ed.), *New immigrants in New York* (pp. 141–172). New York: Columbia University Press.

Zhou, M. (1997). Growing up American: The challenge confronting immigrant children and children of immigrants. *Annual Review of Sociology, 23,* pp. 63–89.

Zhou, M., & Bankston, C.L. (2000). The biculturation of the Vietnamese student. *ERIC/CUE Digest,* 152.

Zhou, M., & Bankston, C.L. (1994). Social capital and the adaptation of the second generation: The case of Vietnamese youth in New Orleans. *International Migration Review,* 28, pp. 821–845.

Zielbauer, P.V. (2003, May 5). A bilingual goodbye to a white-collar past: Hispanic population soaring in Hartford. *New York Times,* p. A23.

Zolberg, A.R. (2001). Introduction: Beyond the crisis. In A.R. Zolberg & P.M. Benda (Eds.), *Global migrants, global refugees: Problems and solutions* (pp. 1–16). New York: Berghahn Books.

Name Index

Subject Index